The social history of Canada

MICHAEL BLISS, GENERAL EDITOR

The Queen v Louis Riel

WITH AN INTRODUCTION BY DESMOND MORTON

UNIVERSITY OF TORONTO PRESS

© University of Toronto Press 1974

Toronto and Buffalo

Printed in Canada

ISBN (casebound) 0-8020-2124-7

ISBN (paperback) 0-8020-6232-6

LC 73-91562

CN ISSN 0085-6207

Social History of Canada 19

This book has been published with the help of a grant from
the Canada Council.

An introduction

BY DESMOND MORTON

In an age when litigation was a prime public spectacle, the trial of Louis Riel in 1885 was followed intently across Canada. The verdict and public reaction to it reflected attitudes to punishment, insanity, and partisan politics as well as fundamental differences of race and religion.

EARLY ON Saturday morning, 16 May 1885, Ottawa learned the good news. The day before, a despatch rider had galloped south from Batoche to Clarke's Crossing. From there, a telegraph line had carried the message, straggling east through Humboldt to Winnipeg, on to Toronto and finally to the desk of the Hon. Adolphe Caron, Minister of Militia and Defence: 'Riel was captured to-day at noon by three scouts named Armstrong, D.H. Diehl and Howrie four miles north of Batoche.'[1] To the government and most Canadians, it was confirmation that the costly, potentially disastrous campaign in the North-West would soon be over. Twice the elusive Métis leader had been at the centre of rebellion against Canadian authority: there would be no third occasion.

In truth the report was a little misleading. Riel had not been captured; he had surrendered. Three days earlier, when Canadian troops broke through the Métis defences and swarmed down the slope toward Batoche, Riel had not stayed with the few who chose to fight and die. Instead, he had joined the general flight to the woods north of the little settlement. He had made up his mind, however, that he would not return a second time to the dreary, hopeless life of an exile. Guided by his own private vision of reality, he would carry his struggle into a new arena. He was not a man of action but he was a man of words. He would go to his enemies and demand the great public trial which he had never received. Single-handed he would confound his opponents and compel them to do him justice. In the poplar bluffs north of Batoche, a scenario was devised for the trial of the *Queen* v *Louis Riel.*

On the night of the 13th, Riel slipped across the river to deposit his ailing, pregnant wife and their two small children with his faithful friend, Moïse Ouelette. By the time he returned to the east bank his last chance to escape had gone. Acting on a rumour that Riel had gone to surrender to the soldiers, Gabriel Dumont, his military lieutenant, and young Michel Dumais had started without him in a desperate journey to the United States border.[2] Already Canadian scouts were patrolling the bush in a wide arc around Batoche and Major-General Fred Middleton, the portly British officer who commanded the militia, had despatched a number of local people into the woods, armed with letters of safe conduct for the Métis leader. 'I am ready to receive you and your council,' Middleton wrote, 'and to protect you until your case has been decided upon by the Dominion

Government.'[3] One of the messengers was Moïse Ouelette and he, alone, managed to find the General's quarry. On the morning of 15 May, a hungry, bedraggled Riel was making his nervous way back to Batoche when he encountered two police scouts, Armstrong and Diehl, and the son of Middleton's halfbreed interpreter, Tom Hourie.

Elaborate precautions were taken to smuggle Riel into the camp, now at Guardepuy's Crossing. While the prisoner and two of his captors hid in the woods, Diehl went back for a horse. Curious scouts were assured that the dark, heavily bearded man was only Riel's cook. In the camp, troops were confined to their tents to discourage any unseemly demonstration.[4] Middleton soon called on his captive for the first of several conversations, later recalling him as 'a mild-spoken and mild-looking man, with a short brown beard and an uneasy frightened look about his eyes which gradually disappeared as I talked to him.' The General even loaned Riel one of his military overcoats as he looked 'cold and forlorn.'[5] To escort the prisoner, he appointed Captain George H. Young of the Winnipeg Field Battery. Fifteen years before, Young's father, a Methodist clergyman, had pleaded in vain with Riel for the life of Thomas Scott.

On 17 May, prisoner and escort set off for Saskatoon on the steamer *Northcote.* From there, Riel, Young, and an escort of sixteen soldiers travelled south by waggon to Moose Jaw. Middleton's original orders were to deliver Riel to the Winnipeg jail but a flurry of frantic telegrams from Ottawa changed the destination to Regina. Under Manitoba law, Riel could have insisted on a mixed jury of whites and halfbreeds. Even if the provincial authorities had the right to confine him, which the federal Minister of Justice, Sir Alexander Campbell, doubted, there appeared to be no legal means of returning him to the Territories for trial.[6] On 23 May, Young delivered his prisoner to Inspector Richard Burton Deane, the adjutant of the North-West Mounted Police and acting commander of the police barracks at Regina.

Middleton and Young had accorded Riel some of the dignity due to a captured enemy general: to Deane he was only a dangerous political prisoner. To forestall the covey of journalists, politicians, and sensation-seekers already descending on Regina to interview the Métis leader, he ordered that no one could visit Riel without written permission from Sir John A. Macdonald. 'I religiously held to this regulation of my own making,' he wrote later, 'and it saved me a great deal of trouble.'[7] More controversial was an order that Riel would have to carry a ball and chain when he exercised in the barrack yard. Inquiries from Ottawa brought the explanation that there was no safe enclosure where prisoners could walk. As Deane explained to Edgar Dewdney, Lieutenant-Governor of the Territories, he also had another object, 'namely to deprecate any act of fanaticism. Riel's chances of escape are obviously so infinitesimal that even a man who had sworn to have his life might well stay his hand & allow the law to take its course.'[8] As partial compensation for the added rigour of his captivity, Deane allowed his prisoner to use the vacant office of the Commissioner. Riel spent his days there pouring out a stream of notes, memoranda, and religious poetry.[9]

During the eight weeks before his trial, Riel had much to occupy his mind. His wife and children had been left penniless and helpless at Batoche and weeks passed before Riel learned that his brother, Joseph, had set off from St Boniface to bring them home. Desperate to find means for their support, he suggested to Deane that he might be photographed in his cell wearing his ball and chain or between two guards. The prints might be sold, with suitable inscriptions, to earn money. His poetry, too, might be sold to provide something for his family. Deane was unresponsive.[10] An even greater concern was the forthcoming trial. His voices had assured him that his life was not at stake: instead, he was approaching his moment of apotheosis, when the entire world would watch and listen. Grievances which had so burdened his mind that he had been committed to insane asylums at Longue Pointe and Beauport from March 1876 to February 1878 might now be set right.

Of course, to stage his drama in a tiny courtroom in a raw prairie town would hardly suit the importance of the occasion. On 24 June, in a letter sent through Deane to Dewdney, he asked that his trial be transferred to the Supreme Court of Canada and that his entire career be submitted to judgement. Had he been a rebel in 1869? Was he a murderer of Thomas Scott? Had he plundered the Hudson's Bay Company stores? Was he a fugitive from justice when he entered the House of Commons in 1874? Had he been guilty of more than self-defence in 1885? If the government granted his request, there would be a bonus: his testimony would pillory their Liberal opponents. 'La force des preuves fera voir de la manière la plus évidente,' he promised, 'que je me défends, selon la rectitude des droits des gens, contre le Parti Libéral du Haut Canada, qui me fait depuis quinze ans, une guerre injuste sous tous les rapports.'[11] Three weeks later, as the date of his trial approached, he appealed again, this time to Macdonald. His sole reward for destroying Blake, Mackenzie, and the Ontario Liberals, he assured the Prime Minister, would be a fair indemnity and reinstatement in Manitoba politics. Anticipating that he would be called upon to form the provincial government, he suggested that no one could make a finer lieutenant-governor than his jailor, Inspector Deane. 'Ce noble officier connait mes façons de penser.'[12] Far from being flattered, Deane concluded that the letters only demonstrated that Riel was 'cracked.'[13]

The government's plans for the judicial aftermath of the rebellion were naturally a little different. Insurrection had to be punished but it did not seem fair to government officials in Ottawa or the West that the simple unsophisticated Indians and halfbreeds who had abandoned their allegiance should pay a heavy price. Guilt lay primarily with the few clever agitators who had seduced them into revolt. A year earlier, hotheads in the Manitoba and North-West Farmers' Union had talked of seizing arms and of annexation to the United States; some of them might well be found behind the uprising. 'Nothing in the whole duty entrusted to you is, I apprehend, more important,' Campbell instructed the government lawyers, 'than that we should, if possible, find out some of the men who have, with far better knowledge than' the Indians and half-breeds, stirred them up to rebellion.'[14] 'Do not spare money if you can only get hold of one or two men, such as you described to me at Ottawa ...,' Campbell directed his deputy minister, George Burbidge. 'You probably will be able to fasten guilt upon some of the Prince Albert men.'[15]

It was easier said than done. Apart from William Henry Jackson, the young Ontarian who had begun as Riel's secretary and ended as his prisoner, no one even remotely fitted Campbell's description.[16] By deliberately turning to the Indians for assistance, Riel had horrified even the most alienated white settlers. Indeed all the evidence, including the large collection of papers seized by the troops at Batoche, kept returning to his central role in the outbreak. No one else could have taken his place. Dumont, an able tactician and redoubtable hunter, certainly had the will and the courage but events had demonstrated how little self-confidence he possessed.

Charles Nolin, the former Manitoba cabinet minister, had once been the ablest spokesman for the Saskatchewan Métis but his refusal to join in the rebellion had cost him his reputation, his freedom, and almost his life at Riel's hands. As the Crown's star witness at his cousin's trial, he would have his revenge. If further testimony were needed, the clergy provided it. A fervent letter from Bishop Grandin of St Albert, accompanied by a petition from most of the Oblate missionaries in the affected area, insisted that the entire responsibility for the waywardness of their flock and for the resulting suffering lay with the heretic Riel.[17]

History has unearthed no rival to Riel as the man who inspired the 1885 uprising; it has merely endorsed the judgement of the government lawyers without, perhaps, joining them in charging him with the crime of high treason. It was a crime clothed in the archaic majesty of fourteenth-century legal language and of five centuries of British constitutional history. Until the codification of the criminal law in Canada in 1893, the Statute of Treasons, first adopted in the twenty-sixth year of the reign of Edward III, still applied. Indictment for treason evoked memories of Tudor and Stuart tyranny, of state trials, acts of attainder, and the grisly punishment of hanging, drawing, and quartering. Those responsible for framing the indictment had a more prosaic responsibility: to ensure that the accused did not escape through some obscure technicality. Since treason could be defined as levying war on the Sovereign, charges were prepared for each of the three occasions when the Métis had battled government forces, at Duck Lake, Fish Creek, and Batoche. Next, taking note of Riel's acquired American citizenship, the lawyers prepared three identical charges against Riel as 'living within the Dominion of Canada and under the protection of our Sovereign Lady the Queen.' To avoid the trouble of finding a specific informant for each charge, the government selected a single symbolic citizen who would lay all the charges in connection with the rebellion—A.D. Stewart, the British-born police chief of Hamilton, Ontario.

'We shall take great care, I think, to satisfy the Country that the prosecution is well done,' Campbell had promised the Prime Minister, 'any want of thoroughness in this respect would be unpardonable.'[18] Both men had chosen the government lawyers with characteristic appreciation of legal talent. Christopher Robinson, a sixty-year-old Toronto barrister with an impressive reputation in the common law, would lead for the Crown. Perhaps by coincidence, he was the third son of John Beverley Robinson, pillar of the Family Compact and Crown Prosecutor at a famous earlier set of treason trials, the Ancaster Assizes of 1814. The son's manner was different. 'His style is not oratorical or declamatory,' the Toronto *Globe* informed its readers, 'but rather conversational.'[19] He had already refused judicial office and, in due course, would refuse a knighthood. To do the detailed work of marshalling the evidence, Campbell chose Britton Bath Osler, 'a very clever, good lawyer' even if he was a Liberal.[20] B.B. was one of the leading criminal lawyers in Ontario and one of a renowned set of brothers including a leading financier, a judge, and Canada's best-known physician. G.W. Burbidge, a Maritimer, had been appointed deputy minister of justice in 1882. French Canada was represented, at Caron's insistence, by Thomas-Chase Casgrain, a young partner in the Minister's own law firm. As a local voice, the government chose Lieutenant-Colonel D.L. Scott, the mayor of Regina.

The government had spared nothing to assemble an impressive legal team; the defence was technically penniless. However, help was in sight. At the oubreak of the rebellion, French-Canadian opinion had stood, for the most part, solidly with the rest of the country. The horror of an Indian war was very much part of French Canada's historical memory while the Church's indignation at Riel's religious aberrations also helped to overshadow the support the Métis leader had once enjoyed in Quebec. However, once the Indians had been crushed and Riel was a helpless prisoner, he rapidly regained his status as a popular hero. Shrewd politics hastened the process. Under the leadership of Honoré Mercier, a former Conservative, Quebec Liberals discovered that Métis grievances were powerful ammunitiion against their *bleu* opponents federally and provincially. Even the Castor faction, ultramontane and ultra-conservative, found the issue a popular cause against their former Conservative colleagues. In time, Mercier would use Riel as a device to bring two apparent political opposites together against a common enemy. Meanwhile, the Liberals busied themselves with collecting funds and selecting lawyers for Riel's defence. The good news came through Dr. J.B.R. Fiset, a former Liberal MP and a friend from Riel's Montreal school days.[21]

Leader for the defence was François-Xavier Lemieux, a thirty-five-year-old lawyer with a brilliant record of mistrials and acquittals for his clients. He had already launched his career in the Quebec legislature and, in time, he would become Chief Justice of Quebec. Charles Fitzpatrick was destined to become Laurier's Minister of Justice and Chief Justice of Canada. In 1885, he was a respected Quebec City lawyer and, despite his Liberalism, a brother-in-law of Adolphe Caron and a partner in the Minister's firm. Riel's third lawyer was James Greenshields, reputedly one of the ablest members of the Montreal bar, and, for local advice, the defence recruited T.C. Johnstone, a Winnipeg lawyer who would also, in due course, be raised to the bench.

By early July, both Crown and defence lawyers had settled down in the dreary little prairie town to begin their work. In a letter thanking Fiset for the help from Quebec, Riel had intimated a possible line of defence. He had, he claimed, been intending to return to Montana, despairing of ever convincing the government by peaceful means, when news was brought by Lawrence Clarke, an abrasive Hudson's Bay Company factor, that 500 police were coming to attack Batoche. Allegedly, the furious Métis had virtually compelled Riel to assume the leadership.[22] Unfortunately, such a plea was hopeless. From Riel's private papers and from the mass of documents produced by his Exovedate government, lawyers could easily demonstrate his prominence. A series of witnesses, many of them Riel's prisoners during the uprising, could corroborate his central role. After interviews with their client, the Quebec lawyers concluded that the only effective defence must be insanity. The two years in asylums, the fantasies about dividing the West among the nations of Europe, the outpourings against the Holy See and the Catholic Church, the visions and dreams, all added up to lunacy. To Lemieux and his colleagues, Riel was 'un maniaque religieux'; to Fitzpatrick, he was either 'un fou ou un sacré hypocrite – peut être les deux.'[23]

First, the defence was determined to challenge the legitimacy of the court itself. By not forwarding Riel to Winnipeg as it had first intended, the government may have saved itself from what Campbell was afraid would be 'a certain miscarriage of justice'[24] but it had guaranteed itself certain other problems. A frugal administration had not yet provided the sparsely settled North-West Territories with a full panoply of judicial institutions. The highest local judicial officials were three stipendiary magistrates. To avoid insoluble

problems in tiny frontier communities, juries were limited to six
members. Appeals might be carried to the Manitoba Court of
Queen's Bench, sitting *in banco* and thence, if permitted, to the
highest tribunal of the British Empire, the Judicial Committee of the
Privy Council. As Riel himself obviously felt, it seemed unfitting that
so modest a court should enjoy the same powers of life and death as
a judge in all his majesty and twelve good men and true.

The responsibility did not particularly upset Lieutenant-Colonel
Hugh Richardson, a dry, bearded man who, at sixty-four, was at last
to find his moment in Canadian history. Born in London, he had
come to Canada as a child when his father became manager of the
Bank of Upper Canada in Toronto. Trained in the law, he had practised for twenty-five years in Woodstock. In 1866, as a militia
colonel, he had been responsible for defending the St Clair frontier
agains the Fenians. In 1872, a Conservative government had
appointed him chief clerk of the Department of Justice; in 1877, a
Liberal government had sent him west as a stipendiary magistrate.
Since 1880, he had presided over the police court at Regina and, if
liquor offences were the most common item on his docket, he had
already convicted an Indian for cannibalism and two halfbreeds and
a white man for murder. The last, a man named Connor or Kohner,
had carried his appeal to the Manitoba court; in rejecting it, the
Queen's Bench had disposed of most of the issues on which Richardson's court might be challenged.[25]

At 11 AM on Monday, 20 July, the trial began. The usual courtroom at the barracks would have been far too cramped for the
throng of journalists, lawyers, and prominent spectators, so the
government had rented the offices of a Regina land company. Still
the court was jammed, men sweltering under heavy broadcloth and
military serge, a scattering of well-connected ladies perspiring under
layers of petticoats. Richardson, his clerk, Dixie Watson, Henry
LeJeune, a Quebec-born justice of the peace who would share the
bench, and a cluster of stenographers, interpreters, and officials sat
at one end of the room. Behind them, to save space, were chairs for
the six jurors. In front stood the dock, flanked by tables for the
lawyers and the press. All around and pushed into the vacant spaces
were the on-lookers, already half-suffocated by the mid-summer heat.

To them and their contemporaries, almost any major trial was an
event, a morality play in which the outcome was always in doubt,

even when the evidence was as overwhelming as it appeared to be against Riel. In nineteenth-century Canada, a good murder trial could drive almost any other event from the newspapers and major Canadian dailies were braced to inform their readers of every word uttered in the Regina courtroom. If the *Queen v Louis Riel* is the most famous trial in Canadian history, it occurred in an age of connoisseurs.

It seemed all the more disappointing, therefore, that the first business of the defence was to deprive people of their excitement by challenging the proceedings and the statute on which they were based. An enormous brief, prepared largely by Fitzpatrick and reaching back as far as Magna Carta, argued that the Canadian parliament could never have had the authority to allow capital cases to be decided by a mere stipendiary magistrate and six jurors. Equally well-rehearsed, Robinson disposed of that contention, and of a less agile attempt to introduce Riel's American citizenship, to Richardson's predictable satisfaction. By 4:30, the magistrate was ready for an early adjournment.

Next day, Riel, Lemieux, and Fitzpatrick arrived armed with affidavits claiming the 'utter impossibility' of conducting a proper defence without the presence of a long list of witnesses. Riel demanded the presence of Dumont, Dumais, and Napoléon Nault, all fugitives in the United States, Father André and Father Fourmond, Oblate missionaries who had once been sympathetic to his cause, and the deputy-ministers of the Interior and of Indian Affairs, together with documents and Métis claims. The court bluntly refused to summon the government officials or to grant what, in effect, would be pardons to fugitives under indictment, but the priests would be summoned. Fitzpatrick was more successful when he asked for the attendance of three medical witnesses. Robinson even volunteered the Crown's assistance in paying their way. However Fitzpatrick's request for a month's adjournment was refused: a week was all that Richardson would allow. On 28 July, the trial would resume.

It was apparent by now that Riel and his counsel were proceeding on different tracks. With his witnesses, he might have struggled to justify his actions during the year since his return from Montana, arguing, as he sometimes still did, that Dumont and Dumais had forced him to participate in the rebellion. Medical testimony could only be used to support his lawyer's forthcoming plea of insanity.

He already had an intimation of their strategy when he wrote to the Prime Minister on 16 July. His lawyers were good men and well-intentioned, he assured Macdonald, but they did not understand. Renewing a plea he had made earlier, Riel asked that Conservative lawyers also be sent to help him. There was, of course, no reply.

If the defence lawyers had any hope of saving Riel, they must have been raised on 24 July. Richardson had taken advantage of the adjournment to dispose of the case of Riel's former secretary, W.H. Jackson. Everyone agreed that the man who now called himself Honoré Jaxon, and who had solemnly invited Dewdney to meet with him and Riel to settle all the outstanding problems of the North-West, was crazy.[26] Even the Crown collaborated in securing a verdict of not guilty on grounds of insanity. Dr Frederick Jukes, the Mounted Police surgeon, and Dr Cotton, a local practitioner, provided the evidence and, within half an hour, Jackson, still protesting his sanity, had been committed to the Selkirk asylum near Winnipeg.[27]

However, there were serious differences between the cases; not simply that one was a former Ontario Protestant, the other a French-speaking Métis. Jackson had struck almost all who met him as obviously insane whereas Riel had impressed Middleton, Young, Jukes, and other custodians as a clever, charismatic man, quite capable of manipulating simple-minded Métis and Indians into insurrection and equally capable, should he choose, of shamming insanity. Later generations of Indians and Métis have found it insulting to be told that their ancestors accepted the leadership of a lunatic. Perversely, Canadian officials in 1885 may have found it equally difficult to accept that so many men had died and so many millions had been spent to overcome a madman. Moreover, if Riel was unbalanced, most of his wanderings were in a domain where his largely Protestant captors could hardly be expected to follow. Denunciations of the Bishop of Rome and suggestions that he should be replaced by Archbishop Taché or Bishop Grandin might shock Oblate missionaries but they hardly persuaded a mounted policeman to send for a straitjacket. However, if a parallel between Jackson and Riel seemed inappropriate in Regina, conclusions about their contrasting treatment were soon to rage across French Canada.

Meanwhile, the trial had to run its course. On Tuesday, 28 July, the crowd returned to the little makeshift courtroom. The initial legal jousting at an end, a jury could at last be selected. Thirty-six farmers, merchants, and contractors had been empanelled from as far away as Brandon. Only two, or at most three, bore French names. The defence challenged five English names and the Crown an Irish Catholic before the six chosen jurors filed into their seats behind Richardson. Two were merchants, Henry Painter from Broadview and Edwin Brooks from Indian Head; the rest were farmers, Walter Merrifield and Francis Cosgrove from Whitewood, Bell Dean from Broadview and Edward Everett from Moose Jaw. Cosgrove, a dark, bearded Irishman, was chosen as foreman.[28]

Now the trial could begin in earnest. A procession of Crown witnesses came forward to testify to Riel's leadership in the uprising, his threats against the police, his role at Duck Lake and before Fish Creek, and his overall responsibility for the unfolding of events. For its part, the defence – chiefly Fitzpatrick – sought admissions that Riel had behaved unusually or eccentrically. On Wednesday, the succession of hostile testimony continued until the appearance of Charles Nolin. So far, Riel had taken little interest in the proceedings, occasionally scribbling notes and passing them to his lawyers. Nolin was different. His cousin, his host, and his closest associate in 1884, Nolin, in Riel's opinion, had deserted the cause in March 1885. Now he appeared as the Crown's most devastating witness.

In the first dramatic moment in the trial, Riel jumped to his feet, pleading for a chance to intervene. Richardson tried to quiet him. It was not time to speak. Fitzpatrick rose to insist that Riel not be heard. The Métis would not be silent. 'If you will allow me, Your Honour, this case comes to be extraordinary, and while the Crown, with the great talents they have at its service, are trying to show that I am guilty – of course it is their duty – my counsellors are trying – my good friends and lawyers who have been sent here by friends whom I respect, are trying to show that I am insane.[29] Again Richardson tried to stop him; again Riel persisted. An exasperated Fitzpatrick burst out that his client was systematically trying to destroy his own case. The argument continued with rising anger until the judge granted a brief adjournment, hoping that the matter could be settled in private. The interval made little difference. Robinson interjected that the Crown would have no objection to Riel putting questions. Obviously neither would Richardson. The dispute was between the prisoner and his own lawyers. If Riel had once imagined that counsel had been sent from Quebec to help him stage his great moment, he was now aware that they had come to take the case from his hands, to orchestrate the evidence in their way. Could he be allowed to ask Nolin the questions he wished to ask? Only, Richardson explained, at the risk of instantly losing the services of his lawyers. The wrangling continued until Richardson offered a brief adjournment. Nothing was resolved. 'If it were an ordinary criminal case,' Richardson interjected, 'I should not hesitate but this is beyond the ordinary run of cases that I have had to deal with in my whole career.'[30] Riel slumped back in the dock to endure his cousin's damning testimony. Somehow, he could not bring himself to dispense with his lawyers.

On the third day of the trial, it was the turn of the defence to summon witnesses. Father André was first, the superior of the Oblates and a man in deep sympathy with the Métis and Indians to whom he had dedicated his life. Both he and Father Vital Fourmond were convinced that Riel was mad and their opinion was reinforced by Philippe Garnot, the young French-Canadian who had succeeded Jackson as secretary. Next came professional testimony. Two of the three alienists whom Fitzpatrick had summoned from eastern Canada had made the long journey; the third had demanded $500 for his services and had been excused.[31] Dr François Roy was superintendent at the huge, notorious asylum at Beauport where Riel had spent more than a year; Dr Daniel Clark ran the Toronto Asylum for the Insane. Both were experienced witnesses and both were convinced that Riel was out of his mind. There is no doubt that Osler's able cross-examination reduced their impact on the jury. If he bullied Roy on the management of his asylum, it is worth noting that the institution was run as a profitable speculation and that, within two years, a Royal Commission would substantiate the appalling consequences of neglect and brutality on the inmates.[32] Clark was a different matter. A bluff, able man, a future president of the American Psychiatric Association and several other international bodies, he had advanced views on criminal insanity. Jurisprudence in 1885 accepted the so-called McNaghten Rules — that insanity was only a defence if the criminal, in committing the offence, did not know right from wrong. McNaghten, who had attempted to assassinate a British prime minister, had benefited from the formula. Now Clark struggled to expand the rules to cover Riel. However, he was also an honest man and Osler's questioning forced him to admit the possibility that Riel's conduct could be consistent with deception. It was enough for Osler and he made sure that it was enough for the jury.

It was fortunate for the government's case that Osler had been so effective, for the Crown's witnesses were by no means as powerful. Dr James Wallace, the superintendent of the Hamilton asylum, was not the equal of Clark in learning or experience and he had spent a mere half-hour interviewing Riel. Dr Jukes, the police surgeon, had never even attempted a psychiatric examination. On the other hand, he was an able courtroom performer, the kind of shrewd, practical physician who probably had far greater impact on the jury than the more eminent witnesses.[33]

By Friday, there was little to add. Middleton, Young, Deane, and a clergyman who had travelled with Riel in the *Northcote* returned to the stand to emphasize their belief in Riel's sanity. Now it was time for the defence and prosecution to sum up their cases. In utterly contrasting ways, the addresses by Fitzpatrick and Robinson were masterpieces of courtroom oratory; each still stands as a remarkable presentation of the opposing cases which had brought conflict and bloodshed to the North-West. The importance of the trial is not limited to the tragedy of Riel or the people he had led to ruin or even to the enduring consequences for Canada as a whole; the *Queen v Louis Riel* was also a contest of legal giants, arguing with a dignity and a force rare in the mundane annals of our country's history.

Fitzpatrick's speech was emotional, launched with praise for the volunteers who had left their homes to put down rebellion, moving forcefully on to the grievances of the North-West, grievances which most of the six jurors must have shared. How many of them, he wondered, would have been alleviated without the act of resistance? Finally, Fitzpatrick mustered the evidence of lunacy, the sudden changes of fortune which, he insisted, had tripped Riel's uncertain mental balance and deprived him of responsibility for all he said and did.

On Fitzpatrick's heels, as Richardson had promised, came Riel, free at last to speak for himself. After Lemieux had jumped to his feet to disavow all that his client would say, the Métis leader began. It was not an ordered speech. There were no notes and little evidence of a plan, but there was eloquence and pathos combined as

the big, powerfully built man struggled simultaneously to plead his
sanity and the wrongs of his people. For an hour he continued,
sometimes quickly, sometimes slowly, struggling for the English
words. By now, as a practised orator, he could sense that the lawyers
and journalists were growing bored. The air was too warm, eyelids
too heavy. Fitzpatrick's speech, with its more conventional tugging
at emotions, had drained whatever feeling had survived the heat. At
last Richardson interrupted. 'Are you done?' No, a few minutes more.
Weakly, searching for a peroration, Riel concluded.

Christopher Robinson rose for the Crown. Two emotional
speeches were followed by strict, frigid logic. Three days of testimony, an array of documents, a series of apparently unconnected
assertions were pulled together and set in place. Nolin had given
damning testimony of Riel's eagerness for money. Father André had
recalled that, for $35,000 or perhaps even less, the Métis leader had
been willing to abandon his people and return to Montana. Were
these the calculations of a madman? If, he continued, Riel was
insane as the defence contended, what did that say about the
Métis people who had followed him with such apparent devotion?

Late on Friday afternoon, Richardson began his own address to
the jury. At 6 PM the court adjourned, and at 10 AM on Saturday he
resumed. It was a cautious speech, by a man well aware that better
legal minds than his own would be searching his words for the
chance of a mistrial. Mostly, he read from the evidence, perhaps
trying to purge the jury of the emotion of the previous day. At 2:15
the jury withdrew. An hour passed as Riel prayed, journalists drafted
their despatches and a hum of conversation rose and fell. At 3:15
the six men filed in. The foreman, Francis Cosgrove, was
weeping – 'crying like a baby,' the *Globe* correspondent contemptu-
ously observed – as he pronounced the verdict. 'Guilty.' Then, hesi-
tantly, he added: 'Your Honour, I have been asked by my brother
jurors to recommend the prisoner to the mercy of the Crown.'
Coldly, Richardson noted the jury's request and then, after the
routine question, it was again Riel's opportunity to speak.

It had come late, but at long last he could give the kind of speech
he had perhaps rehearsed among the clicking poplar leaves north of
Batoche. He was more in control of himself than on the previous
day, and his arguments flowed more coherently. Riel began by
rejoicing that the verdict had at least cleared him of the stigma of

madness. Then he turned to travel again through the tangled events of 1870 and 1885. Once more he found himself without an audience. The jury's decision had ended the drama. Now the packed, sweating courtroom sat in silence, respecting a condemned man's traditional right to be heard but waiting patiently for him to finish. Riel, as exhausted and drained as any of his listeners, sensed the futility of his efforts, slowed, and stopped. Magistrate Richardson looked squarely at the prisoner and began. There was not the slightest concession to the oratory that had come before. There could be no excuse for what Riel had done and there could be no reasonable expectation of clemency. On 18 September, at the police barracks at Regina, Louis Riel would be hanged.

Of course that was not the end of the *Queen* v *Louis Riel*. However exasperated they might be by their client – Dewdney assured Macdonald that the Quebec lawyers were 'pretty well disgusted with him'[34] – the process of appeal had to be carried through. In taking their case to the Manitoba Court of Queen's Bench, Lemieux and Fitzpatrick were joined by the youthful John Skirving Ewart, at the outset of his career as a principled controversialist. It was to little avail. The Manitoba judges were unanimous – a French-Canadian member of the bench and former friend of Riel preferred to absent himself in Montreal – in rejecting every ground of appeal: the jurisdiction of the court, the size of the jury, even Ewart's suggestion that the law did not allow the evidence to be recorded in shorthand. Above all, there could be no question of the lower court's finding that Riel was responsible for his acts. Of Father André's evidence that the Métis leader was willing to bargain for money, Chief Justice Wallbridge noted scornfully: 'In my opinion, this shows he was willing and quite capable of parting with this illusion if he got the $35,000.'[35]

As both government and defence lawyers had always been aware, Riel's fate had depended more on politics than the law. As his lawyers prepared to carry their case a final step to the Privy Council, the clamour over Riel's fate rose in eastern Canada. With time, the government's nerve might break. To allow the weeks needed to bring the appeal before the Judicial Committee, the government reprieved the condemned man, first to 16 October, then to 10 November. At each announcement, the uproar grew as supporters and opponents of execution imagined that the government was retreating before the onslaught.

In Regina, General Middleton could follow the course of the agitation through the eyes of his French-Canadian wife. 'The fact that he is a French speaking subject or man, and a Roman Catholic is quite enough to ensure the sympathy of a large number of the French population, even though he professes to have set himself up as a Roman Catholic reformer,' he wrote to the Duke of Cambridge. 'There is still a strong antagonism between the English & French speaking Canadians. It died out a good deal but I am very much afraid lest this Riel affair resuscitate it.'[36] Middleton's fears were justified. In the fate of the lonely Métis, surrounded by English-speaking enemies, French-Canadians saw a test of their own effectiveness as a minority. If Riel was insane, why had he not been treated like Jackson? If he was sane, did civilized countries still hang men for treason? Mad or not, he was the spokesman for an oppressed minority of their kinsmen.

In Ottawa, Macdonald and most of his colleagues had long since made up their minds that, if the courts so decreed, Riel would die. They were not vengeful men and if, like their Liberal opponents, they had played politics with Riel, they despised the racial and religious fanatics of both English and French Canada who had forced them into those games. Nor would they have cheerfully executed an obvious lunatic, though their definition of such a state was obviously stricter than that of Dr Daniel Clark. What had terrified the government and most of the people of Canada had been Riel's deliberate attempt to foment an Indian war in the Canadian west. For that and that alone, Riel must hang 'though every dog in Quebec bark in his favour.'[37] That the Macdonald government had been insensitive and reluctant in coping with the west's problems is demonstrable; that it was unaware of them or that it deliberately withheld obvious solutions is nonsense. If it is hard now for governments to cope with massive indigence and permanent dependence, it was even more difficult in 1885. Land grants for the Métis (inevitably transferred to white land speculators), larger rations for the Indians, and a general restoration of the buffalo were not serious answers to the bitter discontent of 1884; better answers were not readily available. In the government's eyes, Riel had come with deliberate self-interest to exploit misery and grievance at a time of painful transition. His demands rejected, he had threatened the west with the kind of massacre and ruin which had been the grim accompaniment of

American expansion. Riel would die not to avenge Thomas Scott – his ghost had never risen at the trial – or to humble Quebec but because agitators with or without hallucinations had to be deterred.

That French-Canadian opinion would be at odds with the rest of Canada was surprising, unfortunate and, Macdonald and his colleagues believed, transitory. Confidence in the correctness of their judgement of Riel was reinforced by confidence in the attitude of the Church. Warned by Taché and Grandin, the hierarchy stood firm, deploring the violence of the outrage which now swirled around Macdonald and especially around his three French-Canadian ministers, J.A. Chapleau, Sir Hector Langevin, and Caron. Only Bishop Laflèche of Three Rivers, a former missionary among the Métis and an ardent Castor, was uneasy. In the end he too held back, largely because of his suspicion that the whole agitation was the work of hated Liberals.[38]

Laflèche had a point. Mercier's ingenuity had given the Liberals of Quebec their first successful issue in more than a generation. In judging both Quebec's anger and the government's response to it, its partisan credentials must be recognized. Of course, Mercier's strategy had limitations. To arouse French Canada, there had to be an enemy – vengeful, bloodthirsty, and united Ontario. Aided by a notorious editorial in the Toronto *News*[39] and a succession of marginally more restrained comments in the Toronto *Mail*, Mercier could make his case to his contemporaries and, to an astonishing extent, to posterity. That Riel was hurried to the gallows by bigoted Orangemen is certainly a durable part of Canadian historical mythology.

Proving it, as D.A. Kubesh has pointed out, is another matter. Perhaps it is not even desirable to try. A myth which suggests that the Liberal party is the sole mediating agency between the warring elements of Canadian society serves so many political interests that it should not be challenged. To ask, as Kubesh does, whether the Riel affair was 'a smoke screen behind which contending factions in Canadian life struggled for power' is to suggest that coarse ambition crouches behind every great cause.[40]

At the outset of the rebellion, opposition spokesmen had made the customary renunciation of partisan bickering for the duration of the emergency and had vied with government ministers in enthusiasm for the national cause. Of course patriotism itself demands honest criticism of official bungling and maladministration. Soon both parties and their journalistic allies were blaming each other for the outbreak, with Edward Blake and the Liberals enjoying a clear advantage. A general election was expected in 1886 and Blake was understandably eager to use the Conservatives' mismanagement in the North-West to accomplish their defeat. A spur to partisanship was Macdonald's Franchise Bill, an attempt to provide standard voting qualifications across the Dominion and, in Liberal eyes, to secure built-in advantages for the party in power. Inevitably, Riel's trial and sentence became part of the political struggle. In Quebec it was a unique opportunity to transform the Liberals into the guardians of French Canada's sense of insecurity. In the rest of Canada, it was an opportunity to force the government into the dock with Riel. If it was indefensible to take up arms against Macdonald's misgovernment, at least it was understandable. The jury's recommendation of mercy was immediately interpreted as condemnation of Ottawa. 'If the jury had looked high and low for some form of words with which to express the direct censure of the Dominion Government,' exclaimed the *Globe*, 'they could not have found anything that so eloquently condemns the real malefactors as does this recommendation to mercy of redhanded Riel.'[41] The government had been guilty of gross misconduct in the North-West, insisted the London *Advertiser*, 'and nothing that the Ministry can do as to the convicting of Riel will relieve them from their responsibility.'[42]

As months passed, Liberal tactics in English-speaking Canada had to be altered. Faced with an apparent Quebec insistence that Riel be saved essentially because of his race and religion, English-Canadians reacted. Could a properly convicted criminal escape justice simply because he happened to be French-speaking and Catholic? Atavism was not a Quebec monopoly. However, the basic task of the Liberal press remained unaltered: smite the government. In an editorial welcoming the verdict and drawing appropriate conclusions from the recommendation for mercy, the *Globe* suggested that a rescue attempt by Dumont might be deliberately encouraged by the government: 'Then there would be the chance for the veteran histrionic to wring his hands and elevate his eyes to heaven as he measured out the time-honoured words, "Would to God I could catch him".'[43]

In Ottawa, Macdonald accepted Liberal charges as part of the business of politics and waited for the uproar to subside. After all, basic economic interests were not at stake and emotion could not subsist on sentiment alone. Much depended on the Prime Minister's French-Canadian colleagues. Caron, freshly knighted for his services in the rebellion, was firmly with Macdonald both from conviction and personal policy.[44] So was the senior Quebec minister, Sir Hector Langevin. If, as his biographer insists, he shared the prevailing French-Canadian bitterness about Riel's fate, he held his peace and his portfolio for the larger cause of avoiding French Canada's isolation.[45] For J.A. Chapleau, the choice was more difficult. By far the ablest of the French-Canadians in the ministry, his resignation could have guaranteed him leadership of the growing nationalist movement. His heart and his political advisers pulled him in that direction; his judgement pulled him back. Macdonald did his best to help them. To the dismay of some English-speaking colleagues, he ordered lengthy reprieves to allow Riel's case to be taken to London. On 22 October, the Judicial Committee declared that it would not even entertain the appeal: the grounds were too flimsy.[46]

By now, Riel was fully prepared to die. His personal anguish had been increased by news from St Boniface that his third child had died within a few hours of being born. However, there was yet a further stage. Since September, the French-Canadian ministers had been pressing for the appointment of a commission to determine, once and for all, whether Riel was sane.[47] The verdict of three successive courts that Riel was sane enough to be tried and sentenced could not be set aside, but there was a little-travelled section of the law which would prevent sentence being carried out on an insane man. On 31 October, Macdonald authorized a commission of two doctors — F.X. Valade, official analyst of the Department of National Revenue and the choice of Langevin and Chapleau, and Michael Lavell, warden of Kingston Penitentiary and, in Sir Alexander Campbell's opinion, 'the man in whom I should have the greatest confidence.'[48] Their instructions from Macdonald were straightforward: representations had been made to the government that Riel's mind had given way since his trial; the two doctors were to determine whether it was true. 'I need scarcely point out to you,' Macdonald added, 'that the inquiry is not as to whether Riel is subject to illusions or delusions but whether he is so bereft of his reason as not to know right from wrong, and as not to be an accountable being.'[49]

The terms of reference determined the conclusion. Lavell and Dr Jukes, who had also been directed to examine the prisoner, agreed that Riel was sane. 'There is no difference between his condition now,' Jukes insisted, 'and his condition when he was uniformly regarded by those who knew him best as the most capable leader of the half-breeds in the recent insurrection.'[50] Lavell, admitting that Riel held 'foolish and peculiar views, concerning visions as to prophecy and General Government,' insisted that he was an accountable being. Moreover, he added, Father André evidently thought so too, for Riel was receiving the sacraments.[51] The difficulty came with Valade. Pressed first by Father André and then by Lavell, the unhappy French-Canadian equivocated. His telegraphed report, followed by a thirty-four-page written submission, illustrated his struggle. His conclusion was that Riel was 'not an accountable being, that he is unable to distinguish between wrong and right on political and religious subjects which I consider well marked typical symptoms of a kind of insanity under which he undoubtedly suffers, but on other points I believe him to be quite sensible and can distinguish right from wrong.'[52] It was sufficient admission. The few lines of Valade's report which appeared in print supported the opinions of his fellow investigators and, if the doctor ever protested, it was inaudible.

If Riel was now receiving the sacraments, as Lavell reported, it was because he had formally recanted his heresies. At Deane's request, a succession of priests had been sent to minister to the prisoner, but it was three veteran missionaries, André, Cochin, and Fourmond, who returned him to the Church. Their victory was incomplete: Riel never entirely abandoned his belief in his mission or his role as a prophet, but the priests were satisfied to regard these aberrations as symptoms of insanity. To Jukes, however, they suggested a new thesis from which to argue Riel's insanity. At the trial, Robinson and Osler had attempted to equate his leadership with that of other prophets in history: could the defence argue that all prophets were mad? Now Jukes compared Riel to Emmanuel Swedenborg, the Swedish mystic and theologian who was enjoying a posthumous Victorian vogue. Perhaps, he suggested in a long letter to Macdonald, Riel's letters should be collected and judged by competent experts. However, by the end of a long letter written to provide the Prime Minister with further arguments for execution, the police surgeon's own uncertainties were manifest. The enormity of his responsibility rushed in on him as he wound up his recommendations: 'Mistakes are possible to all,' he confessed, 'but should examination of these papers *after* Riel's execution establish the fact that he was insane, those whose evidence to the contrary had sent him to the gallows, however conscientiously they may have done so, would have much to think upon for the remainder of their life with unavailing pain I regret.'[53]

It was now too late for second thoughts. On 15 November, a special train brought A.P. Sherwood, commissioner of the Dominion Police, armed with the warrant for the execution. The gallows used to execute Kohner had been re-erected in a walled enclosure beside the guardroom, but only by chance did Father André, who had agreed to remain with Riel to the end, learn that the sentence would be carried out on the following day. He was with Riel when the Sheriff, Major S.E. Chapleau, a brother of the minister, arrived to read the warrant. By now, Riel was perfectly calm, far more composed than Father André or Father Charles McWilliams, another school friend who had joined him at the end. When Jukes asked for his final request, all he wanted was an extra ration of three eggs. That night he prayed, wrote letters, forgave his enemies – Grandin, Taché, Pope Leo XIII, even Macdonald – and thanked his priests and his jailors for their kindness.[54]

Next morning, Sheriff Chapleau failed to appear; his deputy filled his place. Shortly before 8:00 AM he unlocked the cell door and the little party filed out, led by McWilliams. At the entrance to the guardroom they halted for twenty minutes of prayers and absolution. Then the hangman appeared, Jack Henderson, a teamster who had once, years before, been among Riel's prisoners. As the group shuffled toward the scaffold, André broke into tears. 'Courage mon père,' Riel said calmly. The rope was adjusted around his neck. 'Was there any reason why the sentence should not be carried out,' Deputy Sheriff Gibson asked. Should he speak, Riel asked his confessor. No. Instead, for two more minutes they prayed. Finally, as they had arranged, Riel and McWilliams began to recite the Lord's Prayer. As they reached 'deliver us from evil,' the trap fell.

Below, Dr Cotton and Dr Dodds, the local coroner, were waiting. After two minutes, Riel was officially pronounced dead.
Almost at once, there was a dispute about possession of the body.
Tradition condemned it to an unmarked grave in the prison yard and
that, Dewdney argued, would be the safest place for it until passions
had cooled and it might be quietly transferred at Archbishop Taché's
invitation to a corner of his cathedral graveyard.[55] Instead, Father
André claimed the body, the two Chapleaus insisted that he
should have it, and Macdonald cheerfully gave way. Although
Dewdney feared lest the body be buried in Regina, creating a
shrine for Métis and Indians or a target for local Orangemen, Riel's
remains were soon on their way to his native St Vital and a final
resting place in St Boniface.[56] First, however, the coffin had to be
opened to repudiate a rumour that a policeman had stamped his
boot on the face.[57]

Across Canada, reactions differed. The *Globe* proclaimed that it
was Macdonald who was directly responsible for all the evils of the
rebellions, including the executions, and pleaded that the eight
Indians, due to be hanged on 27 November, might be spared.[58] On
the Toronto streets, John Beaty, a former Conservative MP, found
that even Grits congratulated him on the Prime Minister's firmness.[59]
In Quebec, shops were draped in mourning and Conservative MPs led
protests or laid low. In Montreal, there were preparations for the
mass rally in the Champs de Mars which would, in turn, launch the
movement to break the Conservative hold on French Canada.
Honoré Mercier's political calculation paid off; Edward Blake's did
not. In 1887, his bid for national power was rejected and he gave
way to a younger leader whose lesson from the Riel affair was not
Mercier's – that Quebec must draw away from Canada – but
Cartier's – that French Canada must not be isolated. Instead, by a
new allegiance to a failing Conservative party, it was Ontario which
would be left out of the Liberal Canada Laurier would create.

The nature of Canadian politics has helped guarantee that the
issues of the *Queen* v *Louis Riel* are still alive. A play, an opera, two
statues, and a postage stamp help to assure French Canada that its
version of the facts has triumphed, at least in popular folklore. The
execution of Riel is officially treated as one of a list of guilty
memories for the majority culture.

It is a comfortable use for history. To test one's ancestors by one's own wisdom and morality is to emerge a certain winner. Just as the McNaghten rules had once marked a notable advance in humane jurisprudence, so our own age would judge Riel differently. We might judge his mysticism and faith as symptoms of insanity. Or we might, in the light of treatment of a prominent defendant after the October crisis of 1970, grant him an income and launch him in a political career – the apparently bizarre request Riel made of the government from his prison cell. However, history is not simply an exercise in Couéism but an effort at understanding. Each generation, our own included, faces its problems with no more than its own stock of wisdom and knowledge. From the community morality play in the little Regina courthouse, three questions emerge: was Riel guilty; was he legally insane; and were there mitigating circumstances which should have reduced his penalty?

That he was essentially guilty as charged not even his lawyers attempted to deny. That he was the author and inspiration of an armed uprising against the government was amply demonstrated by witnesses and documents. His own intermittent attempts to blame Dumont or to claim half-heartedness in his cause were neither consistent nor convincing. Assuming the authority of the Canadian state to protect itself (and at least one British petitioner for Riel's life was prepared to deny it), Riel had committed treason.

That Riel was insane enough to satisfy modern legal and medical criteria hardly now seems in question.[60] That he was shamming, as the Crown had inferred during the trial, seemed impossible, even to Jukes, by November. That he was insane by the standards of his own day remains open to doubt. 'To render a person irresponsible for a crime on account of unsoundness of mind, the unsoundness should, according to the law as it has long been understood and held, be such as rendered him incapable of knowing right from wrong.' That was Mr Justice Maule's version of the rules, widely quoted during the trial and appeal, and two powerful speeches by Riel clearly showed that he knew what he was doing. In an interview after the execution, Dr Clark compared him with Charles Guiteau, assassin of President James Garfield in 1881. In Clark's view, Guiteau was merely a permanent crank, not insane. Riel's madness was demonstrated by the sudden alternation of moods of violent rage with periods of calm, gentle lucidity.[61] On the other hand, Father McWilliams, once so convinced of Riel's insanity that he had warned both Macdonald and the Governor-General that they would have the blood of an innocent man on their hands, later changed his mind. In the time before his execution, he explained to Macdonald, 'no man could have appeared more sane than he, both word and action.'[62] The real dilemma had rested with the six jurors for their decision, in effect, was final. According to the correspondent for the Toronto *Mail*, three of them later explained their plea for mercy on the grounds that while Riel was 'not absolutely insane in the ordinary accepted meaning of the word, he is a very decided crank.'[63] To be a crank, however, as even Dr Clark must had admitted, was not to enjoy the protection of the McNaghten rules.

Finally, could Riel claim justification? That was the plea he would have made for himself if his counsel had permitted, and it was the burden of both of his long addresses to the court. However, his lawyers did not reject the approach from perversity — as partisans it would have suited their purposes admirably — but because it is not a defence against the charge of high treason. No grievance or injustice could entitle a subject to take arms against his sovereign. At best it was a plea in mitigation of sentence.

As such, it might seem persuasive. Certainly it is the Riel version of government policy in the North-West which occupies the history books. A generation which faces the genuine dilemmas as well as the rhetoric of aboriginal rights and native claims should have more sympathy for the difficulties which confronted Macdonald and his colleagues. However, the problems of politicians and officials were not the concern of Indians, Métis, or westerners generally. They could not afford patience and they would not wait for insights. The rebellion brought answers and if, as native people might now argue, they proved to be wrong and even disastrous, they seemed at the time to be a vindication of Riel's actions. The Liberal press may have been right: the recommendation of mercy did condemn the government. Later, Blake would read the House of Commons a letter from one of the jurors: 'had the Government done their duty and redressed the grievances of the half-breeds of Saskatchewan ... there would never have been a second Riel Rebellion, and consequently no prisoner to try and condemn.'[64]

NOTES

1 Desmond Morton & R.H. Roy, *Telegrams of the North-West Cam-paign 1885* (Champlain Society 1972) 284
2 See G.F.G. Stanley, *Louis Riel* (Toronto 1963) 338-9; G.F.G. Stanley, 'Gabriel Dumont's Account of the North-West Rebellion' *Canadian Historical Review* XXXVIII 3 (September 1949) 268. See also B.A.T. de Montigny, *Biographie et récit général de Gabriel Dumont sur les évènements de 1885* (Montréal 1889) 142.
3 Morton & Roy, *Telegrams* 278
4 *Ibid.* 285-6, 290, 297; C.A. Boulton, *Reminiscences of the North-West Rebellions* (Toronto 1886) 199-200; Department of Militia and Defence, *Report upon the Suppression of the Rebellion in the North-West Territories, and Matters in Connection Therewith in 1885* (Ottawa 1886) 33
5 G.H. Needler, *Suppression of Rebellion in the North-West Territories of Canada* (Toronto 1948) 56
6 Morton & Roy, *Telegrams* 288, 308; Campbell to Macdonald, 14 April 1885, Macdonald Papers, Public Archives of Canada, v 197, pp 82799-800; Campbell to Macdonald, 21 May 1885, *ibid.* 82819-21
7 Capt. R.B. Deane, *Mounted Police Life in Canada: A Record of Thirty-One Years' Service* (London 1916) 185
8 Deane to Dewdney, 13 June 1885, Public Archives of Canada, Dewdney papers II 465
9 Deane, *Mounted Police Life* 186
10 Riel to Deane, nd, Macdonald Papers, vol 107, pp 43192-207. On Riel's family, see Stanley, *Riel* 340-2
11 Riel to Dewdney, 24 June 1885, Macdonald Papers, vol 107, pp 43210-16.
12 Riel to Macdonald, 16 July 1885 *ibid.*
13 Deane, *Mounted Police Life* 190
14 Campbell to Messrs C. Robinson, QC, B.B. Osler, QC, etc., 20 June 1885, Canada, *Sessional Papers* 43c, p 12
15 Campbell to Burbidge, 20 June 1885, Macdonald Papers, vol 197, p 82880
16 Campbell to Macdonald, 14 July 1885, *ibid.* p 82898
17 Vital Grandin to Macdonald, 11 July 1885, *ibid.* v 106, p 42513, and petition from Fathers André, Touré, Moulin, Fourmond, Vegre-ville and Lecoq, nd, *ibid.* 42501-2

18 Campbell to Macdonald, 18 May 1885, *ibid.* vol 197, p 82814
19 Toronto *Globe,* 11 July 1885
20 Campbell to Macdonald, 23 May 1885, Macdonald Papers, vol 197,
    p 82832. On Osler's reputation as a criminal lawyer, see Hector
    Charlesworth, *Candid Chronicles* (Toronto 1925) 212-32.
21 J.P.R. Fiset to Riel, 22 May 1885, Macdonald Papers, vol 107,
    p 43108. On the reaction in Quebec, see, for example, G.F.G.
    Stanley, *The Birth of Western Canada* (Toronto 1960) ch. xvii.
22 Toronto *Globe,* 3 July 1885
23 Stanley, *Riel* 344 and n19
24 Campbell to Macdonald, 16 July 1885, Macdonald Papers, vol 107,
    pp 43221-2
25 Toronto *Globe,* 18 July 1885 (Osler and Burbidge were sent to Winni-
    peg to help ensure that the appropriate precedents were established.
    See Campbell to Macdonald, 17 June 1885, *ibid.* vol 197, pp 32862-7
26 See Jackson to Dewdney, nd (26 June 1885) *ibid.* vol 107, p 43220.
27 Toronto *Globe,* 25 July 1885. Stanley, *Riel* 347. (On Jackson, see
    W.J.C. Cherwinski, 'Honoré Jaxon, Agitator, Disturber, producer of
    plans to make men think and Chronic Objector' *Canadian Historical
    Review,* XLVI 2 [June 1965]
28 Toronto *Globe,* 29 July 1885. (The list in *Queen* v *Louis Riel,* 000 is
    incomplete and incorrect.)
29 *Queen* v *Louis Riel* 000
30 *Ibid.* 000
31 'The Execution of Louis Riel: speech by the Hon. John S.D.
    Thompson, March 22, 1886' in Macdonald Papers, vol 107, p 44102
32 On the Beauport Asylum, see T.J.W. Burges, 'A Historical Sketch of
    Our Canadian Institutions for the Insane' *Transactions of the Royal
    Society of Canada* 1898 Section IV 55-7, citing the Royal Commis-
    sion on Lunatic Asylums in Quebec.
33 For an evaluation of the psychiatric aspects of the Riel trial, see E.R.
    Markson, Cyril Greenland, and R.E. Turner, 'The Life and Death of
    Louis Riel: A Study in Forensic Psychiatry' *Canadian Psychiatric
    Association Journal* X 4 (July-August 1965). For a sidelight on
    Clark's testimony, see also G.H. Young to C.E. Hamilton, 5 Decem-
    ber 1885, Macdonald Papers, vol 106, p 42763.
34 Dewdney to Macdonald, 7 August 1885, *ibid.* vol 212, p 90288
35 C.J. Wallbridge, *Queen* v *Louis Riel, Manitoba Law Reports* XI 11
    (November 1885) 329

36   Middleton to Cambridge, 31 July 1885, Royal Library, Windsor,
       Duke of Cambridge Papers
37   This famous phrase is cited only by George Parkin, *Sir John A. Mac-
       donald* (Makers of Canada Series, Toronto 1908) 244. The
       anonymous political neutral who reported it to Parkin might pos-
       sibly be G.M. Grant.
38   On the arguments of the French-Canadian cabinet ministers, see
       Caron's draft letter to his constituents (Macdonald Papers, vol 200,
       pp 84785-91) and 'The Riel Question, Letter by the Hon. J.A.
       Chapleau' 28 November 1885 (*ibid.* vol 107, pp 44061-72) See also
       'Report of Sir Alexander Campbell in the Case of Louis Riel con-
       victed of treason and executed therefor,' 25 November 1885, *ibid.*
       44050-60. On French-Canadian reaction, see *ibid.* vol 108 and
       Mason Wade, *The French Canadians* (Toronto 1968) II 412-19
39   The notorious editorial by E.E. Sheppard is in the *News*, 18 May
       1885.
40   D.A. Kubesh, 'Ontario Press Reaction to the Northwest Rebellion of
       1885' in J.M. Bumsted, *Documentary Problems in Canadian History*
       (Georgetown 1969) II 97. See also pp 95-128 for argument and
       evidence.
41   Toronto *Globe*, 3 August 1885
42   London *Advertiser*, 7 November 1885
43   Toronto *Globe*, 3 August 1885
44   Campbell to Macdonald, 27 November 1885, Macdonald Papers, vol
       197, p 42622; Caron to Macdonald, 26 November 1885, *ibid.* vol 200,
       p 84778
45   Andrée Desilets, *Hector-Louis Langevin: un père de la Conféd-
       eration canadienne* (Québec 1969) 377-9
46   London *Times*, 23 October 1885
47   A. Power to Campbell, nd, Macdonald Papers, vol 106, p 42616
48   Campbell to Macdonald, 23 October 1885, *ibid.* 42613
49   Macdonald to Lavell and Valade, 31 October 1885, *ibid.* 42638
50   Jukes to Dewdney, 6 November 1885, *ibid.* 42631
51   Lavell to Macdonald, 8 November 1885, *ibid.* 42648-9; and *ibid.* 9
       November 1886, 42671-86
52   Valade to Macdonald, 8 November 1885, *ibid.* 42650-1. See also
       Markson et al., 'Life and Death of Riel' 258
53   Jukes to Macdonald, 9 November 1885, Macdonald Papers, vol 106,
       p 42668. (In fact, Riel's prison papers were either destroyed or

carried off by Father André. See Dewdney to Macdonald, 18
November 1885, *ibid.* 42724.)

54 Toronto *Globe*, 16 November 1885; McWilliams to Macdonald, 4
December 1885, Macdonald Papers, vol 106, pp 42753-4
55 Toronto *Globe*, 17 November 1885
56 Dewdney to Macdonald, 18 November 1885, Macdonald Papers, vol
106, pp 42714-16
57 Deane, *Mounted Police Life* 231-2; N.F. Davin to Macdonald, 19
November 1885, Macdonald Papers, vol 106, pp 42739-40
58 Toronto *Globe*, 17 November 1885
59 J.H. Beaty to Macdonald, 16 November 1885, Macdonald Papers, vol
108, p 43744
60 See Markson et al., 'Life and Death of Riel.'
61 Toronto *Globe*, 18 November 1885
62 McWilliams to Macdonald, 4 December 1885, Macdonald Papers, vol
106, pp 42753-4; Toronto *Globe*, 30 November 1885
63 Toronto *Mail*, 3 August 1885. (Macdonald was informed by Robinson's law partner that the foreman of the jury had explained to A.D.
Stewart 'that he would not like to see a dog hanged & I suppose it to
be one of those things wh. softhearted men will do to make the
performance of a painful duty more tolerable.' Henry O'Brien to
Macdonald, 21 August 1885, Macdonald Papers, vol 108, p 43375)
64 Canada, House of Commons, *Debates*, 19 March 1886, p 255

RECOMMENDATIONS FOR FURTHER READING
The student of Riel must always be indebted to George F.G.
Stanley, whose magisterial contribution is apparent in so many areas
of Canadian historiography. Of particular value is his biography,
Louis Riel (Toronto: Ryerson 1963). For a documentary record of
the events in the North-West in 1885 see D.P. Morton and R.H. Roy,
Telegrams of the North-West Campaign 1885 (Toronto: Champlain
Society 1972), and for a narrative account, see the author's *The Last
War Drum: The North-West Campaign of 1885* (Toronto: Hakkert
1972). A dramatised version of the trial was written by John
Coulter, *Riel: A Play in Two Parts* (Toronto: Ryerson 1962). An
examination of the psychiatric considerations can be found in E.R.
Markson et al., 'The Life and Death of Louis Riel' *Canadian Psychiatric Association Journal* X 4 (July-August 1965). The most complete account of reaction in French Canada to the trial and
execution of Riel may be found in Robert Rumilly, *Histoire de la
province de Québec* (Montréal, nd) V. For an account of the aftermath of the rebellion and the trials, see Jean Larmour, 'Edgar
Dewdney and the Aftermath of the Rebellion' *Saskatchewan History*
XXIII 4 (Autumn 1970).

The Queen v Louis Riel

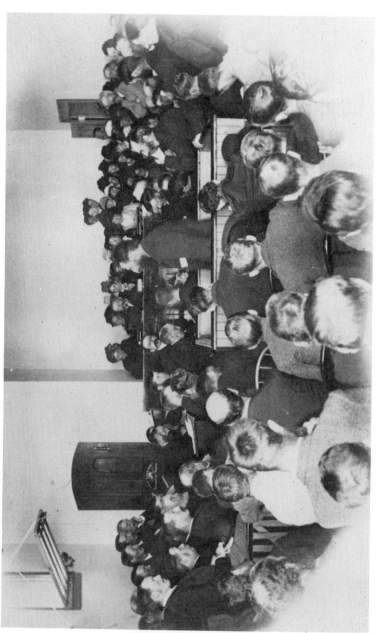

Louis Riel addressing the jury in the courthouse, Regina, 1885
(Public Archives of Canada)

The Court assembled at 11 AM, 20th July 1885.

MR JUSTICE RICHARDSON: I have to announce that Mr Henry Le
Jeune will be the associate justice for the approaching trial; Mr Dixie
Watson, clerk; Wallace McLean, J.S. Monahan, James T. Parkes and
F.R. Marceau, official reporters. Mr Sheriff, will you return the
precept.

Precept handed by the sheriff to the clerk who reads the return
and calls the list of jurors.

HIS HONOR MR JUSTICE RICHARDSON: The clerk will open the
court.

Court opened by the clerk.

MR JUSTICE RICHARDSON: Mr Sheriff, will you bring in the
prisoner.

Prisoner brought in and placed in the dock.

MR JUSTICE RICHARDSON: Louis Riel, have you been furnished
with a copy of the charge, of the panel of jurors, of the list of witnesses for the prosecution?

PRISONER: Yes, your Honor.

MR JUSTICE RICHARDSON: Arraign the prisoner.

The clerk reads the indictment as follows:

Sixth day of July, in the year of Our Lord 1885, at the Town of
Regina in the North-West Territories;

Before me, Hugh Richardson, one of the stipendiary magistrates
of the North-West Territories, exercising criminal jurisdiction under
the provisions of the North-West Act, 1880.

Louis Riel, you stand charged on oath before me as follows:

'The information and complaint of Alexander David Stewart, of
the City of Hamilton, in the Province of Ontario, in the Dominion of
Canada, chief of police, taken the sixth day of July, in the year of
our Lord one thousand eight hundred and eighty-five, before the
undersigned, one of Her Majesty's stipendiary magistrates in and for
the said North-West Territories of Canada, who saith:

1 That Louis Riel being a subject of our Lady the Queen, not
regarding the duty of his allegiance, nor having the fear of God in his
heart, but being moved and seduced by the instigation of the devil as
a false traitor against our said Lady the Queen, and wholly withdrawing the allegiance, fidelity and obedience which every true and
faithful subject of our said Lady the Queen should and of right

ought to bear towards our said Lady the Queen in the year aforesaid,
together with on the twenty-sixth day of March divers other false
traitors to the said Alexander David Stewart unknown, armed and
arrayed in a warlike manner, that is to say with guns, rifles, pistols,
bayonets, and other weapons, being then unlawfully, maliciously
and traitorously assembled and gathered together against our said
Lady the Queen at the locality known as Duck Lake in the said the
North-West Territories of Canada and within this realm, and did then
maliciously and traitorously attempt and endeavor by force and
arms to subvert and destroy the constitution and government of this
realm as by law established, and deprive and depose our said Lady
the Queen of and from the style, honor and kingly name of the Imperial Crown of this realm, in contempt of our said Lady the Queen
and her laws, to the evil example of all others in the like case offending, contrary to the duty of the allegiance of him, the said Louis
Riel, against the form of the statute in such case made and provided
and against the peace of our said Lady the Queen, her Crown and
dignity.

2   And the said Alexander David Stewart further saith: That the
said Louis Riel, being a subject of our Lady the Queen, not regarding
the duty of his allegiance, nor having the fear of God in his heart,
but being moved and seduced by the instigation of the devil as a
false traitor against our said Lady the Queen and wholly withdrawing the allegiance, fidelity and obedience which every true and faithful subject of our said Lady the Queen should and of right ought to
bear towards our said Lady the Queen, on the twenty-fourth day of
April in the year aforesaid, together with divers other false traitors
to the said Alexander David Stewart unknown, armed and arrayed in
a warlike manner, that is to say, with guns, rifles, pistols, bayonets
and other weapons, being then unlawfully, maliciously and traitorously assembled and gathered together against our said Lady the
Queen, most wickedly, maliciously and traitorously did levy and
make war against our said Lady the Queen at the locality known as
Fish Creek in the said the North-West Territories of Canada and
within this realm, and did then maliciously and traitorously attempt
and endeavor by force and arms to subvert and destroy the constitution and government of this realm as by law established, and deprive
and depose our said Lady the Queen of and from the style, honor
and kingly name of the Imperial Crown of this realm, in contempt of

our said Lady the Queen and her laws, to the evil example of all others in the like case offending, contrary to the duty of the allegiance of him, the said Louis Riel, against the form of the statute in such case made and provided, and against the peace of our said Lady the Queen, her Crown and dignity.

3 And the said Alexander David Stewart further saith: That the said Louis Riel being a subject of Our Lady the Queen, not regarding the duty of his allegiance nor having the fear of God in his heart, but being moved and seduced by the instigation of the devil as a traitor against our said Lady the Queen and wholly withdrawing the allegiance, fidelity and obedience which every true and faithful subject of our said Lady the Queen should and of right ought to bear towards our said Lady the Queen, on the ninth, tenth, eleventh and twelfth days of May in the year aforesaid, together with divers other false traitors to the said Alexander David Stewart unknown, armed and arrayed in a warlike manner, that is to say with guns, rifles, pistols, bayonets and other weapons, being then unlawfully, maliciously and traitorously assembled and gathered together against our said Lady the Queen, most wickedly, maliciously and traitorously did levy and made war against our said Lady the Queen at the locality known as Batoche, in the said the North-West Territories of Canada and within this realm, and did then maliciously and traitorously attempt and endeavor by force and arms to subvert and destroy the constitution and government of this realm as by law established, and deprive and depose our said Lady the Queen of and from the style, honor and kingly name of the Imperial Crown of this realm, in contempt of our said Lady the Queen and her laws, to the evil example of all others in like case offending, contrary to the duty to the allegiance of him, the said Louis Riel, against the form of the statute in such case made and provided, and against the peace of our said Lady the Queen, her Crown and dignity.

4 And the said Alexander David Stewart further saith: That the said Louis Riel, then living within the Dominion of Canada and under the protection of our Sovereign Lady the Queen, not regarding the duty of his allegiance nor having the fear of God in his heart, but being moved and seduced by the instigation of the devil as a false traitor against our said Lady the Queen, and wholly withdrawing the allegiance, fidelity and obedience which he should and of right ought to bear towards our said Lady the Queen, on the

twenty-sixth day of March in the year aforesaid, together with divers
other false traitors to the said Alexander Stewart unknown, armed
and arrayed in a war-like manner, that is to say with guns, rifles,
pistols, bayonets and other weapons, being then unlawfully, maliciously and traitorously assembled and gathered together against our
said Lady the Queen, most wickedly, maliciously and traitorously
did levy and make war against our said Lady the Queen at the locality known as Duck Lake, in the said the North-West Territories of
Canada and within this realm, and did then maliciously and traitorously attempt and endeavor by force and arms to subvert and
destroy the constitution and government of this realm as by law
established, and deprive and depose our said Lady the Queen of and
from the style, honor and kingly name of the Imperial Crown of this
realm, in contempt of our said Lady the Queen and her laws, to the
evil example of all others in like case offending, contrary to the duty
of the allegiance of him, the said Louis Riel, against the form of the
statute in such case made and provided, and against the peace of our
said Lady the Queen, her Crown and dignity.

5 And the said Alexander David Stewart further saith: That the
said Louis Riel, then living within the Dominion of Canada and under the protection of our Sovereign Lady the Queen, not regarding
the duty of his allegiance, nor having the fear of God in his heart,
but being moved and seduced by the instigation of the devil as a
false traitor against our said Lady the Queen, and wholly withdrawing
the allegiance, fidelity and obedience which he should and of right
ought to bear towards our said Lady the Queen, on the twenty-
fourth day of April in the year aforesaid, together with divers other
false traitors to the said Alexander Stewart unknown, armed and
arrayed in a warlike manner, that is to say, with guns, rifles, pistols,
bayonets and other weapons, being then unlawfully, maliciously and
traitorously assembled and gathered together against our said Lady
the Queen, most wickedly, maliciously and traitorously did levy and
make war against our said Lady the Queen at the locality known as
Fish Creek, in the said the North-West Territories of Canada and
within this realm, and did then maliciously and traitorously attempt
and endeavor by force and arms to subvert and destroy the constitution and Government of this realm as by law established, and deprive
and depose our said Lady the Queen of and from the style, honor
and kingly name of the Imperial Crown of this realm, in contempt of

our said Lady the Queen and her laws, to the evil example of all others in like case offending, contrary to the allegiance of him, the said Louis Riel, against the form of the statute in such case made and provided, and against the peace of our said Lady the Queen, her Crown and dignity.

6 And the said Alexander David Stewart further saith: That the said Louis Riel, then living within the Dominion of Canada and under the protection of our Sovereign Lady the Queen, not regarding the duty of his allegiance, nor having the fear of God in his heart, but being moved and seduced by the instigation of the devil as a false traitor against our said Lady the Queen, and wholly withdrawing the allegiance, fidelity and obedience which he should and of right ought to bear towards our said Lady the Queen, on the 9th, 10th, 11th and 12th days of May in the year aforesaid, together with divers other false traitors to the said Alexander David Stewart unknown, armed and arrayed in a warlike manner, that is to say, with guns, rifles, pistols, bayonets and other weapons, being then unlawfully, maliciously and traitorously assembled and gathered together against our said Lady the Queen, most wickedly, maliciously and traitorously did levy and make war against our said Lady the Queen at the locality known as Batoche, in the said North-West Territories of Canada and within this realm, and did then maliciously and traitorously attempt and endeavor by force and arms to subvert and destroy the constitution and Government of this realm as by law established, and deprive and depose our said Lady the Queen of and from the style, honor and kingly name of the Imperial Crown of this realm, in contempt of our said Lady the Queen and her laws, to the evil example of all others in like case offending, contrary to the duty of the allegiance of him, the said Louis Riel, agains the form of the statute in such case made and provided, and against the peace of our said Lady the Queen, her Crown and dignity.'

Sworn before me the day and year first   A.D. STEWART
above mentioned at the town of Regina in
the North-West Territories of Canada.

HUGH RICHARDSON

A Stipendiary Magistrate in and for the
North-West Territories of Canada

CLERK: Louis Riel, are you guilty or not guilty?

MR JUSTICE RICHARDSON: Who appears for the prosecution?

MR CHRISTOPHER ROBINSON, QC: I appear with my learned friends B.B. Osler, QC, G.W. Burbidge, QC, D.L. Scott and T.C. Casgrain.

MR F.X. LEMIEUX: I appear for the prisoner with Mr Charles Fitzpatrick, J.N. Greenshields and T.C. Johnstone.

MR LEMIEUX: I hold in my hand a plea to the jurisdiction of the court, supported by the usual affidavits, and we have agreed that Mr Fitzpatrick shall argue that part of the case. Will your Honor be kind enough to have the prisoner swear to the affidavit supporting this plea?

MR JUSTICE RICHARDSON: The clerk may swear him now as the court is open.

Affidavit sworn to by the prisoner.

MR FITZPATRICK: May it please your Honor, I will now proceed to read to the court the plea to the jurisdiction of the court in this case and affidavit.

The *Queen* v *Louis Riel* Charged under the North-West Territories Act, 1880.

And the said Louis Riel in his own proper person cometh into a court here, and having heard the information and complaint of Alexander David Stewart, of the city of Hamilton, in the Province of Ontario, in the Dominion of Canada, chief of police, taken the sixth day of July, in the year of our Lord one thousand eight hundred and eighty-five before Hugh Richardson, one of Her Majesty's stipendiary magistrates in and for the North-West Territories of Canada saith:

That Hugh Richardson, Esq., one of Her Majesty's stipendiary magistrates of the North-West Territories of Canada, exercising criminal jurisdiction in open court with a justice of the peace and a jury of six, under the provisions of the North-West Territories Act, 1880, ought not to take cognizance of the offences in the said information charged and specified, because protesting that he is not guilty of the same, nevertheless, the said Louis Riel saith that the offences with which he is charged are punishable with death, and he should be committed for safe custody and sent for trial to Upper Canada, or to any court constituted in British Columbia taking cognizance of like offences committed therein, and because in virtue of the laws in force in the place where the said offences are charged to have been committed, the said Hugh Richardson, in open court with a justice of the peace and a jury of six, has no jurisdiction to try the offences charged in the said information.

Wherefore the said Louis Riel prays judgment if the said Hugh Richardson, in open court with a justice of the peace and a jury of six, now here, will take cognizance of the charges aforesaid.

MR ROBINSON: I think it would be better to have an adjournment for a quarter of an hour or so in order to consider the plea. If we had a copy of the plea an adjournment would not be necessary.

MR JUSTICE RICHARDSON: At this point we might determine what hours the court will sit.

MR ROBINSON: What hours would your Honor suggest as most convenient to the court?

MR JUSTICE RICHARDSON: I would like to do a fair day's work. Commence at 8 o'clock in the morning, how would that suit?

MR ROBINSON: That is rather too early. As far as counsel are concerned, they would suggest from 10 to 6.

MR JUSTICE RICHARDSON: With an intermission?

MR ROBINSON: Yes.

MR JUSTICE RICHARDSON: I suppose if I don't yield quietly you will make me in the end.

Court here adjourned till 1 o'clock.

Resumed after adjournment.

HIS HONOR MR JUSTICE RICHARDSON: Before you proceed I understand there are quite a number of prisoners in custody.

MR OSLER: Seventy-three.

HIS HONOR: Going through all these will take a very long time. A great number of days. The prospects are that this case, if it does not close at once will take a considerable time and will be followed by the others. I think it would be unfair to the prisoners to keep them longer in custody than necessary, and I propose therefore, as there are other gentlemen having the same jurisdiction as myself, to ask the Government to send one of them to hold court so as to have the two courts sitting at the same time, if you gentlemen have no objection to that course.

MR ROBINSON: We have no objection to that. We were talking about it this morning.

MR FITZPATRICK: I will proceed to read our plea to the jurisdiction of the court as amended in some respects.

HIS HONOR: This will be substituted for the one put in my hands this morning.

Mr Fitzpatrick reads the plea as amended. (See plea p. 000.)

MR ROBINSON: In our view a formal plea to the jurisdiction is not necessary, nor a formal answer, we thought it only necessary for them to state their objection and for us to answer them.

And the said Christopher Robinson, one of Her Majesty's counsel learned in the law, who for our said present Sovereign Lady the Queen, in this behalf prosecuteth as to the said plea of him the said Louis Riel by him above pleaded as aforesaid for our said present Sovereign Lady the Queen saith:

That the said plea and the matter therein contained are not sufficient in law to preclude the court here from their jurisdiction and to hear and determine the offences charged mentioned and specified in the said charge and above charged upon him the said Louis Riel in and by the said charge.

Wherefore for want of a proper and sufficient answer in this behalf he prayeth judgment and that the said Louis Riel may answer in court here to our said present Sovereign Lady the Queen touching and concerning the premises aforesaid.

Answer handed to the clerk and filed.

HIS HONOR: We have the plea to the jurisdiction and we have the demurrer.

MR FITZPATRICK: We join issue upon the demurrer. In excepting to the jurisdiction of the court I beg leave to remark that it is an objection of counsel of the prisoner only, our opposition does not arise from apprehension as to the verdict of the jury ultimately being that Riel is innocent; but your Honor knows that even of technical objections where the life of a man is at stake it is the duty of his counsel to avail himself, and although we entertain no doubt of the acquittal of the prisoner, yet in the duty which we, as legal advisers, have to perform we feel ourselves compelled to neglect nothing that by possibility can lead to it. At the same time I must say on behalf of our client that it is his desire while declaring the respect for your Honors to take advantage of the opportunity now afforded him to claim for the people of the North-West Territories such full and ample enjoyment of the privileges of the British constitution as

British subjects are entitled to have. This may perchance be the closing scene of his eventful career, but Louis Riel will not have lived and died for nothing if trial by jury, the palladium of our liberties, the bulwark of our constitution, the fairest mode of trial which the wisdom of centuries has been able to devise is guaranteed in all its purity to his fellow subjects. We therefore except to the jurisdiction of this court.

The proceedings here are instituted under the Act of 1880. It is my intention to examine how far the provisions of this Act are in force in this Territory. I shall, therefore, in the first instance, proceed to ascertain the laws in force in this country in 1763, and it shall be my endeavor to show what is meant by 'trial by jury.' I will examine the provisions of the Statute of 1880 and see in what respect they are repugnant to the provisions of the Magna Charta, how far they have been followed. I shall proceed to examine the power of Parliament to pass such an Act as that of 1880, and see if power does not exist elsewhere for the trial of the accused.

I may assume that the North-West Territories form part of the British Dominions either as having been part of the territory covered by the Hudson Bay charter of 1670, or as part of Canada ceded to the English by the French in 1763. That is a point which has been debated but is not of sufficient interest in this case. If we consider the North-West Territories as forming part of the British Dominions by the original charter to the Hudson Bay Company, we must look upon the provisions of the Magna Charta guaranteeing trial by jury as the birthright of every British subject. Story 2, p 540, 'The right constitutes one of the fundamental articles of Magna Charta, in which it is declared *nulus homo capiatur, nec imprisonetur, aut exulet aut alique modi destruatur, etc., nisi per legale judicium parium suorum vel per legum terrae* − No man shall be arrested, nor imprisoned nor banished, nor deprived of life, etc., but by the judgment of his peers, or the law of the land.' A trial by jury is generally understood to mean, *ex vi termini*, a trial by a jury of twelve men, impartially selected, who must unanimously concur in the guilt of the accused before a legal conviction can be made. Any law therefore dispensing with any of these requisites may be considered unconstitutional. If we consider these Territories as forming part of Canada ceded to England by France, then the criminal law of the conquering power became the criminal law of these Territories.

As to that it is not necessary for me to cite any authorities. I may, however, refer you to *Regina* v *Coote* L.R. 4, P.C. 599. If it is possible to have any doubts, I will call your attention to the debates on the Quebec Bill, which I hold in my hand. The question there arises as to whether trial by jury in civil matters is to form part of the law of the land. Lord North says: 'If the Crown is interested in any question concerning a jury it is in criminal matters, and having duly considered the great protection afforded the subject by juries, we have universally given them a jury in all criminal cases.' I say we may take it for granted that from 1763 trial by jury was an essential requisite in all criminal proceedings, especially when punishable by death. It becomes necessary to see what is the meaning of these terms in Magna Charta, 'trial by jury,' 'due process of law.' I shall proceed to examine that question. Story, 2nd vol, p 541, in the footnote: 'A trial by jury is understood to mean *ex vi termini*, a trial by a jury of twelve men, impartially selected, who must unanimously concur in the guilt of the accused before a legal conviction can be had. Any law, therefore, dispensing with the requisites may be considered unconstitutional.' 2nd Kent, p 13 (footnote): 'The law of the land in bills of right, says Chas. J. Ruffin, in the elaborate opinion delivered in *Hoke* v *Henderson*, 4 Dev., N.C. Rep. 15 (and one replete with sound constitutional doctrines) does not mean merely an act of the legislature, for that construction would abrogate all restriction on legislative authority. This clause means that statutes which would deprive a citizen of the rights of person or property without a regular trial, according to the course and usage of the common law, and in private suits at common law, would not be the law of the land in the sense of the constitution. And the judgment of his peers means, trial by a jury of twelve men according to the course of the common law' – *Taylor* v *Porter*, 4 Hill, p 140; *Wilkinson* v *Leland*, '2 Peters 657,' the words 'law of the land' do not mean a statute passed for tracking the enemy, that construction would render the restriction absolutely nugatory, and turn this part of the constitution into mere nonsense. See '*Wyndham* v *The People*,' 13 N.Y. Appeals 484; Potter on 'The Constitution p 469, edition of '85, 'The article is a restrain on the legislative as well as the executive and the judicial power of the Government.'

Lord Coke says the words mean by the due process of law, which he afterwards explains to be by indictment or presentment of good and lawful men when such things be done in due manner or by writ

original of the common law, *per legem terrae*, not *per legem et con-*
suetudinem regis Anglicœ populi Anglicœ, so as to bind both King
and people. 37 Edward III, chap. 8, gives the true sense and meaning
of these words. Hurd on the *Habeas corpus*, p 73, Mr Spencer in his
essay on the trial by jury, after an elaborate examination, critical
and historical of the question states the legal import of the chapter
as follows: 'No freeman shall be arrested, or imprisoned, or deprived
of his freehold, or his liberties, or free customs, or be outlawed or
exiled, or in any manner destroyed (harmed), nor will we (the King)
proceed against him, nor send anyone against him, by force of arms,
unless according to (that is in execution of) the sentence of his
peers, and (or as the case may require) the common law of England'
(as it was at the time of Magna Charta, 1215).

Leaving this branch of the case which I have treated at some
length and which goes to show, and by which I have endeavored to
show, what is the meaning of 'trial by jury,' I will draw your attention to the Imperial Act in reference to treason trials. No court but a
superior court having original jurisdiction can try a case of treason.
You will also find it laid down in section 2 of the bill of rights that
there is a special provision made that in case of treason the jurors
shall be freeholders. In section 2 you will also find that the Crown is
to furnish a copy of the indictment and a list of the witnesses, a
precaution taken in no other case except treason. The importance of
the selection of a jury in the case of treason is obvious; in a case of
that kind more than in any other case the Crown is a party to the
suit and therefore special provision is made for the protection of the
individual as against the Crown. So far do they go in England upon
that point, that originally the appointment of the sheriff was taken
out of the hands of the King and given to the people, so that, as
Lord Coke says, it could not be suspected that the sheriff would be
interested and would return a corrupt jury.

It will not be necessary for me to dwell any longer on these
points. I think I have shown what are, under the provisions of the
Magna Charta, the requirements of trial by jury. A special enactment
provides for the case of treason. In the view of these decisions, and
in the light of these authorities, let us examine the statute of 1880
and see in what respects the statute complies with these conditions. I
wish to call your attention to section 74 of the Act: 'The Governor
may from time to time appoint by commission under the great seal

one or more fit or proper persons, barristers-at-law or advocates of
five years' standing in any of the Provinces, not exceeding three, to
be and act as stipendiary magistrates or stipendiary magistrate within
the North-West Territories, who shall hold office during pleasure,
&c.' The third paragraph of section 76 provides for certain offences,
and sub-section five leaves it optional with the magistrate to exercise
his jurisdiction or refuse, as he sees fit, and sub-section 9: 'Persons
required as jurors for a trial shall be summoned by the stipendiary
magistrate from among such male persons as he may think suitable
in that behalf; and then the jury required on such trial shall be called
from the persons so summoned as such jurors and sworn by the
stipendiary magistrate who presides at the trial.' Now that section
goes to the basis of the jury system, because the number is imma-
terial, whether 12, 20 or 25, if the summoning of the jury is not of
such a nature as to guarantee a proper and fit trial. That is the point
Lord Coke refers to when he says the appointment of the sheriff is
taken out of the hands of the Crown, because, in a case in which the
Crown might be a party, he might be suspected of having returned a
corrupt jury, and surely this is one of these cases. Section 2 of the
bill of rights says the jurors shall be freeholders; section 9 here says
you may have the jurors you think suitable. I do not wish anything I
may say to apply to the court as now constituted. I am arguing on
abstract principles; it might be that a Scroggs or a Jeffries might
occupy your place. I speak in that sense and with the intention, as I
am instructed, of paying due respect to this court. I say there is no
qualification required; the only qualification is that the jurors shall
be male. American citizens may be brought here, people may be
brought here from Quebec, who have no interest or knowledge of
the country; such jurors might be brought here to try this case. Is
that such a trial as there should be, according to the proper interpretation of the British constitution? The jury has been called the
bulwark of our constitution. Now the magistrate can take any jurors
he may think fit. What is the meaning of such a jury system? What
can a jury mean when chosen under these circumstances? What does
it mean, except that the jury is chosen not to try the case, but simply to register the decrees of the person who has chosen them. This is
the position in which we now find ourselves. Is that trial by jury
according to the law of the land? I submit it is impossible to put any
such interpretation upon the law. It is impossible to read that

section of the statute in the light of the authorities I have given your Honor and say that this is a provision for trial by jury.

The challenges are next provided for, under sub-section 10, the number being limited to six as against twenty under the English system. I have gone through these provisions which I thought it necessary to call the attention of the court to. I will also refer your Honor to page 642, 2nd volume of Story. 'Mr Justice Blackstone, with the warmth and pride becoming an Englishman, living under its blessed protection, has said: "A celebrated French writer, who concludes that because Rome, Sparta and Carthage have lost their liberties, therefore those of England in time must perish, should have recollected that Rome, Sparta and Carthage, at the time when their liberties were lost, were strangers to trial by jury." ' I hardly think if trial by jury was under the statute of 1880 that Justice Blackstone would have spoken thus about it? It is true that we have trial by jury. But it is the shadow and not the substance; chosen in such a way the jury is as worthless as the human body when the living one has fled. Have they the right to deprive us altogether of the right of trial by jury? It becomes us to examine whether the Federal Parliament can take away trial by jury. It is a moot point whether even the Imperial Parliament can take it away. According to some authorities Parliament can do anything except make a man into a woman, or a woman into a man. Harmon says that it possesses absolute power, and is as arbitrary in England as in Prussia, but there are other men, eminent statesmen, who hold there are restrictions and limitations upon the legislative power. Whether the Imperial Parliament has the power to do this is of very little moment. This statute was passed by the Federal Parliament here, and it becomes necessary to examine by virtue of what authority the Parliament has legislated for the North-West Territories. Counsel may say the North-West Territories formed part of the Dominion of Canada under section 146 of the North America Act. It is doubtful whether the North-West Territories were admitted under that Act. There is no enactment, nor any provision under the British North America Act which permits the Government to admit the North-West Territories on a different basis to the other Provinces. Presuming they were admitted under the British North America Act, we find in the very preamble that the Provinces are guaranteed a constitution similar in spirit to that of the United Kingdom. If there is any doubt as to that I would

refer you to what was said by Lord Carnarvon at the time the Bill
was introduced. If admitted under the Confederation Act I submit
that the Confederation was in reality a treaty scheme between all the
Provinces, and to which they were all parties, and that when the
North-West Territories entered into this treaty they acquired the
same rights as the other Provinces. Sir John Macdonald said that we
must consider this scheme in the light of a treaty. Therefore that
treaty is binding upon the high contracting parties, and it is not in
the power of Parliament to alter any of the provisions guaranteed at
that time. Now what would be said in the Province of Quebec, or in
the Province of Ontario, if it pleased Parliament to deprive both or
either of them of the right of trial by jury? Why then should the
North-West Territories be deprived of the rights and privileges guaranteed to the other Provinces? Is there anything in the Act that says
that Magna Charta, the right of trial by jury, shall not extend to
these territories, but shall be given to the other Provinces? Is it because the North-West Territories have no voice in the legislation,
because they have no power to send a representative to defend their
rights? I say it is contrary to the British Constitution, it is contrary
to the sound principles which should guide British statesmen, to
imagine that her statesmen would have said: We give you power
which shall be used in one way towards one set of subjects and in
another towards another. It is impossible to imagine such a spirit
guiding the British Parliament. It is a very doubtful point whether
the North-West Territories form part of the Dominion of Canada
under section 117 of the British North America Act, and it became
necessary to pass the British North America Act of '71. Now if we
consider that this statute of 1880 is passed by virtue of the powers
conferred under section four of that Act, it must be read in the light
of the Confederation Act. The Confederation Act granted the
Federal Parliament certain well-defined powers, and the Local Parliaments, deriving their powers from the same source, are as absolute
within the limits of the powers given them. But you take section 4
of this Act confers on the Federal Parliament not already conferred
upon it, it is nothing more than adding additional powers to those
conferred. To show that the powers given by the Confederation Act
are not absolute, your Honor will find that it became necessary to
pass the Act of 38 and 39 Vic. to remove any doubt as to the power
of Parliament. Then in *Kielly* v *Carson*, 72 Doutre, you will see the

powers of the Legislature are limited. The power of the Federal Parliament is delegated to them by the Imperial Parliament, and on that
point I will call your attention to *Taylor* v *Porter*, 4 Hill, p 140: 'The
Legislature can only exercise such powers as are delegated to it, and
when it transcends these limits its acts are entirely void.' Mr Story
says: 'The fundamental maxims of a free Government seem to require that the rights of personal liberty and private property should
be held sacred; at least no court of justice in the country would be
warranted in assuming the power to violate and disregard them, a
power so repugnant to the common principles of justice and civil
liberty, a power so repugnant lurked under any general grant of legislative authority, or ought to be implied from any general expression
of the will of the people. The people ought not to be presumed to
part with rights so vital to their security and well-being without very
strong and direct expression of such an intention.' As to the unalterable character of the Confederation scheme I would refer to 118 and
119 Doutre: 'As to the unalterable character of the Bill, Lord Carnarvon repeatedly expressed himself.' And Sir John Macdonald said,
119 Doutre, 'As I stated in the parliamentary discussion, we must
consider this scheme in the light of a treaty.'

There may be reference made by my learned friends to the case
of *Regina* v *Bradshaw*, in which Mr Justice Gwynne sat. Your Honor
will see that in that case there is no reference whatever to the right
of the Federal Parliament to legislate on the question of trial by
jury. It was simply the case of an appeal from the quarter sessions,
whether the two parties to the appeal might either consent or dispense with the right to a jury. Both parties consented to it, and
when the matter came before Mr Justice Gwynne he said the party
having given his consent it did not lie with him to afterwards object
to the fact that he hadn't had trail by jury.

But you will also probably be told that in civil cases the right
exists to limit the number of the jury. For instance, in New Brunswick a jury of five may sit in civil cases.

MR BURBIDGE: Five or seven.

MR FITZPATRICK: All these difficulties disappear in view of the
remarks of Lord North which I have already quoted. With reference
to the jury in civil cases, under the Quebec Act it was decided that
this question should be left to the exclusive jurisdiction, to the
exclusive control of the Local Parliaments of the colonies at that

time. It was decided that principle should be left entirely in their
control, because that was a matter with which the Imperial Parliament had nothing to do. But a matter affecting civil rights is not a
matter affecting the liberty of the subject. The people of different
Provinces of New Brunswick assemble in their Parliaments and decide that in matters affecting purely civil rights that they, between
themselves, will be satisfied with a jury of five or six. But how does
that apply to the North-West Territories? Have the people of those
territories been asked whether they would be content with a jury of
six in cases of treason or where the penalty of the offence is death? I
say there is no analogy between the two cases, and it is impossible
that any such reasoning can apply to the present case.

Then, I know we may be told also that in view of the peculiar
circumstances of this country, in view of the fact that there might be
great difficulty in securing a jury of twelve in the territories, in view
of all such difficulties, that it would be impossible for them to provide a jury such as is required under the English Act, and being
impossible no one is obliged to do it. Now, if we take that reasoning,
and they may possibly be disposed to go further and assert that the
Imperial Parliament, with a full knowledge of the difficulties attending the situation must necessarily have desired to confer on the Parliament the right to modify trial by jury — but how can that
argument stand in view of the fact that the North-West Territories
have already been legislated for by the Imperial Parliament? These
territories were no further advanced when the Acts of the Georges
were passed than they are to-day. At that time they were no better
able to provide a jury system than they are to-day. Why should the
Federal Parliament, under delegated powers, assume to itself powers
which the delegating powers didn't assume? If the Imperial Parliament didn't legislate in this way, why should the Federal Parliament
assume to do it?

You will also hear from my learned friend, Mr Greenshields, a
complete argument on another point: Here we have 22 and 23 Vic.
on the Statute book, in force to this day, providing that this case
should not be tried before your Honor, but either in the Province of
Upper Canada or in British Columbia. You will find it still in force in
the Revised Edition. You will find that statute still in force, and on
the other hand we have our own statute for 1880. Now, which of
these two statutes is to have force? Which of these two statutes is to

prevail? The statute 28 Vic. says which is to prevail. It says the Imperial statute is the one that is to prevail, but as I said, it is not my intention to argue that question fully; the learned counsel who succeeds me will go into the matter in a very few minutes. I am now speaking to the argument which I had the honor to lay before this court. I have nothing further to say, except to repeat in substance what I have already pointed out. That is, that all we require, all we ask, is a fair trial by a jury of our peers; that is all any man can expect, and I say, that with men who are British subjects, having a knowledge of the British constitution, the descendants of those sturdy barons who wrung from their king on the plains of Runnymede that great charter, the inviolable birthright of every British subject, I say with men such as these we can have nothing to fear. But in this case here at the present time, we plead not so much the case of Louis Riel, but a case which has great interest for every subject in these North-West Territories. This is destined to be a great country, fruitful with promises of a brilliant future but these promises will only be realized in so far as the principles of the British constitution are respected, those principles which made of the Mother Country the greatest land the sun has ever shone upon.

MR GREENSHIELDS: The learned counsel who has just preceded me has gone very fully into the constitutional question of this case. The demurrer filed by the defence raises in effect here two questions before the court. The first is whether the court constituted as it now is, has authority under the statute of 1880 to try this case; and secondly, whether that statute, couched in the language in which it is, and by reason of the provisions contained therein, does not interfere and override entirely the provisions of Magna Charta. The learned counsel has gone into the latter point very fully. The first I shall now deal with. Previous to Confederation the North-West Territories were governed by the Imperial Parliament. The statutes providing for their government were passed by that Parliament, and in examining the statutes that are in existence and were in existence, and not repealed previous to Confederation, and since repealed, we find we have now on the Imperial statute book the statute of 1st and 2nd, George IV, chap. 66; the statute 22 and 23 Vic., chap. 26, and 28 and 29 Vic., chap. 23.

Now, on the one hand, we have these statutes of the Imperial Parliament remaining on the statute book and unrepealed, and we

have, on the other hand, the statute of 1880 passed by the
Dominion Parliament.

Now, let us see what is required and what courts are constituted
by the Imperial statutes I have just alluded to. The first statute of
the 1st and 2nd George IV, is entitled: 'An Act for regulating the fur
trade and establishing a criminal and civil jurisdiction within certain
parts of North America.'

MR JUSTICE RICHARDSON: That has been repealed.

MR GREENSHIELDS: Clause 5 has been repealed, but that is the
only clause that is repealed, and in the chronological index to the
statutes that statute appears, the index being issued in 1884 by the
Imperial Parliament, as being still in force and on the statute book.
Now, sections 10, 11 and 12 provide for the constitution of courts
and the appointment of justices of the peace, who shall have certain
jurisdiction as in the statute mentioned. Section 10 provides for the
appointment of justices of the peace, who shall have jurisdiction to
investigate, upon a commission issued from the courts in Upper
Canada, any evidence that may be required in a case sent from those
Territories to Upper Canada for trial, and that their report on that
shall avail as evidence. Section 11 provides that commissions may be
issued to justices of the peace to hold courts of record for the trial
of civil and criminal cases. The section is as follows: 'And be it further enacted that it shall be lawful for His Majesty notwithstanding
anything contained in this Act or in any charter granted to the said
Governor and Company of Adventurers of England trading to Hudson Bay, from time to time, by any commission under the great seal,
to authorise and empower any such persons so appointed justices of
the peace as aforesaid to sit and hold courts of record for the trial of
criminal offences and misdemeanors, and also of civil causes, and it
shall be lawful for His Majesty to order, direct and authorise the
appointment of proper persons to act in aid of such courts and
justices within the jurisdiction assigned to such courts and justices in
any such commission; anything in this Act or in any charter of the
Governor and Company of Merchant Adventurers of England trading
to Hudson Bay to the contrary notwithstanding.'

Section 12 then determines what the jurisdiction of the court so
appointed is: 'Provided always and be it further enacted, that such
courts shall be constituted, as to the number of justices to preside
therein, and as to such places within the said territories of the said

company or any Indian territories or other parts of North America
as aforesaid, and the times and manner of holding the same, as His
Majesty may from time to time order and direct; but shall not try
any offender upon any charge or indictment for any felony made
the subject of capital punishment, or for any offence or passing sentence affecting the life of any offender, or adjudge or cause any
offender to suffer capital punishment or transportation, or take
cognizance of or try any civil action or suit in which the cause of
such suit or action shall exceed in value the amount or sum of £200,
and in every case of any offence subjecting the person committing
the same to capital punishment or transportation, the court or any
judge of any such court or any justice or justices of the peace before
whom any such offender shall be brought, shall commit such offender to safe custody, and cause such offender to be sent in such
custody for trial in the court of the Province of Upper Canada.'

Now, we have that statute on the statute book, appointing a
court of record and authorizing justices of the peace to preside over
that court and to try cases up to a certain amount and offences up
to a certain degree, but we have a positive enactment prohibiting the
justices of the peace so appointed from trying any offence involving
the death penalty.

Now, that section and that statute are still on the statute book so
far as the North-West Territories are concerned. The statute I have in
my hand is the Revised Statutes, volume 5, which states by foot
notes here such portions of the statute as are repealed. Sections 6 to
13 are repealed as to Vancouver's Island and British Columbia, clearly showing that those sections are in force as to the North-West Territories, unless we can find they are repealed in some other way.
That statute providing for this court gives the justices of the peace
jurisdiction to try up to a certain amount, but absolutely prohibiting
him from trying an offence involving the death penalty, but providing what they shall do, viz.: 'The court or any judge of any such
court shall commit such offender to safe custody and shall cause
such offender to be sent in such custody for trail in the court of the
Province of Upper Canada.' There was clearly delineated the rights
and authorities under this statute which the justices of the peace
enjoy. They could only try up to a certain amount, and offences of a
certain kind. That statute remained on the statute book, and later
on, the Act 22 and 23 Victoria, chapter 26, was passed. Now, your

Honors will notice in reading this statute that the first statute referred to, gave the justices of the peace jurisdiction to investigate as
it were, merely, and then to try as provided in section 12. The statute 22 and 23 Victoria, recites in the preamble this very statute of
the 1st and 2nd George IV, and by the first clause extends the jurisdiction of the justices of the peace under certain limits and conditions and gives them a summary jurisdiction for certain offences that
are mentioned in section 1. This section 1 has a proviso too, in the
same sense that section 12 had, viz.: 'Provided always that where the
offence with which any person is charged before any such justice or
justices is one which is punishable with death, or one which in the
opinion of such justice or justices ought, either on account of the
inadequacy of the punishment which such justice or justices can
inflict, or for any other reason, to be made the subject of prosecution in the ordinary way, rather than to be disposed of summarily,
such justice or justices shall commit the offender to safe custody,
and cause him to be sent in such custody for trial to Upper Canada,
as provided by the said Act of King George IV, or where such justice
or justices may see fit, to the Province of British Columbia; and such
offender may be tried and dealt with by any court constituted in
British Columbia having cognizance of the like offences committed
there; and such courts shall have the like powers and authorities for
this purpose as under the said acts are given to any court in Canada
in the like cases.'

Now that statute was merely an extension to the powers of the
justices of the peace. It gave the justice of the peace the right to send
an offender to British Columbia, and gave them a summary jurisdiction for certain offences, excepting, of course, the offences as excepted in the statute of George IV; but it, in no way, repealed any of
the provisions of the statute of George IV, and it constituted another
court, by section No. 1; and section No. 2 comes in as a saving proviso for the court of record, which might be constituted under section 12 of the statute George IV, Section 2 is as follows: 'Provided
that nothing hereinbefore contained shall be taken to repeal or affect
the provisions of the said Act of King George IV, concerning the
establishment of courts of record in the said Territories; and where
such courts are established, any offenders within the limits of the
jurisdiction thereof, may be committed for trial to such courts,
instead of the courts of Canada or British Columbia.' Now this

section 2 is put in this statute here for the purpose of avoiding any ambiguity or uncertainty that there might be with the powers given justices of the peace under the Act 22-3 Victoria, and might not be taken to supersede the powers enjoyed or granted them under the statute George IV, and the saving clause here is put in, which states that, notwithstanding the extended jurisdiction which is given here to the justices of the peace under section 1; that it will not in any way interfere with the courts of record that are provided for under the statute George IV, and that these courts of record as constituted under George IV, will have the jurisdiction to try the offences which they are given jurisdiction of under that statute.

It might be contended, on the part of the Crown, that the terms in which this proviso is couched, gave the courts established under George IV an extended jurisdiction to try all cases, on account, perhaps, of the wording which appears in the section, viz.: 'Where such courts are established, any offenders within the limits of the jurisdiction hereof, may be committed for trail to such courts, instead of the courts of Canada or British Columbia.' Now, the interpretation and meaning of that clause, which is put in here merely as a saving clause, is, as I previously explained, in order that there might be no uncertainty as to the powers that are intended to be given to justices of the peace under this statute, and the marginal note which I see here, reads: 'Saving provisions of 1 and 2, George IV, as to courts of record'; but there is nothing in that section which states in any way that it is intended as an extension of the jurisdiction of the magistrates as they enjoy them under the statute George IV.

Now the words in section two are merely general terms, referring to the statute George IV, and I refer your Honors to Dwarris, on Statutes, p 656: 'for a statute which treats of things or persons of an inferior rank, cannot by general words, be extended to those of a superior'; and also Maxwell, p 297, reads: 'That is, these general words must be construed, the general words as used in this section, must be construed as applicable only to the provisions of statute George IV to which it refers; so that we have them coming up to 22-3 Victoria; we have these two statutes which are in no way contradictory, the first giving justices of the peace certain powers, and the second extending the power of such justices of the peace, and we have a complete form established here in these two statutes for the

trial of all kinds of offences, that is, offences involving a death penalty are to be sent to Upper Canada or British Columbia, and offences
of a minor nature to be tried here. This was the law as contained in
these two statutes, at least until the passing of the British North
America Act, and particularly the amended Act of 1871. These two
statutes were the only statutes under which criminal offenders could
be tried in these Territories.

Now, my learned friend who has preceded me has shown that the
powers enjoyed by the Dominion Parliament with regard to their
legislation for the North-West Territories are delegated powers from
the Imperial Parliament, and, being delegated powers, the Dominion
Parliament cannot exceed the powers that are clearly given them
under the Imperial statutes forming the Confederation.

Now, we find the Dominion Parliament, in 1880, enacts the statute under which this court is now constituted. And this statute goes
so far. It does not refer in any way to the Imperial statutes. It does
not pretend in that statute to repeal it, which we do not admit it
would have the power; but there is no provision that they repealed
these two Imperial statutes.

We have the statute of 1880 passed which gives your Honors in
court, with a jury of six, the right to try for capital offences, and to
try offences to which the death penalty is attached. That statute —
our contention is on the constitutional question — is entirely *ultra
vires* of the Dominion Parliament, but the statute is there. We have,
therefore, the statute of 1880 which gives your Honors the right to
try all criminal cases involving the death penalty.

We have, on the other hand, these two Imperial statutes unrepealed, which, in positive terms, order the magistrate holding criminal jurisdiction in the North-West Territories, in all offences
involving the death penalty, to send the criminal to Upper Canada or
British Columbia.

Now, here it seems to us is a direct conflict of the question of the
powers that might be enjoyed by the justices of the peace in these
territories. Which statute is to prevail? Are we to follow the Imperial
statutes, or are your Honors to take the provisions of the statute of
1880 as overriding the provisions of the Imperial statutes, and follow
them? Now we have, fortunately for the court, an Imperial statute
passed after the statute 22-3 Vic., chap. 63, Imperial statutes, in-
tituled: 'An Act to remove doubts as to the validity of Colonial

Laws.' The preamble of this statute reads as follows: 'Whereas
doubts have been entertained respecting the validity of divers laws
enacted or purporting to have been enacted by the legislature of
certain of Her Majesty's colonies and respecting the powers of such
legislation, and it is expedient such doubts should be removed, &c.,'
and then follow certain interpretation clauses defining what a colony
is, what legislature and what colonial law is. Now the term legislature
is defined here to signify the authority, other than the Imperial Parliament or Her Majesty in Council, competent to make laws for any
colony. The term 'colonial law' shall include laws made for any
colony either by such legislature as aforesaid, or by Her Majesty in
Council. Now this interpretation clause clearly brings this statute of
1880 within the purview of the statute 28-9 Vic., providing for the
interpretation of it.

Section 2 of that statute meets the case exactly. Any colonial law
which is or shall be in any respect repugnant to the provisions of any
Act of Parliament extending to the colony to which such law may
relate or repugnant to any order or regulation made under authority
of such Act of Parliament, or having in the colony the force and
effect of such Act shall be read subject to this Act, order or regulation, and shall, to the extent of such repugnancy, but not otherwise,
be and remain absolutely void and inoperative.

Now our contention there is this, your Honors, that the statute of
1880 is the statute of a Colonial Legislature such as is defined by 22
and 23 Victoria; that that statute is passed under the delegated
authority from the Imperial Parliament to the Dominion Parliament;
without the amended Act of 1871 we contend the Dominion Parliament could have no possible right, would have no right whatever to
pass this statute of 1880 or to legislate for the North-West Territories, and the fact that it was so construed till the Amendment
Act of 1871 was passed, that they had not the right to legislate is
clear from the fact that the Imperial Parliament in passing the statute of 1871 ratifies certain statutes that had been passed previously
by the Dominion Parliament affecting the North-West Territories,
and gives the Dominion Parliament, under section 4, all the rights it
could have for the purpose of legislating for the North-West
Territories.

Section 4 is this: 'The Parliament of Canada, &c.' Now we have
there a delegated power to legislate for the North-West Territories.

This statute, if it had been the intention of the Dominion Parliament to override all the provisions of the previous Imperial statute by the very statutes extending those powers, it naturally would have repealed that statute, and when they extended this delegated power to the Dominion Parliament, to legislate for the North-West Territories, it cannot be pretended that the Imperial Parliament did not intend that these two statutes of George the 4th and 22 and 23 Victoria should not remain in force. The Dominion Parliament therefore passed this statute of 1880 under the delegated authority given them by the 4th section of the amended constitution. Now that statute is a colonial statute within the terms and meaning of 28 and 29 Victoria, and we have, therefore, these two statutes, and the Act of 1880 on the statute book and the interpretation Act or the Act to remove doubts.

Which of these statutes is the court to follow? It seems to me the explanation is clear. The Imperial Parliament has limits placed upon the jurisdiction and right of the justices of the peace to try offences in this country. When they delegated that authority, they did not take from the justices of the peace in these territories the limits that they placed on their jurisdiction and we have therefore the two statutes directly repugnant, the one to the other, the one saying you shall not try and the other you shall try or you may try. The Statute of 1880 does not say that the magistrate shall try but that he may try.

Well, your Honors, if it was not the intention of the Imperial Parliament that these two statutes of George IV and 22 and 23 Victoria should remain on the statute book, and having merely the provision there that the justice of the peace may try, which is an optional right he has — and we may suppose a condition of affairs like this — supposing these two statutes are repealed, and that the Statute of 1880 is the only statute which governs the North-West Territories, and the magistrate under that statute exercising optional jurisdiction, he might say, I have an optional jurisdiction to try this case, I won't try this offence. It is purely optional on my part, I won't try this. What would be the outcome in a supposition of this kind? If, under the Imperial Statutes, the magistrate would not have the right to send the offender to Ontario or British Columbia, what would then be the result? If the magistrate said he would not try, then there would be no provision for the trial of criminals charged with such offence as this before us.

I say, then, we have these two statutes, and we have the Dominion statutes, and there is a repugnancy of jurisdiction, and the
statute of 28 and 29 Vic. comes in clearly to solve the doubt as to
what course can be followed; and that the court here has no jurisdiction whatever to try this man under these two statutes; that the
court as now constituted has not by law the right to try this man,
and it does not seem to us, where there are Imperial statutes on the
one hand saying what shall be done, and with this statute of 1880
infringing, as it does, on the rights granted by Magna Charta, it does
seem to us that if there is the slightest doubt in the minds of your
Honors as to the right to try this case, as to the jurisdiction your
Honors may have, that it is the duty of the magistrates in such a case
as this to give effect to such a doubt as this, and not act under a
statute so repugnant to the well known ideas and principles of the
common law and the right of trial by jury. We do not say anything
against the constitution of this court. We have the utmost respect for
the court as well as for the gentlemen of the jury, but I say it is possible, under the provisions of this statute, that a Government desirous of ridding itself of particular men in these Territories, can, by a
servile creature appointed as magistrate, with the absolute right to go
out on the highway and streets and select his jury as he saw fit –
might accomplish its ends in this way.

MR JUSTICE RICHARDSON: Suit the jury to the occasion.

MR GREENSHIELDS: Suit the jury to the occasion – exactly. Contending as we are for the abstract principle of trial by jury, as given
us in this country; and inasmuch as this is a trial of great importance
in the North-West Territories, and as it is a trial that will form a precedent for the future, it is only proper that the justices should,
charged as they are here, guardians of the peace and liberties of the
people, administer that law in the way that will be most conducive
to the interest and liberties of the people of the North-West
Territories.

MR ROBINSON: We entirely agree with the remarks of my learned
friend. It is clearly their duty to see that this prisoner is tried before
a legal tribunal, properly constituted, and by no possibility that it be
implied that there is any want of deference towards this tribunal in
taking the objections they have taken before it. That was not merely
the right of my learned friends, but the plain duty incumbent upon
them, and no one will say that that duty has not been performed in

the best possible spirit or that they have not brought to the performance of it all the zeal and ability which it was possible to bring. Now, if our answer to our learned friends' argument is comparatively short, it will not be from any want of respect for the arguments they have urged, but it will be because the principle upon which we think the question is to be determined is one which eliminates a very great deal of the arguments. In our opinion there is but one simple question, or I might perhaps say two questions – what had the Dominion Parliament a right to enact? and what have they enacted? As regards, therefore, the larger portion of my learned friends' argument, which was addressed to the reasonableness or unreasonableness of those different enactments, we decline to follow them into that argument at all. We have nothing to do whatever with the question whether what the Legislatures have enacted, if within their power, is reasonable or unreasonable. Those laws are Acts of Parliament, passed by British subjects for British subjects; they have existed for years, and until the past few months their validity has never been questioned. As regards their reasonableness or unreasonableness, I would say this also, that we must have regard always to the circumstances and conditions of the country for which the laws are enacted, and it is impossible that everything which my learned friend calls the fundamental principle of the British constitution can be extended to all parts of the Empire; but if they rely upon that argument, it is a further answer to say that there is no fundamental principle of the British constitution than the supremacy of Parliament. Neither the right of grand jury nor the petit jury, nor the right of a jury of any kind, is so much a fundamental principle of the British constitution as the supremacy of Parliament. It is not because we rely upon our own judgment that we decline to follow our learned friend into any discussion of the reasonableness or unreasonableness of enactments which have been passed by the Imperial or Dominion Parliaments. Very soon after Confederation this question came up in our courts, and over and over again sustained by a long series of decisions. It has been held that the Legislature of the Dominion of Canada or of any of the Provinces, acting within the subjects entrusted to their jurisdiction, are just as supreme as the Imperial Legislature. In 1872 the case of Queen against Goodhue, 19 Grant, decided in the Province of Ontario, by the Courts of Chancery and Appeal that it was not open to a court of justice to question an Act of Parliament passed, not, I may observe, by the Dominion Parliament, to which different reasons might apply, but by a Provincial Parliament, on the ground that it was unreasonable or contrary to natural justice. When I say different reasons might apply, I refer to what your Honors know is a well-known distinction between our constitution and that of the United States. With us the reserve powers are left with the Dominion. In the constitution of the United States it is exactly the reverse. The reserve powers rest with the sovereign States, and it is by them that powers are granted to the Federal Parliament. The Federal Parliament is, in a certain sense, subservient. Here every power not given to the Provinces is given to the Federal Legislature. This was the earliest case I know of; but I could, with very little trouble, refer your Honors to several cases in the Supreme Court where the principle has been enunciated beyond question. Now, perhaps it is just as well I should take up first, shortly, that branch of the subject which my learned friends have discussed last, because it comes first in chronological order. The question is, whether there was any power to send this prisoner for trial to the courts of Upper Canada. I need hardly say that the question of the best tribunal and the proper tribunal, the legal tribunal, before which this offence should be tried, is one that has engaged the anxious consideration of all who have had the responsibility of advising the Crown, and admitting all the force and thoroughness and ability of my learned friends' argument, it has not brought to our attention any argument which has previously escaped our consideration. It was thought, beyond all reasonable doubt, that there was no power to send this prisoner or any of the other prisoners to Upper Canada for trial, and I believe it is thought, and justly thought, also, that if there was a choice on the part of the Government of this Dominion whether these prisoners should be sent to Ontario for trial or tried in this country, it would not be consistent with public opinion nor with what would be regarded as the proper administration of justice that they should not be tried in these Territories. There are elementary principles of the criminal law just as there are fundamental principles of the British constitution, and one of these is, that crime should be tried in the territories where they are committed; another is, that it is always most desirable to pass any special legislation with a view to crimes which have been already committed. It was thought it was possible, and if it had been possible it would have been most undesirable, to take

advantage of any enactment which would empower the Crown
to send persons accused of this crime for trial to the Province of
Ontario and out of the territory where the offence was
committed.

Assuming that the statute of George IV has not been expressly
repealed, our view was that it was so affected by subsequent legislation that it became impossible to act under it, and your Honors will
find, that under the Statute Law Revision Act of 1872 and 1873
there is a class of statutes which are repealed as having ceased to be
in force or become unnecessary, and we all know perfectly well that
there is a large number of statutes which, though not expressly repealed in words, are in effect repealed, because, by virtue of subsequent legislation and of their inconsistency with the legislation, they
have ceased to be in force and have become unnecessary.

Having explained that it was thought impossible, and if possible it
would have been thought undesirable to attempt to take advantage
of that statute, let us see whether there is any question that the subsequent statute removed all doubt as to the jurisdiction of this court.
It would have been a sufficient answer to have reminded your
Honors that within the last few weeks the jurisdiction of this court
has been asserted in a capital offence and has been unanimously
confirmed by the only Court of Appeal existing from it, the Court
of Queen's Bench of Manitoba. It would be amply sufficient for us
to cite this case unless my learned friends can point to some distinction between treason and murder.

Now, that there is no intention to except the crime of treason —
on the contrary that the crime of treason was intended to be included in the jurisdiction of this court — your Honors will find in
section 76, sub-section 10, where the enactment is that any person
arraigned for treason or felony may challenge peremptorily so many
jurors — being the plainest indication and enactment on the part of
the legislature that it was intended to include within the jurisdiction
of this court the crime of treason. It is very possible that that was
put in by reason of what you are aware was the law, that a larger
number of challenges were allowed to persons in treason than in any
other felony, and it may perhaps have been thought that if it only
said felony, although treason is felony, that special extension applying to the case of treason would not have been superseded; and
therefore very possibly whoever framed the Act included the crime
of treason in words.

Let us see then whether there is any serious room for doubt that by the effect of subsequent legislation on the part of the Imperial Parliament and of the Parliament of Canada the jurisdiction of this court is unquestioned. I do not know that the British North America Act has very much bearing on the case. Nothing, as I understand, affects it except section 146, and that shows that it was in contemplation of the Imperial Parliament at the time when they formed this Confederation that the North-West Territories and Rupert's Land would at a future time be admitted into the Confederation. I do not think it has any further bearing on the arguments.

Then the next statute is the Rupert's Land Imperial Act, 31 and 32 Vic., chap. 105, passed in 1868 (I am taking them in chronological order). That is to be found in the statute of 1869 at the beginning. It was passed, as your Honors are aware, as a matter of history when negotiations were going on for cession of the Hudson Bay Company's charter and for the admission of Rupert's Land into the Dominion, and section 2 says that for the purposes of this Act the term 'Rupert's Land' shall include the whole of the land or territories held or claimed to be held by the said Governor or company. I may say here, and probably it is not contested, that that definition clearly includes the district between which these crimes were committed. That is shown plainly by an Imperial Order in Council which enumerates the posts then held by the Hudson Bay Company, for example, Edmonton, which is very far westward of the district in question.

So, then, having enacted that Rupert's Land should include the whole of these territories, it proceeds, it shall be competent for Her Majesty by Order in Council to declare that Rupert's Land shall from date to be therein mentioned be admitted into and become part of the Dominion of Canada, and thereupon it shall be lawful for the Parliament of Canada from the date aforesaid 'to make, ordain, and establish within the land or territory so admitted as aforesaid, all such laws, institutions and ordinances, and to constitute such court and officers as may be necessary for the peace, order, and good government of Her Majesty's subjects and others therein, provided that, till otherwise enacted by the said Parliament of Canada, all the powers, authority and jurisdiction of the several courts of justice now established in Rupert's Land and of the several officers thereof and of all magistrates and justices now acting within the said limits, shall continue in full force and effect therein.'

Now is it possible to devise words more plainly conferring upon the Parliament of Canada the undoubted power then possessed by the Imperial Parliament to make laws for the good government of this country, both criminal and civil as they should think right.

That has always appeared to us to put the matter beyond question, not because we are disposed to adopt any doubtful construction of the Act, but because we cannot see how you could confer more ample and full power upon the legislature of Canada to be the law-givers for this country — to constitute such courts and to ordain such laws as they may think right for the Government.

Then the next statute, which we find is 32 and 33 Vic., chap. 3.
MR JUSTICE RICHARDSON: That is a statute of Canada.
MR ROBINSON: Yes. I am taking the statutes in chronological order. Your Honors will observe that first comes the Imperial Act which says that as soon as Rupert's Land is admitted the Parliament of Canada shall make laws for it. Let us now see what Parliament did under that power. That statute was passed on 22nd of June 1869. It says that, whereas it is possible Her Majesty pursuant to the British North America Act, 1867, may admit Rupert's Land and the North-West Territory into the Union or Dominion of Canada before the next Session of Parliament, and whereas it is expedient to prepare for the transfer of the territories at the time appointed and to make some temporary provision for the civil government of the Province until more permanent arrangements can be made; therefore, in the first place said territories, both Rupert's Land and the north-western territory, when admitted shall be styled and known as the North-West Territories. Secondly, it shall be lawful for the Governor by the advice of the Privy Council, and subject to such conditions and restrictions as may seem mete to authorize and empower such officer as he may appoint Lieutenant-Governor of said territory to make provision for the administration of justice therein, and generally to make, ordain, and establish all such laws, institutions, and ordinances as may be necessary for the peace, order and good government of Her Majesty's subjects and others therein; provided that all Orders in Council, and all laws and ordinances so to be made as aforesaid shall be laid before both Houses of Parliament as soon as may conveniently may be after the enactment thereof respectively. That was the first provision made for temporary government.

MR JUSTICE RICHARDSON: That was to govern by Order in
Council?

MR ROBINSON: Yes. Then the next enactment which we have is 33
Vic., chap. 31, which carves out of Rupert's Land and the North-
West Territories the Province to be called Manitoba. All that I think
is important in that statute is the 35th and 36th sections, 'and with
respect to such portions of Rupert's Land and the North-Western
Territory as is not included in the Province of Manitoba, it is hereby
enacted that the Lieutenant Governor of the said Province shall be
appointed by commission under the great seal of Canada, &c.' And
except as hereinbefore enacted and provided 32 and 33 Vic., chap 3,
is re-enacted, extended, and continued in force until the 1st day of
January, 1871, and until the end of the Session of Parliament then
next succeeding.

Then we have the Imperial statute, 34 and 35 Vic., chap. 28, the
British North America Act of 1871, by which the two Acts of the
Parliaments of Canada already mentioned, 32 and 33 Vic., chap. 3,
and 33 Vic., chap. 3, shall be and be deemed to have been valid and
effectual for all purposes whatsoever from the date at which they
respectively received the assent in the Queen's name of the Governor
General of the said Dominion of Canada.

So that we have this court of legislation. First, we have the Imperial Legislature saying to the Parliament of the Dominion, you can
make such laws as you think proper for the government of Rupert's
Land. Next, we have the Parliament of the Dominion under that
power making laws, and then we have the Imperial Parliament again,
in view of the enactments which they have passed, making this enactment valid.

Now is it possible to conceive any legislation more clearly enacted
and validated both by the Imperial Parliament and by the Dominion
Parliament?

It is not a question, therefore, of what the Dominion Parliament
had power to do under the general power given to them by the
Imperial Legislature, but it is a question of what the Imperial Parliament itself had power to do, for they have confirmed the enactment.

Then as your Honors are aware under those provisions we have a
series of statutes beginning in '68 which, from time to time, have
been passed for the government of the North-West Territories. I

don't propose to call your attention particularly to these, because you are familiar with them all and because they are simply statutes enacting laws under which this court is now constituted. 32 and 33 Vic., chap. 3, is the first of them. 34 Vic., chap. 16, is the next. Then 36 Vic., chaps. 34 and 35, and then 38 Vic., chap. 48, and then the present Act, 40 Vic., chap. 7.

It is, however, to be observed that the argument of my learned friend, Mr Greenshields, has addressed to Your Honors would have been equally valid and strong against the Act which allows trials of a particular class to take place before the Court of Queen's Bench in Manitoba where all the procedure to the absence of which they object so strongly is to be found because your Honors are aware that up, I think, to 37 Vic., cases of certain importance were to be tried before that court.

MR JUSTICE RICHARDSON: That is the Act of '75 and '77.

MR ROBINSON: Yes. They would have no more power to direct that the trial should take place in the Province of Manitoba or Lower Canada or anywhere else than to say that the trial shall take place here, because they would have been bound, according to the argument, by the Imperial enactment which says that for all time to come, notwithstanding the leave we have given to you, notwithstanding the power which we have conferred upon you, you must send all criminals of a certain class for trial to Upper Canada.

For these reasons it has been thought on the part of the Crown that nothing could be plainer than the course of legislation under which this court is constituted and from which it derives its jurisdiction, and we have referred to these statutes, not because we thought it necessary to go over this argument at length, for, as I have said, the question is already determined by the authoritative jurisdiction of the court at Manitoba, but because we think in a case of this gravity and importance it is desirable that the public should know that all who are interested in the administration of criminal justice should know that this court is not sitting in the exercise of doubtful jurisdiction, and this not merely in view of the cases we are here now to try, but in view of other capital cases which have already been tried, and in which sentences have already been pronounced and carried out within these territories.

MR OSLER: I have a word to add to the argument of my learned friend, Mr Robinson, which I think covers all the ground.

I simply refer to the two Imperial statutes that my learned friends
are relying upon – 1 and 2 George IV, chap. 66, and 22 and 23 Vic.,
chap. 26. I point out that by the recital to 1 and 2 George IV, it was
an Act for a special purpose, an Act reciting the troubles that had
arisen between the Hudson Bay Company and the North-West
Company of Canada, and the administration of justice being in the
Hudson Bay Company providing an independent forum before
which the crimes that had theretofore been prevalent could be tried,
and that Act called for the appointment of special officers to carry it
out.

MR JUSTICE RICHARDSON: An independent tribunal?

MR OSLER: An independent tribunal. Those officers do not exist.
The Act itself saves all the power of the Hudson Bay Company
which they are by law entitled to exercise. They had full judicial
power over the territory granted to them. It became important that
when they were parties there should be an independent forum. This
Act created that forum and pointed out officers through whom the
Act should be carried out, and the prisoners conveyed to the Province remained for trial.

Then my learned friends have omitted to point out to your
Honors that the Statute on which they rely so much, 22 and 23 Vic.,
chap. 26, is distinctly limited to the territories not in the possession
of the Hudson Bay Company. Nothing herein contained shall extend
to the territories heretofore granted to the Hudson Bay Company
trading under that name, and nothing herein contained shall extend
to the colony of British Columbia save as herein expressly provided.

Now as my learned friend who has preceded me has pointed out,
it is unquestionable that these offences were committed – the offences charged here were committed, if committed at all, in the
territory that had been immediately in possession of the Hudson Bay
Company – Fort Carlton, for instance. Edmonton, and other forts
are immediately in this territory.

So that we say that the Statute 22 and 23 Vic., Imperial Act does
not apply territorially, and we say that 1 and 2 George IV was an Act
limited in its scope and passed for a special immediate purpose, the
necessity for which is over, and that they are not therefore Imperial
Statutes clashing in any way with the authorized legislation of the
Dominion. We admit the proposition of my learned friend that
where an Imperial Act and a Colonial Act clash, the interpretation

law has to guide, and there is the interpretation law which is to
guide – the Imperial Statute referred to.

MR JUSTICE RICHARDSON: That is to govern.

MR OSLER: That is to govern. But we say there is no such a position, and we say that the matter is in great simplicity. The power is
delegated by the Imperial Legislature to the Dominion Parliament in
the Acts referred to by my learned friend. The Dominion Parliament
has exercised that power in the various Acts, the law now being contained in the Act of 1880. My learned friend's argument goes too
far. It would vitiate the Acts under which justice in Manitoba is
administered, for if these laws are still in force they remain unrepealed as to the territory that is now the Province of Manitoba.

The point being clear and one so fully covered and as we don't
propose to reply to my learned friend's argument of convenience, I
don't think that I need take up the time of the court by further
remark. I might only add that as far as the unconstitutionality is
concerned the law as to treason throughout the largest territory of
the British Empire or the most populous India is administered without the aid of a grand or petit jury. The law of treason in India is
administered by a stipendiary magistrate sitting unaided, who himself charges the accused and one who tries him for the offence. That
is the legislation approved of by the Imperial Parliament and administered in a country where they have found it difficult to institute
the ordinary and regular courts that are to be found in all older and
more established countries. The jury system is essentially a court
system, essentially impossible where a territory is of the extent of
these territories not divided into judicial districts. This is not a question of convenience; that is not what you are administering here. We
are seeking the proper interpretation of the Statutes. We take them
as we find them, and we say this court is properly constituted,
having full power, and we pray that there may be judgment for the
Crown upon the plea that has been put in.

I would just call your Honor's attention to the Imperial Order in
Council of the 23rd June 1870. It recites the surrender by the Hud-
son Bay Company and it sets out in the schedule a lot of posts, in
fact defines the territory then in the possession of the Hudson Bay
Company. There is in the Saskatchewan District the Edmonton
House, Fort Pitt, Carlton House – this very territory.

MR FITZPATRICK, in reply: The argument made use of by the
learned counsel who leads for the Crown, sets out, in the first instance, the supremacy, the absolute supremacy, of Parliament, that
is, of the Imperial Parliament, I apprehend. He sets that out as one
of the fundamental principles of the British constitution.

Now, I said in my opening address that in so far as the Imperial
Parliament is concerned, it was a very debatable point whether or
not the Imperial Parliament was absolutely supreme. Your Honors
will look at the treatise on Statutes, Dwarris, p 480, where you will
see that that has been more than once put in doubt. If a statute says
a man shall be judge in his own case, such a law, being contrary to
natural equity, shall be void. Such was the opinion of Lord Chief
Justice Cockburn, influenced by the same powerful sense of justice.
Lord Coke, when Chief Justice, fearlessly proclaimed that when an
Act of Parliament was contrary to natural right or reason, &c., the
common law shall control it, and adjudge it void; and Lord Holt, in
the *City of London* v *Woos*, expressed the opinion that the observation of Lord Coke was a very reasonable and true saying.

So that in any case, with all due respect for what was stated by
the counsel for the Crown, that is a debatable point, and I say that
there are authorities which assert that the power of Parliament is
absolutely supreme; but, as I have had occasion to say in my opening
address, there are, on the other side, people, eminent jurists and
eminent judges, who put that question beyond doubt.

However, let that be as it may, presuming the Imperial Parliament
to be absolute — and here I might as well remark that the tribunal
provided for the case of treason in India is a tribunal provided by the
Imperial Parliament, if I mistake not, or by a statute passed in India
subject to the approval of the Imperial Parliament.
MR JUSTICE RICHARDSON: In that respect is not the constitution
of India the same as that of Canada?
MR FITZPATRICK: I am not in a position to say whether it is the
same. I am doubtful of the point. I think it is not, however, but I am
not in a position to give any very positive opinion upon that point.
No doubt, under the Imperial Federation Act, the statutes of the
federation are reserved for allowance or disallowance by the Queen.
There is no doubt about that. They are subject to disallowance
within a certain period of time; but supposing all that to be the case,

here we have a statute passed by the Federal Parliament, under certain delegated powers, powers delegated to it by the Imperial Parliament. The learned counsel for the Crown referred to the case of Goodhue, where it is asserted that Local Legislatures within their own jurisdiction are absolute. There can be no doubt about that, and on that point I would just give the opinion of Lord North, when he introduced the Quebec Act. He says: A matter concerning civil rights is a matter with which the Imperial Parliament has no concern, but when it comes to be a case of trial by jury in a criminal case, then we have the right guaranteed of trial by jury. When it comes to be a matter of civil rights, that is a matter essentially within the purview of the Local Legislature, and, of course, is a matter left entirely to their control; but the question of delegated powers is one that is very strongly insisted upon by the Crown counsel. They say we have the most absolute power.

The statute 31 and 32 Victoria, chap. 105, the Rupert's Land Act, 1869, which delegates the powers, was read by him, the learned counsel for the Crown, and insisted upon by him as giving the most absolute power it is possible to convey. He insisted that the statute gave the Federal Parliament identically the same power as the Imperial Parliament, and it was impossible to give them any greater powers. If that be the case, if that statute gave the Federal Parliament the most absolute power that the Imperial Parliament had itself, why did it think it necessary to pass the statute of 1871 to ratify the Acts passed by virtue of that delegated power? If this power were so absolute, if those powers of such an absolute character as to put the Federal Parliament in exactly the same position as the Imperial Parliament, why did it become necessary to ratify the legislation which had been had under this delegated power? Why was the statute of 1871 passed?

MR ROBINSON: To ratify the formation of Manitoba.

MR FITZPATRICK: In my opinion, which I give respectfully as it is contrary to that of my learned friend, Mr Robinson, it is a matter of undoubted law that powers delegated as in this instance are always delegated subject to certain rights; for instance, as Judge Story says, where people assemble together and give to their representatives whom they elect to the Legislature certain powers, they say that this power must be exercised subject to the principles of the common law, and subject to certain restrictions. Now why should those powers delegated and transferred to the Federal Parliament be exercised with any greater freedom and without those same restrictions? Why should the powers delegated by the Imperial to the Federal Parliament be exercised in such a way that you can interpret them as meaning one thing with reference to one province, and a different thing with reference to another? It is all very well for the learned counsel to say this is not a case of convenience, that we are not to argue for convenience, but I say that these Acts, the Act of 1871 and the Federal Act, must all be read together, that it is impossible to separate them. Those Acts were for the purpose of forming federation of the different provinces and territories. They entered on an equal basis. The British subjects who composed this federation all had equal rights, and it is impossible for this court or any other court to decide in this country that what is law in the Province of Quebec, in so far as the criminal law is concerned, shall not be the law here; that the Legislature of the Province of Quebec shall have certain rights guaranteed to them by this treaty of federation, and that the inhabitants of the North-West Territories shall not have the same rights.

The learned counsel who leads for the Crown also said that it is impossible to find the tribunal before which this man can be tried, if not the tribunal now here. I say that, in my humble opinion, the tribunal can be found, and that tribunal can be found in the Imperial Statute 22 and 23 Victoria, which provides for the appointment of magistrates with certain defined powers. That statute also provides that those magistrates shall not go beyond a certain limit. The statute of 1880 provides another delegated power, provides for the appointment of magistrates. Now, in what respect are the Imperial Act and the Federal Act in conflict? They are in conflict purely and simply when it comes to be a question of deciding finally on those capital cases. Until such times the question of committing for trial is the same. Let the magistrate be appointed under the statute of 1880, or under the Imperial Act, he is appointed legally in either case, his powers are identical in either case, but when it comes to the question of trial then the powers are repugnant, and the two statutes are in conflict, and the Imperial Act must override the Federal Act. Mr Osler, who argued last for the Crown, said that the Act 22 and 23 Victoria does not apply to the Hudson Bay Company territories at all, but that the

Act of George IV does apply. If it is possible to read sections 1 and 2
of this Act so as to show that this Act does not apply to the same
tribunal and territories as the Act of George IV, it is impossible for
me to read anything in the statutes. This statute provides expressly
that courts be appointed under George IV, the appointment of which
is in the hands of the Imperial Parliament, and nothing in the previous Act contained shall be construed to be or be considered a
repeal of that clause of the other statute.

Now if it does not apply at all to the same territories, what is the
necessity for the saving clause? Why should section 1 say that the
magistrate may be appointed under the first Act, and shall have
more extended jurisdiction under this Act than they had before?
What is the necessity of all that? I say that section of the statute
must be read in connection with the other section. This statute
begins in its preamble by saying, whereas certain statutes are passed,
among others the very statute that the learned counsel said was
passed expressly for the Hudson Bay territory, and in view of that
Act so passed those other enactments are made. It seems to me it is
impossible to construe anything if we are to say that the statute of
George provides for the appointment of magistrates in a court of
record, and this statute says that nothing in the previous Act contained shall be construed to mean a repeal of that clause.

Now, if they are not to be read together, it is impossible to rely
upon any statute. According to the learned counsel's reading of that
statute, it is that this statute here was not intended to provide for
the appointment of magistrates at all, that this court of record which
is provided for by George IV should not exist in the Hudson Bay
territory. It is impossible, to my mind, to put any such construction
upon the statute, but even if this statute was not in force at all, the
statute George IV provides for the method in which this trial should
take place, and to what tribunal the prisoner should be sent.

The 'Dwarris on Statutes' I refer to is not Potter's Dwarris. One is
the English edition, the other the American.
MR JUSTICE RICHARDSON: Now, if I understand the contention
of Mr Fitzpatrick, it is that this Act of 1880, so far as it relates to
the trial of criminal offences such as this, is *ultra vires.*
MR FITZPATRICK: My contention is that the Act of 1880, in so
far as it relates to the trial of capital cases, is *ultra vires.*

MR JUSTICE RICHARDSON: Well, as I cannot hold that, I must sustain the demurrer. I must now call upon Louis Riel to plead.

Prisoner pleads not guilty.

MR JOHNSTONE: With the permission of the court, I beg leave to demur to the information. It might be sufficient to demur *ore tenus*, or by oral exception to the information; yet as the information laid by the prosecution is itself formal, and a departure from the procedure hitherto of this court, I think it necessary to put in a written general demurrer as follows:

CANADA – NORTH-WEST TERRITORIES
Queen v *Louis Riel*,
now charged before his Honor Hugh Richardson, stipendiary magistrate, and Henry Lejeune, Esquire, a justice of the peace, and a jury of six under the provisions of subsection 5, section 76 of the North-West Territories Act, 1880, on the information of Alexander David Stewart, the said Louis Riel, in his own proper person, cometh into court here and having heard said information read, sayeth that the said information and the matters therein contained in the manner and form as described and above stated and set forth, are not sufficient in law, and that the said Louis Riel is not bound by law of the land to answer the same;

Wherefore, for want of sufficient information, the said Louis Riel prays judgment.

MR ROBINSON: You assign no special grounds of demurrer.
MR JOHNSTONE: No; it is the general form of demurrer prescribed by Archbold. It is given in the case of *Queen* v *Connor.*
MR ROBINSON: I am not objecting to the form, but I am only pointing out this, that if it is intended to rest on any ground not already discussed, and you think it is desirable to point them out, we will answer them, but in the absence of that indication, we cannot do more than put in a general joinder. If he can point out in what respects he thinks it is insufficient, it will be proper.
MR JOHNSTONE: If the Crown choose to join in the demurrer, they will argue after the joinder is filed. I think the Crown should join or else it will have to remain as it is.
MR ROBINSON: Then we put in a general joinder.

MR JOHNSTONE: The information, your Honors, contains in all six overt acts. Three of them purport to be laid against the prisoner as a British subject; the other three are silent as to the nationality of the prisoner. The overt acts laid in the last three charges are identical with the overt acts mentioned in the first three clauses of the information. Admitting for the purpose of argument, the information can contain more than one charge, I contend that if my learned friends intended to rely upon the last three clauses of the information, and they also intended to prevent evidence being given of citizenship of the prisoner as a citizen in a foreign state, these clauses of the information should specify that the prisoner is a citizen of that foreign state and that that foreign state is at peace with Her Majesty. That question is settled by an address of a very eminent lawyer, the Hon. John Hillyard Cameron, in *Queen* v *School*, 26 U.C. Q.B. 212. The prisoner was one of the Fenians of 1866.

MR JUSTICE RICHARDSON: Settled by Mr Cameron, or did he represent the Crown? It was Judge Wilson who gave the judgment. I prefer you should read from the judgment instead of Mr Cameron's opinion.

MR JOHNSTONE: Mr Cameron proceeds to detail the case to the jury, and says the indictment declares that we are at peace with the United States. That is a fact known to all, but as a matter of form I will have to ask the question of one of the witnesses, in order to place it legally before you.

MR JUSTICE RICHARDSON: Was that a prosecution under Edward III Act? Wasn't it under the 31 Victoria?

MR JOHNSTONE: It was under the Fenian Act. The clauses are the same.

MR OSLER: Totally different on that point.

MR JOHNSTONE: As I understand it, you are proceeding under 31 Victoria.

MR OSLER: You are misunderstanding us then. 25 Edward III is the one.

MR JUSTICE RICHARDSON: I don't know that I comprehend the point that you are raising, Mr Johnstone; will you put it to me again?

MR JOHNSTONE: Admitting that the information can contain more than one charge, the first three charges are proper in stating that the prisoner is a subject of Her Majesty, but in that respect the

forms are identical with the forms given in works on criminal procedure; but the three last charges do not allege that the prisoner –
MR JUSTICE RICHARDSON: What you say is that because the three last do not contain a nationality, they are bad?
MR JOHNSTONE: The information is double. If my learned friends have decided to leave the information in that shape and not declare against the prisoner as a subject of a foreign state at peace with Her Majesty, I say the information is double in this respect, that the overt acts mentioned in the three last clauses of the information are identical with those mentioned in the three former clauses which allege that the prisoner is a subject of Her Majesty.
MR JUSTICE RICHARDSON: They cannot lay the same offence in different ways?
MR JOHNSTONE: Not in different ways, your Honor. The only difference is this that it does not allege – the several charges do not allege – that the prisoner is a British subject. Then it must be presumed that he is a British subject, and presuming that, then the information is double. It contains these charges twice over in the same words, the same identical words, the same overt acts.
MR JUSTICE RICHARDSON: Then what do you want me to do?
MR JOHNSTONE: Well, we have demurred to the indictment, and we want your Honors to hold that the information is bad because it is double, or that is not double, that is just it.
MR JUSTICE RICHARDSON: Have you the School case here? (This is to be produced.)
MR ROBINSON: There is a McMahon case.
MR JOHNSTONE: In the School case, there are three counts.
MR JUSTICE RICHARDSON: The case I refer to has six counts.
MR JOHNSTONE: They all charge the prisoner with being a subject of a foreign state at peace with Her Majesty.
MR BURBIDGE: I think my learned friend is misapprehending the nature of the charge from the fact that he states that we have laid six overt acts in the charge. We have not done that. He is probably thinking of a count for compassing to levy war. In three counts we have charged him as a British subject and having violated his natural allegiance, and in three counts we have charged him with having acted contrary to his local allegiance. It is quite sufficient that a man may live in a country to be guilty of treason. With reference to the

two sets of counts, I need do no more than refer to School's case. In that case, counsel for the prisoner were called upon to say whether their prisoner would be tried as an alien or a British subject, before the Crown was called upon to amend or to make any election. I need not pursue this question further I think.

MR JUSTICE RICHARDSON: *The Queen* v *School* is the case I refer to. The prisoner was indicted on two separate counts; this was under the Fenian Act. I don't think there is anything in the objection of Mr Johnstone, and I overrule it. Are there any other demurrers?

MR OSLER: The clerk will ask the prisoner whether he is guilty or not guilty?

CLERK: Louis Riel, are you guilty or not guilty?

PRISONER: I have the honor to answer the court I am not guilty.

CLERK: Are you ready for your trial?

MR FITZPATRICK: I have now to state that I have to ask an adjournment till to-morrow morning, to enable us to prepare some affidavits we require to produce, to show why we are not in a position to proceed with the trial at the present moment. It is possible that these affidavits should have been in court now, but, unfortunately for the defence, they have been at a disadvantage and have not been in a position to do work of any importance. I have therefore to ask the indulgence of the court. As soon as the affidavits are prepared, we will hand them to the learned counsel on the other side.

HIS HONOR: You propose that the court should rise, with a view of enabling you to prepare the necessary affidavits to ask for an adjournment?

MR ROBINSON: To what time do they propose to ask the adjournment?

MR FITZPATRICK: That is a matter that will have to be decided by the court when we have furnished the affidavits showing the witnesses we require and how we intend to produce them, and how it is we have not got them now. Some of the witnesses are in Montana, and the adjournment will not be a long one.

HIS HONOR: Montana is out of our jurisdiction, and we cannot bring them here.

MR FITZPATRICK: It is to give us an opportunity of bringing them here.

MR ROBINSON: Do I understand my learned friend that they will
ask for an indefinite adjournment, not an adjournment to a definite
day?

MR GREENSHIELDS: Perhaps a month.

MR ROBINSON: They must produce affidavits of the strongest possible character, and they must not consider we are not at liberty to
oppose such an adjournment.

HIS HONOR: It is simply a matter of convenience this evening
whether we adjourn now or go on for an hour and a half till 6
o'clock. Can't we make it early to-morrow morning?

MR ROBINSON: I do not know that that will facilitate matters, as
we have to consider the affidavits and prepare answers.

HIS HONOR: Jurors will understand that they are to be continually
in attendance, as also witnesses on both sides. We will adjourn till 10
o'clock to-morrow.

Court then adjourned.

21st July 1885

The clerk opened the court at 10 o'clock.

HIS HONOR MR JUSTICE RICHARDSON: Call the jury.

The clerk calls over the list of jurors.

THOMAS PULL — one of the jurors: Your Honor, on account of
being postmaster and contractor to carry the mails, I beg to be
relieved.

HIS HONOR: I fear I have no power to relieve you now — you were
fairly drawn out of a large number of names, and I do not think that
I can discharge you now. I have noticed several jurors who were
summoned do not appear. Is it the desire that proceedings should be
instituted against them?

MR ROBINSON: Not if we can get on without them.

MR LEMIEUX: Mr Watson, will you please swear the prisoner to
these affidavits.

The clerk swears the affidavits.

MR GREENSHIELDS: Please your Honor, we renew the application
made yesterday afternoon for an adjournment of this trial. In the

interval since the adjournment we have had three affidavits prepared, two of the senior counsel, Messrs. Lemieux and Fitzpatrick, and one of the accused. We base our application to a large extent upon those affidavits.

HIS HONOR: Have they been shown to the counsel for the Crown?

MR ROBINSON: We have seen them just lately; we will look over them again.

Mr Greenshields read the three affidavits annexed hereto. These are the affidavits upon which we base our application for an adjournment of this trial, as the counsel for the defence feel that it is utterly impossible to do justice to the prisoner, if we are forced on at the present time with this trial. The charge is the most serious that can be preferred against a subject, that of treason, involving, as it does, the death penalty. We excepted to the jurisdiction and think the procedure of this court is an extraordinary one. The prisoner is arraigned yesterday for the first time, and is asked if he is ready to proceed immediately with his defence. In ordinary cases time is given for the preparation of the defence, and we do not see why this court should differ from the practice followed in the other courts of justice throughout Canada and the British Empire. We have put in three affidavits, and these establish it is an utter impossibility for the counsel for the defence, and an utter impossibility for the prisoner to make his defence before this court, because we could not obtain the attendance of these witnesses upon whom the defence rely. The prisoner is a man of little or no means, and we propose to make application to the court, to order its officers to issue subpoenas to the witnesses whose names we will give, and that the expenses be defrayed by the court.

HIS HONOR: The court is in possession of no funds.

MR GREENSHIELDS: It is not usual that the court is in possession of funds for that purpose, but it is often the case that courts of justice on application to the Government have the funds provided for the defence. I did not suppose that your Honor had the funds in your pocket, but that it could be so obtained. We are defending this man on a very serious charge. Your Honor is appointed by the Government, and any representation made by this court as regards the defence of this man would be followed by the Government. It would be based on the affidavits, and with that would be an application for assistance to obtain those witnesses who are to be here.

Now, we must take into consideration the affidavit of the prisoner. He swears in this affidavit that Dumont, Dumas and Nault
who were in Montana — these men are those who went to Montana
at the solicitation of the half-breeds, and asked the prisoner to assist
them in petitioning the Government, and have proper representation
made that their rights might be obtained. It will no doubt strike the
court as it does the counsel for the defence, that these matters are
important for the defence of the prisoner. It is important that it be
shown that this prisoner was in a foreign country, following his usual
avocations, that these men came to him, and made representations as
a committee representing the half-breeds, and asked him to assist
these poor people in asking for their rights. It seems to me important
to prove, as we can show by these witnesses, that when the prisoner
came to the North-West Territories, he came upon the honest solicitation of the half-breeds and citizens of these territories who felt
themselves aggrieved by the policy pursued by the Government as
regards the lands. We want to prove that at the time the prisoner
came into this country he came with pure and good motives, his
motive being to assist these people in obtaining redress of the
grievances which they unquestionably had, grievances which every
public man, be he of either political party, will admit. We want these
men to show that the prisoner came to this country honestly, to
assist his fellow citizens in obtaining redress of those grievances.
Dumont, Dumas and the others I have named will come here on the
assurance of counsel that they will be protected. Now we want these
witnesses, we think we are in a position to obtain the attendance of
these witnesses if the delay we ask is given. We also intend to ask this
court to order that all documents, petitions, writings and representations — prayer after prayer, petition after petition was presented to
the Government by the people asking for redress — be brought before this court. All these papers are in the possession of Mr Burgess,
the Deputy Minister of the Interior, and of Mr Vankoughnet the
Deputy Superintendent of Indian Affairs. Our desire in having these
documents is to show that when the prisoner was asked in 1884 to
come to the North-West Territories he was asked to come simply as a
last resort of these people to whose petitions the Government, for
some reason, did not take notice. We want these papers to show the
state in which most of these people were, and to show that the
prisoner came into the country in a legal and proper way to aid in

redressing the grievances the half-breeds had been complaining of to
the Government for years. In addition to that, there is the evidence
of the doctors from Quebec. This defence, we are instructed by
others than the prisoner to make.

MR JUSTICE RICHARDSON: There are three in Montana.

MR GREENSHIELDS: Two at Helena, and one at the Turtle Mountain. It is an undoubted fact, competent of proof, that the accused
was confined in the Beauport asylum for a period of three years,
from 1872 to 1875. The doctors whose names have been mentioned
in the affadavits are to prove those facts, and also the condition of
the prisoner's mind at that time.

MR JUSTICE RICHARDSON: That is from Quebec.

MR GREENSHIELDS: And Dr Clark of Toronto. We desire that
these witnesses should be here. When we left we expected that these
gentlemen would be present here in Regina, but they are not here.
The correspondence or communication we have had with them has
been of the most limited kind, by telegraph, and we have not been
able to arrive at a proper explanation as to why they are not here.
We have also the affidavit of Mr Lemieux who says that if time is
given, he will immediately return to Quebec, and will return before
this court with these three medical gentlemen. The court can see
the necessity in a trial of this kind where life is involved, that we
should be given the fullest opportunity to make a proper defence.
What we want is a fair trial. That is what we are here for, and we
should obtain the fullest and fairest trial, and if after a full and fair
trial, the court and the jury find that the prisoner is guilty of the
offence charged, we will have done our duty before the court and
the people. The people of this country will be satisfied that no injustice has been done. If, after the production of such affidavits as
these, the prisoner is forced on to trial on the charge of high treason,
public feeling will not be satisfied. A trial of this kind in which the
public are all interested must be a fair and impartial trial.

It seems to us there is every reason why the application should be
granted, and no reason why it should be refused. The delay need not
be the cause of any inconvenience, as it has been remarked that
there are some sixty or seventy other prisoners awaiting trial, and
their trials can be proceeded with.

MR JUSTICE RICHARDSON: The convenience of counsel should
not be considered in a case of this kind.

MR GREENSHIELDS: I am referring to this only to show that there
is no other reason why the application should not be granted. It is
purely a matter of convenience. The witnesses can be kept here; they
are under the control of the Crown; we find them here all the time.
Witnesses whose names were given us by the prisoner give some testimony, but the moment we approach them to speak to them they
stand back as though we were tainted with a plague, and say we are
instructed to have no conversation with the defence. Our endeavors
to obtain information have been frustrated by the counsel for the
prosecution or some one for the Government, who have instructed
every person not to recognize the counsel for the defence, and –
MR OSLER: You have no right to make such a statement.
MR ROBINSON: There is nothing of that kind in the affidavit.
MR GREENSHIELDS: We can furnish affidavits to that effect. I do
not wish to make any charge that the counsel have instructed the
witnesses to that effect. I say that the witnesses for the Crown
would not talk to us because they said they had been instructed to
have no conversation with the counsel for the defence. The names of
many of them were the names given by the prisoner as witnesses for
the defence, but we were unable to see them or to have any conversation with them, for what cause we do not know, but they said
they were instructed not to have any conversation with us. We are
unable to enter upon the trial now, and we ask that the trial be adjourned for a month from this time. There are some other witnesses
who are in the country in addition to those whom we have named,
and we ask that subpoenas be issued for them at the expense of the
Government or the court or such other procedure as your Honor can
take to procure their attendance. The witnesses from Quebec we do
not ask the Crown to bring at their expense; we will bring them here
ourselves. The other witnesses –
MR JUSTICE RICHARDSON: The law in regard to witnesses is laid
down. I think my powers are defined.
MR GREENSHIELDS: I think upon proper representation being
made to the Government –
MR JUSTICE RICHARDSON: Have you seen the order of the 17th
of June? The old one is repealed and a new one issued.
MR GREENSHIELDS: I have not seen the one of the 17th June.
MR JUSTICE RICHARDSON: It is simply a little more
liberal.

MR GREENSHIELDS: If we are forced on with this trial now we
really have no defence to make; we could not have the witnesses
here; we have no witnesses.

MR FITZPATRICK: May it please your Honors. In connection with
this case, I will simply say that at the time we were retained for the
defence, it had been made to a very large extent apparent in our
Province, that it would be almost impossible to secure such a trial
for the prisoner as public opinion appeared unanimously to require.
So far as we could gather from the press, and other modes of ascertaining the opinion of the public, the desire was that this man should
have a full, fair and impartial trial, that every possible means should
be afforded to him to make a full and complete defence, that after
he had made his defence and had a fair chance of exculpating himself or explaining his position, then that the law should take its
course; but that if a full and free and impartial trial, such as the public absolutely required, was not had, no satisfaction would be given
to the public, and the public would not be in a position to say that
Louis Riel was really guilty of the charges laid at his door.

With this object in view, and in view of the fact that the press
throughout the country required and besought the Government to
interfere in this case, for the purpose of forcing the Government to a
certain extent to secure for the defendant all the means that might
be considered necessary to have the trial, we were sent to Ottawa,
and we went to Ottawa, and there had an interview with the Minister
of Justice, and, being there, he replied very naturally: There is no
provision in the law which enables me to furnish you with the means
necessary to defend, but he also added that on a recommendation by
the court, certain witnesses being produced, that it would be proper
that their expenses would be paid, and action would be taken. This
being the answer from the Government, of course then we had to go
to the parties who were acting and who were really our clients in this
case.

We then found ourselves in this position, that the Government
were desirous of paying witnesses after they had been brought here,
on recommendation by the court, and then we said: What is the use
of that to us? How are the witnesses to be produced? Of course I can
understand such an order as that being given in the Tichborne case
for instance. In that case such an order was given, such a thing was
done, but where, as in England, the distances to be covered are very

short, where the means of getting witnesses is very simple, one can understand such an order. In a country like this where we have thousands of miles of territory to cover in order to get witnesses, such an order as that which the Government were anxious to give us, and which the court now says is in existence, and which the court now says applies to this case is perfectly useless to us. It is perfectly useless for us to know that when the witnesses are here they will be paid. How are we going to get them here? that is the point. In view of those facts, subscriptions were organized throughout the Province of Quebec, and your Honor knows that it takes necessarily some time for the public to properly realise the importance of a case of this kind. It takes some little time for the public mind to be properly seized of the importance of a case of this kind. Before we had the answer from the Government, subscriptions were organised, and now, from telegrams received from Quebec, we believe that we can honestly come before this court, and say that a certain number of witnesses that are required will be produced before this court. Of course I don't wish to come before the court and say here that we can produce all the witnesses that are necessary for the defence, but I am instructed that the witnesses who are required from Quebec, will be sent here from Quebec. As to the other witnesses, I have nothing further to say than what has been already said by Mr Green-shields, except, perhaps, that I have a letter which I communicated to the learned counsel for the Crown, from a gentleman who is in personal communication with Dumont and Dumas, from which I gather that these witnesses are ready to give us every assistance in their power, and I infer from that it will be possible if they are properly instructed as to the immunity which is guaranteed them by our laws, it is possible to infer from the letter that those men will be brought here, that they can be brought here, and that we may possibly be able to have them if the adjournment takes place.

Of course, I don't wish to bind myself here, standing as counsel for the defence; I don't wish to bind myself to anything I cannot do, and I would not undertake for the defence, under any circumstances, to say here I shall produce so and so. I do not bind myself that I can do it. All I say, all I can say as counsel, is that I am instructed that such witnesses can be produced, and I infer from the letter which I have and which I placed in the hands of the learned counsel for the Crown, and which I am prepared to lay before the

court, that if it is possible I can say that a witness, Dumont or
Dumas, can be brought here with immunity, we can produce them
before this court. Those witnesses I am instructed will prove facts
that are of the highest importance for the defence; they will prove
that Mr Riel if he had been listened to, not one drop of blood would
have been shed.

MR OSLER: Confine yourself to the facts on the affidavit.

MR JUSTICE RICHARDSON: I will hear anything that has not
already been said.

MR FITZPATRICK: As to speaking to the facts, I think the statement I made is covered by the affidavit, that the alleged rebellion
was commenced and conducted under the direction of a council of
fourteen persons, of which council the prisoner was not a member;
that he did not participate in any engagement or permit or countenance any act of overt treason.

Of course it would be very humiliating for a counsel to be said to
be not confining himself to the facts, to statements not already sworn
to, but I have endeavoured in all that I have said, as I shall endeavor
all through this case, to restrict myself, so far as lies in my power, to
the facts as they appear before the court, and I think the statement
is borne out by my affidavit.

I don't wish to detain the court any further in this case, and so
far as we are concerned, we think it is necessary for the accused that
the postponement should be had, and we leave the matter with
entire confidence in the hands of the court.

MR JUSTICE RICHARDSON: What I understand you to suggest, at
least the facts which you have put forward are these, that some witnesses who are not here ought to be here for the proper defence, and
that some of them cannot be here because they have not got the
funds?

MR FITZPATRICK: Some of them we have not been able to procure, up to the present time, because we have not had the funds, but
if a delay is granted to us, we are in expectation that we shall be able
to produce those witnesses.

MR JUSTICE RICHARDSON: There are three points covered by
your application; firstly, necessary and material witnesses are not
here; secondly, with regard to some of them they have not the
funds; thirdly, if a reasonable postponement is given, they can be
produced, or rather, you believe they can be produced.

MR FITZPATRICK: Yes, I believe they can be produced.

MR ROBINSON: These affidavits we saw, at least I myself, only a few minutes before the court opened, and I have had time only to glance at them. I desire to give such answer as we think proper to give to them on the part of the Crown after proper consideration, and I ask your Honors, under the circumstances – I think it would be better to ask your Honors to allow us an interval of ten or fifteen minutes to consider what course it is right for the Crown to take. Court postponed for a few minutes.

MR ROBINSON, resuming: We have considered together the course which the Crown will take in answering this application. We have considered the matter with some anxiety, because we are quite aware that a serious responsibility rests upon us either in acceding to or opposing such an application. In the first place I must be permitted to say that I regret extremely that my learned friend, Mr Greenshields, should have departed so far from what I regard as professional courtesy and professional etiquette, as to make the remarks which he thought it right to make in the discharge of his duty, and I must say that it is wholly new to me in the course of a very long professional career to hear a simple practice application of this kind, such as this application for adjournment or postponement of a trial, urged in such a tone and in such a spirit. As to part of his remarks, I understood, and I think everyone else must have understood that if they meant anything, they certainly meant to imply a threat against those acting for the Crown, that if they declined to accede to the contention, public opinion would be brought to bear upon them, and public opinion would not support them. We are answerable to public opinion, and we are perfectly content to be answerable to public opinion, but I repeat again my surprise that that tone of spirit and sort of address should have been thought necessary in a case of this description.

I will now say what I have to say, in answer to the application made. As to the application for postponement which is asked for, those who represent the Crown think it their duty to oppose it. To a certain extent, we think it right to accede to it so far as we have any voice in the matter. I will discuss the different grounds in a few moments on which this application is based. As regards what I am inclined to think is the main portion of the application and main grounds urged, I think it is an application made under circumstances

and based upon grounds which are wholly without precedent. I
speak now of the application for the postponement of this trial
under Gabriel Dumont, Michel Dumas, and a Mr Nault, should be
brought from the United States where they are said now to be, to
give evidence for the prisoner. It is a matter of history that a rebellion has broken out in this country. It is a matter of notoriety that
those three men were not only participators in that rebellion, but
were leading and active spirits concerned in it. It is a matter of
notoriety that the result of their connection with that rebellion has
led them to flee from justice. I don't believe there is an instance of
any application having ever been made, still less of such an application ever being granted, as an application for adjournment of the
trial of those who have not been successful in escaping from justice
until those who have escaped are brought back under a safe conduct
from the Crown to give evidence in their favor. We have no authority
at all events, and we have no power whatever to give to any of those
persons who have fled from justice anything approaching protection
or safe conduct, if they choose to enter this province. If they enter it
in innocence, they can prove their innocence. If they enter it guilty,
they must take the chances of all others who are guilty.

There are other grounds which are urged. It is said that Mr Vankoughnet and Mr Burgess, two gentlemen employed in the public
service of the Crown at Ottawa, have the custody of a large number
of petitions and documents which it is necessary the prisoner should
have for the purposes of his defence, and the purport of those petitions and documents is stated. They are petitions to the Government, applications to the Government, asking for redress of what
were alleged to be certain grievances. Those documents and those
petitions I believe to be utterly inadmissible under any circumstances, as a defence in this case. We hear, for the first time, that an
application for redress on constitutional grounds is evidence to form
a justification for armed rebellion. If those documents were here they
would be opposed as wholly inadmissible, and so far as we can judge,
they are wholly inadmissible, as having any bearing whatever on this
case; but I am not aware that any application was made to the
Government to send Mr Vankoughnet or Mr Burgess here to allow an
inspection or production of any of those documents, or to produce
any of those documents at the trial. With regard to another application which my learned friends say they will think it right to make, or

which they do make now, an application for an order for the production of all correspondence which was found in possession of the
prisoner at Batoche, all I can say is, that we regard those documents
as state documents, and many of them necessarily implicate others,
and that we, in the discharge of our duty, should feel it necessary to
refuse to any person acting for the prisoner an inspection of anything which can be in the nature of treasonable correspondence, or
which could implicate others in any matter, and which it is in the
public interest and in the interest of society to see properly
punished.

With regard to the certificate of naturalization which the prisoner
says is necessary for his defence, in our view the law is clear that the
existence of that certificate would make no difference whatever. We
have not that certificate ourselves. I am told we have never known
where it was until we got a telegram this morning, and we heard that
a certified copy of the certificate or the certificate itself is at Winnipeg. All that we can say with regard to that is, that we shall telegraph. We have telegraphed for it to Winnipeg, and it shall be got and
produced, and they shall have the use of it. We can do nothing more
with regard to that.

With regard to those witnesses who, it is said, will come from
Quebec and will prove the state of the prisoner's mind ten or twelve
years ago, it is not for me to say or to conjecture what possible
weight that can have on the question of the state of prisoner's mind
six months ago; but, however that may be, what we are told here is,
that they desire, not a postponement of a few days until those witnesses can be telegraphed for and brought up, but the leading counsel for the defence comes and says he thought the witnesses would
be here, and if you will allow him to go back to Quebec, he will go
and bring them. I don't think an application based upon those
grounds can be listened to. My learned friend, Mr Greenshields, for
whatever object I do not know, has recurred, to a certain extent, to
an argument addressed to your Honors yesterday, and has endeavored to point out that his trial contrasts unfavorably with other
trial in fairness, because the prisoner is now, for the first time, asked
to go on with his trial at once. Far from that being the case, this trial
contrasts most favorably with all other criminal trials in point of
fairness with reference to the prisoner. The usual course in all
ordinary trials is, that the prisoner is arraigned, and he is asked then

if he is ready for trial, and a day is named at once. It is now 14 or 15 days since the day was named for this trial, and yesterday would be the day on which the trial would take place, and it is now for the first time, on the day after that day named, or rather we hear the contention made about which we heard for the first time the intention to make — declared only yesterday. It must have been well known too, perfectly well known, the very moment that the prisoner was captured, it must have been perfectly well known that his trial would take place as soon as could be made possible under the circumstances. There must have been the most full and amplest notice to all those interested in preparing for the trial, that it was necessary to take whatever steps might be necessary, without delay. Now, I do not desire to place the convenience of any person, for one instant, in the scale to weigh against what my learned friends say here, they are entitled to a perfect, fair and impartial trial of this case. Convenience has little to do with it. But it is not to be forgotten that a panel of 36 jurors are here; that almost as many witnesses have been summoned, and probably more, from all parts of the country, and that there are public officers here, whose detention here is of very great inconvenience to the public service of the Dominion. All those things I suppose must give way to what is necessary to obtain an impartial trial, but it must be only such a delay as will be necessary to obtain that trial, and such a delay as in reason can be said to be desirable, in order to effect it. Under those circumstances, what those representing the Crown have thought, is that it would be right for them to accede to an adjournment or postponment of this case for one week. All those witnesses who are in this country can be got in a week, just as well as in a month or a year. The Crown will do more. The Crown will join with my learned friends in telegraphing to those three gentlemen who are at Quebec, or those three gentlemen who are at Prince Albert. I desire that to come from the Crown as well as from them, and the Crown will pay their expenses.
MR JUSTICE RICHARDSON: With regard to witnesses, Mr Robinson, near any police post in this country, they can be warned on telegraph, verbally warned, and it would simply involve the coming here of the person who warned them, in case warrants be disobeyed. It does not require a subpoena in this country. It would simply require the presence of the officer, or official or constable who warned them, in order to attach them.

MR ROBINSON: I was not aware of that. Then there is no sort of difficulty in regard to witnesses living in these territories, principally at Prince Albert and Batoche. We will join in whatever steps are necessary to procure their attendance, and the Crown will pay their expenses.

MR JUSTICE RICHARDSON: The statute is general – one of the succeeding sections to section 76, I think, applies generally to the Dominion.

MR ROBINSON: Then there is no difficulty at all events about this. As regards the witnesses in Quebec, we take it for granted that my learned friends, having communication with them, will have no difficulty in getting them, on the Government joining in a telegram to them desiring them to come, and if the Beauport asylum is a Government institution, there will be no difficulty in getting them, and in doing that, I think we are doing all that in the discharge of our duty we can be asked to do properly.

In our view, we will consent to the postponement of the trial till this day week, and that will necessarily give the prisoner and my learned friends an adjournment of ten days, because the case for the Crown will no doubt occupy two or three days, and their witnesses will not be required till that is closed. That is the answer.

There is only one other matter to remark upon, which I had forgotten, and which I wish I had mentioned before, but my learned friend made some very strong and very inflammatory remarks about the treatment which he received from certain witnesses whom he alleged were witnesses for the Crown. All that I can say is that if the counsel desire to interview a witness subpoenaed on the other side, they must always take their chances as to the reception they meet from the witnesses. That is a matter in their own judgment and in their own discretion, about which they have no right to complain.

MR GREENSHIELDS: My learned friend will reply to the main question of the application. I merely wish to rise to make a personal explanation.

MR JUSTICE RICHARDSON: I understood you to disclaim any personal imputation.

MR GREENSHIELDS: My learned friend, Mr Robinson, rather stated that he was surprised at the vehemence and warmth with which I had urged the application for the adjournment. It may be true that a due realisation of the obligation resting upon me as one of the counsel for the defence, and the importance with which we deemed the application, I might perhaps have urged it with perhaps more warmth than the learned counsel, who seems much cooler, would have done, but in doing so, I did it because I felt now as we all have felt that unless this application were granted, unless we could obtain a postponement of this trial, this man's life was in danger.

We are charged with this defence, and if the defence is not properly made, and a verdict of guilty should follow and then execution, as counsel for the defence we cannot help but feel the responsibility that rests upon us in making an application of this kind, and far from intending to intimate for one moment that public opinion had anything to do with influencing the learned counsel, or intimidating them, the thing is impossible, the learned counsel are too well known in this country and in the Dominion of Canada to be influenced in any way by any public sentiment or public opinion. What I wished to intimate was that this being a state trial, and the public at large being interested, and the case having gone so prominently before the public, as well as the events preceding the rebellion, that the public naturally expected that a fair trial should be given, and we felt that in the exercise of our duty in defending the prisoner, we had to a certain extent a public trust as well as the learned counsel representing the Crown, and that we wanted to do everything in our power in order that a fair trial should be obtained; and if I urged the application with warmth, it was the result entirely of the responsibility which I feel as one of the counsel, and of the intense importance which we attach to this application, feeling, as we do, that the result of this trial largely depends upon whether this application is granted or refused.

MR FITZPATRICK: May it please your Honors. I on behalf of the defence assume the responsibility of accepting the delay which, as stated by the Crown counsel, the Crown is prepared to offer us.

MR JUSTICE RICHARDSON: I think it is reasonable, Mr Fitzpatrick. I think it is a reasonable time. I might perhaps have gone and stretched it a day or so, but not beyond that, because the means of communication are very quick now compared with what they were, and a witness can be got from Quebec and you are quite able to avail yourselves of the provisions of the Act that I referred to with regard to warnings.

MR FITZPATRICK: I may as well state now as to the offer made by the counsel for the Crown of their concurrence in the way of remuneration of witnesses, we will consider whether or not we will accept that part of it or not.

MR JUSTICE RICHARDSON: You must bear in mind that I am powerless to make any order. There is the Order in Council. It is not a provincial court, and I have no control over funds except in the limited way in which the Order in Council provides.

MR FITZPATRICK: I read the Order in Council as conferring the very limited powers; however, that difficulty is all obviated by the offer made by the Crown.

MR OSLER: My learned friend will understand that that adjournment is necessarily peremptory.

MR FITZPATRICK: That is all right.

MR JUSTICE RICHARDSON: The order will be that the trial stands adjourned, that it proceeds peremptorily on Tuesday morning next, the 28th instant, at 10 o'clock. With regard to the jury I don't feel inclined to keep them in attendance and I propose to caution and warn them to return on Tuesday morning.

TO THE JURYMEN: You gentlemen in the audience who have been warned as jurors will understand from what has been said that your services will not be required now till Tuesday next at 10 A.M., and you are at liberty now to return to your homes if you please. The fees that are usual for the double journey will be paid by the Crown. Perhaps it is not necessary for me to make any remarks touching you personally, but knowing the fact that you are called upon to act as jurors in the case, kindly think of the position you occupy, and neither talk to anybody about the trial, nor allow any person to talk to you or bring you in conversation.

The court was accordingly adjourned at 11:45 A.M. till the 28th July, at 10 A.M.

AFFIDAVITS FILED ON MOTION FOR ADJOURNMENT

Canada, North-West Territories
The Queen v *Louis Riel*, charged under the North-West Territories Act of 1880

I, Louis Riel, the said accused, being duly sworn do depose and say:

That Gabriel Dumont and Michel Dumas, now of Helena, in the United States of America, in the Territory of Montana, are essential and material witnesses to my defence;

That Napoléon Nault, of Turtle Mountain, in the United States, the Rev. Father Touze, of Sacré Cœur, the Rev. Father André, of St Antoine, the Rev. Father Fourmond, of St Laurent, all in the North-West Territories of Canada, L. Vankoughnet and A.M. Burgess, of Ottawa, in the Province of Ontario, are also essential and material witnesses for my defence;

That the said L. Vankoughnet is Deputy Minister of Indian Affairs, and the said A.M. Burgess is Deputy Minister of the Interior, both of whom are, in their official capacity, the custodians of various official documents, petitions and representations made by the half-breeds of the North-West Territories to the Government of the Dominion of Canada praying for the redress of their grievances, the refusal to grant which led to the legal agitation by the people to secure the redress of their wrongs. The said papers, petitions and documents, as nearly as I can now describe them, are as follows: The report of Mr Pearce relating to the settlement of Prince Albert, a letter of the said Pearce addressed to the Minister of the Interior, of date the 17th January 1884; a letter from Mr Deville, addressed to the Deputy Minister of the Interior, of date 7th February 1884; a letter from Father Vegreville, addressed to Capt. Deville, of date 19th January 1884; a petition by the inhabitants of St Louis de Langevin, forwarded to Sir John A. Macdonald, on or about the 19th November 1883; a letter from the Land Commissioner, Mr Pearce, dated 14th September 1883; a letter from Fathers Le Duc and Maloney, addressed to the Hon. D.L. Macpherson, Acting Minister of the Interior; a petition from the settlers of Prince Albert, in the North-West Territories, forwarded during the winter of 1882-3, and signed by a large number of said settlers; a petition from St Antoine de Padua, addressed to Sir John A. Macdonald as Minister of the Interior, of date the 4th September 1882; a petition from Gabriel Dumont and others, of the 4th September 1884, addressed to the Right Hon. Sir John A. Macdonald as Minister of the Interior; a petition presented by the Rev. Father André to the Lieutenant Governor in Council, in the month of June 1881; a petition

presented by the inhabitants of Prince Albert to the Minister of the
Interior; a letter from Land Agent Duck, dated the 13th November
1878, addressed to the Minister of the Interior; a petition by the
French Canadians and half-breeds of Prince Albert, presented by Mr
Laird, to the Government of the Dominion of Canada; a resolution
passed by the settlers of St Laurent, on the 1st February, 1878, forwarded to the Government of the Dominion of Canada; a petition
presented by the Qu'Appelle half-breeds, in August or September
1881, to Sir John A. Macdonald, as Minister of the Interior; a resolution of the Council of the North-West Territories, of date 2nd
August 1878.

That I have reason to believe, and do verily believe, and am informed on reliable authority, that all of the aforementioned documents were duly forwarded to the Government of Canada and are
now in the possession of the various Departments and can be pro-
cured by the above-named witnesses;

That all the above-named witnesses are material and essential to
me in my defence, and will prove that the agitation in the North-
West Territories was constitutional and for the rights of the people
of said North-West;

That without the said witnesses being heard in court, I cannot
make a proper defence to the present charges, and will be deprived
of justice;

That I have no means with which to defray the expenses of the
said witnesses, and to procure their attendance here in court or to
retain counsel;

That unless the Government of this country or this honorable
court do provide the means with which to secure the attendance
of the above-named witnesses, before this court, that it is essential to
my defence that the various papers, writings and documents taken
from me at the time of my surrender to General Middleton, and
taken by him and his officers from my house subsequently, should
be placed in the hands of my counsel for their examination and
consideration, previous to being put upon my trial;

That it is impossible for me to state the exact description of the
said papers, writings and documents, as the excitement under which
I was laboring during the time of my surrender and some days subsequently and previous thereto, rendered it impossible for me to
destroy the said documents; that I believe that among the said

documents is a certificate of the courts of the United States of America that I was duly naturalized as a citizen of the United States, which I was; but if the said certificate is not among the said papers, it is essential to my defence that I should be given an opportunity of obtaining the said certificate, by means of which I can establish, that at the time of the commission of the alleged offences I was a citizen of the United States of America, and not a British subject, as charged in the said information;

That in order to properly prepare for my defence, I require at least a delay of one month, and I have signed

(signed)
LOUIS RIEL

Sworn and acknowledged before me this 21st
day of July 1885, at Regina, in the
North-West Territories
(signed)
DIXIE WATSON, clerk

Canada, North-West Territories
The Queen v *Louis Riel*

François Xavier Lemieux, barrister, one of the counsel of Louis Riel, the accused, being duly sworn deposes and says:

That in the course of last June towards the end of the month he was retained by persons interested on behalf of the accused, to undertake his defence;

That persons were instructed to cause to be brought to Regina, essential and necessary witnesses in the defence of Louis Riel, and believed to be such by the deponent;

That the witnesses above referred to are Dr François Roy, of Quebec; Dr Clark, of Toronto and Dr A. Vallée of Quebec;

That the deponent verily believes that the said witnesses would have reached Regina by this time, but by reason of misapprehension and circumstances beyond control, the said witnesses have failed or not been able to be present in order to give their evidence;

That from his experience as a counsel and advocate, swears that the said Drs Roy, Vallée, and Clark are necessary material and indispensable witnesses for the defence of the accused, and moreover, are the sole witnesses capable of proving certain important facts relating to the said defence;

That the deponent verily believes that if a delay of one month is granted he can procure the said witnesses by going himself to Quebec and Toronto and that at the expiration of the said delay, the above-named witnesses will be present at the court to give evidence in favor of the accused.

And the deponent has signed.

(signed)

F.X. LEMIEUX

Sworn before me at Regina this 21st day
of July 1885
(signed)
DIXIE WATSON, clerk

Canada, North-West Territories, Regina, to wit:
The Queen v *Louis Riel*, on trial under sub-section 5 of section 76 of the North-West Territories Act of 1880, before their Honors Hugh Richardson, S.M., and Henry Le Jeune, J.P., and a jury of six

I, Charles Fitzpatrick, of the city of Quebec, one of the counsel of the above-named Louis Riel, make oath and say:

1 I was retained for the defence of the said Louis Riel in the month of June last past, and immediately thereafter put myself in communication with my said client and others with the view of obtaining such information as would enable me to set up such defence as in the interests of my said client would be most beneficial.

2 Owing to the distance of Quebec from my client it was not until the 29th day of the said month of June I was instructed by the accused, and then only partially.

3 Since the receipt of the said instructions, I have been diligently endeavoring to obtain the attendance of the witnesses for the accused, but as he, the accused, is a man of little or no means and had to raise funds for his defence through his friends in the Province of Quebec, it was an utter impossibility to obtain their attendance in time for his trial.

4 I have been instructed since my arrival in Regina that the requisite funds have been raised to secure the attendance of the said witnesses for the defence, who are material and necessary and without whose evidence we cannot proceed to trial.

5 Some of the facts intended to be proved by such witnesses are that the accused for several years was insane, and had to be

confined in a lunatic asylum in the Province of Quebec, and would get deranged, also the circumstances under which the accused left his home in Montana, and came to this country at the solicitation of his friends, was in the year one thousand eight hundred and eighty-five; the nature of the agitation in the North-West, and the constant advice given by the accused to limit the agitation to constitutional means and peaceful measures; the desire expressed by the accused to leave the country in the month of February now last past, and the objection of the people to his returning to Montana aforesaid; that the alleged rebellion was commenced and conducted under the direction of a council of fourteen persons of which council the prisoner was not a member, and that he did not participate in any engagement or commit or countenance any overt act of treason.

6 These facts can be proved by Gabriel Dumont, Michel Dumas, Napoléon Nault, Dr Roy, of Quebec, Dr Clark, of Toronto, and Dr Vallée, of Quebec, whose attendance at the trial I verily believe can be secured if sufficient time for that purpose is granted to the defence.

(signed)
C. FITZPATRICK

Sworn before me at Regina this 21st day
of July 1885
(signed)
DIXIE WATSON, clerk

Tuesday, 28th July 1885

The court opened at 10 o'clock.

After, the following were challenged on behalf of the prisoner: Demetrius Woodward, John McIntyre, Thomas Rogers, Thomas Howard and William Braley; and on the part of the Crown, Michael Sullivan. The following jurors were sworn and empannelled: Edward Erratt, Edwin J. Brooks, Walter Merryfield, Peel Dean and Francis Cosgrave.

MR OSLER: May it please your Honors, gentlemen of the jury: The prisoner stands before you charged with the highest crime known to the law, and you are charged with passing upon his life or death. It is for you to remove from your minds any impression you may have had, or possessed from the knowledge of public facts, as to his guilt or innocence. You must endeavor to bring upon the evidence, and upon the evidence alone, your reasoning; and upon the evidence, not upon your knowledge of that which is public property, you must pass upon his guilt or innocence. He is to be presumed, as everybody is in the criminal dock, innocent until the evidence brings home, to your satisfaction, guilt.

He is charged under six counts, the three last being in fact a repetition. He is charged first as a subject of our Sovereign Lady the Queen, not regarding his duty and allegiance, with levying war at Duck Lake, Fish Creek and Batoche.

Again he is charged with high treason, not as a subject, but as a person living within the protection of the law and owing that local allegiance which the law demands from everyone living in the country. He is charged in those two ways, because it has been said, or suggested, and may be made out by the prisoner's counsel if they think it worth while, that he is an American citizen and is not under allegiance to the British Crown. And it is for that reason and as a mere matter of precaution, that there are six counts instead of only three in the indictment, a precautionary measure that it might be seen that this point had not been overlooked. Anyone may be guilty of treason who is living in the country, and so far has the law gone in that respect, that an alien enemy, although his country was at war with England was held, is held by English law to be guilty of high treason by reason of his domicile, although his duty to his country made him an alien enemy; and if you think it out it is necessary that it should be so.

Now, gentlemen, it may be proper for me, before considering the facts of the case, to point out shortly how you, sitting here as a jury of six, instead of as we generally see a panel of twelve, are charged with so serious a trial; the most serious trial that has ever probably taken place in Canada, and why you are here charged with such a duty without the preliminary of an ordinary enquiry by a grand jury of the county. I need not and do not intend to go into a lengthy discussion of the legal matters that were argued at the opening of the court. It is sufficient to say to you that by an Act of the Imperial Parliament passed in 1871, the Dominion Parliament were charged with making laws for the peace, order, and good government of these territories, from this Act from the supreme source of all power in the British realm is delegated power to the Dominion Parliament. The Dominion Parliament then passed various Acts regulating the government of these territories. The law is contained in the statute of 1876, and by that statute stipendiary magistrates are provided for, men learned in the law and of certain standing at the bar. They are charged with the administration of justice in serious cases, cases involving the penalty of death, with the aid and assistance of an associate justice of the peace, and with the intervention of a jury of six. By that statute that court is entitled to try any man on any charge, and by that statute treason is specially named as one of the charges which that court is competent to try.

A great deal has been said about there being no grand jury; it is only necessary for me to point out that the grand jury is essentially a feature of county organization. The grand jury is an accusing body, gathered fairly from the county, and charged to enquire as to the crimes committed in that county. From the nature of these territories it is impossible that grand juries can be summoned in the ordinary way, there are no criminal divisions, this territory is but one as far as the administration of criminal justice is concerned, and it would be impossible in the organization of courts of justice in these territories to organize them upon the same basis upon which, no doubt, they will be organized as soon as the country is more settled. Parliament has had to organize just such courts as they thought would fairly administer justice in the territories, having reference to the circumstances and sparseness of the population, and such as would administer justice, having regard to reasonable economy. I believe in this case the mileage of the jury panel brought together comes to something like 1,500 miles, so you see it would be impossible, until these North-West Territories are more settled, to have those organizations which we have in the older provinces. It has been suggested, however, that there were other methods of trial. It has been suggested that there are Acts in force enabling these trials to take place where there are grand juries and juries of twelve, that is to say in Upper Canada, or British Columbia. It has been also suggested that the Crown has the power to issue a special commission, and that by that commission such important crimes as the one now before us should be disposed of. There is grave doubt, as far as the Crown is concerned, whether the Acts in reference to trial in Upper Canada, or British Columbia, now apply. In reference to a special commission, the Crown have been unable to see their way towards organizing any court, although, no doubt, the prerogative rests in the Crown to issue a special commission for the delivery of any gaol from trial for any crime. The officers of the Crown have taken the responsibility of saying that the proper court is the court in the territories where the offence was committed. That the ordinary courts organized in the land should be the courts in which justice should be administered to the insignificant criminal, or to the one of greater prominence and I think you will consider that that is the proper conclusion to arrive at. It is always to be avoided, if possible, the organizing of special courts for special purposes. Well, then you see, gentlemen, you are charged regularly and in a proper way with the duty of enquiring into this offence. The offence of treason, and treasonable crimes, has been the subject of a great deal of legislation. There are several Acts under which the Crown, in this case, could have proceeded; there is the Act known as the Fenian Act. That Act provides for the punishment of an alien, who, belonging to a country at peace with this country, endeavors to levy war or make a raid upon this country. Under that the Crown could have proceeded in this case if they chose to do so, but had they done so the burden of proof would have been on the Crown to make out that the accused here was an alien, a responsibility the Crown did not choose to assume.

There are other statutes for the protection of the Crown, such as the Act in relation to treason-felony which we have not thought it advisable to proceed under.

The prisoner has been indicted upon the statute of treason passed in the reign of Edward III, a statute that has been in force ever since that day, and which has been the foundation of the law of treason since that early period. And, under that clause in that Act declaring that a person who levies war against the king is guilty of high treason, the prisoner here stands charged. The charge, as I have already explained, is in the alternative position of subject or alien.

Now, I proceed, as shortly as consistent with the importance of the case, to open to you the facts which the Crown will sustain, or endeavor to sustain, by the evidence.

The prisoner is said to have resumed his domiciel in this country sometime in the year 1884. About the beginning of July, or the

latter end of June 1884, we find him living in this country, in the
district of the Saskatchewan. In that district there were supposed to
be some 700 or 800 French half-breeds, and a good many more
English half-breeds, and there were several Indian reservations not
very far from where the prisoner made his headquarters. We first
find him acting in concert with prominent men of both the English
and French half-breeds and holding meetings. At those meetings
apparently for some time nothing more than ordinary constitutional
agitation for the redress of grievances, supposed or real, took place.
The first overt act which we find against the prisoner is his calling his
immediate friends – the French half-breeds – to bring their arms at
the last of this series of public meetings; that meeting was held, I
think, on the evening of the 3rd of March. At that meeting arms
were brought. That is the first act that we find indicating that the
prisoner intended to resort to violence. Now we find matters getting
worse and worse, and on the 17th of March, we will give evidence of
a statement made by the prisoner to the effect that he intended
effecting a change in the government of the country, probably referring to that particular section of the country known as the Saskatchewan district; he stated that he intended to become the ruler of
that country or perish in the attempt. We find him progressing from
that until the 18th of March, when we find him sending out armed
bodies of men, who took prisoners the Government Indian agent, Mr
Lash, and some store-keepers. We find them looting or taking possession of the contents of stores at and near Batoche; we find armed
men stopping freighters and taking their freight from them. Matters
had become very serious, and the authorities much alarmed. On the
21st of March the French half-breeds, speaking generally, may be
said to have been in arms under the guidance of the prisoner, and
they were then joined by Indians, Indians incited to rise, as I think
the evidence will satisfy you, by the prisoner. On the 21st of March,
Major Crozier, desiring to do all he could to avoid bloodshed, did all
he could to get the armed men to disperse and go home. For that
purpose two well known citizens of Prince Albert, Mr McKay, I
think himself a half-breed, and Mr Hilliard Mitchell were asked to go
and see the people. Well, on the morning of the 21st of March, there
was a meeting. These two gentlemen proceeded to Batoche and met
the prisoner and others there, they urged to the extent of their
power and influence that the rank and file who had been induced to

take up arms should disperse and go to their homes, and said: I believe that if the leaders were given up, no blood having been shed,
the rising in arms of these men would be overlooked. The result of
the embassy was unfortunate, they remained in arms, the prisoner
guiding their ideas and keeping them in rebellion. That morning it
was arranged that McKay and Mitchell should go back for definite
instructions to Major Crozier and that Major Crozier himself should
meet Riel and endeavor to adjust matters on a peaceable ground; this
did not take place, and it was arranged that two French half-breeds
should meet McKay and Mitchell or two others whom Major Crozier
should appoint, and these parties should be empowered to carry out
any arrangements. As a result of that, Charles Nolin, a justice of the
peace, and a French half-breed who will be called as a witness, with
Lepine, were appointed to meet McKay and Mitchell; they did meet
about eleven o'clock that night. Now, upon that occasion Nolin and
Lepine were instructed by the prisoner in writing, and as this is a
most important document containing a demand to Major Crozier to
surrender Fort Carlton, I propose to read it to you. This document is
in the prisoner's handwriting, it was written by him, and by him
given to Charles Nolin to deliver. The terms of the half-breeds were
that Carlton should be unconditionally surrendered, and that the
police should be sent home under a safe conduct pass. That was the
sole condition the prisoner and his associates dictated as the terms of
peace; that Major Crozier, directed and ordered to keep the peace,
should deliver up one of the forts of the country to rebels. The instructions of McKay and Mitchell were about the same as those they
acted on in the morning, that is to say, that the rank and file would
not be pursued if the leaders were given up. The emissaries being so
far apart, this document was not delivered, and it was afterwards
found among the papers captured after the fight at Batoche, in the
council house of the so-called Provisional Government of the Saskatchewan. I will now read this paper:

St Antoine, N.W.T., 21st March 1885
To Major Crozier, Commander of the Police at Forts Carlton and
Battleford
Major: The Councillors of the Provisional Government of the Sas-
katchewan have the honor to communicate to you the following con-
ditions of surrender: You will be required to give up completely the

situation which the Canadian Government placed you in at Carlton
and Battleford, together with all Government properties.

In case of acceptance you and your men will be set free on your
parole of honor to keep the peace. And those who choose to leave
the country will be furnished with teams and provisions to reach
Qu'Appelle.

In case of non-acceptance we intend to attack you, when to-
morrow, the Lord's day is over, and to commence without delay, a
war of extermination upon those who have shown themselves hostile
to our rights.

Messrs. Charles Nolin and Maxime Lepine are the gentlemen with
whom you will have to treat.

Major, we respect you. Let the cause of humanity be a consolation to you for the reverses which the governmental misconduct has
brought upon you.

LOUIS 'DAVID' RIEL, Exovede

Then follow the names of some of the prominent sympathizers of
the prisoner and after them follows the signature of Philip Garnot,
Secretary. Then on the other side is written:

St Anthony, 31st March 1885
To Messrs. Charles Nolin and Maxime Lepine
Gentlemen: If Major Crozier accedes to the conditions of surrender,
let him use the following formula and no others: 'Because I love my
neighbor as myself, for the sake of God and to prevent bloodshed,
and principally the war of extermination which threatens the
country, I agree to the above conditions of surrender.'

If the Major writes this formula and signs it, inform him that we
will receive him and his men Monday.
Yours,
LOUIS 'DAVID' RIEL, Exovede

Now, gentlemen, that document in itself, in the handwriting and
over the signature of the prisoner, is direct evidence of treason, delivered, as it was, to gentlemen demanding the surrender of the fort.

It will be important to bear in mind throughout the evidence you
hear that a few days before this, on the 18th of March, the prisoner
declared himself to be about to proceed to create himself ruler of
the country or perish in the attempt; then we find that followed up

by arming and by this demand. It has been suggested that when the
first conflict took place it was not with the consent of the prisoner,
but that he was forced to it. This evidence would be a most complete refutation of that theory. That brings us to the 21st of March,
when the four gentlemen met and failed in any way to come to
terms. On one side the prisoner and his followers were insisting upon
the capture of Carlton, and on the other Major Crozier insisting on
the surrender of the leaders and the dispersal of the armed men. I
will not go into the details, which you can best follow as the evidence is given. We will pass from the 21st to the 26th of March. On
that day Thomas McKay, whom I have already named, being at
Prince Albert with the Prince Albert volunteer company, which had
been hastily formed, started out, under the direction of Major
Crozier, to bring in some stores which were at Duck Lake, at
Mitchell's store. On their way they were met by a body of armed
men, and with the greatest possible difficulty bloodshed was then
avoided by the prudence and great discretion of Mr McKay. On that
occasion matters went so far that some Indians entered the sleighs
that McKay had for the purpose of bringing back the stores, and one
of the leaders of that party fired, presumably over the heads of the
men who were with McKay. The result was both parties turned back,
and there was no actual contest. McKay sent forward a man to the
fort to say that the enemy were in force, and as they came near the
fort they met Crozier and the residue of the men coming out to their
assistance. McKay's party turned back with Major Crozier, and they
proceeded to about where the smaller party had turned back in the
morning, and there took place what is known as the Duck Lake
fight, the battle or contest of Duck Lake. There this man took on
himself the terrible responsibility of ordering his armed men to fire
on the police, and we will bring home to this man in the dock the
personal responsibility of that act. The dead loyal lay on the field.
The loyal men, outnumbered and crippled by the deep snow, in a
position impossible to guard themselves or to make that contest
which, under other circumstances, they would have been able to
make, were forced to retire. That act of war constitutes the first and
fourth counts with which the prisoner is charged. No constructive
treason is the crime we seek to bring home. No treason such as may
be made out from meetings, treasonable acts or letters, but we seek
to bring home on those counts treason, involving the shedding of

brave men's blood; treason which roused the whole country, treason sounding from the dead bodies lying on the blood-stained snow, and which brought a response from end to end of the land, which would make any man with treasonable ideas in his head tremble at the thought of the power invoked by such crime; that act of treason brought an armed force from the east, from every town and city; men rallied to protect the integrity of the country. The country prepared itself for the contest, rendered serious by the number of men in arms, and by the influence of the prisoner on the material he had to work upon. The seat of the trouble was in a distant part, and winter still binding the country, rendered communication difficult; nevertheless, a response was made, and a force of volunteers approached the rebels. Then we find the prisoner and his men organizing their forces, inciting the Indians and bringing them into their camp, endeavoring to arouse up the north, south and west. It will be shown that the prisoner, reckless of the results, endeavored to rouse the Indians, it will be shown to you under his own hand. All these acts will be brought home to the prisoner. These preparations on his part occupied about a month. The troops had been from various causes delayed in their advance. However, a little before the 24th of April last, they approached the place where the rebels were entrenched, and on the 24th of April a contest takes place, the first contest between the volunteer forces under General Middleton and the armed rebels led by the prisoner and Gabriel Dumont, at all events directed by the prisoner. If he was not personally present at the fight at Fish Creek, it is the same thing. We charge him with levying war, and if you find he directed the body, gave orders and organized, it is the same thing as if he had a musket in his hand or gave the order to fire. We hold him responsible for the contest at Fish Creek, the particulars of which I need not detail to you; it is sufficient to say that many lives were lost on both sides, and a check was given, I do not say in any way a defeat to the loyal troops. It was absolutely necessary for the troops to remain where they were for some time after that before proceeding.

We find them, at the same time that the Fish Creek fight was going on, fortifying and preparing at Batoche, and the prisoner goes back the day of the Fish Creek fight from that position to Batoche, with a party of men, to finish the rifle pits they were preparing.

The further progress of the volunteers is staid until the advance of the 8th of May, and on the 9th opened the contest at Batoche, continuing the 10th and 11th, and which was ended on the 12th by the charge we have all heard of, resulting in the complete rout of the rebels and the complete victory of General Middleton and the troops under him, and the breaking up of the so-called Provisional Government. In that contest we will bring home to the prisoner active work. He was seen giving directions; he was heard giving directions. We will show to you that upon that occasion that the prisoner was the one who opened negotiations with General Middleton, and we will produce to you letters signed by him as being the person in authority, correspondence between himself as the leader on the one side, and General Middleton on the other. We will show you that upon that occasion as the rebels were being driven from the field, the prisoners, whom they had gathered together and kept confined till that time, were released.

On that occasion, immediately after the charge, were found the papers to which I have alluded, the one I have read and various other papers that will bring home to the prisoner the charge of treason, that will absolutely prove leadership on his part. These, then, gentlemen, are the counts charged in the indictment, and as I am instructed they will be amply sustained by very many witnesses as well as by the documents which I have alluded to. As the documents will be put in evidence and read I need not more than refer to them in a very short way. The first document we find is the one I have read to you, next we find a document in the prisoner's writing asking the authorities to come and take away their dead at Duck Lake. We find next a document evidently written after the Duck Lake fight to the half-breeds of Qu'Appelle, telling of the victory as he claimed and described it; there is a draft letter to the half-breeds of Fort Pitt and Battleford; a letter to the half-breeds and Indians of Battleford, in which he says amongst other things: 'Justice orders us to take up arms.' There is another document, it is not very clear where it was to go, but it is addressed 'Dear Relatives,' which I take to mean half-breeds, informing them of the Duck Lake fight and asking them to join the movement. There is a letter to the Indians and half-breeds at Fort Pitt and Battleford, in the writing of Octave Regnier, acting as secretary or in some capacity. That will be proved to have been dictated by the prisoner, that is the letter of the 1st of May 1885, and is a letter inciting the Indians to rise; another letter describing them as under arms at St Anthony, that is in the prisoner's writing, another document which shows the treasonable intent to form a new government. There was a letter found in the camp of Poundmaker, the Indian, a letter written by the prisoner, a letter which will be read to you and which shows a deliberate attempt to bring on this country the calamity of an Indian war with all its attendant horrors. There are other papers which will be produced before you, but which I need not now refer to.

I believe the facts as I have opened them to you, will be fully and thoroughly sustained by the evidence. And there will be this further matter appear in evidence, that the prisoner was not there for the purpose so much of aiding the half-breeds, as he was there for the purpose of utilising the half-breeds for his own selfish ends. You will find throughout the evidence in this case that it was not so much the rights of the half-breeds he was seeking as the power and benefit of Louis Riel, and money that Louis Riel wanted to extract from the Government. It will appear that this so-called patriot, leader of an oppressed people, was willing to leave the country and go wherever the Government wanted him if he got a sum of money from the Government.

Gentlemen, when he found that the church to which he belonged, to which his principal supporters belonged, was against him in the movement, he had more ground to play upon his material and to feed his own vanity and ambition, had himself named as the leader and prophet of his new religion. The prophet of the Saskatchewan was the cry under which his poor dupes, and many of them should have known better, were supposed to rally, intending by combining religious power to follow on the North Saskatchewan, the methods of eastern leaders.

I think, gentlemen, you will be satisfied before this case is over that it is not a matter brought about by any wrongs and grievances that have existed, so much as a matter brought about by the personal ambition and vanity of the man on trial.

I think you will find the evidence shows that he was utterly careless of his methods, and had but one object, his own power, or money, and he did not care whose lives he sacrificed.

The Crown will show that the prisoner wanted to try everyone not in accord with his ideas, for high treason. He wanted to shoot them at once without even the intervention of a stipendiary magistrate and a jury of six; his associates had great difficulty in restraining him, and had he had his way, McKay would not be here today. The evidence will show that he desired blood, that his only object was to obtain money, or gratify his desire for power and he was altogether reckless of the means he employed to further his ends.

DR JOHN H. WILLOUGHBY sworn
Examined by MR ROBINSON:

Q. You are a medical man? A. Yes.

Q. Where are you practising? A. At Saskatoon.

Q. How long there? A. I have been there since two years last May.

Q. How far is Saskatoon from Batoche? A. About fifty miles.

Q. Do you remember going to Batoche about the 16th March last? A. I do.

Q. Did you go alone? A. No; I was accompanied by —

Q. By whom? A. A half-breed named Norbert Welsh.

Q. And at what house did you go to stop when you got to Batoche? A. I stopped with George Kerr.

Q. Is that the Kerr Brothers? A. Yes, at their store.

Q. Did you hear anything of any anticipated difficulty? A. I did.

Q. Where? A. I heard it at Mr Kerr's store.

Q. How long did you remain at Batoche then? A. Two days.

Q. You went on the 16th; when did you leave it? A. I remained over the 17th and left upon the 18th.

Q. Did you see anyone on the 17th? Did you hear anything then of any disturbance anticipated? Did you hear any more of possible difficulties? A. I did hear rumors.

Q. When you left Batoche whom did you go with? A. I left with Mr Welsh and Mr McIntosh.

Q. Had Welsh any object in view? Did he desire to see any one from Batoche? A. We were leaving Batoche for Saskatoon.

Q. You were with Welsh? A. Yes.

Q. Was he desirous of seeing anyone as far as he explained to you? A. He was desirous of seeing Riel.

Q. Did you go with him for that purpose? A. I did.

Q. Where did he expect to find Riel then? A. I hardly know where
he expected to find him; he was informed on the road by Gabriel
Dumont as to Riel's whereabouts.

Q. Did you find Riel? A. Yes.

Q. Where? A. At the house of a half-breed named Rocheleau.

Q. What is his christian name? A. I don't remember.

Q. How far south of Batoche was that? A. Six or seven miles.

Q. Did you know Riel at that time? A. I had met him before.

Q. How long before? A. About four months.

Q. About the December or January before? A. Yes; in November, I
believe.

Q. Whereabouts? A. I met him at the house of Moîse Ouellette.

Q. Had you been introduced and spoken to him then? A. I had
spoken to him then.

Q. You knew him by sight? A. Yes.

Q. When you met him at Rocheleau's did he say anything to you?
A. He did.

Q. What did he say? A. Well, he told me the time had come for the
half-breeds to assert their rights.

Q. Do you mean that was the first thing or almost the first he said to
you? Did he ask you any questions at all? A. When I entered the
house I spoke to him. I sat opposite to him, and very little was
said for a few moments. Presently he got up and passed in front
of me and he suddenly stopped and turned to me and said, the
time has come when it would have been well for a man to have
been good, or to have led a good life.

Q. Did he say any more then? A. I replied to that.

Q. What did you say; do you remember? A. I cannot remember what
I did say — something to the effect it would be better for a man
to always lead a good life and be prepared for any emergency.

Q. What took place next? A. Just at that time a large crowd of men
drove up to the door of Rocheleau's house.

Q. How many do you think? A. I would judge about sixty or
seventy.

Q. Were they half-breeds? A. Half-breeds.

Q. Were they armed? A. They were.

Q. All armed as far as you observed? A. No; there were some who
were not armed.

Q. Were the majority armed? A. The majority were armed. I only
remember seeing one who was not armed.

Q. What were the majority armed with? A. The majority, I believe,
had shotguns – appeared to me to be shotguns. They were outside and I was in the house.

Q. This would have been on the 17th March, if I understand it
rightly? A. The 18th. It was on a Wednesday, I believe the 18th.

Q. When this crowd came, did the prisoner say anything to you?
A. It was just as they drove up he addressed me. He then said the
half-breeds intended (he and his people I believe he put it) to
strike a blow to gain their rights.

Q. Did you make any answer? A. Yes; I replied there were different
ways to gain their rights, the white settlers took a different way
of having their grievances settled. He replied no one knew better
.than he did as to the grievances of the settlers, and he said I and
my people have time and time again petitioned the Government
to redress our grievances, and he said the only answer we received
each time has been an increase of police.

Q. He said they had time and time again petitioned the Government
for redress and the only answer they received each time was an
increase of the police? A. Yes.

Q. What next did he say? A. He said, now I have my police, referring
to the men at the door.

Q. Those sixty or seventy men? A. Yes; he pointed to them and he
said, you see now I have my police; in one week that little
Government police will be wiped out of existence.

Q. Well, what next? A. I believe I said if he intended to attack the
police or raise a rebellion, they should look after the protection
of the settlers; there was no ill-will among the settlers towards the
half-breeds.

Q. What next? A. He told me I was from Saskatoon, and as a settler
of Saskatoon I had no right to speak for the welfare of the
settlers, and charged the settlers at Saskatoon with having offered
to aid the Mounted Police at Battleford to put down an Indian
rising last autumn.

Q. Repeat that? A. He said that I, as a citizen of Saskatoon, had no
right to ask protection, because –

Q. Because the people of Saskatoon had aided the police? A. He said
they offered men to kill the Indians and half-breeds.

Q. That is the reason why he said the settlers of Saskatoon had no right to protection? A. He said we will now show Saskatoon, or the people of Saskatoon, who will do the killing.

Q. Go on? A. He made a statement as to my knowledge of his rebellion, that is of the former rebellion in 1870, and he said that he was an American citizen living in Montana and that the half-breeds had sent a deputation there to bring him to this country.

Q. What else? A. That in asking him to come they had told their plans, and he had replied to them to the effect that their plans were useless.

Q. Did he say what the plans were? A. No, I believe not, but that he had told them that he had plans, and that if they would assist him to carry out those plans he would go with them.

Q. Did he tell you what those plans were? A. Yes, he did.

Q. What were they? A. He said the time had now come when those plans were mature, that his proclamation was at Pembina, and that as soon as he struck the first blow here, that proclamation would go forth and he was to be joined by half-breeds and Indians and that the United States was at his back.

Q. Did he tell you anything more? A. He said that knowing him and his past history he might know that he meant what he said.

Q. Anything else? A. He said that the time had come now when he was to rule this country or perish in the attempt.

Q. Go on? A. We had a long conversation then as to the rights of the half-breeds, and he laid out his plans as to the Government of the country.

Q. What did he say as to the Government of the country? A. They were to have a new Government in the North-West. It was to be composed of God-fearing men, they would have no such Parliament as the House at Ottawa.

Q. Anything else? A. Then he stated how he intended to divide the country into seven portions.

Q. In what manner? A. It was to be divided into seven portions, but as to who were to have the seven, I cannot say.

Q. You mean to say you cannot say how these seven were to be apportioned? A. Yes, he mentioned Bavarians, Poles, Italians, Germans, Irish. There was to be a new Ireland in the North-West.

Q. Anything more? Did he say anything more about himself or his own plans? A. I recollect nothing further at the present time.

Q. You say he referred to the previous rebellion of 1870. What did
he say in regard to that? A. He referred to that and he said that
that rebellion – the rebellion of fifteen years ago would not be a
patch upon this one.

Q. Did he say anything further with regard to that? A. He did. He
spoke of the number that had been killed in that rebellion.

Q. What did he say as to that? A. I cannot state as to what he said
but it was to the effect that this rebellion was to be of far greater
extent than the former.

Q. Did he speak to the men who were there or they to him when
you were there? A. There were several men there when the cutter
drove up to the door. The majority of them stayed outside in the
sleighs and some of them came in.

Q. Yes? A. They spoke in French, which I did not understand very
well; but I understood him to tell them to go down to Champagne's house, and I understood him to be sending them there.
Most of the men then drove off and a few staid behind.

Q. You cannot say what they asked him as your knowledge of
French does not enable you to repeat the questions they asked
him? A. No, I cannot say.

Q. Now what did you do then? Who left first, you or him?
A. We had dinner.

Q. This conversation took place before dinner or during dinner?
A. Partly before, during and after dinner.

Q. You had dinner and what took place next? A. Riel prepared to go
then to follow the others.

Q. Well, what next? A. As he was leaving he asked me, he stated
personally he had no ill-feeling towards me but that I was a
Canadian, but he put it in his way as a Canadian I was a part of
the Canadian Government, and in our hearts there could be no
friendship towards each other.

Q. Well did you go before or after him? A. He left before me.

Q. Did he say where he was going? A. No, he did not.

Q. What did you do? A. I left immediately after he did and went on
towards Clarke's Crossing, at the telegraph office.

Q. For what purpose? A. To make known what I had heard.

Q. To whom? A. My intention was to communicate with Regina, but
when I got to Clarke's Crossing, the wire was down between
Clarke's Crossing and Qu'Appelle.

Q. How far was it from Clarke's Crossing that you had taken
dinner? A. Something over forty miles.

Q. Was that on your way to Saskatoon? A. It was.

Q. Then you intended to communicate with Regina but when you
got to Clarke's Crossing the telegraph was down? A. Yes.

Q. What did you do? A. The only communication was with Battleford and I informed Colonel Morris.

Q. Who is Colonel Morris? A. He was in charge of the police at
Battleford at that time.

Q. You informed him of what you had heard? A. Yes.

Q. What was Mr Welsh doing all this time? Was he present at your
conversation with Riel? A. He was.

Q. Did he, in Riel's presence, tell you anything or not? A. No, I
believe not.

Q. Have you told me your whole conversation with Riel as far as you
remember? A. I remember one point in regard to Orangeism.

Q. What was that? A. As Riel was leaving he expressed an opinion,
he stated they would have no Orangeism in the North-West. I said
I hoped by Orangeism he did not mean Protestantism. He turned
excited and said he was glad I had mentioned it, that he certainly
understood the difference between Protestantism and Orangeism,
and he then spoke of the different religions and beliefs and illustrated it by the example of a tree; he took a tree – the true
church was the large branch at the bottom of the tree, and the
others as they departed from it got weaker, up to the top of the
tree.

Q. He illustrated his ideas of the different religious bodies in that
way? Have you told me now all you can remember of your conversation with him? A. Whilst speaking of sending a telegram last
fall offering to aid the police –

Q. Sending which telegram? A. He stated of the Saskatoon people
that he had been furnished with a copy of the telegram sent by
the Saskatoon people to Battleford last fall, offering to kill off
the half-breeds and Indians, and that in consequence the Saskatoon people had no right to ask for any protection; and that that
was not the only telegram they had sent, that about eleven days
before, I think he said, that they had again made such an offer. I
mean that the people of Saskatoon had again made such an offer.

Q. Now, is there anything else he said to you that you can remember, or have you told me everything? A. I believe I have told you everything.

Q. You went back to Clarke's Crossing and communicated what you had heard to Colonel Morris, and from that time onwards where were you? A. I was at Saskatoon and Clarke's Crossing.

Q. Then do you know anything more of your own knowledge of Riel in connection with this rebellion, I mean not what you have heard? A. No, I know nothing further.

Examined by MR FITZPATRICK:

Q. If I mistake not, you said you saw Riel for the first time about the month of November, 1884? A. About November.

Q. Did you see him for any length of time then? A. I did not.

Q. Did you — you never saw him again till the 17th of March 1885? A. I believe not.

Q. During that interval of time you are aware there was an agitation going on throughout that section of the country? A. I was perfectly well aware of it.

Q. The first time you ever heard of any reference to an appeal to arms in connection with this agitation was during this interview in March last with Riel? A. That was the first I heard.

Q. Riel was not armed on that occasion? A. He was.

Q. What had he with him? A. As he left the house —

Q. I am speaking of the time you had the conversation in the house. Was he armed then? A. He was not armed at that time.

Q. When you first began talking with Riel, he first mentioned to you the fact that it now became necessary for all men to reflect that it is a good thing to live well? A. That was the first remark.

Q. Shortly after he made that remark he paced up and down the floor? A. That was before he made the remark.

Q. Then he began telling you about his intention to sub-divide these provinces into seven? A. He did not.

Q. He told you he intended giving the Province of Quebec to the Prussians or Germans? A. He did not.

Q. Did he say anything as to the manner he was going to divide? Did he refer to the Bavarians, Hungarians and other people? A. He did.

Q. What did he say he was going to do with these people? A. They were going to assist him in the rebellion, before this war was over, and that they would have their portion of the country.

Q. By country, what did he allude to? A. The North-West Territory.

Q. Exclusively? A. As I understood it.

Q. Would you now indicate to us the different people he expected to assist him? A. The Irish of the United States, the Germans, the Italians, Bavarians and Poles, and Germany and Ireland.

Q. We have had Germany and Ireland twice? A. Well, he put it twice. He put the Irish and Germans of the United States — then Germany itself was to come into line.

Q. Bavarians also? A. Yes.

Q. The Hungarians? A. I don't know. I don't believe he said anything as to the Hungarians.

Q. The Poles — did he intend to give them a chance too? A. He did.

Q. He also stated to you he was giving the Jews a portion of the province? A. Not that I remember. He did not mention them while I was there.

Q. Did he explain to you at that time as to what progress he had made towards completing the negotiation he had had with these people for their assistance? A. He did not.

Q. You did not think it necessary to ask him how he intended to carry out this agreement, or if he had made any endeavors to have an understanding about this? A. I did.

Q. What did he say about this? A. I tried to find from him his plans, to get what information I could, and he seemed unwilling. He took good care to unfold none of his plans.

Q. You said he had unfolded his plans as to sub-dividing the province? A. Yes.

Q. Did you ask him if he had entered into any negotiations with these different people mentioned, in order to get their assistance? A. No, I did not ask him that.

Q. You did not ask him how he expected to get these people into the country either, did you? A. No, I did not.

Q. Don't you think that would have been a very necessary question to put in order to get at the bottom of his plans? A. I believe not.

Q. You thought all these plans were very reasonable and acceptable? A. I had my own opinion regarding them.

Q. What is that opinion? Be good enough to let us know it? A. My opinion at that time was, that that was about the last that would be heard of it.

Q. You never heard anything of those plans before? A. From him?

Q. From him or anyone else? A. Nothing of that kind in regard to this country.

Q. In regard to the plan he submitted to you, did you ever hear of such a plan before? A. No, I never did.

Q. Did it strike you as being at all peculiar? A. Rather; a little.

Q. When he spoke to you on religious subjects, did you understand him to tell you that in his religion Christ was the foundation, and represented the trunk of the tree, and the different religions might be considered as representing the branches of the tree? A. I did.

Q. Did he say what position he occupied with reference to the trunk, or with reference to Christ? A. He stated his church was the strongest branch.

Q. During all this time, during all this conversation, I think you stated Mr Welsh was present; was he not? A. He was.

Q. Where is Mr Welsh now? A. I believe he is at Fort Qu'Appelle.

Q. That is about forty miles from here? A. About fifty miles.

Q. When you said Mr Riel explained his religion was the strongest branch, did he say what his religion was? A. He did. He said the Roman Catholic church.

Q. He did not say anything further than that about his religion? A. No.

Q. Did he speak anything about the Pope? A. No, I believe not. Nothing that I can remember.

Q. You don't remember anything further of this conversation with Riel except what you have stated? A. I remember nothing further.

Q. Of course the plan he unfolded to you about the conquest of the North-West did not strike you as anything extraordinary for a man in his position to assert? A. It did, certainly.

Q. It appeared to you a very rational proposition? A. No, it did not.

Examined by MR ROBINSON:

Q. You said Riel was not armed in the house – did you see him armed at all? A. I saw him armed as he drove off from the house. He was supplied with a gun as he got into the sleigh.

Q. Do you know by whom he was supplied with the gun? A. No, I don't know. I could not say by whom it was given him.

THOMAS MCKAY, sworn

Examined by MR ROBINSON:

Q. Mr McKay, where do you live? A. Prince Albert.

Q. You were born in this country? A. Yes.

Q. How long have you lived in Prince Albert? A. I have been in Prince Albert district since July 1873.

Q. You remember, of course, the disturbance which took place in March last? A. Yes.

Q. Can you tell me when you first heard of that, and when you first took any part in consequence of it? A. I had heard of the agitation for some time in the early part of March. I heard that the prisoner was inciting the half-breeds to take up arms.

Q. Well? A. On the morning of the 20th, Capt. Moffatt and Capt. Moore came to my house between two and three o'clock in the morning, and they brought a letter from Major Crozier stating he had been informed on good authority that the French, under the leadership of the prisoner, had risen and taken Mr Nash and some other prisoners and had robbed the stores of Walter and Baker, and Kerr Brothers. He also, in the same communication, asked for a detachment of some sixty or seventy volunteers to go up and reinforce the police at Fort Carlton.

Q. Well? A. I went down to the town and went to a number of the people there and told them what we had heard and asked them to meet us in James Elliott's rooms in town. We met there and decided — we thought that we could not spare the number of men as we had to look after the town and our families. We went out with something like forty men. Capt. Moore enrolled about forty men and we started about 2 o'clock in the afternoon of that day.

Q. For what place? A. Fort Carlton.

Q. How far was Fort Carlton from Prince Albert? A. Between forty and fifty miles.

Q. When did you get to Carlton? A. We arrived at Carlton between ten and eleven o'clock that night.

Q. What day was that? A. The 20th.

Q. Fort Carlton was then held by a force of mounted police under Major Crozier? A. Yes.

Q. You reported to him? A. Yes, reported to him.

Q. Did you remain there that night? A. When I arrived there, I found
Mr Mitchell, from Duck Lake, was at Fort Carlton. He had a
letter from Mr Riel, I believe. The letter I think was regarding the
surrender of Fort Carlton. I did not see it. When I left Prince
Albert, I had decided to go on to Batoche's where the rebels had
made their headquarters. When I found Mr Mitchell there, he
asked me to go along with him that I might be of some use.

Q. For what purpose did you decide to go to Batoche's? A. To see if
I could point out to them the danger they were getting into in
taking up arms. I knew a great many of them were ignorant and
did not know what they were doing, and I thought I might induce
them to disperse. I went to see if I could be any use in preventing
any outrage. An hour after I got there we went to Duck Lake and
we found two or three of Riel's men there, Joseph and Baptiste
Arcand. They had come from Batoche to meet Mr Mitchell. I had
a long conversation with them, and I invited them and tried to
induce them to drop the movement. I told them at the same time
that I had enrolled as a volunteer, that I was one of the first to
put down my name as a volunteer, and at the same time I told
them that anything they should say I should report to the commanding officer, and if there was anything they did not wish me
to hear they should prepare themselves accordingly. After an
hour or two's conversation with them, they went on to report at
their headquarters that I was coming with Mr Mitchell.

Q. They went before you to report that you were coming? A. Yes.

Q. What took place? A. We arrived at the river about eight or nine
o'clock in the morning.

Q. You had travelled all night? A. Yes.

Q. You did not arrive that night? A. No. When we got to the river I
found a number of armed men around Walter and Baker's store.
A sentry hailed us and took us to the guard.

Q. How many armed men did you find? A. Twelve or fifteen outside. There were some more in the store.

Q. They took you to the guard? A. There was a sentry about fifteen
or twenty yards on this side of the store.

Q. Did he stop you? A. He stopped us and took us on.

Q. Do you know his name? A. No.

Q. Where did he take you to? A. To the guard that was stationed
around Walter and Baker's store.

Q. Well? A. Philip Garriépy came out and said he was deputed to
show us across the river.

Q. You were then on the north side of the river? A. Yes. He got into
the sleigh and took us across to their council room.

Q. Where was their council room? A. The council room at that time
was a little building just south of the church. I do not know who
it belonged to. It is burned down now. It was just near the
church.

Q. Whom did you find in the council room? A. A number of men.

Q. Armed? A. Yes; they were armed.

Q. These twelve or fifteen men you have referred to, were they
armed? A. Yes. Philip Garriépy was not armed but the rest were.
We went into the council room and I went around the table and
among them, and finally was introduced to the prisoner. That was
the first time I had seen him.

Q. Where were you introduced to him? A. In the council room.

Q. You say that was the first time you had seen him? A. Yes.

Q. Who were in the council room when you were introduced to
him? A. Quite a number. They were moving out and in.

Q. Would you say there was a dozen men in the room? A. Yes, more
than that.

Q. Who introduced you to the prisoner? A. Mr Mitchell introduced
me to Mr Riel as one of Her Majesty's soldiers.

Q. That is, Mr Hillyard Mitchell? A. Yes. I shook hands with Mr Riel
and had a talk with him. I said, there appears to be great excitement here Mr Riel. He said, no; there is no excitement at all, it
was simply that the people were trying to redress their grievances,
as they had asked repeatedly for their rights, that they had
decided to make a demonstration. I told him that it was a very
dangerous thing to resort to arms. He said he had been waiting
fifteen long years, and that they had been imposed upon, and it
was time now, after they had waited patiently, that their rights
should be given, as the poor half-breeds had been imposed upon. I
disputed his wisdom, and advised him to adopt different measures.

Q. Did he speak of himself at all in the matter? A. He accused me of
having neglected my people. He said, if it was not for men like me
their grievances would have been redressed long ago; that as no
one took an interest in these people he had decided to take the
lead in the matter.

Q. Well? A. He accused me of neglecting them. I told him it was
simply a matter of opinion, that I had certainly taken an interest
in them, and my interest in the country was the same as theirs,
and that I had advised them time and again, and that I had not
neglected them. I also said that he had neglected them a long
time, if he took as deep an interest as he professed to. He became
very excited, and got up and said, you don't know what we are
after – it is blood, blood, we want blood; it is a war of extermination, everybody that is against us is to be driven out of the
country. There were two curses in the country – the Government
and the Hudson Bay Company.

Q. Yes? A. He turned to me and said, I was a traitor to his Government; that I was a speculator and a scoundrel, and robber and
thief, and I don't know what all.

Q. He used very violent language to you? A. Yes. He finally said it
was blood, and the first blood they wanted was mine. There was
some little dishes on the table, and he got hold of a spoon and
said, you have no blood, you are a traitor to your people; your
blood is frozen, and all the little blood you have will be there in
five minutes, putting the spoon up to my face and pointing to it.
I said, if you think you are benefitting your cause by taking my
blood you are quite welcome to it. He called his people, and the
committee, and wanted to put me on trial for my life, and Garnot
got up and went to the table with a sheet of paper, and Gabriel
Dumont took a chair on a syrup keg, and Riel called up the witnesses against me. He said I was a liar, and he told them that I had
said all the people in that section of the country had risen against
them. He said it was not so, that it was only the people in the
town. He said he could prove I was a liar by Thomas Scott.

Q. Was Thomas Scott there? A. Yes; he said so.

Q. Well? A. He called for Garnot, the secretary, and called for the
witnesses, and they would assent to what he said.

Q. Which of the two Arcands was there? A. Baptiste. He was putting
words into their mouths, saying things I did not understand at all.
When I saw what he was driving at, I says, I am here, and if you
wish to hear me speak for myself, I will do so. I says, there is no
necessity for Mr Riel telling what I have to say. If you wish to
hear me, I will speak, and if not, I wont. They said yes. I says, Mr
Riel, I suppose you understand Cree. He says yes. I did not speak
French, and I says, I will speak in Cree. I spoke in Cree.

Q. You spoke in Cree, and told them what you have said? A. Yes, and what had occurred. Champagne got up and said — I told them Riel was threatening to take my life. I said, if you think by taking my life you will benefit your cause, you are welcome to do so. He said, no; they did not wish anything of that kind. They wanted to redress their grievances in a constitutional way. Riel then got up and said he had a committee meeting of importance going on upstairs, and he went upstairs.

Q. Did he return? A. I spoke to them for quite awhile and he occasionally came down and put his head down stairs and said I was speaking too loud, that I was annoying their committee meeting. When I said what I had to say, I asked for something to eat, that I was pretty hungry. I got something, and after I got through there was a lot of blankets in the corner, and I lay down there till Mitchell was ready.

Q. Where was Mitchell at the time? A. Up stairs. When he got through he came down with the prisoner and I told him to stay there awhile, and we left for Fort Carlton. When he came down, he apologized to me for what he had said, that he did not mean it to me personally, that he had the greatest respect for me personally but that it was my cause he was speaking against, and he wished to show he entertained great respect for me. He also apologized in French to the people there and he said as I was going out that he was very sorry I was against him, that he would be glad to have me with them and that it was not too late for me to join them yet. He also said this was Crozier's last opportunity of averting bloodshed, that unless he surrendered Fort Carlton, an attack would be made at twelve o'clock.

Q. He said if Major Crozier did not surrender, the attack would be made at twelve o'clock that night? A. Yes.

Q. Was there anything more? A. That was all I had to do with him then and I then left.

Q. What did you then do? A. I went to Carlton.

Q. That would have been on the morning of the 21st? A. Yes.

Q. About what time? A. One or two in the afternoon of the 21st.

Q. What happened on the way? A. I met a number of armed people coming into Batoche.

Q. How far from Batoche? A. About two miles.

Q. You met a number of armed people in sleighs? A. Yes, in sleighs, Indians and half-breeds.

Q. Indians from what reserve? A. I did not recognize the Indians.

Q. How many sleighs full? A. Five or six. Five or six I met on the road, I spoke to them. I knew two or three of the men who were there. I asked them what all this was about. They jumped out of the sleigh and shook hands with me, and told me they had been sent for and taken by Albert Monkman who was driving the team.

Q. How many altogether were there? A. In one sleigh there were five and I think in another there were six. Altogether there must have been twenty or twenty-five.

Q. Were they all armed? A. I could not say because they were sitting down. I saw rifles and guns among them.

Q. You went back to Carlton? A. Yes.

Q. Did you meet many men on the way? A. That is all we met on the road. When we got to Duck Lake there was a trail coming from the east and west and we saw some sleighs passing there and some sleighs passing along the lake.

Q. Then when did you get to Duck Lake, or to Carlton, rather? A. About four o'clock.

Q. What was your object in returning to Carlton? A. I was just returning. As I was going away from the council room I overtook Emmanuel Champagne. He was walking along on the road with Jackson who was with Riel at that time. I told him to get into the rig and I thanked him for the stand he had taken. I told him if I could be of service to him in any way, I would never forget the services he had rendered me. He told me then they had decided to send two men to Major Crozier but they were afraid of treachery, that they were afraid they would be arrested. I says, you need not be afraid, I will be one of the party that will come out, and you may tell them they will not be interfered with at all. When we got to Carlton, Mitchell delivered the letter to Major Crozier, and I think it was asking him to meet him half way some time that night, and that Riel did not choose to meet Major Crozier himself but that he had sent two men.

Q. Did you go as representing Major Crozier? A. Yes. About an hour after we had reached there Charles Nolin and Maxime Lepine came up driving in a cutter. We were mounted. We told them what Major Crozier had said — that they should give us the names of the leaders of the movement, and that they would have to answer to the law, but that a great many of them who had been forced into the movement that they should be dealt leniently with. Nolin said Riel and his council demanded the unconditional surrender of Fort Carlton, and nothing else would satisfy them, and if they did so no harm would be done them, that they would give a safe conduct home. We said there was no use discussing the matter at all, as we said the matter could not be entertained at all — that all we had to say was to advise them to disperse and go home, and that the leaders of the movement would have to be answerable to the law. He then said he had a letter which he was told to hand us, but that it would be no use to hand it as Fort Carlton was not to be surrendered. I thanked them for the stand they had taken when I had been there that morning, and I returned to Carlton.

Q. Is that all that passed between you and Capt. Moore and Nolin and Lepine? A. Yes.

Q. Then what did you do? A. We returned to Carlton.

Q. How long did you remain there? A. I remained there until the night of the 24th.

Q. You had got as far as the 23rd. You gave me an account of your interview in the council chamber, of your trial. You spoke of Garnot, Philip Garnot, I think, you said? A. Yes, Philip Garnot.

Q. What capacity did he act in? A. As secretary.

Q. Of the council? A. Yes, taking notes of the evidence.

Q. Which was given against you? A. Yes.

Q. Well, did anyone ask him to act? A. Riel called for the secretary, and then Garnot came forward.

Q. And took his seat at the table? A. Yes, as secretary of the council.

Q. Now, on the 21st you got back to Carlton — how long did you remain there? A. Till the 24th.

Q. What did you do then? A. On the night of the 24th, between ten and eleven o'clock, Crozier asked me to go and see if I could hear anything of Major Irvine.

Q. Was he expected? A. We heard that he left Regina with reinforcements, but nothing had been heard of him.

Q. You heard that he had left Regina? A. That he was to leave at a certain time.

Q. And nothing had been heard of him up to that time? A. Yes.

Q. On the 24th Crozier asked you to go and see if you could find anything about him? A. I started and took the trail to Prince Albert. The wire was tapped about half way between Batoche to see if anything had been heard of him at Prince Albert before going any further. When about twenty-three miles out from Carlton I met two messengers with a note for Crozier. I opened the note and found that it was a note from Inspector Moffatt stating that he heard he was at the South Branch, and that he expected him that night. I found out that he had reached Prince Albert. I saw him and told him that I was sent by Major Crozier. I then returned to Fort Carlton, travelling all night, and got into Carlton about four o'clock in the afternoon.

Q. With Colonel Irvine? A. No, I left him. They had made a march that day of about seventy miles and he did not know whether he could make Carlton that day from there.

Q. You returned to Carlton? A. Yes.

Q. You got there between three and four o'clock? A. Between four and five.

Q. Having gone out and got tidings of Colonel Irvine you returned at that time? A. Yes.

Q. What did you do next? A. I overtook a messenger with a note from Colonel Irvine to Crozier saying that he could not leave that day, that he would the next, the 26th. I had been travelling all night and turned in early. After I turned in I was told that Crozier wanted to send Sergeant Stewart with teams and an escort for the purpose of getting some provisions and flour from the store belonging to Mitchell at Duck Lake, and that he wanted me to accompany the party, and we were to start at four o'clock the next morning, that would be the 26th. The next morning came and we got up and got ready. Sergeant Stewart sent out an advance guard of four men on ahead towards Duck Lake to see if the road was clear; we followed with the teams and sleighs. I was riding on about a quarter of a mile ahead of the teams looking out. When I got within three or four miles of Duck Lake I noticed on the road some people lying in the snow; there were marks; I took them to be Indians. I noticed them communicating the signal by walking backwards and forwards. I suspected they were watching the trail. I got to within about a mile and a half of Duck

Lake. There is a ridge there a little to the north of the mail
station. When I got there I saw some mounted policemen riding at
a full gallop, and immediately after them there were some
mounted men following them. I wheeled around and rode back as
hard as I could make my horse go. There was a hill about a quarter of a mile away I wanted to get to before they came. When I
got within sight of the men I threw up my hands and told them
to prepare and get their rifles ready. I told them that they were
following the mounted police. I told them to get their rifles and
said not to fire, whatever they do I can ride out and if they want
to fire they can have the first chance at me and you can defend
yourselves. They were coming round the bluff. They were pretty
close to the men. I saw they would overtake them. I knew they
were excited, so I rode out as hard as I could. They then hauled
up all but one man, who came right on and who never hauled up
at all. It was Patrice Flary. I asked them what they were about.
They said, what are you about? I said that we were going to Duck
Lake to get Mitchell's provisions. They said there were a great
many there. I asked whether they were at Duck Lake; they said
yes. They said we had better go back. I turned around and went
towards the sleighs. As I was getting near the sleighs a party of
perhaps thirty or forty of them, very excited, came upon us.
They were yelling and flourishing their rifles. They were very
excited. Gabriel Dumont was of the party; he was very excited;
jumped off his horse and loaded his rifle and cocked it and came
up to me and threatened to blow out my brains. He and some
others threatened to use their rifles. I told them to be quiet, that
two could play at that game. Dumont talked very wildly; he
wanted us to surrender. He said it was my fault that the people
were not assisting them, and that I was to blame for all the
trouble. I told them that we could not surrender, that I thought
we had the best right to this property. Some of them jumped off
their horses and went into the sleighs. I rode up and told the
teamster to hold on to his horses. They made one or two
attempts to snatch the lines. Finally he fired his rifle over our
heads. They all stepped off the road and we went on the road to
Carlton.

Q. Had any of the men got into the sleighs? A. Two of them went
   into one sleigh and they went to a second team to try and get the
   lines.

Q. Then there was nothing but the one shot fired? A. That is all.

Q. You returned to Carlton? A. Yes.

Q. How many teams had you upon that occasion? A. Seven or eight.

Q. How many policemen? A. A policeman in each team, Sergeant Stewart and some others.

Q. How many altogether? A Fifteen or sixteen. There were twenty-two of us altogether; fifteen policemen I think.

Q. You returned to Carlton? A. Yes.

Q. What time did you get there? A. About ten o'clock.

Q. In the morning? A. Yes.

Q. What did you do then? A. As we returned to go back Sergeant Stewart sent a man to report what had taken place.

Q. You had sent in a man in advance to report what had taken place? A. Yes.

Q. Well? A. When we got near Carlton we met an advance guard coming out of Carlton. There were a number of teams. They were coming out of Carlton, and we wheeled around and went out with them.

Q. Who was in command of that party? A. Major Crozier.

Q. How many were there? A. Ninety-nine.

Q. How many constables? A. Fifty-six.

Q. Of the party that first met you, the time you turned back, you stated there were thirty-five or forty? A. Yes.

Q. How many were Indians and how many were half-breeds? A. There were some Indians and some half-breeds. I cannot tell you the proportion at all. I was not paying much attention. I kept my eye on Jim Owen and one or two others.

Q. You met the advance guard coming out of Carlton, in all there were ninety-nine? A. Yes.

Q. Major Crozier was in command? A. Yes.

Q. Were there any sleighs? A. Yes.

Q. How were the men? A. Some mounted and some in sleighs.

Q. What is the distance from Carlton to Duck Lake? A. About fourteen miles.

Q. Did you join and go back with them? A. Yes, the whole party.

Q. This would be on the 26th? A. Yes. We went on till we came to a house about four miles from Duck Lake, when the advance guard returned and reported that there were some Indians in the house (I believe it was Beardy's house), he was in the house.

Q. Was it upon his reserve? A. Yes.

Q. Well? A. The interpreter went over and he came back again; I do not know what occurred between them. We went on, and when we got to the same place where I returned back that morning, we saw the advance guard coming over the hill in the same way as in the morning.

Q. Was the advance guard retiring? A. Yes, at the same place as in the morning, and there was a number of men following them.

Q. About how many? A. I cannot tell you, they were coming over the hill and they were scattered all along the road; there appeared to be quite a number of them. Major Crozier told us to unhitch the horses and make a barricade and take the horses to the rear. When they came near, within half a-mile, they made use of a blanket as a flag.

Q. White blanket? A. Yes. Crozier went out and called his interpreter, and the two parties came near each other. They began to talk; in the meantime they were running on to the road behind us and getting behind the hills.

Q. They were changing their positions? A. Yes.

Q. Well, what then? A. While placing the sleighs I heard some one calling out that they were firing upon us, and let them have it. I said wait till we get hurt. Just then I turned my head kind of this way, and saw Major Crozier lift his hand in the direction the firing was from, and he said "fire now," and the firing began then and there was quite a skirmish for thirty or forty minutes after that.

Q. How long did it last? A. Thirty or forty minutes. I did not take time into consideration.

Q. How many were killed on your side? A. We left ten men upon the field, but one of them was wounded, and turned up afterwards.

Q. Who was that? A. Newett.

Q. The other nine? A. Were dead. One mounted policeman was killed and several were wounded; two died just after we got to Carlton.

Q. You brought two back with you? A. One, the others died after we got back to Carlton.

Q. What time did you get back to Carlton? A. It must have been about four o'clock in the afternoon.

Q. How many were killed on the other side; you did not know at the time? A. No.

Q. During the engagement how many men would you judge to be engaged upon the other side? A. We could not see them. I cannot tell that. Some were in the house, some were behind the hills. There were two sleighs with two Indians in each behind us, and one Indian who was mounted, that was the Indian that was talking to Major Crozier; he was killed when the firing began.

Q. Would your observation enable you to say how many were engaged upon the other side? A. The road seemed to be pretty well covered with them.

Q. Can you form any idea as to the number? A. The road was straight, and they seemed to cover a greater space than we covered, but I cannot say as to the number. They seemed to cover a greater space than we did.

Q. You cannot say the proportion of Indians and half-breeds? A. I cannot say. I saw five Indians; these Indians got behind us, one of them was killed.

Q. You did not recognize any of the people that were there? A. I did not recognize any person.

Q. You returned to Carlton and got there about four o'clock? A. Yes.

Q. What did you do then? A. They were some time attending the wounded. Colonel Irvine got in about half an hour after we got in, and I think it was that afternoon or the next morning that he decided to leave Carlton and go down to Prince Albert.

Q. Did you go with him? A. Yes.

Q. Was Carlton burnt? A. Yes; I believe it took fire accidentally, and part of it was burnt then.

Q. He decided to evacuate Carlton with his forces? A. Yes.

Q. And to retire on Prince Albert? A. Yes.

Q. What distance is that? A. Forty-six or fifty miles.

Q. Did you go with him to Prince Albert? A. Yes.

Q. What day was that? A. We left on the morning of the 28th, about one or two o'clock, and we got down that evening.

Q. You remained at Prince Albert during the rest of the rebellion? A. Yes.

Q. You have told me all you know about it? A. Yes. There may perhaps be some things which I have omitted. When Mitchell introduced me to the prisoner, he asked Mitchell whether I came of my own accord, or whether I came with him. When he heard I came with him, he said I was entitled to the same protection as he was, but if I came of my own accord, he would look after me, or something of that kind. The prisoner said I was entitled to the same protection as he was.

Q. Is there anything else that you remember? A. No, I cannot remember everything that took place; I do not remember anything else.

By MR GREENSHIELDS:

Q. The first time that you met the prisoner was in the council chamber? A. Yes.

Q. And before that you never saw him? A. No.

Q. Nor did you see him after that till in court? A. I saw him in court when he was first brought into court.

Q. You had no conversation, nor did you see him from that time till he surrendered to General Middleton? A. No.

Q. You never had any personal quarrel or trouble with him before? A. No, I never had any communication with him.

Q. Did he appear excited when you were introduced by Mitchell? A. No, not at the time; a while after he became excited.

Q. How long after was it till he got excited? A. I cannot tell.

Q. Five or ten minutes? A. Perhaps a quarter of an hour.

Q. During that interval you were talking to him all the time? A. He went away for a little while, and then he came back again; he went up stairs and came back again.

Q. Tell us what he said when you were first introduced and shook hands with him. Did he speak first, or did you? A. I spoke first. I told him that we would shake hands, or something to that effect, and he said yes.

Q. Now, what did you first begin to talk with him about? A. I told him — I said there appears to be great excitement here. He said, no excitement at all; everything was quiet, or something like that.

Q. You said something about his having spoken about wanting to get their grievances redressed? A. Yes, I think I said there seemed to be a number of men armed, and he said that they had been, asking for their rights for fifteen years, and they had not yet been granted, and they had decided to make a demonstration.

Q. Did you have any conversation as to what their rights were?
A. No, I had not with him.

Q. Whom did you talk about it with? A. The rest of the people that
were in.

Q. That is, the council? A. Yes.

Q. What was their statement to you regarding their rights? A. They
did not seem to know — that they were entitled to scrip, and
never got it.

Q. Did they speak of having made any petitions to the Government
for their rights? A. Yes, we discussed the matter. I had taken part
myself in the petitions that were sent forward, and knew more
about it than they did. It came out in this way: Gabriel Dumont
said that I had taken no interest in the matter before; that I never
advised them; that it was only now when matters had gone so far,
that I advised them in the matter.

Q. That was reproaching you because you had been instrumental in
getting the rights of the half-breeds, the English half-breeds?
A. We were entitled to scrip, but we never got it yet.

Q. Have you got it since? A. No.

Q. There is a commission sitting now? A. Yes.

Q. Riel said that the only answer they got to every petition was an
increase of police? A. No.

Q. What was on the table when you went into the council chamber? A. Some tin dishes and some spoons; some fried bacon and
some bannocks.

Q. Any blood in the dishes? A. No; I did not see any.

Q. Will you swear that there was not? Will you swear that some of
them were not eating cooked blood at the time? A. Not that I saw.

Q. How long after the conversation with him till he used the words
"he wanted blood"? A. He left me and came back again. It was
then he said it.

Q. Was he in a very excited state of mind when he talked about
blood? A. He became very excited. I told him that I did not think
that he had adopted a wise way to redress their grievances.

Q. In what position was he at that time? A. Standing, striking
the table.

Q. What did the prisoner say to you when Mitchell stated you were
entitled to the same protection as Mitchell was? A. It was Riel
said that, not Mitchell.

Q. Didn't he say you were at liberty to return? A. He said I was entitled to the same protection as Mitchell.

Q. What did you understand? A. That I was at liberty to go as I pleased.

Q. You did not go as you pleased? A. Yes, I did.

Q. Was that before or after the conversation about the blood took place — was it before Riel told you he wanted blood that he told you you were free to go? A. It was before I had any conversation with him at all.

Q. The first thing he did on being introduced to you was to assure you that you were at liberty? A. Yes.

Q. You had no fear but that you were at perfect liberty to return? A. It did not make any difference to me.

Q. After telling you that you were at perfect liberty he spoke to you of his desire for blood? A. Yes, certainly.

Q. Did you have any other conversation with him that day? A. He said what I said at the time he went up stairs, he went up and he would occasionally put his head through and say that I was speaking too loud. After he came down he apologized and said that he had great respect for me personally, but it was my cause.

Q. On the whole he treated you civilly? A. No, he made use of language to me that was never before used to me.

Q. Did he have any conversation with you as to the object of the rebellion? A. He said they wanted their rights.

Q. Did he tell you anything about the administration of the North-West Territories? A. No.

Q. About a new church? A. No.

Q. No conversation about either of these matters? A. No.

Q. When he called for blood was it after he went down? A. He went away and came back and called for blood.

Q. And then he went upstairs? A. Yes.

Q. When he came down the next time he apologized for the language he used? A. Yes.

Q. Shortly after that you went away? A. Yes.

HIS HONOR: Any juror that desires to ask the witness any questions is at liberty to do so.

JOHN W. ASTLEY sworn
By MR BURBIDGE:
Q. You reside at Prince Albert? A. Yes.

Q. How long have you resided there? A. About three years.

Q. What is your occupation? A. Civil engineer, land surveyor, and explorer.

Q. In March last you were employed by Major Crozier? A. I left with the volunteers to go to Carlton.

Q. How were you employed? A. As volunteer and then I was used as scout.

Q. What time in March? A. About the 18th March.

Q. How long were you scout? A. I was scouting through the French settlement, the half-breed settlement, and the reserves till two o'clock on the morning of the 26th.

Q. Were you alone? A. Part of the time; part of the time H. Ross was with me.

Q. You posted a proclamation? A. Yes, I posted a proclamation from Crozier telling those who had been forced into rebellion that if they gave themselves into the charge of the police, they would be protected. I posted those as far as Lepine's and back by the other road in the most conspicuous places where I thought there would be a chance of their being seen, one in English and the other in French. I noticed in passing the road afterwards that these notices were nearly all torn down. I went over the road on the morning of the 26th to see if the French half-breeds were trying to intercept Major Crozier; Ross was with me. We were about the place where the battle took place. I was about thirty or forty yards on ahead of Ross, an Indian suddenly jumped along-side of me and pointed his rifle or shotgun at my breast. I turned round to see if my partner was prisoner too, I saw that he was and that there were some sixteen or twenty of them all armed and as he was captured first I thought it best to give up quietly.

Q. Who appeared to be the leader of the party? A. Gabriel Dumont. There were about sixteen or twenty of them, part half-breeds and part Indians. We were taken to Duck Lake and put in the tele-graph office till the morning; an armed guard was placed outside the building that night. Albert Monkman seemed to be in charge of Duck Lake at that time.

Q. How many men would be at Duck Lake at that time? A. Eighty or 100, that is taking into consideration those who were acting as outside guard. In the morning we were removed into the upstairs in what had been Mitchell's house.

Q. During that day did any more come in? A. After we were placed
   upstairs about noon or shortly after – before a lot of half-breeds
   and some Indians came from Batoche with the prisoner in
   command – that would be some time about noon.

Q. The accused was in command – how did you come to that conclusion? A. That morning he interviewed me and Ross and talked
   to us. He brought Bourget with him. He seemed to control and
   asked the questions. I was downstairs afterwards for a few
   minutes and I saw the prisoner beckoning to the men to fall in
   line and they fell in line.

Q. He was giving commands? A. Yes.

Q. After they were reinforced how many men had they altogether?
   A. I should say about 400 taking both Indians and half-breeds.

Q. How many Indians? A. About 150 Indians altogether.

Q. Did you see any other prisoners on the 26th? A. Lash, Tompkins,
   Simpson, McKean, and Woodcock were brought up into the same
   room. We heard some report of McKay having come near the
   building and being ordered back by Dumont. In the afternoon
   looking towards the west we noticed them running towards
   Carlton: Shortly after that all that were there except what I
   would call a fair sized guard, who remained around the building,
   went in the same direction. Shortly after the prisoners heard
   firing. I myself did not hear it. I heard the sound of a cannon that
   is all I can swear to. In about an hour or an hour and a half they
   returned bringing a wounded prisoner, Newett, with them. He was
   shot through the leg and hammered on the head with a musket or
   something. I dressed his wound and the prisoner came upstairs
   and talked to us about this battle. He said that ourselves as
   prisoners might have been sent into his hands to show future
   people in what way he had conducted the war – pointing to the
   wounded prisoner and saying that he used that man humanely.
   He said the volunteers and the police fired first. I told him that
   from what I knew of Major Crozier he did not intend to fire first,
   that he had told me so. I suggested that perhaps a gun had gone
   off by accident and the prisoner admitted that that was perhaps
   so. He called on his men in the name of God or the Supreme
   Being, 'I say unto you fire,' and he explained that the troops were
   beaten by the bravery of his own soldiers.

Q. At this time were the stores looted? A. They were not looted
   when we went there, but before we left they were cleared out.

Q. You were taken to Carlton on what day? A. On the 31st of March
   we left Duck Lake for Carlton. When we got out in the yard Riel
   was there in person, some were getting into sleighs when he told
   us to march.

Q. Who was in command of the party that took you? A. Monkman.
   When we got to Carlton we remained there till the 3rd of April,
   we were then moved to Batoche.

Q. Who was in command taking you to Batoche? A. Andrew Jobin.
   In Batoche we were placed in a room in the lower floor of the
   store, afterwards we were put in the upper flat of the same store.
   Soon after I sent a communication to Riel in reference to Ross
   and the other prisoners, seeing what I could do towards getting an
   exchange. Riel came upstairs and told me he could not see things
   in the same light, but he would exchange us for Clarke, Sproat
   and McKay.

Q. The Hon. Lawrence Clarke? A. Yes; I said that could not be done.

Q. How were you treated as a prisoner? A. In the early part, well –
   as well as men could be under the situation, but after that when
   we were taken down into the cellar we could not have been
   treated worse.

Q. Did they take extra precautions at the time of Fish Creek?
   A. There was always a home guard left around the buildings. Just
   after the Fish Creek fight the Indians came back earlier and
   alarmed me as regards the safety of the prisoners. I thought as
   long as the half-breeds were there the Indians could not get at us,
   but if the home guards were taken away when the Indians came
   back earlier they might massacre the prisoners. After the Fish
   Creek fight I wrote to Riel asking him for an interview, that
   would be about the 26th of April. I had a long talk with him
   about the prisoners. I told him about the fears I entertained
   about the Indians and asked him if he would allow me to see the
   general or Irvine to try and effect an exchange. He refused to
   exchange.

Q. What did you say to him? A. I said, what do you want to keep us
   for? I said I suppose you wish that if you or your council get into
   danger you will want the prisoners for that purpose. Riel said,
   yes, certainly. I said to him to allow me to go and see either
   Irvine or the general about getting an exchange. I said: 'You claim
   a victory at Fish Creek and Duck Lake, and I said let me go and
   see and try for terms.' He said that he had gained two victories. I

asked him if he would not allow me to do that. He said we must
have another battle and he said: 'If we gain another battle the
terms will be better and he said if we lose it the terms will be the
same as now.' He said that after another battle he would allow me
to go. From that day I was waiting, expecting that another battle
would occur. On the last day, that would be the 12th of May, he
came to the cellar and called my name in a hurry, and as I was
getting out he told the rest of the prisoners what he was sending
with me to the general in that message. I think the paper is there.

Q. Is that the paper? A. Yes, that is the message I carried out that
morning (paper shown to witness).

Q. Did you see the prisoner right after that? A. Yes, right at the
council chamber at Batoche. At the same time that he wrote that
he wrote another message for Jackson to take. I took the message
to the general. I also saw him write that one for Jackson.

Q. Is that it (shown witness)? A. Yes, that is the one that Jackson
carried.

Q. He gave that to Jackson the same time he gave you yours? A. Yes,
at the same time. One of us was supposed to go one way and the
other the other. I rode to the general with that on horseback. The
prisoner went with me until he passed me through his own lines. I
went on, reached the general, and gave him the note. He read the
note and took a few minutes to consider. I asked him to write a
note to Riel. He wrote that note and I took it back to Riel. I
think that note is among the papers there. Instead of allowing me
to go back into the cellar the prisoner made me go into the
church and he put an English speaking half-breed and an Indian
to guard the church. In about half an hour or so Riel called for
me again and I went with him among the women and the children. He wrote several notes but none of them seemed to please
him and he tore them up, except one which seemed to suit him. I
sat talking with him till he had finished writing and then I began
to ask him whether it would not be better to let me see and try
what terms I could get. I said that he could come with me and see
the general. After talking a long time he left me and came back in
a short time with Gabriel Dumont, but as I do not talk French I
had to let the prisoner explain to Gabriel what we were talking
about. Finally he said there was a great deal to consider. It would
then be about one o'clock. About half-past one o'clock he had

nearly agreed to what I proposed he should do. The firing then
began and he at once turned to me and asked me what that
meant. I told him that some of the Indians must have started it.
I told him if he would write a note to the general thanking him
and say nothing about fighting, but leave it to me, I would get
the firing stopped, if possible. Anyway I would see what could
be done. He then wrote a note and asked me to take it. I asked
him to pass me through the lines.

Q. Is that the note (shown witness)? A. That is the note just as an
excuse for me to get the firing stopped.

Q. That is the note? A. Yes; he wrote that in a tent or the council
chamber and gave it to me. He went part of the way with me
through his lines. In the position outside his own rifle pits the
firing was pretty heavy. Riel went down into a low place till I
overtook him; he was on horseback. Some of his men had left the
rifle pits and gone to where he was. When I came up to him Riel
asked for the note and put it into an envelope.

Q. Is that the envelope? A. Yes.

Q. Are those the words he wrote upon the envelope? A. Yes. He
took the note out of my hands and wrote those words on the
outside in my presence. He ordered the men who had left the rifle
pits to go back again, and they went back along with me. I continued on, went to the general, and gave him the note. I did not
call his attention to the memorandum on the outside of the note
till the night time. I asked him how the fire began and he said the
Sioux started, but that if Riel would get his men to stop firing
that he would order his men to remain where they were and they
would not advance any further. There was not time to write a
letter. I went back and it took a long time to find Riel. I went
among the women and the children and I found him. The firing
was getting warm. I told him what the general had said, that if he
would order his men to stop the firing he would do the same, and
that he could come with me personally to the general. He hesitated for a time. At last I said there are not many minutes to
waste; if you want to call the council together call them and let
me address them. At last the prisoner said, 'It is not necessary to
call the council.' He said he would do as I wished. I said you
acknowledge you have the power to do as I wish without the
council. He said, 'Yes.' I said for him to give the order to stop

firing. He said, 'You know the men I have; I cannot go among
these men and tell them to stop firing.' He said, 'You know that.'
I told him I would go back and explain how everything stood and
see if it was possible for the general to stop his men at a certain
position; if he was willing to do as I wished. He was.

Q. That is willing to surrender? A. Yes, I went back and told the
general what he said. He said that he could not accept it as a surrender unless Riel ceased firing. I knew he could not get his men
to cease firing. I went back to try and keep the troops from
getting at the women and children. I got the general to send a
note to Riel offering the same terms as I had offered, that is that
he should be kept safe till he had a fair trial.

Q. Did he speak to you of his personal safety? A. He had very little
to say about the half-breeds. As far as regards himself seemed the
principal object.

Q. What did he ask you in regard to himself? A. If I would explain
what risk he ran personally himself. He said to me that we knew
he never carried a rifle, of course, at the same time we had seen
him carry a rifle on one occasion. I told him he ran no danger as I
could look at it. He suggested that I should broach the subject of
the church to the general and it would give him a chance to
broach the subject when he came to be interviewed by the
general. He would say that he was not to blame, that the council
was to blame.

Q. During the time that you saw the prisoner there did you see him
in command? A. He ordered the men into the pits on that occasion when some of them were leaving them. He took one half-
breed and made him go back, saying that he would be able to do
some fighting with the troops at all events.

Q. When did you see him armed? A. Some time before the Fish
Creek fight, it must have been about a week before, I was talking
to Riel before the council chamber one day, when a French half-
breed came up with the report that the troops were coming.
Shortly after, myself and the rest of the prisoners saw him passing
the front of the house quickly with the half-breeds going towards
the river, armed.

Q. During the eight days you were in the cellar were you bound at
any time? A. They used to tie us up about supper time and leave
us that way till next morning, that was for the last eight days.
Delorme came down and threatened to shoot us if we were loose

when he returned. They used to tie our hands behind our backs and then release us in the morning again.

Q. It is suggested to ask you if when you were released on the 12th if anything was said to the prisoners? A. He told the other prisoners the message I took to the general that if the women and children were hurt or were wounded by the troops he would massacre the prisoners, or words to that effect, just the same as was in the note.

By MR JOHNSTONE:

Q. Was the 26th of March the first occasion on which you saw the prisoner? A. No, I saw him in the settlement since last summer off and on, but not to know him as I know him now.

Q. How often did you see him from that time? A. Perhaps ten or twelve times.

Q. Where did you see him? A. At the Batoche settlement, Prince Albert and different parts of the Prince Albert district.

Q. Were you present at any of the meetings? A. I never attended any. I was at the Prince Albert meeting a few minutes but I took no interest in it at all.

Q. A few minutes at Prince Albert? A. Yes, just walked into the hall and saw the prisoner at the end of the hall.

Q. When did you commence to take an interest in him? A. When I went to Carlton as a volunteer, and when I undertook scouting.

Q. You went up from Prince Albert with the volunteers? A. Yes.

Q. How long did you remain at Carlton? A. About a day and then I went through the settlement.

Q. When you left Carlton where did you go? A. Past the Indian reserve, Duck Lake, and through the principal part of the French half-breed settlement. I did not go quite to Batoche.

Q. You returned when? A. Sometimes at night and sometimes in the day time.

Q. Did you see the prisoner at Batoche till the 26th? A. I did not go to Batoche.

Q. Now you were prisoner – who took you prisoner? A. Sixteen or twenty half-breeds took me. Gabriel Dumont was in charge of the scouting party.

Q. How long were you prisoner before you saw Riel and his men? A. From two o'clock that morning till about noon the same day, that is when he came in person from Batoche.

Q. How long was he at Duck Lake before you saw him? A. I saw him coming in the yard.

Q. Was he the first man that came into the yard? A. You could not see the yard. He was the first man I noticed. I knew him by sight.

Q. Were there others besides him? A. Yes.

Q. Was he mixed with the others? A. No, he was more advanced than the others; he was by himself.

Q. How was he dressed? A. A large check, common looking trousers, as well as I remember, about the same kind of tweed he wore most of the time. Riel was never very particular about his dress.

Q. How long was he there before he came to interview you and the other prisoners? A. I would say it might be perhaps half an hour.

Q. Did he come to see you or did he send for you? A. He came to see Ross and myself.

Q. To whom did he address himself first? A. I do not know. I may have been the spokesman.

Q. What did you say to him? A. I did not tell him exactly what I was there for. I gave him another story.

Q. What was the story? A. That I was travelling through the country making enquiries if that outfit was stopped at his headquarters.

Q. What was your object in telling him that? A. To get away from the place.

Q. Was the prisoner excited at that time? A. Not that I could see, he talked reasonably, as rather a clever man.

Q. What did he say. How long were you engaged in conversation with him at that time? A. Just while I explained to him.

Q. Did he tell you afterwards he found out you were not telling the truth? A. I don't think he found it out for five weeks.

Q. Did he say anything about church and state at that time? A. Not at that time.

Q. Did he talk about the rebellion? What did he say? That was the last you saw of him till you returned from Duck Lake? A. No; after the battle was over he came up and saw us.

Q. Did he say he was at that battle? A. Yes, that he had ordered the men to fire.

Q. He said that Crozier fired the first shot? A. He said that the volunteers or policemen fired the first shot. I said that I knew that Crozier would not fire the first shot, that perhaps one went off by accident, then he admitted that it might be so. He laid no stress on the first shot being fired.

Q. How long did you talk with him at that time? A. Quite a long time.

Q. How long? A. I would not say as to the time at all.

Q. How long did you converse with him? A. He talked to us
prisoners.

Q. How many of you? A. Myself, Lash, the two Tompkins, Ross,
McKean and Woodcock.

Q. Were the wounded prisoners with you at this time? A. Charley
Newett. I dressed his wounds. The prisoner asked him some
questions.

Q. What did he ask him? A. He asked him whether he knew if the
Hon. Lawrence Clark was among the volunteers. That was the
principal thing.

Q. Did he give directions how the wounded man was to be treated?
A. He left that in my hands, he hoped and expected I would do
the best I could for the wounded prisoner.

Q. You say you were speaking to him for a considerable time, did he
at this time strike you as being excited or excitable, or was he
calm? A. He was cool enough, a little elated at his victory.

Q. Did he speak of dividing the territories? A. He mentioned about
the half-breeds making certain claims and told us we had no business in that part of the country, that we belonged to Canada and
that this country belonged to the Indians and half-breeds. I did
not take much interest in what he was saying as I was dressing the
wounded prisoner.

Q. Did you hear him talking of defeating the Government that
time? A. Not as far as defeating the Government is concerned.

Q. What did he say about it? A. He told us what the ordinary claims
were and said that we might have been sent to show how we conducted the war.

Q. Do you know did he say anything about saving the life of this
wounded man? A. He said that he himself had stopped an Indian
from killing that man. I told him that was the effect of raising the
Indians and that was the way the Indians fought to kill a man
when he was wounded.

Q. When had you a conversation with him again? A. The next day. I
was downstairs a short time and I met him and had a talk with
him about the Indians. I told him it was a bad thing to have anything to do with the Indians. He said that he could not help it
that he was compelled to use the Indians. I told him that he was
aware that he could not control the Indians.

Q. Who was present at that conversation? A. I was by myself just coming out of the door.

Q. Were there others around? A. Some half-breeds were stationed as guards, they were armed.

Q. During that occasion or on any occasion, did he speak of the church or of the Dominion of Canada? A. No, not of any importance except as regards Batoche.

Q. What did he say at Batoche about his church? A. He said he wanted me to mention to the General that he was to be recognized as the founder of the new church and that if the subject was mentioned to the General he could continue the subject when he met him.

Q. What did you understand by founding a new church? A. I understood it as a sharp trick to get the upper hand of the unfortunate half-breeds.

Q. Did you understand that before? A. I looked upon it in that light.

Q. Were there other half-breeds listening at this conversation at Batoche? A. Lots of them were standing around but only an odd one could talk English, he spoke in English to me.

Q. When did you think it was to get advantage of the half-breeds? A. I considered that he was using them for his own ends.

Q. Did you consider his actions eccentric? A. He seemed intelligent and in many respects a clever man.

Q. What did you say to General Middleton about this man? A. I told the general exactly what I knew about the matter.

Q. Did you tell the general that you had considerable influence over Riel and that he was a simple-minded man? A. No.

Q. You have had considerable to do with the working up of the evidence against Riel? A. Not that I am aware of.

Q. Have you been engaged in that line for the last month? A. Not working up evidence.

Q. Working up the case? A. No; I am here as a simple witness — I am no more than the others.

Q. Have you given instructions to the Crown about this prosecution? A. Not in any other light. I gave no instructions — it would be rather strange if they received instructions from me.

Q. Had you anything to do with preparing the papers or giving information? A. No; not in preparing the papers. I have only given my own information.

Q. Did Riel appear to have been engaged in these fights or was he afraid to fight? A. As far as I could see he was too much afraid to run his neck into unnecessary danger.

Q. You were not alarmed that you would receive injury at the hands of Riel or the half-breeds? A. At the hands of the Indians.

Q. Not injury from Riel? A. Not as far as the half-breeds were concerned. I knew Riel's object in keeping us, he admitted himself that that was his object.

Q. How many interviews had you with General Middleton altogether? A. One in the morning, one a little after the fire began and one after. I could not get back.

Q. How many altogether? A. Three.

Q. During that time you had made arrangements as to the surrender of Riel to Middleton? A. He said he would do as I wished, but I could not get back because by that time the charge had begun and Riel was gone.

Q. What reason can you give for Riel's willingness to surrender himself? A. I told him what a kind man the general was, and he thought from the words of the note that what I said was true.

HAROLD ROSS sworn
Examined by MR SCOTT:

Q. Where do you live Mr Ross? A. At Prince Albert.

Q. What is your occupation? A. I am deputy sheriff.

Q. Where were you on the 20th March last? A. I was at Carlton.

Q. In what capacity? A. I went up as a volunteer under Capt. Moore.

Q. When did you go there — on the 20th? A. On the 18th, I think.

Q. On the 18th March you went there? A. Yes.

Q. Do you remember the 20th March? Were you doing anything on that day in your capacity of volunteer? A. Nothing, nothing particular at all.

Q. What duty were you engaged in after you went to Carlton? A. Chiefly volunteer.

Q. What description of duty? A. Just staying there, waiting for an attack on Carlton.

Q. How long did you stay there? A. I was there — we went on Thursday, and I was there until the 21st. The 21st would be on Sunday — on the 21st.

Q. What did you do at Carlton? A. I saw Major Crozier and he asked
me if I would go out to Stoney Lake, between three and five
miles from Carlton, and see certain English and Scotch half-
breeds living there and ask them to come into the fort.

Q. Did you go? A. I went and they came in with me.

Q. When did you come in? A. We came in the same evening, or
about, I suppose, six o'clock that night.

Q. Were you out after that again? A. On the following Monday
morning I left with Mr Astley. I went out scouting on Monday.

Q. Monday the 22nd? A. Yes, we went to Duck Lake, and from
Duck Lake we went to the St Laurent church mission.

Q. When did you go back to Carlton? A. Tuesday night, about eleven
o'clock.

Q. On the 23rd? A. Yes, the 23rd, and on Wednesday I stayed there
all day, and about eleven o'clock in the evening, half-past ten or
eleven, Mr Astley said that Major Crozier wanted us to go out and
see if the half-breeds would intercept Colonel Irvine on the route
from Regina to Carlton, and we went out.

Q. About what time? A. Between half-past ten and eleven, as near as
I can judge.

Q. On Wednesday night? A. On Wednesday night; yes.

Q. How far did you go? A. Well, somewhere near where the battle of
Duck Lake was fought, and about a mile or so — between Duck
Lake and Carlton — close to Duck Lake.

Q. Did anything happen there? A. We were taken prisoners by
Gabriel Dumont, and between sixty and one hundred men.

Q. Did you know any of those besides Gabriel Dumont? A. No, I
could not recognize any.

Q. Will you describe how you were taken prisoner? A. I heard a sort
of noise behind me. The horse at first drew my attention to it by
pricking up his ears, and a sort of stopping, and I turned around
and saw a body of men behind me, and I called Mr Astley's attention to it, and I wheeled my horse around and I was surrounded
by half-breeds and Indians. And he told me to dismount. Gabriel
Dumont came to me and recognized me and said, how are you,
you are a scout, and he told me to dismount, that I was his
prisoner, and I refused to dismount and they pulled me off the
horse.

Q. Were they armed? A. They were all armed, everyone of them.
Gabriel Dumont then felt my revolver, he felt it under my coat,

and he got quite excited, and he went to take it away from me, and I drew the revolver out myself (witness showing how it was held, holding his right hand to his stomach), and I was covered by an Indian on my right with a gun, and there were two more behind me.

Q. Guns were pointed at you? A. Guns were pointed at me, and Mr Astley called on me not to shoot; better hand over the revolver.

Q. And did you surrender? A. I did.

Q. And what was done with you? A. We were taken to Duck Lake and put into the telegraph station.

Q. What was the aspect of Duck Lake at this time? A. Full of armed men, all around the post, guards all around the post, wherever we went, in front of the building, on the road, all around the building where we were imprisoned.

Q. Where were you put? A. In the telegraph office.

Q. What kind of a building is that? A. A very small building.

Q. How many storeys? A. A small little building, as large as an ordinary porch —

Q. How many storeys? A. One.

Q. Was there anybody else in there besides you and Astley? A. No.

Q. I suppose Astley was taken with you? A. Yes; only the two of us.

Q. How long were you kept there? A. Till about nine o'clock the next morning, as near as I can judge.

Q. Did anything occur next morning? A. No, nothing particular.

Q. How long did you continue alone there? A. With Mr Astley?

Q. Yes. A. Well, we were there until we were removed to Mitchell's house, upstairs.

Q. And when was that? A. That same morning about nine o'clock.

Q. This was on the 26th? A. On the 26th, we were there until the rest of the prisoners came over from Batoche.

Q. And what time was that? A. They came somewheres about noon.

Q. This was in the upper storey of Mitchell's house? A. Of Mitchell's house.

Q. And the other prisoners were sent up there too? A. Were sent up with us.

Q. Did you see any people about that morning? A. Outside?

Q. Yes. A. The square was full of armed men all the time.

Q. Was there a larger crowd there when the other prisoners were brought in than there was in the forenoon before? A. Yes, there was a good many came over with the other prisoners.

Q. How many armed men did you see there altogether? A. I should say there would be between 300 and 350 men, as near as I could judge; I did not count them.

Q. Of what nationality? A. French half-breeds and Indians.

Q. What proportion would be Indians? A. I should say near 100 — between 75 and 100.

Q. Did anything occur that afternoon? A. That afternoon the battle of Duck Lake took place.

Q. How do you know? A. We could hear the shots.

Q. About what time? A. About half-past three or four in the afternoon, I should say.

Q. Did you see any of the men, armed men, going? A. I saw them all going; I saw about 300 going.

Q. In the direction of the battlefield? A. Yes. The first intimation I had that the battle was taking place was Albert Monkman coming upstairs where we were, and we asked him what was the matter, and he said there was a little fight going on. At that time they were all going then —

Q. All this armed force you had seen were hurrying in that direction? A. Hurrying in that direction.

Q. Did you hear any shooting and firing before going in Mitchell's? A. No, after that we heard rifle shots.

Q. Anything else? A. No, nothing else. I did not hear the cannon. They had a cannon there. I did not hear the gun.

Q. What occurred that afternoon after you heard the firing? A. Well, after we heard the firing, about half an hour afterwards they came back, some of them came back. Some of the men came up stairs, one Fiddler in particular.

Q. Did you see the prisoner Riel that afternoon? A. Yes, I saw Mr Riel that afternoon.

Q. Where? A. He came upstairs.

Q. When, after the firing or before? A. He came up before the firing and he spoke to me upstairs.

Q. What did he say? A. He called me by name, and asked me how I was, spoke to me and said that I need not be afraid, that I would not suffer at his hands, something to that effect. I forget the exact words he said now, but then after the fight he came up.

Q. And what did he say then? A. The first thing he said was something about Newett, one of the men that was brought in as a prisoner.

Q. What did he say about that? A. He said he thought he would be better with us than anybody else. We were his friends and we could look after him better than anybody else, and he put him upstairs, and then he and Mr Astley were speaking something about the battle.

Q. Did you hear the conversation between them? A. I heard the conversation.

Q. What was it? A. Mr Riel said the troops fired first, and Mr Astley suggested that perhaps the shot went off by accident and Mr Riel said — well he did not agree with him for some time afterwards, he said perhaps that was the way.

Q. Did he say anything else? A. And he said, when I heard the shot I called on my men in the name of God to fire, and he seemed quite proud of it.

Q. Did he say so? A. No, judging from his actions, that is all.

Q. How long did you remain in the upper storey of Mitchell's store? A. Until the 31st. The morning of the 31st we were sent to Carlton.

Q. By whom? A. By Mr Riel himself; we came out in sleighs; he said we were going to Carlton.

Q. How did you go to Carlton? A. In sleighs.

Q. Did you go alone? A. No, seven of us together.

Q. Seven persons? A. Yes.

Q. Anybody besides the prisoners? A. The Indian and half-breed guards.

Q. You were taken under guard to Carlton? A. Yes, under guard.

Q. How long did you remain at Carlton? A. Until 3rd April.

Q. Who was in command at Carlton? A. Albert Monkman.

Q. Were there many men there? A. About 150 to 200.

Q. Armed? A. All armed.

Q. You were kept there until what day did you say? A. Until 3rd April.

Q. What was done with you then? A. We were then ordered from Carlton. We were called up about two o'clock in the morning.

Q. Ordered up where? A. For Batoche. We were called up about two o'clock in the morning, and we started for Batoche, and when we were leaving the buildings were set on fire.

Q. Then the fort was deserted at the time you left? A. Yes, they deserted the fort.

Q. And they marched to Batoche? A. Yes.

Q. What was done with you when you reached Batoche? A. We were put in the lower flat of a house owned by Baptiste Boyer for that day and we were put up stairs in the second flat.

Q. And how long did you remain there? A. We were there till the end of the campaign; that was our prison at the time of peace, and if there was any excitement, we were shoved into the cellar of an adjoining building.

Q. How many times were you put down in the cellar? A. Three or four times.

Q. Do you remember how long you were there the last time? A. About ten days.

Q. Continuously? A. Yes.

Q. In the cellar? A. In the cellar.

Q. How many prisoners were there in the cellar? A. Seven.

Q. What was the size of the place? A. About 16 feet square and 9 feet deep.

Q. Any other precautions taken to prevent your escaping besides putting you in the cellar? A. Always a guard upstairs, and the trap was very well secured, so there was no chance of us escaping by knocking the trap up.

Q. Anything else; were you shackled? A. We were tied every night, with our hands behind us.

Q. When did you first see the prisoner after you were taken to Batoche? A. I saw him different times. I saw him every day nearly.

Q. What was he doing? A. He would be out addressing the men, talking to them.

Q. Could you say what was said to them? A. No, it was in French. I don't understand French — apparently giving orders.

Q. You don't know? A. No, I couldn't say that.

Q. Did he ever visit you during the time you were confined there? A. He came, I think it was two or three times — I am not sure of the number of visits — once in particular he came, and I asked him for a little exercise, and he said he would see about it. He did not come back for some days, perhaps two days after that, and I heard him talking outside, and I went out, and he said that under the circumstances he couldn't allow us to go out at all, that we would have to stay in.

Q. Was that all the conversation you had with him? A. Yes, that is about all.

Q. When did you last see him? A. I saw him –

Q. That is, at Batoche? A. About eleven o'clock of the 12th, or a little earlier than that. It was at the time they called Mr Astley, on the 12th of May, the day of the charge.

Q. Did he say anything to you that day? A. He came and opened the hatch in the cellar and called Mr Astley. Mr Astley, he said, come up and stop the troops advancing, for if they hurt any of our families, we will massacre all the prisoners in the cellar.

Q. That is what he said? A. That is what he said.

Q. Do you remember having any conversation with the prisoner after the Fish Creek battle? A. After the Fish Creek battle, I remember Riel one time – I can't tell you the day or date – saying that they had gained two victories, and they wanted to gain a third, and they could make better terms with the Government.

Q. That was after the Fish Creek fight? A. Yes, after the 24th of April.

Q. Where were you confined at this time – in the cellar or in the building? A. We were taken out of the cellar and we were in the building.

Q. This was during one of his visits to you? A. Yes, during one of his visits.

Q. Was the building in which you were confined attacked, or the building above the cellar in which you were confined? Did they attack it at any time? A. No, not at all.

Q. Do you remember the shell? A. That was done by the troops. I think it was on the 11th May there was a shell went through the building.

Q. Did you see Riel shortly after that? A. I did not see him. He came to the cellar, the hatch, and asked me if we were all safe. I knew his voice, and we said we were, and he said, I am glad to hear it, and he went out of the building and came back again. We could hear him walking along the floor and he said I forgot to tell you you had better call on God for you are in His hands.

Q. Was that all he said? A. That is all he said.

By MR FITZPATRICK:

Q. Mr Riel was not with the party that arrested you was he? A. He was not.

Q. The first time you saw Mr Riel was after you were put in Mitchell's house was it not? A. I had seen him a year before that.

Q. On the occasion in question we are talking about? A. That was the first time I saw him.

Q. You say you saw the troops leave for the Duck Lake fight also? A. His troops yes, the rebels.

Q. Did you see Riel with them? A. No, not going away I did not see him.

Q. If he had been there, of course, you would have seen him? A. I saw him outside.

Q. When they were going away did you see Mr Riel with them, going away to Duck Lake? A. I did not.

Q. Had he been with them you would have seen him would you not? A. I might not. There was a big crowd going away.

Q. There were 300 going out? A. Yes.

Q. And you said they were half an hour away, half an hour elapsed from the time they left till the time they came back? A. About half an hour I should say, perhaps a little more.

Q. When Mr Riel saw you in Mitchell's, the first thing he said was that he was glad to see you? A. No, he did not say he was glad to see me. He said how do you do, you shan't suffer.

Q. Who wanted you to go down to the cellar at the time you were put in the cellar at Batoche. Who put you there? A. We were down different times. At one time or twice Delorme, another time it was a French half-breed, his name I have forgotten.

Q. Neither of those times was Riel present when you were put down in the cellar? A. No, he was not.

Q. At the time you asked to go outside for exercise, Riel said to you that you had better not go out, because the Indians wanted to kill you did he not? A. He did not.

Q. Did he not give you to understand at that time that that was the reason? A. He did not.

Q. Did you not know that was the reason? A. I had a sort of an idea, the Sioux were rather dangerous at that time. It was not from any information from him.

Q. You knew very well the protectors you had there were the half-breeds as against the Indians? A. Certainly we did. We looked to the half-breeds for protection.

By MR SCOTT:

Q. You say, Mr Ross, that Gabriel Dumont was the leader of the party who took you prisoner? A. He was.

Q. Did you see him afterwards? A. Yes.

Q. Where? A. I saw him at Batoche. I saw him at Duck Lake. I don't remember whether I saw him at Carlton or not.

Q. Did you see any others of the party who took you prisoner afterwards? A. One Indian is all I can remember.

Q. Then Gabriel Dumont formed part of the same party that you saw Riel in company with afterwards? A. Certainly.

PETER TOMPKINS sworn

Examined by MR CASGRAIN:

Q. Where did you live in the month of March last? A. At Duck Lake.

Q. Do you remember the 18th of March last? A. Yes.

Q. What happened on that day? A. Nothing particular happened to me on that day, till towards evening.

Q. Well, what happened towards evening? A. Towards evening I was up at the mail station, and the telegraph operator came up there for me and wanted me to go and repair the line. The telegraph line was down.

Q. Well, what did you do? A. I told him I would go.

Q. Did you go? A. I did.

Q. Well, what happened? A. I went and got a horse and rig and tried to get another man – I had considerable difficulty in getting another man – and finally I got my horse and brought it up to Duck Lake to the telegraph office, and the miller, Mr McKean, volunteered to come along with me, and the operator got a message that we were to start for Duck Lake at 12 o'clock at night. Start about midnight at Duck Lake to repair the line.

Q. You repaired the line didn't you? A. I repaired the line in two different places.

Q. Well, what happened after you repaired the line? What happened to you? A. When we were repairing the line, there were about thirty half-breeds came rushing down on to us and arrested us.

Q. Did you know any of them? A. Yes.

Q. Who were they? A. I know the man that was in charge.

Q. Who was it? A. Joseph Delorme was one of the men arrested me, and Jean Baptiste Paranteau was the other.

Q. What did they do with you? A. They told us to surrender, in French, at least that is what I understood them to mean, and they took us down by Walters' & Baker's store.

Q. Well, did you see anything strange at Walters' & Baker's store? A. I saw them going through the store, looting everything there was in it.

Q. Who was going through the store? A. The half-breeds and Indians. There were not many Indians there.

Q. Were they armed? A. Yes, they were all armed.

Q. Whom else did you see there? Did you see in particular there anybody that you recognized? A. I saw quite a few there that I recognized. I saw Gabriel Dumont, and when we were sent upstairs I seen Mr Lash, the Indian agent.

Q. You were taken upstairs in Walters' & Baker's store? A. Yes, we were sent upstairs and I seen Lash, Marion, Joseph Gagnon, Mr Walters, William Tompkins and quite a few others upstairs.

Q. What were they doing there? A. Most of them were prisoners. George Ness, was another man.

Q. Was there a guard there? A. Yes.

Q. Could you let yourself out of the house, could you have gotten out of the house? A. Not without a guard following us.

Q. There was a guard over you all the time? A. Yes.

Q. Well, how long did you stay there? How long were you kept there? A. We were kept there till about nine o'clock, I should judge, the next morning.

Q. That would be the 19th? A. Yes.

Q. Where were you taken to then? A. We were taken to the church across the road.

Q. What was the church used for at the time you were taken there? A. It appeared to be used as a council room and barracks and prison and a restaurant and everything else.

Q. Well, whom did you see there? A. I seen a whole church full of people there. I knew some of them and some of them I didn't know.

Q. Were the people armed? A. Yes.

Q. Were there any Indians there? A. Yes.

Q. What took place when they took you to the church? Was there anything done there by the rebels whom you saw? A. Yes, they brought some freighters there and the prisoner addressed the people there.

Q. What did he say? A. Well, he spoke in French and I did not understand what he said except towards the last. The last thing he said – I understood him to say – to tell his men – he asked them what was Carlton, or what was Prince Albert? They're nothing. March on my brave army. I understood him to say that.

Q. You heard the prisoner say that? A. I understood the prisoner to say that.

Q. To a crowd of people who were standing before him? A. Yes.

Q. Was this in the church or outside the church? A. In the church. He was addressing them from right in front of the altar.

Q. Well, who appeared to be the leader of the crowd there? A. The prisoner.

Q. Did anything else take place in the church that day? A. Yes, we had our dinner in the church, and there were two men tried or I understood them to be tried.

Q. Who were they? A. Tried by the prisoner.

Q. What for? A. For not being with him and his movement. They were Wm. Boyer and Charles Nolin.

Q. Well, were they acquitted or sentenced or what became of them? A. I don't know what became of Nolin, I didn't hear his trial, but Boyer, Mr Riel had a talk with and when he was through talking, Mr Boyer spoke in his own defence, and the prisoner said that instead of it being a dishonor to him, it was an honor. I understood him to say so. He was talking French.

Q. It was an honor to whom? A. To Boyer.

Q. Was this trial carried on before Riel only or before any others acting with him? A. No, Riel was standing on the platform and Boyer stood up from among us men and spoke in his own defence from there.

Q. Did you hear or see anything about that council while you were in that church? A. Yes, I understood them to be electing a council there.

Q. Did you see the council elected? A. Yes.

Q. Who were the councillors? A. I can name some of them. I can't name them all.

Q. Name some of them? A. Gabriel Dumont was the man who called them out. He called Baptiste Boyer, Joseph Delorme, Moise Ouellette, and several more I don't remember.

Q. Well, was this before or after this trial took place? A. I think it was after the trial took place.

Q. Well, where did you go from that church? How long were you
kept there? A. We were kept there till about nine o'clock the next
evening, and then we were sent down to Garnot's place.

Q. Philip Garnot's place? A. Yes.

Q. What capacity was he acting in, do you know? A. He was acting as
secretary to the council.

Q. To Riel's council? A. Yes. We were told that we would be sent
down there, and there would be a few men sent with us to look
after us, that our word of honor would be taken that we would
not escape. So about nine o'clock that evening we were sent
down there, and there was about in the neighborhood of fifteen
men came down to see whether we had kept our word of honor.

Q. Were these men armed? A. Yes.

Q. Well, how long did you stay in Philip Garnot's house? A. Well, I
couldn't say. I don't remember how low we stayed there. We
stayed there quite a while.

Q. Where did you go from Batoche? A. To Duck Lake.

Q. Did you go there of your own free will? A. No.

Q. How were you taken there? A. Taken there as prisoners, and by a
strong guard.

Q. By whom? A. One of the guards told me it was by —

Q. You were taken there anyway to Duck Lake, under a strong
guard? A. Yes.

Q. Of armed men? A. Of armed men.

Q. Where were you placed at Duck Lake? A. We were hurried up
stairs into Mitchell's residence.

Q. Hillyard Mitchell's house? A. Yes.

Q. Did you meet anybody upstairs? A. Yes.

Q. Whom did you meet? A. Harold Ross and John Astley.

Q. The witness, Ross, who has just been heard? A. Yes.

Q. And what was done to you there, or what took place while you
were there? A. Just as we were coming to Duck Lake, Albert
Monkman galloped out of the yard and came to meet us, and he
ordered his men up to the front, and he said, the police are
coming from Carlton. He ordered some men who were with us to
the front, that the police were coming from Carlton, and in Cree,
at the same time, he called for us again, and wanted to know who
had his gun in our party, and then the man that was driving the

team (the sleigh that we were in) put the whip to his horses, and got in as quick as he could, and then we were taken upstairs.

Q. And what happened while you were up there? A. Well, when we were up there, we could see quite a few of them going off towards Carlton.

Q. Quite a few of the half-breeds? A. Of the half-breeds, yes, and Indians.

Q. And how many were there going off altogether? A. I suppose, probably over 400, all that went.

Q. This was on the 26th day of March, wasn't it? A. I can't swear to the day.

Q. It was in the month of March last? A. Yes.

Q. Well, did you hear anything while you were upstairs in Mitchell's house? A. Yes.

Q. What did you hear? A. Well, I heard a cannon go off a couple of times, and then, when the half-breeds returned, Riel rode into the yard on horseback.

Q. The prisoner rode into the yard on horseback? A. Yes, and turned his horse around to the back of the building – the side of the building – and with his hat he was waving and cheering his men, and he thanked –

Q. He apparently came in with them, didn't he? A. Yes, he came in just along with them; the men came with him, the men behind him and some in front of him, and he waved his hat, cheering and hurrahing, and he thanked Ste Marie, and St Jean Baptiste, and St Joseph, for his victories.

Q. Did anybody come up stairs into Mitchell's house while you were there, on that same occasion? A. After night?

Q. Yes? A. The prisoner came up stairs, and before he came up, Charles Newett, who was wounded on Duck Lake field, was brought to the door, and he helped him up.

Q. Who helped him up? A. The prisoners who were there.

Q. Helped him into the room? A. Garnot helped him up.

Q. Garnot was there too? A. Yes.

Q. Did you see Gabriel Dumont around there? A. Yes; Gabriel Dumont rode into the yard in a little while. I think it was after the prisoner had been cheering, he rode into the yard, and said in Cree, to bring out the prisoners and kill them.

Q. Well, you say that the prisoner went up into Mitchell's house with those some time after the volunteer was taken out, didn't you? A. Yes.

Q. Did he say anything there? A. Yes, I don't remember everything that he said there; I remember him speaking to the wounded man.

Q. Did he speak of the fight that had just taken place? A. Yes; one thing he said about the fight was that the volunteers or police had fired a shot first. They fired first, and when they fired he said — he told me distinctly that he ordered his men to fire in the name of the Father Almighty who created us, 'fire'; — them is the words he used.

Q. Did he say anything else at that time? A. Nothing that I remember just now.

Q. Well, did anything take place after that? Did the prisoner go down then or did he come back? A. Afterwards he went down stairs and sometimes came to see us.

Q. Well, what was he doing there from the appearances from what you could see? A. From what we could see I thought at the time that he was running the whole thing.

Q. Whenever you had any communication to make to anybody, whom did you make it to? A. Well, if ever we wanted anything in particular we generally applied to Mr Riel.

Q. The prisoner? A. Yes.

Q. Was any message sent to anybody at that time? A. I wrote a letter home myself.

Q. Well, was there anything else sent? A. There was one of our men, who was a prisoner there, was sent to Carlton with a message.

Q. By whom? A. By the prisoner.

Q. Who was sent? A. Thomas Sanderson.

Q. What for? A. He was sent to Carlton to tell Major Crozier to send some men and take the dead off the field — to tell them they were allowed to take their men off the field unmolested.

Q. Did the prisoner say anything further to you on that occasion? A. Nothing that I can remember just now.

Q. Well, did you remain at Duck Lake any length of time? A. We remained at Duck Lake quite a while; till after the police left Carlton. We remained at Duck Lake till a day or so after the police left Carlton.

Q. Then where did you go, to Carlton? A. We were taken to Carlton.

Q. By whom, by the half-breeds? A. By the half-breeds.

Q. Then where did you go or where were you taken to? A. When we left Carlton we were taken from Carlton to Batoche, by Duck Lake.

Q. Well, what took place at Carlton? Did anything take place at Carlton before you left? A. Yes; they had set fire to the police stables before we left.

Q. Who had? A. The half-breeds, and the whole place apparently was on fire. Just as we got up the hill we could see by the fire and smoke that there was more than one building on fire.

Q. You say you were taken to Batoche. To where were you taken at Batoche? A. To Baptiste Boyer's store.

Q. How long were you kept there? A. We were kept there till about the time of the Fish Creek fight, when we were removed to the cellar.

Q. Who was with you at that time? A. There was seven of us, Mr Lash, Mr Astley, Mr Ross and Mr William Tompkins, Mr McKean and Mr Woodcock.

Q. Was there a guard over you? A. Yes, always a guard over us.

Q. Well, did you have occasion to see the prisoner during that time; during the time you were there? A. The prisoner used to come in and see us sometimes.

Q. Did he say anything to you? A. Yes; he used to speak with us every time he came in pretty near.

Q. What was he doing there that you could see of him? A. From what I could see of him, I thought that he was apparently the leader.

Q. Well, did you hear anybody giving orders there? A. Giving any orders?

Q. Yes, giving orders? A. Yes.

Q. Whom? A. I heard the prisoner ordering his men to go on guard one night.

Q. Well, if any orders were given, who gave them; who were they given by? A. The orders that I heard were given by the prisoner.

Q. Well, did you stay at Baptiste Boyer's house all the time? A. We stayed there until we were removed to the cellar.

Q. How long were you kept in the cellar? A. I don't recollect how long we were in the cellar the first time, we were kept there for several hours.

Q. Were you at liberty to go all round the cellar or were you tied
up, or how? A. We were not tied till the time of the Fish Creek
fight, or about that, before it, the day of the fight. Delorme came
down to the cellar and ordered three guards to come down after
him, and he ordered them to cock their guns, which were double-
barrelled shot guns, and covered the men while they tied me hand
and foot, and we were left that way till eleven o'clock next
day — supposed to be that way.

Q. Did anything happen after that, before you were released?
A. Every night we were tied, that we were in the cellar, mostly.

Q. How were you released? A. I was released by General Middleton's
men.

Q. Before you were released, did you see the prisoner at all have any
conversation with anybody in your presence? A. The day he
came to the cellar after Mr Astley, he did; the day that Batoche
was taken.

Q. The day that Batoche was taken you saw him come to the cellar
to see Mr Astley? A. Yes; he came for Astley. He came there in a
very excited manner; he was very much excited, and so were the
men who were with him. We could tell by the way they flung the
stones off the cellar door; they just sent them rolling all over the
building, and he came to the door of the cellar, and the first
words I heard him say was, Astley, Astley, come here and go tell
Middleton if they — I think 'massacre' was the word used — if
they massacre our women and children, we will massacre your
prisoners.

Q. Well, from that time till your release, did anything happen
between you and the prisoner? A. No; I did not see the prisoner
afterwards.

Examined by MR FITZPATRICK:

Q. You speak Cree very perfectly, do you not? A. Not perfectly. I
speak Cree pretty well.

Q. You were arrested on what day? A. I was arrested about four
o'clock of the 19th March.

Q. You saw Mr Riel for the first time when? A. I ain't positive
whether I saw him at Walter's store or at the church for the first
time. I am certain of seeing him at the church, but I don't remember whether I saw him at Walter's or not.

Q. You saw him at the church? A. I seen him at the church, but I
ain't positive whether I seen him at the store or not.

Q. Did you have any conversation with him? A. Yes.

Q. At the church? A. Yes.

Q. What did he say to you, and what did you say to him? A. I asked him if he would respect my property, and he said my property would be respected, and he gave me leave to take my horse out of the cutter, that some half-breed had kindly hitched him up to.

Q. Some half-breed had taken your horse and you told the half-breed to deliver your horse up to you and you got him back? A. No; some half-breed had hitched him up to a cutter and tied the horse up to a post, and I asked leave to undo him and feed him some hay, and he gave me permission to do so.

Q. And he told you your property would be respected? A. He told me it would.

Q. Now you heard Mr Riel make a speech to his men, did you not? A. Yes.

Q. You heard him tell that Carlton and Prince Albert were nothing? A. Yes.

Q. And did not amount to anything? A. Yes.

Q. Was he very far from you when he made that little speech? A. No; he was about as far as you are from me now.

Q. That little speech was delivered by him to his men in French, was it not? A. Yes.

Q. You would have no objection now to repeat the little speech, the substantial words he used, would you? A. Well, as near as I can repeat the words he used – I don't know whether I can repeat them now or not – he said: 'Qu'est-ce que c'est que Carlton? Qu'est-ce que c'est que Prince Albert? Rien. Marchons mes braves.' Something pretty near that.

Q. You next heard him make that speech to his men after the men had come back from Duck Lake, did you not? A. Yes.

Q. Where was he at the time? A. He was sitting on horseback outside in the yard.

Q. And where were you? A. Upstairs in Mitchell's house looking out through the window.

Q. You were in the second storey of Mitchell's house, were you not? A. I was in the upstairs of the house.

Q. And he was down in the yard? A. Yes.

Q. And you heard all that he said no doubt? A. Well, I heard mostly all that he said, but I did not understand him – at least I did not understand all he said.

Q. Of course the windows were closed and he was down stairs?
A. No; the windows were not closed; there was a pane of glass
partly knocked out of the window and through this pane I was
looking.

Q. Through the pane you were looking down at him? A. Yes,
through the broken pane.

Q. And you heard what he said out in the yard? A. Yes, I heard what
he said.

Q. You heard him make his speech there, saying he thanked the
Lord and the Virgin Marie for his successes? A. I don't remember
him thanking the Lord. I remember him thanking the Virgin
Marie.

Q. Whom else did he thank? A. St Jean Baptiste, St Joseph and
several other saints.

Q. He went through the whole list, didn't he? A. What do you mean
by the whole list?

Q. How many more did he repeat? A. I don't remember how many
more he said. He mentioned other saints.

Q. You next were present at the choosing of the council in the
church, were you not? A. I was present at the council before I
was to Duck Lake.

Q. That was in the church at Duck Lake, was it not? A. No, it was in
the church at Batoche.

Q. Were there very many people there? A. Yes, the church was full.

Q. Did Riel take any part in the election? A. In the election of the
council?

Q. Yes. A. I don't think he took much part, except he spoke in one
man's favor whom somebody else rose objection against.

Q. As far as you can now recollect, that is all the part he took in the
election? A. That is all.

Q. What he said of course was in French and you understood what
he said? A. No, I don't understand French.

Q. Well you understand sufficiently to know what Riel said on that
occasion do you not? A. I understand some of it. I didn't understand everything he said.

Q. Did Riel at any time prevent Gabriel Dumont or anybody else
from killing prisoners? A. Well, I don't know who prevented
Gabriel Dumont at Duck Lake, he did not seem to act as a man as
though he wanted to kill prisoners very bad. He just simply

ordered them out, and then he seemed to quit there when he had ordered them out.

Q. That was Dumont? A. Yes, he did not seem to push matters ahead very much to try to get them out.

Q. Riel took no part in your arrest did he; was he present when you were arrested? A. No, he was not present when I was arrested.

Q. Was he present when you were put down in the cellar at Batoche; you were put down with the other prisoners of course? A. Yes. No, he was not present then.

Q. He was not down in the cellar at the time you were pinioned and tied there, either was he? A. No, but I have sent men to tell him we were tied. I have asked the guards to tell him we were tied.

Q. But he was not present at the time? A. No.

Q. At the time that the shell fired by the troops struck your house, he went there and asked after your safety, did he not? You were there with the other prisoners of course, in the cellar? A. Yes, I was there with the other prisoners in the cellar.

Q. You know the house was struck with a shell do you not? A. Yes, I know and I ought to know.

Q. Do you know also Riel came there after the house was struck? A. I don't know whether he came there after the house was struck or before the house was struck, but I am inclined to think it was before it was struck, and he asked if we were safe and alive and went out of the house and afterwards returned and spoke through the floor, and he says, I forgot to say a good word to you. Remember the Almighty, he said, we have all got religion, and then he went off.

Q. Very good advice? A. Kind of cool advice coming through the floor at that time.

Q. I suppose it would have been cooler had it gone through an ice-house, wouldn't it? A. Probably.

Q. You know that he gave a prisoner that had been wounded at Duck Lake into the custody of the prisoners that were at Mitchell's house do you not; or do you think you can remember that; a man named Newett? A. Newett was brought to us. I don't think Riel brought him there. I don't remember Riel bringing him there.

Q. You are quite sure also that Riel did not say anything to you about him when he was brought there; you are quite sure now on your oath that Mr Riel did not tell Mr Astley in your presence to take good care of that man? A. I can't swear that he didn't.

Q. You don't think he did do it, don't you? A. I can't swear he did nor yet I can't swear that he didn't.

Q. Your impression is that he didn't do it? A. No, I ain't got no impression about it.

Q. That fact did not remain sufficiently on your memory to be able to remember it of course? A. No, it did not. I don't remember him telling me —

Q. You don't remember anything about him at all; but you remember about the angels he gave praise to after the victory at Duck Lake? A. Yes.

WILLIAM TOMPKINS sworn:
Examined by MR ROBINSON:

Q. You are a brother of the last witness, I think, are you not?
A. A cousin.

Q. You have been in the employment of the Indian Department in these territories, have you not? A. Yes.

Q. For how long? A. I have been in their employment now on and off for this last five years.

Q. In what capacity? A. As assistant farmer, and interpreter also.

Q. You were at Fort Carlton in the month of March, last, I believe?
A. Yes.

Q. For how long had you been stationed there? A. Since the 15th August, up till that time.

Q. Do you recollect the 18th of March, last? A. Yes.

Q. Do you recollect leaving the fort on that day? A. Yes.

Q. With whom did you go? A. Mr Lash, the Indian agent.

Q. And for what purpose? A. I did not know that.

Q. Did he ask you to go with him? A. Yes, he said I was to go.

Q. You were ordered by him to go, then? A. Yes.

Q. You were under his instructions, were you not? A. Yes.

Q. He was the Indian agent there? A. Yes.

Q. Just tell us what happened, you went with him I suppose? A. I went with him.

Q. Where to? A. One Arrow's reserve he started for.

Q. About how far from Carlton? A. Twenty miles.

Q. On horse-back or driving? A. Driving.

Q. Both in the sleigh? A. No, I was separate.

Q. Each had your own sleigh? A. Yes.

Q. What took place then? A. When we came as far as Duck Lake Mr
Lash stopped there a few minutes, and then he went on to the
river and stopped at Walters & Baker's, and finally we got to the
reserve and found the farm instructor not at home, and we fed
the horses there, and the farm instructor drove up, and Mr Lash
stopped a little while, and then we started back. He wanted to buy
some potatoes or something for the Indians, as far as I could
understand, and we came to this place where I was taken prisoner, at Kerr's store.

Q. Who were you taken prisoner by? A. Mr Riel.

Q. And were there others with you? A. Yes, there was Gabriel
Dumont and a lot of others.

Q. About how many others? A. I should judge between sixty and
one hundred.

Q. Were they half-breeds? A. Yes principally.

Q. Were they armed? A. Yes, not them all. They were not all armed
at the time.

Q. Were the majority of them armed do you think? A. No, I don't
think they were.

Q. And what were those armed with that were armed, as far as you
observed? A. Guns.

Q. Well, who first stopped you? A. Gabriel.

Q. What did he say to you? A. He told us to remain there awhile.

Q. What happend then? A. Mr Riel drove up and said he would detain us a few hours.

Q. Well, what happened? A. Well, we stopped there, remained there
for about ten minutes I should think, and finally we were taken
to the church.

Q. Under a guard? A. Yes.

Q. Did all these men go with you to the church, or only a small
guard? A. They all went with us, as far as I could see.

Q. And what was done then? A. Well, we went to the church, and of
course I don't understand the French language, but I understand
the Cree, and as far as I could make out from the Indians they
were trying to elect a council there, and we remained there all
that night.

Q. Who was engaged in trying to elect a council? Was Dumont there?
A. Gabriel was appointed to elect them, as far as I could find out.

Q. Was Mr Riel there? A. Yes.

Q. And what part did he seem to be taking? A. Well, I couldn't say as he was taking any part.

Q. Then you were put in the church? A. Yes.

Q. Were you kept in the church that night? A. No; we were taken across to Walter's store, and we were kept there up stairs until the morning, and then they returned us back to the church again, and we remained there that night — not that night; we stopped there that night, and we were removed down to Philip Garnot's restaurant at Batoche. He was cooking there.

Q. Yes; and what happened then? A. First there was one of the councillors; he took our name as a word of honor, to go down there, if we would not try to escape; and we put down our names on the word of honor, and then they sent some guards along to be sure.

Q. How many guards did they send in addition to the word of honor? A. Well, there were two with me. I don't know how many there were with the rest.

Q. How many of you were sent down? A. Well, there were Mr Lash and I, and George Ness and McKean, and Mr Tompkins, my cousin.

Q. Were the guards armed? A. Yes, the guards that were with me were armed.

Q. What happened then? A. Well, we remained there until we went to Duck Lake.

Q. And what day did you go to Duck Lake? A. It was the 26th.

Q. And who took you there? A. The half-breeds took me there.

Q. Did you go with the other prisoners? A. Yes; all in one sleigh.

Q. And how many half-breeds went with you? A. Well, I should judge there were about sixty.

Q. Any Indians? A. Yes; some Indians.

Q. How many Indians do you think? A. I should think there would be about ten or twenty.

Q. Were the Indians also armed? A. Yes.

Q. What did they do with you at Duck Lake when you got there? A. They put us up stairs in Mr Mitchell's house.

Q. Tell us what happened next? A. Well, the next thing that I heard was, we were ordered down to be shot in the afternoon. I met Mr Astley and Mr Ross there.

Q. The next thing you heard you were ordered down to be what?
A. To be shot.

Q. In the afternoon – who by? A. Gabriel was the man that I thought ordered us.

Q. Was that before or after the affair at Duck Lake? A. After the affair.

Q. Well, tell us anything you can that took place before that affair. Did you see them going out to Duck Lake? A. Yes, I saw them going out.

Q. Where did they come from? A. The principal part of them were ahead when we got there.

Q. How many do you think were ahead of you? A. I should judge about 300.

Q. And then there were how many with you? A. Well, about sixty or seventy altogether – Indians and all.

Q. And of the 300, how many do you think were Indians? A. About 150.

Q. Well, they were ahead of you; did you get to Duck Lake before they left it, to the place where the fight took place, before they went out to where the fight took place? A. No, they were just going out. How I knew they were going to fight, Monkman came running by, and he said in Cree, asked an Indian where was his gun, or had he brought his gun with him, and he ordered them to the front, so I thought by that there was going to be a fight.

Q. Did you see Riel at that time? A. No.

Q. Well then did you hear any firing? A. Yes.

Q. How long after they had gone out did you hear the firing?
A. I should judge about an hour or hour and a half, to the best of my knowledge.

Q. Did you hear many shots fired? A. I heard quite a number.

Q. You heard it plainly, I suppose? A. Yes.

Q. What happened next? A. Well, then they all returned, and we were ordered out to be shot the next. Gabriel got wounded. I heard them talking about it downstairs.

Q. Well, who interfered to stop that, anyone that you know of? A. A half-breed told me, by the name of Magnus Burstein that he interfered.

Q. Well, you were not taken out and what happened next? A. Well, we were removed to Carlton next.

Q. Before that did you see Riel? Did you see Riel at Duck Lake?
A. Yes, he came with the prisoners.

Q. And what did he say to you? A. He did not make any remark at all to me.

Q. Did he make any remark to anyone else in your hearing? A. He made a remark to Astley, or Astley made a remark to him. They were talking about the fight. He said that the police fired on them first, and Mr Astley said that probably the gun might have gone off accidentally, and he said, perhaps so.

Q. Did he tell you anything more about the fight? A. The next day he allowed me to go out. Ross and I to take the bodies off the field.

Q. Before that he told Mr Astley the police fired first, and Mr Astley said, perhaps the gun went off accidentally, and he said perhaps so. Was there anything else spoken of as regards firing? A. He said he gave the word in the name of God to fire.

Q. He said he gave the word to whom? A. To his men.

Q. Did he say anything more about his men? A. No, he brought this Charles Newett up.

Q. Did he say anything more about his men or what any of them had done at the fight? A. No, nothing that I heard.

Q. Nothing that you remember? A. No.

Q. Well, did he say anything about yourselves? A. Oh, he said that probably we were brought in there for our life, to have our lives saved. Whereby if we had been out I suppose we would have been shot. That is the way I understood it.

Q. He said that probably you were brought in there for your lives' sake that if you had been out you might have been shot? A. Yes.

Q. Well, how long did you remain at Hillyard Mitchell's? A. We remained there until the 31st.

Q. And where were you taken then? A. To Carlton.

Q. By whom? A. Taken there by Baptiste Laplante. When he was driving the team. There were three guards in the cellar, as far as I can think.

Q. How many other half-breeds were there with you there?
A. I should judge about fifteen altogether, twelve to fifteen.

Q. Any Indians? A. Yes.

Q. How many? A. Two.

Q. About fifteen half-breeds and two Indians? A. Yes.

Q. What was done with you there? A. We were placed in a house there up stairs.

Q. When you got there whom did you find in possesion of Carlton? A. Monkman.

Q. With how many men? A. I should think about sixty.

Q. Were they armed? A. Yes.

Q. And how long did you remain there? A. We remained there till the 3rd April.

Q. What was done with you then? A. We had to go back to Batoche.

Q. What distance is that? A. Twenty miles.

Q. Under a guard? A. Yes.

Q. How many were in the guard? A. We went with all the crowd.

Q. The whole that were at Carlton? A. Yes.

Q. Did they burn before leaving? A. It was afire before I left. I could see the flames when I had left.

Q. Then the whole force went over with you to Batoche, about 100? A. Yes.

Q. They were armed as I understand? A. Yes.

Q. Then when you got to Batoche what was done with you? A. We were put in Baptiste Boyer's house.

Q. How long were you kept there? A. Kept there till the battle of Fish Creek.

Q. That would have been on the 24th April? A. 24th April.

Q. Under guard? A. Yes.

Q. And what happened on the 24th April? A. Well, before we were taken to the cellar I saw a man get up there and wave to the other party that were across the river to come on this side, and they started, and we were taken down to the cellar, and we did not hear anything more.

Q. Who took you into the cellar? Who was in command of the guard if there was one? A. I couldn't say who was in command.

Q. How long were you kept in the cellar? A. We were kept in till the battle of Fish Creek was over, and then we were taken out.

Q. That would only have been a day or two I suppose at that time? A. Yes.

Q. Well, how long were you left out of the cellar after that? A. Well, to the best of my knowledge, I think we were put down either that day or the next – I am not sure which.

Q. Now, while you were in Baptiste Boyer's house did you see Mr Riel at all? A. Yes, I saw him around.

Q. Did he ever speak to you? A. No, he never had any conversation with me at all that I know of.

Q. Did he ever have any conversation with other persons in your presence? A. Yes.

Q. With whom? A. He used to converse with Mr Astley.

Q. What did he say to Mr Astley in your presence? A. Well, Mr Astley told me —

Q. Never mind what Mr Astley told you, but what did you hear him say to Mr Astley? A. Well, I heard him say that he would exchange us for the Honorable Lawrence Clark and Mr Thomas McKay and Col. Sproat.

Q. What did Mr Astley say to that? A. Well, I don't know exactly what he said to that.

Q. You don't remember what the answer was? A. No.

Q. Then during all this time were you in the custody of an armed guard? A. Yes.

Q. Who appeared to be in command of the people there, the armed men? A. Riel, as far as I could see.

Q. Did you ever see him armed? A. Yes.

Q. What with? A. A Winchester rifle.

Q. You were left out of the cellar for a short time, and when were you put back there? A. I think we were moved back, but we came out — I think we were moved back either that day or the next.

Q. He came out about the day of the battle of Fish Creek, 24th? A. Yes.

Q. You moved, were moved back you mean on the 25th and 26th? A. Yes.

Q. How long did you remain there? A. The 24th was the battle of Fish Creek, and we were out on the 25th, I think, and then we were put back again right that next day.

Q. Then you were put back on the 26th, and how long did you remain there then? A. Remained there till I was released.

Q. That would be the 12th May? A. Yes.

Q. Who was there with you? A. In the cellar?

Q. Yes? A. There was Mr Astley, Mr Ross, Mr Lash, Mr McKean, Mr Woodcock and myself.

Q. Was there any light in this cellar, or what sort of place was it?
A. No, no light.

Q. No light at all? A. No.

Q. How did you get into it? A. Through a trap door.

Q. And that was closed, I suppose? A. Yes.

Q. Were you at liberty, or confined or tied in any way? A. We were tied for the last three nights.

Q. Hands, or hands and feet, or how? A. I was tied hands and feet; the others were only tied hands.

Q. Who was it ordered you to be tied? A. Well, Delorme was the man that tied me.

Q. How was it done – was he armed? A. Yes, he was armed.

Q. Did he say anything when he did it? A. He said if he found us unloosed he would shoot us.

Q. Do you remember seeing Riel on the 12th, the day you were rescued? A. Yes.

Q. Where did you see him? A. He came to the trap door and took Mr Astley out.

Q. What did he say to him? A. He said go and tell Gen. Middleton that (as far as I can understand) if he did not stop shelling the houses he would massacre the prisoners.

Q. Did Astley go? A. Yes.

Q. Were you there when Astley returned or did you see him? A. No.

Q. Then, have you told me all you know about the matter? A. Yes.

Q. Had you known Riel before this? A. I had seen him. I never was acquainted with him.

Q. How often had you seen him before this? A. I had seen him just once to my knowledge.

Q. And when would that have been? A. He was holding a meeting at a settlement.

Q. When? A. I forget the date.

Q. How long before this? A. I should judge about six months.

Examined by MR GREENSHIELDS:

Q. Were you present at the meeting? A. Yes.

Q. Did you hear any of the speeches at the meeting? A. Yes.

Q. What was the meeting held for? It was grievances, as far as I could find out.

Q. Grievances that the half-breeds contended against the Government? A. As far as I could understand, that was it. I wasn't there long.

Q. I think you stated in your examination-in-chief you did not understand French but you did understand Cree? A. Yes.

Q. And when you state what Mr Riel said, did he speak in French or English then? A. When Mr Riel was speaking?

Q. Yes? A. He was talking French.

Q. Somebody interpreted it for you? A. I asked an interpreter that had it interpreted to him; he told me; an Indian.

Q. So that what you know, then, is the statement you have proved that Mr Riel made was interpreted to you by an Indian? A. An Indian that understood French.

Q. But you did not know what he said himself personally? A. No; I did not say I did.

Q. I think you said, also, that at the meeting of the council where you were present, when they were electing a council that Riel did not seem to be taking very much of a part in it? A. Yes.

Q. Now, you understood, did you not, that half-breeds during your arrest were really standing between you and the Indians — that is, you looked to them for protection? A. Yes, I did.

By MR ROBINSON:

Q. These conversations with Astley, were they in English, or how did Riel address him? A. In English.

Q. So that you understood them? A. Yes.

JOHN B. LASH sworn:

Examined by MR OSLER:

Q. I believe you are Indian agent for the Dominion Government at Fort Carlton? A. Carlton district.

Q. You had not been there very long at the time of the occurrence in question? A. No, I went there in January.

Q. On the 18th of March I believe you were with the last witness? A. He was my interpreter.

Q. And you were taken prisoner? A. Yes, I was taken prisoner at Batoche.

Q. Relate how you were taken prisoner? A. I was returning from One Arrow's reserve, and when near Batoche I came down upon a crowd of armed men. Gabriel Dumont came forward and said Mr Riel wanted to see me. While he was talking Riel drove down at a furious rate. He came forward and addressed me as Mr Agent. He says 'I will have to detain you.' I asked on what grounds he was going to detain me and he said the rebellion had commenced and that they intended fighting until the whole of the Saskatchewan valley was in their hands.

Q. That is what Riel told you himself? A. Yes.

Q. What else passed between you? A. Then he told me to give up my arms if I had any, to hand them over to Dumont.

Q. Then what was done? A. From that we were taken to the church.

Q. Who seemed to be in authority when Riel came up? A. He seemed to command the whole thing. It was by his orders that the mules I was driving were unhitched and he took possession of them and the trap.

Q. It was he told you the intentions of the Party? A. Yes.

Q. About how many men were there in arms? A. I should say there was about forty or fifty in the mob.

Q. How were they armed? A. With guns, chiefly guns, and a variety of arms, rifles.

Q. Do you mean they were all firearms? A. Yes, all firearms.

Q. Then where were you put? A. We were taken down to the church, and remained there till about eight o'clock.

Q. The church at what place? A. At Batoche. Then we were sent to the south side of the river, to Walters' & Baker's store.

Q. About what time on the 18th? A. Between eight and nine in the evening.

Q. What was going on at Walters' & Baker's store? A. The store was being pillaged by the armed mob. We were put up stairs.

Q. Did you see Riel there that evening? A. No.

Q. You were put up stairs and whom did you find there? A. I found Walters, and his clerk, Mr Hannipin. They were prisoners.

Q. Anyone else in the house? A. Not at that time.

Q. On the 19th what took place? A. That evening there was another prisoner brought in, Louis Marion.

Q. On the 19th what took place? A. Early in the morning there were two more prisoners brought in.

Q. Who were they? A. Tompkins and McKean.

Q. The men who had been repairing the telegraph lines? A. Yes, they stated so.

Q. What happened further on the 19th? A. We were then removed to the church and kept there all day.

Q. What happened at the church? A. There was a great deal of
   excitement going on, but it was spoken in French chiefly and I
   didn't understand it.
Q. Whom did you see at the church? Did you see the prisoner at the
   church? A. Yes.
Q. What was he doing? A. Addressing the crowd.
Q. Anything else? A. There was nothing I know of particularly.
Q. Who was in charge that day so far as you saw? A. The prisoner.
Q. Then, where did you go from the church, and when? A. They kept
   us there till about eight o'clock, and we had no blankets or any-
   thing, and a man by the name of Monkman came along and I
   spoke to him. He said he would see Mr Riel, and see what could
   be done, and we were removed to Philip Garnot's house.
Q. How long did you stay there? A. We remained there till the morning of the 26th.
Q. Of March? A. Yes.
Q. During that time had you any conversation with the prisoner?
   A. Several.
Q. Can you give us anything of importance he said to you as to his
   intentions? A. On one occasion he said he had three enemies, and
   he enumerated them as the Government, the Hudson Bay Company and the police. He also stated to me he would give the
   police every opportunity to surrender, and if they didn't do so
   there would be bloodshed. On another occasion he told me he
   had heard the Lieutenant Governor was on his way up, and that
   he had sent an armed body to capture him.
Q. Anything else? A. I cannot remember what his ordinary conversation was. On one occasion he said he would not release me on any
   account, as I was a Government official — that he would hold me
   as a hostage.
Q. Anything else? Anything personal of himself, as to motives?
   A. Yes, he talked about as soon as they had the country, it would
   be divided up, and so forth. He was going to give a seventh to the
   Indians, a seventh to the half-breeds, and I don't know what was
   to become of the balance.
Q. It was only two-sevenths he was going to give away apparently?
   A. That was all he stated to me.
Q. Was anything said as to his intentions or movements? A. No, not
   that I am aware of. On one occasion he wanted me to join the

movement. He said he would guarantee me a position in the service if I fell in with him.

Q. What did he say? A. He said he would give me a position in the Government that they were to form.

Q. Did he say anything about the Indians? A. Nothing out of the way.

Q. Did he say what position they were taking? A. No; I don't remember any particular conversation about the Indians.

Q. Was there anything said as to the length of time he had been considering these matters? A. Yes; he told me he had been waiting fifteen years, and at last his opportunity had come.

Q. Then, where were you taken on the 26th? A. To Duck Lake.

Q. And where were you put there? A. We were put above Mr Mitchell's store — above his house, I should say.

Q. That is, with the other prisoners? A. Yes.

Q. Did you see Riel there at all before the fight? A. No; the main body had gone to the fight when we arrived there.

Q. Did you see him after the fight? A. I saw him returning with the mob.

Q. Who was he returning with? A. If my memory serves me, he was on horseback.

Q. How many men about him? A. I should say between 300 and 400.

Q. How were they armed, if armed? A. They were partly armed; armed with guns, rifles, and so forth.

Q. Then did you hear Riel after that say anything? A. He came up with the wounded prisoner (the wounded volunteer), and he said, he will be better in your hands, as he is one of yourselves, or words to that effect.

Q. Then what conversation took place in which the prisoner took part? A. On another occasion he came up, and was anxious to find out if Mr Lawrence Clark was at the Duck Lake fight. I don't know that there was anything else particularly said by him.

Q. Was there anything said by him as to which fired first? A. Yes, he claimed the police fired first, and then he told his men to fire — that is what he claimed.

Q. Did you hear him make that claim, that he told his men to fire? A. Yes, I did.

Q. Was that all you heard him say? A. That was all I remember at present.

Q. Did you remain there any length of time, at Duck Lake? A. We remained there till the morning of the 31st.

Q. What took place in the interval? A. One of the prisoners, Sanderson, he sent him to Carlton.

Q. Who sent him? A. The prisoner.

Q. For what purpose? A. With a message to Major Crozier, to send for the dead, and that he would not molest any parties coming for them.

Q. Do you remember the day that was? A. Friday.

Q. The Friday after the fight? A. Yes.

Q. Did Sanderson return? A. Yes, he returned on Sunday.

Q. Do you know, personally, of the dead being taken away by Sanderson? A. I didn't.

Q. Then was anything said by Riel, at any time, as to who were with him in the movement? A. No, he never mentioned any names.

Q. Not names, but what peoples? A. Yes; he told me the Indians were all with him, and the half-breeds, both French, English and Scotch.

Q. Were with him? A. Were with him in the movement.

Q. Then you were taken on the 31st where? A. Taken to Carlton.

Q. All of you? A. Yes.

Q. What was done with you there? A. We were kept there till the morning of the 3rd April, and then we were carted or walked the best part of the way to Batoche.

Q. Where were you put in Batoche? A. In the bottom of a store, on arriving, and on the next day we were moved above the store.

Q. You were kept above the store until when? A. We were kept above the store until some excitement sprang up there, and we were put down the cellar for a day or two, and we were taken out and put back again, and we remained there then till Thursday, the 23rd, and we were taken out of the cellar after the Fish Creek fight was over.

Q. How were you treated in the cellar? A. Our hands were tied at nights.

Q. Had you any communication with Riel during your stay at Batoche — any talk with him? A. I spoke to him several times about getting released.

Q. What did he say to that? A. He refused it every time.

Q. Give any reason? A. He said he might release the other prisoners but I was a Government official and he would not release me.

Q. Did you ever see Riel armed? A. I did.

Q. With what? A. It was a rifle of some kind.

Q. When? A. Prior to the Fish Creek fight, I cannot give you the date.

Q. Did Riel say anything about the Fish Creek fight? A. Yes, he claimed the victory there.

Q. In talking to you? A. No, not to me personally. I heard of him claiming the victory and that is all.

Q. Do you remember anything taking place on the day you were released? A. Yes, Riel came to the trap door. It was loaded with stones. He called Mr Astley and says: 'Come quick, go and see General Middleton,' and he turned back and says 'If our families are hurt in any way I will massacre the prisoners,' addressing us all who were left in the cellar, six of us.

Q. What occurred after that? A. Shortly after that we were released by the arrival of the troops.

MR FITZPATRICK: We do not wish to cross-examine this witness.

GEORGE NESS sworn:

Examined by MR BURBIDGE:

Q. You live near Batoche, Mr Ness? A. Yes.

Q. On which side of the river? A. On the east side of the river.

Q. How far from Batoche? A. About two miles.

Q. What is your occupation? A. Farmer.

Q. You are a justice of the peace as well? A. Yes.

Q. You know the prisoner? A. Yes.

Q. When did you first see him? A. Somewhere in the month of July, about that time.

Q. July 1884? A. Yes, 1884.

Q. Where did you see him then? A. I cannot say exactly the first place that I saw him, but I saw him around the settlement.

Q. In the parish of St Antoine? A. Yes.

Q. Was he living there at that time? Yes, somewhere there.

Q. Was his wife and children living there, too? A. Yes.

Q. Do you know if he has continued to live in the country since then? A. Yes.

Q. You know of his holding meetings? A. Yes, sir, I believe he was holding meetings.

Q. Did you attend any of those meetings? A. I attended one of them.

Q. One of the first meetings? A. No, this was on the 24th February.

Q. Where was it held? A. In the church at St Antoine.

Q. Did anything of importance take place at that meeting, and if so tell us? A. I didn't continue all way through the meeting. I left when it was about half way through.

Q. And you say it was conducted principally in French? A. Yes, it was conducted in French.

Q. You understand French? A. Yes, I knew what they were saying.

Q. Was that meeting attended by persons who afterwards remained loyal? A. Yes, several, and also by persons who were in the rebellion.

Q. Did you take any part in the meeting yourself? A. No, sir, I was just listening. I heard there was to be a meeting and I just went out of curiosity.

Q. Had you any reason for not taking part? A. I never did take any active part.

Q. Had you any conversation with Riel soon after he came into the country? A. Yes, I talked to him several times.

Q. In what month of 1884 would that be? A. It might have been the end of July or August.

Q. What were you speaking about? A. He was talking of trying to assist the people in their grievances, to have their grievances righted.

Q. Speaking of getting up an agitation? A. Yes, an agitation or bill of rights.

Q. Did he at that time make any suggestion of using force? A. No, sir.

Q. Did you see him frequently from that time forward? A. Yes.

Q. You live in the same neighborhood? A. Yes. I have seen him there very often.

Q. He attended church regularly? A. Yes.

Q. Did you see anything or hear anything to lead you to suppose they would take up arms? A. No, nothing till the 17th of March.

Q. Now, tell us what took place then? A. As I was proceeding home in the cutter I overtook one of my neighbors on the road. He was on foot and as is the custom of that part of the country I took him into my cutter as far as my place. He said, I believe Gabriel is inciting the Indians on One Arrow's reserve. I went home. I thought probably it might be true and I took and fed my horse and started for Carlton.

Q. This was about three in the afternoon? A. About three, it was getting towards sunset. I went to Carlton and informed Major Crozier what I had heard. I came there that night, it was late. I suppose it is about twenty miles to drive there. I asked permission to camp from the major and the next morning I saw him and he told me if I heard anything more to try and let him know as soon as possible. When I got back to Duck Lake Mr Kerr told me, they are in arms already at the river, and they are going to take Carlton to-night. I thought it was my duty to send back to the major and inform him what was going on.

Q. You did so? A. I did so. I sent a letter by a special messenger.

Q. All this time your own family was about two miles from Batoche? A. Yes.

Q. After sending the message what did you do? A. I started for home to my family as I was anxious about them.

Q. What took place on the way home? A. On my way home, on the north side, or west side of the river at Walters' store, I heard there again that a mass meeting was to be held that evening.

Q. There was something really stirring them? A. Yes, there was something really the matter. I determined to go on.

Q. Did you do so? A. Yes. As I crossed the river I met another man. He was under arms already. He says they have taken up arms already. I said it was very foolish of them. Take the advice of a friend says I and leave that thing alone. So I continued on my way. When I got opposite Kerr Brothers' store I saw a big crowd there.

Q. Is Kerr Brothers' store on the east or west side? A. On the east side.

Q. Or on the south side as some say? A. Yes. As I got close to them I saw them coming on foot to the road. The store is perhaps about seventy or eighty feet from the road. Gabriel Dumont was in front. He says 'bonjour.' I took his hand and I says Gabriel, what is it you wish — it is not for nothing you stop me in this manner. He says, 'where have you been to?' I said I have been to Duck

Lake, and he says you have been doing something, you have been further than Duck Lake. I says, Gabriel, it is none of your business where I have been to. Well, he says, I will take you prisoner. I says you can do what you please. I says, if you want to kill me, I am ready. I asked him if he was at the head of affairs, and he said no, Mr Riel, the prisoner here, was at the head. He says I will have to keep you prisoner till his arrival.

Q. How many people were with Dumont? A. There were probably forty or fifty or sixty.

Q. And they were principally your neighbors? A. Neighbours and Indians.

Q. People you knew well? A. Yes.

Q. And some Indians? A. Yes.

Q. How many Indians do you think were there? A. There might have been twenty or twenty-five.

Q. Did you say anything to these people? A. I asked them who was taking me prisoner, whether they assisted Gabriel or not, and no one would answer me. I said it was a very foolish thing they were doing, that they would all be killed if they went on with it, if they meant rebellion.

Q. You made a speech to them? A. Yes. They said there is some more old men in the house. A young man said that. He says you better go and ask them if they will take him prisoner. They went back to the house and brought along two men.

Q. Who were they? A. Donald Ross and Calice Tourond. Tourond made a jump for my horse and caught him by the reins, and Ross consented.

Q. The people all consented to your arrest? A. Yes.

Q. Where did they take you to? A. Back to the store, about seventy or eighty feet from the road. Gabriel says you can get down and warm yourself; so I went in and warmed myself. While I was in the house I heard the people saying in French, they have taken Captain Gagnon.

Q. Who is he? A. A captain of the police force stationed at Carlton. All the people went out. I went out with them. I saw Mr Lash.

Q. Had the prisoner arrived at this time? A. After I went out I saw Mr Riel, and he was saying to Mr Lash, have you any arms. Lash says, no, I never carry any arms.

Q. Who appeared to be in command after the prisoner arrived? A. Mr
Riel. He told me, he says you go down to the church; and we
started almost immediately for the church.

Q. Did every one appear to obey him? A. Yes.

Q. Dumont and all the rest? A. Yes.

Q. Tell us about their taking you to church. A. When we got to the
church they were in the front of the church. Mr Riel commenced
saying he was a prophet, that he could foresee events.

Q. Before that how many men were in arms – at the time you and
Lash were taken prisoners to the church? A. Well, there might
have been about fifty.

Q. How were they armed? A. With guns.

Q. Had any of them rifles? A. They might have had rifles. I didn't
take that much notice.

Q. They were armed with firearms? A. Yes.

Q. Who was in charge of the church? A. Rev. Father Moulin.

Q. Did you see him on that occasion? A. When the crowd got to the
church he came out and he wished to speak to the people. Mr
Riel says: No, we won't let him speak; take him away; take him
away; we will tie him.

Q. He threatened to tie him? A. Yes. He says: Shall we take him
prisoner? Some of them said: No, we will put a guard over him.

Q. Did he say anything about taking possession of the church at the
same time? A. Yes. Riel says: I will take possession of the church.
Father Moulin says: I protest your touching the church. Riel
says: Look at him; he is a Protestant.

Q. The prisoner said that? A. Yes. Go away, says Riel, go away.

Q. What happened then? A. They went into the church then, and
ordered us to go into the church.

Q. Ordered you prisoners? A. Yes, us prisoners. Mr Riel jumped into
my cutter as I was going to the church. He bowed very politely to
me and said to take my horse.

Q. How long were you in the church? A. Probably quarter of an
hour or half an hour.

Q. Where did they take you then? A. Across the river to Walters' &
Baker's store.

Q. Where did they put you then? A. Up stairs.

Q. Were there any prisoners in that store when you arrived? A. They
took Mr Lash and Tompkins.

Q. Did you find any prisoners when you got there? A. Mr Walters
was a prisoner with his assistant, Mr Hannipin.

Q. Were you kept under guard at Walters' & Baker's store? A. Yes,
all the time.

Q. That would be on the night of the 18th still? A. Yes.

Q. Tell me if anything of importance took place that night. A. They
brought in Louis Marion a prisoner on the 18th about nine or ten
o'clock, and during the night I heard some one call out down
stairs to go and cut the telegraph wire. I heard a noise as if they
were going off to, and then several hours afterwards I heard them
saying they could see a lantern, that some one was repairing the
telegraph. I heard them as if they were starting off again.

Q. Did they bring in any more prisoners that night? A. They brought
back Peter Tompkins and McKean, who had been repairing the
telegraph.

Q. What took place on the 19th? A. On the morning of the 19th
they took us back to the church again.

Q. Were you kept there all the day? A. Yes.

Q. As prisoners? A. Yes, as prisoners.

Q. Was the prisoner giving orders? A. Yes, he appeared to be at the
head of affairs; he was giving orders.

Q. What was the chief event of that day as far as you can remember? A. He was giving orders to go and take William Boyer and
Charles Nolin prisoners.

Q. Did you hear him say why they were to be taken prisoners?
A. Because they would not take up arms.

Q. Did he say anything about because they had been movers up to
that time? A. Because they had been movers and had left it at the
time of the taking up of arms.

Q. Was Nolin tried? A. About his trial I cannot say exactly. I heard
Riel saying he ought to be shot, or that they would shoot him.

Q. You understood Nolin and Boyer were to be shot? A. Yes, both
of them.

Q. And because they would not join in the movement in taking up
arms? A. In not taking up arms.

Q. Where did they take you from the church? A. In the evening they
offered to take our word of honor we would not try to escape
and they gave us a book to put our names down and they told
us we would be more comfortable down at Garnot's house and

they took us down there with a big guard in addition to our word of honor.

Q. Coming to the 20th, the next day, can you tell us anything of importance that occurred on that day? A. Yes, somewhere about the middle of the day Riel came down to see the prisoners.

Q. While you were at dinner? A. Yes, while we were at dinner.

Q. And addressed you all? A. Yes, addressed us all.

Q. Did he say anything to any of you particularly? A. Well, he told Mr Walters — Mr Walters asked him why he was keeping him prisoner — if he would not give him his liberty and Riel said he would think over it, and that he would give him his liberty. He says to Lash: 'We will offer you the same position in our Government which you hold under the Dominion Government as agent, that is if you will accept of it.'

Q. After that did he take you to the council house? A. He told me he wanted to see me at the council house, so I went up to the council house.

Q. What did he say to you there? A. He told me he was going to give me my liberty and they would read me my penalty for my crime, my offence.

Q. Did he make any further promises there? A. Yes, he would let me go on condition I would not do anything against the movement.

Q. What did you say to that? A. I said I preferred he would leave a guard over me, that I could hardly consent to that.

Q. Was anything else said? Did you see Maxime Lepine there?
A. Yes, I saw Maxime Lepine there.

Q. Did he take part in any conversation do you remember? A. Yes, he was one of the councillors.

Q. Do you remember anything he said? A. No, I cannot remember now.

Q. When you told him you would rather he would keep a guard over you what took place? A. They took me in and read my crime to me.

Q. What was your crime? A. Communicating with the police.

Q. Was this before the council? A. Yes.

Q. Who appeared to be in the chair? A. Albert Monkman and Garnot.

Q. What was Garnot acting as? A. Secretary of the council.

Q. They read over to you your offence? A. Yes, they read over to me my offence and my penalty.

Q. What was your offence? A. Communicating with the police and insulting Gabriel Dumont.

Q. What was your penalty? A. They took my horse and cutter and robes.

Q. They were to be confiscated? A. Yes.

Q. You were to be given your liberty on the condition that you would do nothing against them? A. Yes.

Q. That you would be neutral? A. Yes. I had no alternative. I had to take it.

Q. Your wife and family were at home? A. Yes. When I arrived home that evening I found my wife in a great state of excitement about me. It appears Sioux Indians had been through there and told her I was to be shot.

MR GREENSHIELDS: There should be a limit to this hearsay evidence.

Q. From the 20th March till the 14th May where were you? A. I was at home.

Q. Were you within the line of guards of the rebel position? A. Yes.

Q. You had frequent occasion of seeing armed parties? A. Yes, they were passing and repassing all the time.

Q. Did you see Indians in arms too? A. Yes.

Q. Did you have any of the rebels quartered on you during the time? A. Yes, they told me my property was public; everybody's property was public.

Q. The prisoner and others with him took whatever they saw fit? A. Yes.

Q. Did they ever speak with you about what they intended to do, or you with them? A. Well, after the Duck Lake fight most of them were frightened; they saw they had put their foot in it, and they didn't know how to get out of it.

Q. Do you know the day of the Fish Creek fight? A. Yes.

Q. What date was that? A. On the 24th April.

Q. How far is Fish Creek from your home? A. About twelve miles.

Q. Did you see the rebels going down to Fish Creek? A. Yes, I saw them.

Q. Did you see them returning? A. Yes.

Q. Had you any conversation with any of them on returning? A. Yes. When they were returning there was a wounded man brought into my house, one who was wounded at Fish Creek.

Q. Did you see Riel among the men who went down? A. No, sir, I
   didn't. I could not see them well enough to identify them. I would
   not expose myself that much. I was hiding.
Q. Didn't you see Riel returning from the direction of Fish Creek
   before the fight? A. No, sir, I didn't.
Q. Did you ever see Riel armed? A. I saw him with a revolver.
Q. On what occasion was that? A. That was while I was a prisoner.
Examined by MR FITZPATRICK:
Q. You saw Riel in connection with the present difficulty for the
   first time last July or August? A. Yes, somewhere in July or
   August.
Q. You knew the circumstances under which he came into the
   country? A. I believe he was sent for as far as I heard.
Q. At the time you first saw him there was a certain amount of agita-
   tion in the country was there not? A. Yes, sir.
Q. The agitation was to obtain by constitutional means redress for
   certain grievances that the half-breeds pretended to exist? A. Yes.
Q. That agitation had been going on for some years? A. Yes.
Q. Riel told you when you first saw him that he had come for the
   purpose of taking part in that agitation at the request of the
   persons interested? A. Well, I could not say he exactly said that,
   but I understood that he came for that purpose.
Q. You saw him frequently from July last up to the month of
   March? A. Yes.
Q. Did you during all that time hear of anything either from himself
   or any person else which would lead you to believe that anything
   in the shape of a rebellion was pretended by him? A. No, sir, not
   till the 17th of March.
Q. During all that time he lived in the country and took part in all
   the movements that took place? A. I believe he did.
Q. It was a matter of common report he took part in all those movements? A. Yes.
Q. You never heard any extraordinary remarks passed with regard to
   him until the 17th of March? A. No.
Q. You know that different petitions had been in circulation in the
   country and had been forwarded to Ottawa? A. I believe they had.
Q. You are also aware that as late as the month of February last a
   petition was prepared under the direction of the prisoner, which

was signed by yourself, and which was sent to Ottawa, or of which you approved? A. I might have approved of it, but I never signed it. He showed me a petition some time in August, I think, but I never heard of its being taken around to be signed.

Q. Did you hear of anything in February? A. No.

Q. At the time of that meeting which you refer to as having taken place on the 24th of February? A. No. I had heard the Government had refused Riel, that they would not have anything to do with him.

Q. Do you know whether any answer had been given to any petitions that had been sent in; any answer by the Government?
A. I believe not. I never heard of any.

Q. It was a matter of common report previous to the 17th of March that the police force was being increased? A. Yes, there was some talk of it.

Q. That was generally considered among the people there as being the answer to their petition? A. I could not say.

Q. Was not that the general impression formed by the public report circulated at that time? A. I could not say.

Q. After Riel came into the country, at the request of the half-breeds, you know of your own knowledge that he was very poor? A. Yes.

Q. You know a subscription was made for the purpose of enabling him to exist in the country? A. Yes, a subscription was made.

Q. You know he also desired to return to Montana again? A. Yes, there was something said about him returning to Montana.

Q. You said that the first time you heard of anything in the shape of an armed rebellion was on the 17th of March? A. Yes.

Q. Up to that time there had been nothing of that kind spoken of in any way to your knowledge? A. No, there were some reports in the papers.

Q. But among the people, among your neighbors? A. No.

Q. When did you first see Riel after the 17th? A. On the 18th.

Q. You saw him at the time he took possession of the church?
A. Yes.

Q. You heard what he said to the priest at that time? A. Yes.

Q. Up to that time had you heard him make any remark derogatory to the priests? A. Yes.

Q. When? A. In the month of February, I think.

Q. Towards the end of February? A. Somewhere in February.

Q. At that time did he not have a difficulty with Father Moulin? Just state what that difficulty was? A. He accused Bishop Taché and Bishop Grandin of being thieves and rogues.

Q. Made a general onslaught on all parties connected with the Roman Catholic Church? A. Yes.

Q. Didn't you clearly understand at that time that this man declared publicly that he had ceased to belong to the Roman Catholic Church? A. No.

Q. Didn't he say at that time that the priest was entirely outside of the church, that he was a Protestant? A. No.

Q. What about the word Protestant which you used in your examination-in-chief? A. He said that on the 17th of March.

Q. The difficulty with Father Moulin was in March? A. Yes; and in February.

Q. In March he said the priest was a Protestant or something to that effect? A. Yes.

Q. Did you consider at that time he acted as he had acted when you first knew him in July or August with reference to the priests and religion? A. No; he acted very much otherwise.

Q. Now, can your memory enable you to say what he said at that time on the 17th March in his difficulty with Father Moulin? A. It was on the 18th March.

Q. State what took place, the words that were used, and how he acted on that occasion? A. He said the Spirit of God was in him, and Father Moulin said he was making a schism against the church, and Riel said Rome had tumbled. *Rome est tombée.*

Q. Proceed if you please? He said the Pope of Rome was not legally Pope? A. Yes.

Q. He said the episcopate spirit had left Rome and come into the North-West Territories? A. No; he did not say that.

Q. Did he say anything of that kind? A. He said the Spirit of God was in him and that Rome had tumbled, and he could tell future events.

Q. Did he state the reason why Rome had tumbled? A. No; he did not give the reason.

Q. During July, August, September and October, immediately after his return to this country, he attended church as Roman Catholics generally do? A. Yes; he acted very devoutly.

Q. The first time you heard of the rebellion, heard it talked of, was at this time of the 17th March, and it is on that day he gave expression to this extraordinary language you have just told us about? A. Yes; on the 18th of March.

Examined by MR BURBIDGE:

Q. When you told Mr Fitzpatrick you understood the Government had refused Mr Riel, I understand you to be referring to Mr Riel's own personal claims, is that what you mean? A. I said the Government had declined to accede to Riel's terms?

Q. You were referring to Riel's own claims? A. Yes. Yes; from what I understood it was his personal claims.

The court adjourned till 29th July.

Wednesday, 29th July 1885

GEORGE KERR, sworn

Examined by MR CASGRAIN:

Q. You live at Batoche, I believe? A. Yes.

Q. How long have you lived there? A. I went in November, 1884.

Q. Do you know the prisoner? A. Yes.

Q. Well, between November, 1884, and the outbreak of the rebellion what happened at Batoche; did anything happen that you know of? A. No; meetings were held.

Q. What was the first intimation you had of the outbreak of the rebellion? A. Meetings were held alternately at different places and called at our store.

Q. Who held the meetings? A. I do not know, the council I guess.

Q. They called at your store? A. Yes, they called there, we were dealing with them.

Q. Who were they? A. Mr Vandal, and Norbert Delorme. I do not know any more of them I think.

Q. When was this? A. In January and February.

Q. You kept store at Batoche? A. Yes.

Q. In partnership with your brother, John Kerr? A. Yes.

Q. What did they do at your store? A. We traded with them for cattle and furs.

Q. Did they call at your store after this? A. Yes, they always called at the store and traded there as a general thing.

Q. What was the first intimation you had of any outbreak or insurrection? A. The first intimation of any outbreak was on the 18th
March.

Q. What happend on the 18th of March? A. On the 17th March there
was a rumor circulated around the store that a meeting was to be
held at Batoche.

Q. By whom? A. Gabriel Dumont, and Riel, the prisoner.

Q. Well, what happened then? A. That is on the 17th, on the 18th he
came down to the store.

Q. Who came down to the store? A. The prisoner himself.

Q. Who with? A. There was a good many followers of his.

Q. Can you give the names of any? A. Yes, I can. I can name some.
Jean Baptiste Vandal, Joseph Vandal. That is all I can name.

Q. How many were there, about? A. About fifty.

Q. What did they do at the store? A. Riel came in the store and
demanded my guns and ammunition — just asked for them.

Q. What did you say? A. I told him they were up on the shelf, that
the store was with cross beams and the guns were on the cross
beams. I told him to take them.

Q. Did they take them? A. The half-breeds jumped around to take
them, and he says who is boss here? I told him I was, and he said
they have no right to go behind your counter.

Q. Were you boss there at that time? A. Yes.

Q. How did you allow them to take your guns? A. I told them to
take them.

Q. What happened? A. He went away.

Q. Who went away? A. The prisoner. He told me then, he says give
my men what they want and charge it.

Q. To whom? A. He did not say to whom. I told him to take whatever he wanted in the store.

Q. Did he come back to your store? A. No, he did not come back at
all. I wrote him a letter the next morning to know if my brother
and I could go down about three miles to find out where our
cattle were.

Q. Did he give you permission? A. Yes, he sent up word that I could go.

Q. When they went to your store the first time were the men
armed? A. Yes, they were all armed.

Q. How much ammunition did they get at your store? A. A keg of
powder, and six English double-barrelled shot guns.

Q. Anything else? A. Yes, a box of Ballard rifle cartridges.

Q. He gave you permission to go and get your cattle? A. Yes, to go five miles.

Q. Did you go? A. Yes, we went up, and my brother and I stopped about two hours, I think, at Peller's house, that is about three miles from where the store was. When we were coming back we met a lot of half-breed women and Indians with packs upon their backs.

Q. Did you recognise any of them? A. They had some frying-pans which were ours. I said to my brother: Jack, those are ours. He said: No. I said: I think they are. I went to one of the women and asked her, and she said they had broken into the store and taken everything out. We walked on down to the store, and when we went into the store there were four or five Indians pulling the nails out of the beams. The store was upside down, and the Fairbanks' scales were turned upside down. Nothing was left in the store at all.

Q. What day was that? A. On the 18th.

Q. Did anything happen on the 19th? A. No, that was the 18th.

Q. Is this all that happened upon the 19th? A. Yes, that is all that happened on the 19th.

Q. Do you know of anything else that happened on that day? A. No.

Q. What happened on the subsequent day, on the 20th of March? A. No, I don't know. I was not allowed to go away. I promised Riel I would not leave my place of business, and I kept myself reserved.

Q. Did the prisoner give you any orders? A. No, he asked me if I would promise him not to leave my place of business. I told him I would, and I kept my word.

Q. Did you leave your place of business? A. No.

Q. Did you stop there all the time? A. I went down to Mrs Venn's.

Q. What for? A. I was stopping there.

Q. Did you get back from Mrs Venn's on the 19th? A. Yes.

Q. On the 20th? A. Yes.

Q. Did anything happen to you on the 20th? A. Yes.

Q. Were you always at liberty there? A. Yes.

Q. Do you know anything about the council that was formed there at Garnot's? A. Yes.

Q. Under what circumstances did you become acquainted with the council? A. I do not know as I can give you any information. I know the whole of them pretty well.

Q. Were you at any time arrested? A. Yes.

Q. Who by? A. By Solomon Boucher, Modeste Rocheleau.

Q. Were they armed? A. Yes.

Q. Where were you taken to? A. To Mr Ludger Gareau's house, a French Canadian's house.

Q. Whom did you see there? A. All the men were there.

Q. Who were there? A. I cannot tell you all the names, Norbert Delorme, Charles Nolin, and Boyer who keeps the store there.

Q. William Boyer? A. No.

Q. Jean Baptiste Boyer? A. No.

Q. Joseph Boyer? A. No.

Q. A man of that name who keeps store? A. Yes.

Q. How many were in that room? A. I suppose fifty or sixty.

Q. Were there any arms around? A. They were standing at the door with those double-barrelled shot guns.

Q. Did you see the prisoner there? A. No, I did not see him, he was up stairs.

Q. How do you know? A. I met him when I went in first.

Q. Did he say anything to you? A. No, not just then.

Q. Any time on that same day did you see him? A. Yes, he came down stairs and told the council that he had always found us very decent fellows. He said, of course, they may have done something that escaped my memory, but he said if they have, excuse them.

Q. Who was in command? A. Gabriel Dumont, as far as I was concerned.

Q. In command of what? A. He appeared to be in command of the whole outfit, as they say in this country.

Q. What did the prisoner do there? A. I don't know; he was up stairs.

Q. When he came down? A. He came to the council and he says, perhaps something has escaped my memory; if there has, he says, excuse them; and he says, these prisoners are in your hands do as you like with them, and he said they always acted kindly with me.

Q. How was this council constituted? A. Philip Garnot was at the head of the table.

Q. What was he doing? A. He was there, he had a book setting down; he got up and says: Monsieur le conseil, these men have come here and we want to know what to do with them; he talked like that and they came over.

Q. Who came over? A. Dumont and Delorme.

Q. Did you say the council was sitting there? A. Yes.

Q. They were in session? A. Yes.

Q. Were any charges made against you before the council? A. Yes, three charges.

Q. What were they? A. One charge was that my brother had telegraphed with George Ness to Major Crozier; another charge was that we wanted to get our cattle away from Batoche, and that we wanted to get to the telegraph officials and evade the vigilance of the police.

Q. What action was taken upon those charges? A. They could not prove anything and they let us go.

Q. I understood you to say that the prisoner was in the house all the time? A. Yes, up stairs.

Q. Did he know what was going on? A. Yes — No, I do not know; he was upstairs with the priests.

Q. He came down you said? A. Yes.

Q. Did you answer those charges? A. Yes, of course.

Q. You were acquitted? A. Yes.

Q. What was the state of that part of the country? A. Greatly agitated.

Q. Is not that a mild word, was it only greatly agitated, what do you mean? A. I mean that the whole country was excited, something like that.

Q. What do you mean by excited? A. That every man was taking care of himself as near as possible.

Q. Did you see any people under arms other than those you saw in the council? A. Yes, all around the council chamber they were under arms.

By MR FITZPATRICK:

Q. When did you first see Mr Riel? A. I met him in November.

Q. Of last year? A. Yes.

Q. You were aware he was in the country from November up till March, till the fight at Batoche? A. Yes.

Q. Did you have occasion to attend any of the meetings that were held in the country during that time? A. No, I did not.

Q. Do you know the nature of those meetings of your own knowledge? A. No, I do not.

Q. Do you know for what purpose they were held? A. No.

Q. Did you at any time attend any meeting at which Riel was present? A. Yes.

Q. What time was that? A. I think in January.

Q. Last year? A. Yes.

Q. Can you remember what took place at that meeting, was it a political meeting? A. No.

Q. What kind of a meeting was it? A. A presentation to Riel of some money.

Q. Money gathered by the people of that place? A. Yes.

Q. Did you hear anything there about the Government in reference to the grievances? A. No, not a word.

Q. What took place at the meeting? A. My brother and I were invited to go to the meeting. I gave $1 towards it myself. We were invited to the supper and the prisoner was there. I guess the whole people were there. There were about 150 in Baptiste Boyer's house. There was a pretty good spread. After the thing was started he had me and my brother sit up on the first end of the table.

Q. Were any speeches made at the table? A. Yes, Riel proposed the health of our Sovereign Queen Victoria.

Q. Riel did that? A. Yes.

Q. Did you see the prisoner after that meeting? A. I saw him when I left that night.

Q. Did you see him any other time between the time after that meeting and the 19th March? A. No, I did not.

Q. Didn't have any conversation with him at all? A. No.

Q. Have had no intercourse with him? A. Not since then.

Q. Never attended any meeting held by him or the council? A. No.

Q. Do you remember a meeting about the 24th of February at the church? A. No, I was not there at all.

Q. You are quite certain about that? A. Yes.

Q. You said these people broke into your house the time you went away for your cattle? A. Yes.

Q. Did the prisoner approve of their doing that? Did he counsel it? A. No, I wrote to him the next morning about it, and I got a letter back saying that he did not advise them in any way at all.

Q. Protesting against it? A. Yes, protesting against it.

Q. Did Riel take your part before the council? A. Yes, he took my part.

Q. Did you notice anything peculiar about Riel at the time you saw him? Did he give you any explanation as to his plans or programme? A. No, he never spoke about that at all.

Q. He never mentioned his political programme? A. No.

Q. Never gave you to understand what he proposed to do? A. No. I did not know him very well, only sometimes to meet him.

Q. At the meeting where he proposed the health of the Queen, do you remember under what circumstances he proposed it? A. No. Philip Garnot came with that paper and I put my name down for $1, and they asked me to go down.

Q. Riel you say proposed the health of the Queen at that meeting? A. Yes.

Q. Was there any treason talked? A. No, not one word.

Q. They were all pleasant together as loyal subjects? A. Yes.

Q. How long have you been in that section of the country? A. About a year.

Q. You knew that there were meetings being held alternately in the vicinity of Batoche? A. Yes.

Q. By all the people? A. Yes.

Q. You knew that Nolin took an active part in these meetings? A. Yes.

HENRY WALTERS sworn:

Examined by MR SCOTT:

Q. Where were you living in March last? A. At Batoche.

Q. What was your occupation? A. Keeping store.

Q. Was it your own store? A. I had a partner.

Q. What was your partner's name? A. Baker.

Q. And the firm's name? A. Walters & Baker.

Q. On which side of the river was your store? A. On the west side.

Q. Is there any house there besides your store? A. There is only one house close, belonging to the firm.

Q. Batoche proper is on the east side? A. Most of the stores are there.

Q. Were you there on the 18th March? A. Yes.

Q. Anything happened on that day? A. Yes, that evening this thing broke out.

Q. What broke out? A. The rebellion. The first act was committed.

Q. What intimation had you of the breaking out of the rebellion? A. About six o'clock in the evening of the 18th of March I looked out of the store and saw a party of armed men driving towards the door, they came up the hill apparently from the east side.

Q. You say about six o'clock in the evening you saw an armed party driving to your door from the direction of the river? A. Yes.

Q. What did they do? A. They came to the store and entered it. A man came and spoke to me whom I did not know at the time.

Q. A man whom you did not know spoke to you? A. Yes. He asked for the proprietor. I said I was the man.

Q. Who was the man who spoke to you? A. The prisoner is the man. He said, well, Mr Walters, it has commenced.

Q. What did he say to you? A. I said to him, I suppose you are Mr Riel. He said, yes, he was. I asked him what he wanted, and he said he wanted arms and ammunition. I told him he could not have them.

Q. Did the conversation continue? A. Yes. He asked me to give them up quietly and peaceably, and said that if they succeeded in the movement they would pay me, and if they did not the Dominion Government would pay for them. It would be all right either way.

Q. Did you ask him what had commenced? A. Yes. He said it was a movement for the freedom of the people, or something to that effect.

Q. Did you ask him what movement? A. Yes.

Q. He said a movement for the freedom of the people? A. Yes.

Q. Was that before or after he asked for the arms and ammunition? A. It was before.

Q. When you refused to give up the arms, what was said? A. He argued with me and wanted me to give them up, and I told him that I could not do it.

Q. Was anything done? A. Yes, they finally took them.

Q. Did you consent? A. No. They went through some form and put their hands upon my shoulders. Riel ordered the men to do that. I was standing behind the counter and they forced their way past. I did the best I could to stop them.

Q. They got past you? A. Yes, there were fifteen or twenty to one.

Q. Were all the party armed? A. Five, six, seven or eight were armed. I did not count the number.

Q. Was the prisoner armed? A. I did not see anything with him.

Q. Had you any conversation with him — did you say that the intention was to arrest you when they laid their hands upon you? A. I did not think so at the time. I was arrested a few minutes after.

Q. Had you any conversation with the prisoner about the movement? Did he say anything beyond what you have told us? A. No. He did not at the time we talked. I thought he would not succeed, but they thought they would. That was about all.

Q. Had you any conversation with him at any other time about the movement? A. No, not in reference to the movement. He told me what they were going to do when they took the country.

Q. What were they going to do? A. If successful, he told me the way they were going to divide the land.

Q. How was he going to divide it? A. One-seventh for the pioneer whites, and one-seventh for the Indians, one-seventh for the French half-breeds, and one-seventh for the church and school, and the balance was Crown lands — I suppose Government lands.

Q. That is the way? A. Yes, that is the way I understood it.

Q. Lands of which Government? A. Government land; he did not say which Government.

Q. Did he make any charges against you? A. The time I was arrested he said that something had transpired which led him to believe I was in deadly opposition to his cause, and he would have to detain me.

Q. How long did he detain you? A. I was allowed to go on the third day. The first night I was kept over my own store; the next morning I was moved across to the church at Batoche.

Q. And kept there three days? A. Not three whole days; only until the third day.

Q. Were you then released? A. Yes, the prisoner allowed me to go.

Q. You had a conversation with him on the other side of the river? A. Yes.

Q. Did he say anything about the movement there? A. No, he did not say anything very particular about it. He said they would have no opposition from Prince Albert. The people, he said, were friendly. He said if the whites struck a blow, a thunderbolt from Heaven would strike them; that God was with their people.

Q. Did you know of any meeting before the beginning of this movement? A. I only heard of meetings from time to time. I never was at any of the meetings.

Q. Were there any other prisoners besides you detained in the same place? A. Yes. One young fellow that was with me at the time, and during the evening, Lash and his interpreter, Tompkins, George Ness, Tompkins and another man that was repairing the line. That is all I saw.

Q. I suppose they took the guns and ammunition from your store; did they take anything else? A. Yes.

Q. What did they take? A. I don't think they were there at that time; they took it all out before the morning.

Q. Everything out of the store? A. Pretty nearly everything. Some unbroken packages they did not take. They were there when I left.

Q. Do you know who was superintending the removal of the goods? A. Everyone helped themselves to the clothing and moccasins, and in the morning they were carrying away the heavy goods, and Riel was superintending the removal.

Q. You say that the prisoner superintended the removal of the goods in the morning? A. He was giving direction. He was standing up on the seat of his cutter in a prominent position, and the half-breeds were loading up the goods.

By MR GREENSHIELDS:

Q. How long have you been living at Batoche? A. Nearly two years.

Q. Were you aware that there was excitement and agitation going on among the half-breeds some time previous to this time? A. Yes.

Q. It was rumored? A. Yes.

Q. Had you ever seen Riel before the time he came to your store? A. No, not to my knowledge.

Q. Did you know that he came to the country last year? A. I heard at the time that he came in.

Q. You heard that he had been sent for by the half-breeds? A. Yes.

Q. Did you know for what purpose? A. No. I heard that the half-breeds had grievances.

Q. And they wanted Riel to assist them? A. Yes.

Q. When this discussion between you and the prisoner took place regarding the division of the North-West Territories, was that in the store? A. No; in the church, next day.

Q. Did you talk about anything else at that time with him? A. No. What I was thinking about was to try and get away.

Q. Did he tell you that he expected assistance from other powers in this rebellion? A. No, I cannot say he did.

Q. Are you positive he did not? A. I have no recollection of his saying so.

Q. Did he say anything about the Germans and Irish? A. No.

Q. Or the United States? A. No.

Q. Did you have any conversation with him about his religion at that time? A. No.

HILLYARD MITCHELL sworn
Examined by MR OSLER:

Q. What is your occupation? A. Indian trader.

Q. Where were you carrying on business in March last? A. At Duck Lake.

Q. I believe you are a justice of the peace there? A. Yes.

Q. You had a store at Duck Lake? A. Yes.

Q. What was the first you knew of this trouble? A. The first I heard of the actual rising was when I was coming from a place called Sandy Lake to Duck Lake. I was crossing the Saskatchewan when I met one of the priests, and he told me to get back to Duck Lake, as the half-breeds were in arms and intended to take my store.

Q. You heard from him that was the intention? A. Yes.

Q. What was the first you saw of the trouble? A. I went to the fort and saw Major Crozier, and he told me –

Q. He will speak for himself; what date was that? A. I don't remember the day. It was on a Thursday. I don't remember the day of the month, but I think it must have been the 19th.

Q. The Thursday preceding what? A. Preceding the day of the Duck Lake fight.

Q. What was the first you saw of the prisoner? A. The first I saw of the prisoner was sometime after Christmas. He came to my store then, and that was the first I saw of him.

Q. I speak more in reference to the first time you saw him after the trouble commenced? A. I saw him at Batoche. After coming from Carlton, I went to Duck Lake, and from there I went to Batoche.

Q. On a Thursday? A. Yes.

Q. At Batoche whom did you se? A. I met Bernard Paul, and asked him what was the trouble.

Q. You had a talk with him? A. Yes.

Q. We want to come down to the occurrences with which the prisoner was connected? A. I went to the river. Where I met this man was about two miles from the river.

Q. What took place at the river? A. I saw a great many people around the river; it was getting dark. I saw that two or three of the people on this side of the river had guns in their hands, people whom I knew. I recognized some of them, and when they saw me they appeared to be getting out of the way. On the other side of the river, I saw a man standing on the hill. I went to the village of Batoche and saw some English half-breeds waiting with loads of flour. They said they had been waiting all day to be unloaded, and that they had been taken prisoners by Riel. They were loaded with flour. I saw the load, and they were loaded with flour.

Q. What next? A. I tried to get as much information as I could. I did not know whether it would be safe for me to proceed, and did not know how I might be received by these people. I saw Fisher and also Garnot, and their opinion was that I could go into the council room. I asked them where the council room was and Philip Garnot took me to the council room. I did not go into the council room. I went into the priest's house. I saw some people standing outside and I went up stairs in the house.

Q. Whom did you see? A. Charles Nolin, Philip Garriépy, and a small man named Jackson, who was walking up and down.

Q. Did you see the prisoner? A. I saw him after some time. I waited about an hour before I saw him. I said that I wanted to see him that that was what I came for.

Q. Can you place this date more accurately? Do you know the day Walters' store was raided? A. I am told it was on Wednesday, not on Tuesday.

Q. Was this after that store had been raided? A. Yes, I left Duck Lake on Tuesday.

Q. This would be Thursday, the 20th, probably? A. I think it was the 19th.

Q. Had you a conversation with the prisoner? A. I had a long conversation with him, he did most of the talking.

Q. Tell us what the conversation was? A. Someone told me that he was come to see me, I went down below, there was no light, he asked me to sit down and said he was pleased to see me, and that

kind of thing. I told him I came to find out the cause of this
trouble, what it meant, and said that he need not look upon me
as a spy as I simply came as a friend of the half-breeds to give
them some good advice, and try to get them to go home. He went
on explaining the cause of the rising. He said that the half-breeds
had petitioned the Government several times to have their grievances redressed but never got a proper reply, and the reply they
were getting now was, 500 policemen to shoot them. I told him
the whole thing was a false rumor, that no police were coming.
There always had been false reports and I looked upon this one as
not true; he said it did not matter whether it was true or not, that
the half-breeds intended to show the Government that they were
not afraid to fight 500; either he or the others told me that, that
was said. He went on about the half-breeds' grievances and he said
that he had suffered himself, that he had formerly been kicked
out of the country fifteen years ago and kicked out of the House.
He said a great deal against Sir John and the other members of
the Government, particularly against Sir John. He said that he
intended to bring Sir John to his feet, and talked a great deal of
bosh. This was all in the dark, others were in the room, several
half-breeds.

Q. He was talking as well of his own grievances? A. Yes, principally.
All he said about the half-breeds' grievances was that they had
petitioned the Government, and then he went on with a long
string of his own grievances about his being turned out of the
House and having to leave the country. I think he called himself
an outlaw. He said he had been outlawed.

Q. He was particularly hard on Sir John? A. Yes.

Q. Then was there anything else of importance that evening? A. Of
course I asked him to give me some decided answer. I tried to
persuade him and the people to go home. I had to be careful as I
did not know what ground I was treading on. I did not know
what moment they would make me a prisoner, and I did not want
to be made prisoner. He said he was very glad I had come, that
my coming no doubt might stop the thing at once, but he said he
could not give an answer to me as it would take some time to
consider it. He expressed a desire to communicate with the
Government and try to get the grievances redressed, through
telegraph. I said for him to have the wire repaired, as there would

be a great many false reports in Canada. I told him that he had done a foolish thing and asked him to have the wire put up at once, get the grievances redressed if possible and stop the thing in that way. I did not look upon it as serious. I thought the thing would simmer down. He said he would give no answer that day, that it would take some time to consider it.

Q. What did you do? A. I went home.

Q. In going out did you see anything? A. I saw several men, of course it was dark when I was going back. I saw several men around the village loafing about with guns. After I crossed the river, I was stopped by two men on the other side of the hill, one catching hold of my horse. They came alongside the sleigh and asked me if I was free. I said yes, and was allowed to go on. I came back to Batoche the next day to get a decided answer from the people and see what they would do, and see if I had made any impression upon them.

Q. What passed that day? A. I was taken to the council room and I was told they wanted the unconditional surrender of Fort Carlton, and I was asked if I would make that proposal to the police. I told them it was too absurd, but I said I would be happy to arrange a meeting between Major Crozier and themselves, but I would not make such a proposal myself. Before I came that morning I heard they had got some plan of sending for me, I think I was to carry a white flag ahead of those gentlemen to Carlton, and I was to make the proposal to the people in the fort. They said if the police did not surrender, they would go for them. I think the police were to carry a cross. They told me they were 800 strong; it was not Riel that said that, it was at the council that was said. Nolin was the speaker. I asked him to put up the wire and he said he could not, that it was cut below Saskatoon. The two things I asked him about was the release of the prisoners and about the wire.

Q. He refused both? A. He released Walters and his clerk.

Q. Was this the occasion when Thomas McKay was with you? A. No. After that I went to Carlton to try and arrange a meeting between them and the head of the Government (Major Crozier).

Q. The interview you are now speaking of would be on the 20th? A. On Friday, the 20th.

Q. Then you went to Carlton? A. Yes, and reported matters to Crozier.

Q. What next? A. Major Crozier said he was willing to meet Riel man
for man, with or without an escort, and at any place that suited. I
named a place. I asked the major to send a written note to Riel,
but he said it was not necessary, there was no occasion for it.
McKay went back with me.

Q. Was it the next morning that you went? A. We started from
Carlton about one o'clock in the morning. We went to Duck
Lake. I had arranged with the council to have two messengers
ready so that I would not have to go back to Batoche again, and
they would carry the reply of the major. And I found the two
Arcands waiting to get the reply from Carlton.

Q. Did you send it on by them? A. No, I did not say anything at all
about it.

Q. So the interview of the morning of the 21st was arranged, and so
you and Mr McKay went forward? A. Yes, we went over to
Batoche.

Q. Whom did you see there? A. A great many people.

Q. Speaking of the actions of the prisoner, or the words of the
prisoner? Tell us what took place? A. On this occasion he was
very much excited, and he did not like my bringing over Mr
McKay.

Q. What did he say? A. McKay had some conversation with these
people here in my house, and these two men and some other men
were brought up as witnesses against McKay, that he was a
traitor. And they talked pretty roughly to him. Mr Riel talked
very roughly to him, and said that the Government and the
Hudson Bay Company were the two curses of the country, and
that he, McKay, was hand and glove with the Hudson Bay
Company.

Q. That was spoken to McKay? A. Yes, and he said if he was not
careful his blood would be the first blood shed on this occasion. I
told them I had asked McKay to come as my friend. I told the
people he was one of Her Majesty's soldiers, and I told them it
was rather rough for them to speak of Mr McKay in that way.
Riel calmed down and said if Mr McKay came as your friend he is
entitled to the same protection that you are, but that is the only
thing that saves him.

Q. Then what else took place? A. After that, I asked Riel if we
would come to the council chamber up stairs. We went up there

and I told him the message I had from Major Crozier, that he would meet him man and man at a certain place, alone or with an escort, and he got very much excited and said he would not take Major Crozier's word of honor, that I ought to have brought the thing in writing, and he asked me to put it in writing. I objected at first, but finally I did put it in writing to the effect that Major Crozier would meet either Riel or some one sent for Riel's people if he gave him time.

Q. You made a memorandum of it and signed it? A.,Yes, to his dictation.

Q. Then what else? A. He seemed very much excited, and he said something about a war of extermination unless he could come to terms with the Government, and he blackguarded the Government a great deal, and he blackguarded the members of the Government, and he said their word was not worth that (indicating with his thumb). That it was no good. I offered to give myself as a hostage, that Major Crozier's word was perfectly good. He said I had nothing to risk and he refused to take it. In fact, he refused to meet Crozier, but he named two people who would meet him.

Q. Two who would meet him? A. Yes. Of course I carried this message back to Carlton.

Q. Is that about all that took place on that occasion? A. Yes.

Q. Did you see many people around the council house? A. I saw the whole of the population. I saw a great many people there. I considered the whole settlement was there.

Q. Did you see anybody armed? A. Yes, they were all more or less armed.

Q. Any Indians? A. No, I did not see any Indians there, but I met Indians coming down.

Q. Did you go back to Fort Carlton? A. I went back to Duck Lake and then to Fort Carlton with Mr McKay.

Q. Then did any further meeting take place? A. I finished the thing there. I told Major Crozier what they had decided upon.

Q. What did you next do? A. I came back to Duck Lake.

Q. What was the next you knew of it? A. I met two people who had been named by the council to hold a meeting. I did not go to the meeting. I only arranged for the meeting. It was Capt. Moore who went. I met these two people coming and told them to get there as soon as possible, that it was getting dark, and that they should go as soon as possible, and they went on and had their meeting and came back about nine o'clock, and I had some conversation with Nolin then. I advised him to escape. He had been a prisoner before, and he told me he had been forced into the thing and that he had been condemned to be shot. I told Nolin to tell Riel and the people that I had finished with them, and that they must now consider I would have nothing more to do with them, that I had done what I could to quiet them down.

Q. Then was there any formal proceeding, or any attempt at formality on the occasion of Mr McKay and yourself being at the council house? A. I don't exactly understand you.

Q. It is said Garnot was secretary, and that the council was called together; what do you know about that? A. There was a general hurrah given, and people went up to the council table. There was a speaker and a secretary.

Q. Was anyone called upon to act as secretary? A. Garnot was secretary.

Q. Philip Garnot? A. Yes, at that time.

Q. Where were you on the occasion of the Duck Lake trouble? A. I was with the troops.

Q. On the occasion of that fight? A. I was advancing on to Duck Lake with the police and volunteers.

Q. And were you in the fight? A. Yes, I was in the fight.

Q. And the result was that you did not get to Duck Lake? A. No, we had to retreat.

Q. You were not able to take possession of your store? A. We did not get to the store, we were stopped.

Q. By reason of the armed force? A. Yes.

Q. I believe your store was raided afterwards? A. Everything I had was taken away, and the place was burnt down. They made that place their headquarters for two weeks, and they cleaned my store out entirely.

THOMAS E. JACKSON sworn:
Examined by MR OSLER:

Q. Do you live at Prince Albert, Mr Jackson? A. I do.

Q. You are a druggist? A. I am.

Q. You have been there for some years? A. Some six years.

Q. Your brother, William Henry Jackson, I believe, was one of the prisoners? A. He was.

Q. And he had been in the company of Riel immediately prior to these troubles and during the troubles? A. For some time previous to them.

Q. You had known of the movement and the agitation that was in the country? A. Oh, yes, and I sympathised with it.

Q. Did you know of the prisoner being in the country? A. Yes, I knew of his coming to the country. I heard he was coming shortly before he came back.

Q. You knew of him after he came to the country? A. Yes.

Q. I believe you have seen him write? A. Yes.

Q. Do you know his handwriting? A. I know his handwriting.

Q. You went over, I believe, on an occasion shortly after the Duck Lake fight for the bodies of those who were slain? A. I did. I was one of those who went.

Q. How many days after? A. Three days after. It was the Sunday after the fight.

Q. How did you come to go? Under what circumstances did you take that journey? A. Mr Sanderson, who had been a prisoner of Riel, was released by him to carry a message to Major Crozier to remove the dead bodies, and Crozier had taken him prisoner at Carlton, and then took him to Prince Albert. I interviewed Sanderson, and asked him about my brother, and he told me he was insane.

Q. You were inquiring about your brother from Sanderson? A. Yes.

Q. It was arranged Sanderson should go? A. Yes, Sanderson said he was going and I offered to go with him.

Q. And who else went with you? A. William Drain.

Q. You started, I think, on the 31st? A. Sunday the 29th, the Sunday after the fight.

Q. You went to Duck Lake? A. Yes.

Q. Did you see the prisoner there? A. I did.

Q. What passed between you? A. General conversation.

Q. Give us the material part of it? A. He spoke of having taken up arms, that they had done it in self-defence; and in talking about the Duck Lake fight he said he had gone there in person, that after Major Crozier had fired the first volley, he replied and urged his men to fire, first, in the name of God the Father; secondly, in the name of God the Son; and thirdly, in the name of God the Holy Ghost; and repeated his commands in that manner throughout the battle.

Q. That is what he told you about the engagement? A. Yes.

Q. What else did he say? A. He spoke of the people in the town and of the settlers generally. He said he had no desire to molest them, that this quarrel was with the Government and the police and the Hudson Bay Company. He wished the settlers to hold aloof from taking arms in opposition to him, and he said if they held aloof he would prevent the Indians from joining them. If they kept aloof he was to oppose the police himself.

Q. Did he ask you to do anything in reference to that? A. He gave me a letter to the people generally, stating so.

Q. What have you done with that letter? A. I have destroyed it.

Q. It is not now in existence? A. No.

Q. Did you read the letter? A. Yes.

Q. What was in it? What was the purport of it? A. To the effect that if the people would hold aloof and remain neutral, that he would not bring in the Indians, and also to the effect that the last part of it, that if they did hold aloof he believed they would celebrate the 24th of May; but that if they did not, the Indians would come in, and parties from across the boundary, and the result would be they would celebrate the 4th of July, or something like that.

Q. What was he going to do with Prince Albert? A. He said he would give them a week to decide whether they would accept his terms or not.

Q. And in the event of their not accepting his terms? A. Then he would take the place. He said Prince Albert was the key of the position, and that he must attack it. He said that if the settlers did not stay at home, but kept in town with the police, he would attack them all.

Q. Whom did you arrange with to get the bodies of the slain? A. We requested first some assistance from him, that some of the half-breeds would go with us to remove them, but there was some discussion about it, and when they learned Major Crozier was suspicious of them, he refused assistance, and the French half-breeds also he refused to let go. In fact, I believe the suggestion came through some of them in the first place, and in consequence we had to go and remove them ourselves.

Q. Who was in charge there? Who were you taking orders from at Duck Lake? A. Mr Riel.

Q. Who was giving orders? A. Riel.

Q. Anybody else? A. Nobody else.

Q. Then you went to get the bodies? A. Yes.

Q. I believe he showed you the bodies that had been slain on their side? A. Yes, he did, just as we were leaving.

Q. Then you made another visit within the rebel lines? A. Yes, about a week later.

Q. What was the occasion of that visit? A. I heard from a half-breed named Toussant Lussier that Albert Monkman and fifteen men were in charge of the prisoners at Fort Carlton and that my brother was with them and they left them across the south branch to attack General Middleton, and I thought it would be a good opportunity to get my brother away. I knew Monkman and I thought he would give him up. I obtained a pass from Irvine and went after my brother.

Q. What did you find when you got there? A. I went to Carlton first and then to Duck Lake. I found Carlton was burned down and I found Duck Lake in ashes. I went to Batoche and arrived there on the Tuesday after.

Q. What is the date? A. About the 1st of April — no, about the 4th of April probably.

Q. You reached Batoche when? A. That was the time, on the Tuesday.

Q. When had you left Prince Albert? A. On the Saturday.

Q. That was the 4th of April? A. I reached Batoche on the 4th April, on the Tuesday following.

Q. That would be the 7th of April? A. Yes, I suppose so.

Q. Then did you see the prisoner after you got there? A. Yes, I did.

Q. Had you any conversation with him? A. I had.

Q. This was where? A. On the south side of the river.

Q. The day you got there was the day of the fight? A. The day I got there.

Q. You had a talk with him about your brother? A. Yes.

Q. Did he say what was the matter with your brother? A. He said he was sick; he said his mind was affected. He said it was a judgment on him for opposing him.

Q. He seemed to know his mind was affected? A. Oh yes.

Q. Did you find his mind was affected? A. I did.

Q. How were they considering him, as a sane or insane man?
A. Allowing him his own way, but they had a guard over him.

Q. Did Riel speak as to what was best to do with him or what they were doing with him? A. Yes, he thought he would improve there, but I applied for permission to get him away. Riel said he was getting along very nicely there and that he would recover.

Q. He did not let you take him away? A. No, he refused to do so.

Q. Then did you make any formal application to get him away? A. I did to the council.

Q. And it was refused, I believe? A. Yes, it was refused.

Q. What kept you in the camp? A. They refused to let me go or my brother either.

Q. Giving any reason? A. Yes, I heard a discussion. I was upstairs in the council room and I had spoken to Albert Monkman to speak in my favor and I heard them discussing the matter. Of course they spoke in French and I did not understand, but Monkman was speaking in Cree. Riel came down to the room and commenced to eat, and while he was eating Monkman kept on talking, and he rushed up stairs and attacked Monkman and in the course of his remarks he accused him of not doing his duty with the English half-breeds, that he had not brought them up with the twenty men he had sent for them. Monkman defended himself and there was a discussion about. Monkman said the reason he did not bring them was because one man said he would go if another would, and Riel told him he had given him these twenty armed men to bring the leading men of the English half-breeds by force.

Q. And what Riel was complaining about was that the orders had not been obeyed? A. Yes.

Q. And Monkman was excusing himself? A. Yes.

Q. Did you hear any discussion after you arrived there as to what they should do, as to any places that should be attacked? A. They talked about attacking Prince Albert, but I believe they were waiting for the Indians to join them in greater numbers.

Q. Had they Indians there? A. They had Indians there.

Q. At this time, about the 8th of April, could you form any idea as to the number of men under arms? A. I could not say. I was told, when I first arrived there, they had 1,800, but I did not believe it.

They said they were in houses near by. Afterwards I was told by English half-breeds that there was only about 700.

Q. Then, do you remember an occasion of a false alarm – do you remember anything being done by Riel on that occasion? A. On one occasion I remember he rushed to the church and brought down the crucifix, and ran around among the houses calling out the men, and insisting all should come, and I saw him go out and choose the ground upon which to defend themselves, expecting an attack from the Humboldt trail.

Q. He went out and arranged the ground and warned the men? A. Yes, and urged them all to fight, and made preparations for the defence.

Q. Did he ask you to do anything for him? A. Yes; the first night I was there he intimated he would like me to write some letters to the papers, and place a good construction on his acts.

Q. Wanting you to write to the eastern papers? A. Yes; to place a favorable construction on his action in taking up arms.

Q. Do you remember anything, any particular matter he wanted inserted? A. I refused to do so at first, because he had not allowed me my liberty and had taken my brother away. In my application to the council I said unless they showed me some consideration they could not expect any consideration from me in writing letters. After the Fish Creek fight I thought the thing was going to last all summer, and commenced to write for him.

Q. Then, do you remember Riel's asking you to write any particular matter with reference to himself? A. Yes. He claimed that he had applied to the Government for an indemnity through D.H. Macdonald, and in reply the Government had made use of some expressions.

Q. What indemnity had he applied for through Macdonald? A. For $35,000.

Q. For what? A. For supposed losses through being outlawed and his property being confiscated.

Q. That was the money he wanted from the Dominion Government? A. Yes.

Q. He did not tell you how he made up the account? A. No. He claimed in all his claim against the Dominion Government amounted to $100,000.

Q. Did you know from him anything as to his personal motives in taking up arms? A. Yes. He disclosed his personal motives to me on this occasion. He became very much excited and angry, and attacked the English and the English constitution, and exhibited the greatest hatred for the English, and he showed his motive was one of revenge more than anything else.

Q. Revenge for what? A. For his supposed ill-treatment, his property being confiscated and he being outlawed.

Q. Did you hear anything about the half-breed struggle? A. Yes, he spoke of their grievances.

Q. In his communications with you whose grievances were the most prominent? A. I think his own particular troubles were the most prominent. Of course, he spoke of the half-breed troubles.

Q. Were you put in close confinement at any time? A. Shortly after this outburst he placed me in confinement with my brother.

Q. Had you refused to write for him in this way? A. Yes; and it was in reference to discussing that that he became excited, and it was shortly after that he placed me in close confinement.

Q. You were kept with the other prisoners? A. No, I was kept by myself with my brother. They would not allow me to communicate with the other prisoners.

Q. When you were placed in close confinement had you any conversation with him? A. He came in on one occasion and accused me of trying to incite an English half-breed named Bruce to desert. He said I had been seen speaking with him, and if he could prove I had been inciting him it would go hard with me.

Q. Any other interview with him while you were in close confinement? A. Not just then. Shortly after Middleton approached Batoche he placed us in the cellar; in the cellar of George Fisher's house. The first day he took me up to attend the wounded, in case there should be any wounded, and he had some talk then in regard to the wounded, and he asked me if I would attend to them as well as if nothing had happened between us.

Q. Did you attend to the wounded? A. No; they suspected I was going to desert and they put me back in the cellar that night.

Q. Did anything material happen until the 12th of May? A. No.

Q. What happened then? A. On the 12th of May a half-breed opened the cellar and called out and said Riel was wounded. I came up to the council room, and presently Riel entered with Astley, and as soon as he came in he told us Middleton was approaching and if he massacred the families he would massacre my brother and the rest of the prisoners, and he wished to send both of us with messages to Middleton.

Q. Were you to deliver the message? A. I was.

Q. Did you see Riel write the message? A. I did.

Q. Is this the message produced? A. I believe that is the message.

Q. By whom was it written? A. Written by Riel. (The message alluded to is exhibit 2.)

Q. Do you remember what you did with this message? A. I believe I delivered it to General Middleton.

Q. You don't know? A. I don't remember the fact, but I believe I did.

Q. With that message you left the camp? A. I did.

Q. The rebel camp? A. Yes.

Q. And I believe you did not go back? A. I did not go back. I did not go directly to Middleton because he changed his mind at the last.

Q. Who changed his mind? A. Riel. He took us down about a mile and a-half and he ordered me to go to Lepine's house and wave a flag in front of it.

Q. Just to go back for a moment – did you ever see the prisoner armed? A. I did on one occasion.

Q. When was that occasion? A. It was some time after the Fish Creek fight.

Q. Who was in charge at Batoche? A. Riel.

Q. Who instructed the movements of the armed men? A. Well, Gabriel Dumont instructed them immediately, but Riel was over him.

Q. Do you remember what he did on the occasion of the Fish Creek fight? A. He went out with 180 men the night before and re-turned with 20, thinking there might be an attack on Batoche from Prince Albert or Humboldt or from the other side of the river, as he knew General Middleton's forces were divided.

Q. You said you knew the hand-writing of the prisoner? A. Yes.

Q. Look at this document dated St Anthony, 21st March 1885. In whose hand-writing is that? A. Louis Riel's. (Document put in, exhibit 5.)

Q. Is all this writing on the 3rd page his? A. Yes, it is all his writing.

Q. These signatures are in Garnot's writing? A. Yes, they seem to be Garnot's.

Q. In whose hand-writing is this document? A. Louis Riel's. (Document put in, exhibit 6.)

Q. Is this paper in the writing of Louis Riel? A. Yes, that is his writing. (Document put in, exhibit 7.)

Q. Are the two papers attached here in Riel's hand-writing? A. Yes. (Put in, exhibit 8.)

Q. Is this document in Riel's hand-writing? A. It is. (Put in, exhibit 9.)

Q. Perhaps you can tell me the meaning of the word 'exovede'? A. It means one of the flock.

Q. Is this letter in the hand-writing of Riel? A. It is, with the exception of a piece of back-hand which appears to be in Garnot's writing. (Document put in, exhibit 10.)

Q. In whose hand-writing is this? A. Riel's. (Exhibit 11.)

Q. Is exhibit 12 in Riel's writing? A. Yes.

Q. Exhibit 13 and exhibit 14 are both in Riel's hand-writing? A. Yes, it is all Riel's.

Q. Are these five sheets comprising exhibit 15 in Riel's writing? A. They are all in the hand-writing of the prisoner.

Q. Exhibit 16 is in the hand-writing of the prisoner? A. Yes.

Q. And exhibit 17 is in his hand-writing? A. Yes.

Q. Exhibit 18. Is this document in his hand-writing? A. It is, all but the last signatures.

Q. Exhibit 19. Is that in the hand-writing of Riel? A. Yes.

Q. Is it Riel's signature that is to this document? A. Yes. (Put in, exhibit 20.)

Q. The body of the writing, is that Riel's? A. No.

Q. But the signature is? A. Yes.

Examined by MR FITZPATRICK:

Q. You know nothing more of the documents that have been shown you, except that you know they are in the hand-writing of Riel? A. That is all I know.

Q. You don't know if they ever left Riel's possession or not? A. I don't.

Q. You said, at the beginning of your deposition, that you were aware of a certain amount of agitation going on in the Saskatchewan district during last autumn and fall? A. I did.

Q. Will you explain the nature of that agitation? A. That agitation
was for provincial rights principally, also for half-breed claims,
and also against duties and such things as that. We felt the duties
onerous.

Q. A purely political agitation? A. Yes.

Q. You were in sympathy with the agitation? A. Yes.

Q. You were aware Riel was brought into the country for the purpose of taking part in the agitation? A. He was brought to this
country on account of his supposed knowledge of the Manitoba
Treaty.

Q. The people of the Saskatchewan district were of opinion Riel
could be useful to them in connection with the agitation?
A. Well, he was brought in principally by the half-breeds. The
Canadians knew nothing about it till he was very nearly here.

Q. Almost the whole of the people in that district had joined together for the purpose of this agitation? A. They had.

Q. That agitation had been going on for a considerable length of
time? A. For some time.

Q. Can you say for about how long? A. Five or six years or longer.

Q. Did you attend any meetings held by Riel? A. I attended the
meeting in Prince Albert.

Q. You were present during that meeting? A. During the greater part
of it.

Q. You heard what Riel said? A. I did.

Q. What date was that meeting held? A. I could not say exactly,
some time in June or July.

Q. At his first arrival? A. Yes.

Q. He stated he wished the movement to be entirely a constitutional
movement? A. Purely a constitutional movement. He said if they
could not get what they agitated for in five years to agitate for
five years more, that constitutional agitation would get what they
wanted.

Q. You knew he continued assisting in the agitation up to the time
of the difficulty in March? A. He was there as a sort of half-breed
adviser principally. He was not a member of the committee, but
he was there in the capacity of half-breed adviser.

Q. Did you at any time hear that he wished to resort to any means
other than constitutional up to the – March? A. Nothing.

Q. You being an active participator would naturally have heard of any such intention if it had existed? A. Certainly.

Q. There was no such movement up to that time? A. No.

Q. After the 1st of March when did you first see Riel? A. When I went to Duck Lake.

Q. When had you seen him previous to that time? A. Sometime in January he was in the town.

Q. Had you conversation with him then? A. I had.

Q. Did you speak to him about the movement? A. I daresay I did, but I cannot remember.

Q. Did he at that time say anything to you that would lead you to believe he intended to do anything that was not a constitutional agitation? A. Nothing of the kind. He never referred to anything that was not a constitutional agitation.

Q. At the discussions you had had with him previous to March last it always appeared to you that the ordinary means adopted by the settlers were adopted by him? A. Certainly.

Q. When you saw him at Duck Lake you spoke to him about your brother and he told you your brother had become insane? A. He did.

Q. He told you he had become insane because he had opposed Riel, and that he was punished by God for his opposition to Riel? A. That is what he said.

Q. You never heard such a remark by Riel previous to that time in any of your other conversations with him? A. No.

Q. Did it strike you as a peculiar remark? A. No, I don't think so.

Q. You thought it was quite natural such a thing should occur? A. I didn't agree with it, but I thought it was a very nice explanation on his part to make.

Q. He told you at that time the priests were entirely opposed to him and the movement and were entirely opposed to the interests of the North-West settlement? A. No, but he said they were opposed to him.

Q. He gave you then to understand the priests were entirely wrong and he was entirely right? A. Certainly.

Q. In fact they did not know anything they were talking about and he knew it all? A. He said they were working only for their own interests.

Q. Did he explain to you what his intentions were as to the division
of the territories, what he intended doing when he succeeded in
chasing the Canadians out of the country? A. Sometimes, probably when I was a prisoner I heard him talk of dividing the
country in sevenths or giving a seventh of the proceeds to assist
the Poles; a seventh to the half-breeds and a seventh to the
Indians.

Q. Some more to the Hungarians? A. Yes, and so on.

Q. You said when you were Riel's prisoner, that it was after the 17th
and 18th of March you heard him discussing the future division
which he intended making of the territories if he got rid of the
Canadians? A. Something to that effect, but I cannot remember
exactly what it was.

Q. You heard him talking of dividing the country into different
parts? A. I understood it was one-seventh of the proceeds of the
sale of land and 'takes' would be given to these different people.

Q. Did he then say he expected any assistance from these people?
A. No, it seemed to be a scheme of immigration more than
anything else.

Q. His plan as he then unfolded it — did it appear in conformity with
the plans you had heard him discussing at the public meetings at
which you had assisted? A. Oh, no, altogether different.

Q. Would you look at this document called the foreign policy document and say if you can see anything on it which would bear out
that intention to divide up the country (witness looks at exhibit
15)? A. Yes.

Q. Do you recognize the hand-writing as that of Louis Riel? A. It is
scribbled so that it is difficult to say.

Q. What is on the other side of the sheet is certainly in his hand-
writing? A. Yes, it certainly is.

Q. And is the ink on the other side not the same as that? A. I think
it is.

Q. And don't you think the hand-writing is also the same? A. I could
not say.

Q. To the best of your knowledge does it not represent Riel's hand-
writing? A. I think it is.

Q. Riel explained to you what was meant by the word 'exovede'?
A. He did.

Q. That it was meant to convey that he was simply one of the flock? A. Yes.

Q. That he had no independent authority but simply acted as one of the others? A. Yes, it was simply an affectation of humility.

Q. You are aware all the documents signed by him as far as you know bore the word 'exovede'? A. The most of them.

Q. You had several conversations with Riel after the conversion of your brother, on religious matters? A. After I was taken prisoner, but nothing much on religious matters. He used to talk about his new religion, about leaving the errors of the church of Rome out and adopting a more liberal plan.

Q. He explained to you his new religion? A. He explained it as a new liberal religion, he claimed the Pope had no rights in this country.

Q. Did he condescend to inform you as to the person in whom his authority should be vested? A. No.

Q. You believed from him there was some person in this country who would probably take the position of Pope in this country? A. I think very likely he intended himself to take the position, that the Pope was in his way.

Q. This took place after you were made a prisoner — this conversation about the new religion? A. I think so, and he also spoke about it at Duck Lake.

Q. All the conversations you had with him in reference to this political movement never in any way referred to this new religion? A. No; he spoke of religion but merely as ordinary men do.

Q. The first time you heard of this new religion and these new theories of religious questions was after the rebellion had begun? A. Yes.

GENERAL FREDERICK MIDDLETON sworn
Examined by MR ROBINSON:

Q. You are a major-general in Her Majesty's service? A. I am.

Q. What position do you hold in Canada? A. I am commanding the home militia force.

Q. Where do you reside? A. Ottawa.

Q. Were you called upon for service in these territories at any time? A. I was.

Q. When? A. I think it was on the 23rd of March. I was sent for on
the 23rd of March by Mr Caron and told I should have to leave at
once for the North-West.

Q. Mr Caron is Minister of Militia? A. Yes.

Q. What reason was given you? A. He told me they had news which
was of a very bad character; that a rising might take place and I
was to go at once, and he asked me when I could go.

Q. When did you start? A. About two hours afterwards.

Q. What did you do first? A. I went straight to Winnipeg. On the
way to Winnipeg, I think it was on the train, I heard of the Duck
Lake battle. When I got to Winnipeg I found the 90th was almost
ready to march, that a small detachment had been sent to
Qu'Appelle and that the Winnipeg battery was ready. And then I
heard more news about Colonel Irvine afraid to go to Batoche as
it was in the hands of the half-breeds, and I heard a confirmation
of the Duck Lake affair. I went to the town hall and inspected
the 90th, and that evening I went on the train with the 90th and
went straight to Qu'Appelle without stopping.

Q. How long did you remain at Qu'Appelle? A. I cannot exactly
remember. I was there waiting for the formation of the
commissariat.

Q. You left Qu'Appelle and proceeded where? A. To Fort
Qu'Appelle.

Q. And from that you went to Fish Creek? A. Yes.

Q. That was the first occasion on which you met the opposing
rebels? A. Yes.

Q. What force was under your command when you got to Fish
Creek? A. When I got to Fish Creek I had the 90th. I had previously divided my forces and put half of them on the other side
of the river. I had under my immediate command the 90th, the
so-called 'A' Battery with two guns, Boulton's scouts, and I think
that was all.

Q. How many in all? A. On paper there would be about 420 or 450.

Q. That was your force at Fish Creek? A. Yes; as far as I can
remember.

Q. And how many were lost there on your side? A. I think we
had — well I forget the exact number. We lost nine or ten killed
and forty wounded.

Q. That was on the 24th of April? A. The 24th of April.

Q. You remained there for some short time? A. Until I could get rid
of the wounded. We had a large number of wounded and I could
not leave them there. I hadn't sufficient force to leave to protect
them and I was obliged to wait, and I also wanted oats, but the
principal thing was to get rid of the wounded.

Q. Then you proceeded to Batoche? A. Yes.

Q. When did you arrive before Batoche? A. About nine miles from
Batoche I struck the trail from Batoche on the 8th, and on the
morning of the 9th marched straight on to Batoche, leaving my
camp standing.

Q. And when did the engagement begin? A. On the 9th, the instant
we got there.

Q. Do you mean you were fired on almost on your getting there?
A. On our arrival, we came on the top of the plateau and we saw
a large assembly of men, and we opened fire there.

Q. That was the beginning of the engagement? A. Yes.

Q. The engagement continued till the 12th? A. Yes.

Q. When Batoche was taken? A. When Batoche was taken.

Q. I believe you had some negotiations on the 12th? A. Yes. On the
12th I had moved out to the extreme left of the enemy. I moved
to the right in order to draw their attention away, and I left
orders with my second in command, that while I was away, as
soon as he heard firing, he was to retake the old position we had
the previous days, and as I drew the enemy off on the right, he
was to press on on the left. I went off with the cavalry and guns
so as to make as much show as possible, and I kept the enemy
engaged some little time. In the middle of our engagement there,
which was quite at long bowls, I saw a man galloping across the
plains, from the direction of the enemy, with a flag. He came
closer, and it turned out to be Mr Astley. He handed me a letter.
He said: 'I am one of the prisoners. I have been sent by Riel to
communicate with you, and I have brought you this letter.'

Q. Is this the letter he brought you? A. Yes, that is the same letter.
(Letter put in Exhibit 21.) This is my answer on the back of it.

Q. Then what did you do with this letter? A. I took it from Mr
Astley and wrote my answer, and gave it to Mr Astley, who went
away with it.

Q. What took place next? A. The next thing was a man on foot came up.

Q. Do you know who he was? A. Yes, he was Mr Jackson, a brother of the man who was a prisoner. He came up with another document. He had exactly the same story to tell, that he had been sent by Riel, only he was confused. He said he had been told to stand in front of a house with a white flag, and eventually he said he found that was a stupid work, and he came on to me.

Q. Is this the document he brought (Exhibit 22)? A. Yes, to the best of my belief it is. It is an exact copy of it, because it was a little different from the wording of the other one.

Q. Then what did you do in answer to that? A. I took no particular notice of it, as I had already sent an answer back. I looked upon this simply as a copy, and I told Jackson I had sent an answer back by Astley.

Q. How long was it between the time you received the two communications? A. I should say about a quarter of an hour.

Q. And what took place next? A. As soon as that was over, I did what I principally wanted – I had drawn the fire of the enemy. Mr Astley said: 'I think, sir, Mr Riel is in a very great state of excitement, and I should not wonder if he would surrender.' I gave orders, and retired my whole force by degrees and fell back upon my camp.

Q. And what took place next? A. When I arrived at the camp, I was very much put out and annoyed to find my orders had been misunderstood, and that instead of their having taken advantage of my feint and having occupied the rifle pits, they were all quietly in camp.

Q. Did you receive any further communications? A. As soon as I found this, I am afraid I used some pretty strong language. The end of it was we attacked. The men were ordered down. I went down myself to the front to see if there was any of the enemy in the entrenchment. I soon got tangible proof of it. The force that had their dinner were brought up, and we began gradually to force our way on. In the middle of that, when we got the artillery down, Mr Astley came again galloping, having run the gauntlet of both forces. He ran between them, and came with a flag and produced another letter from Riel.

Q. Is this the one he brought you that time? (Producing.) A. Yes,
   that is the same one.

Q. Is this the envelope it came in? A. Yes. (Exhibits 3 and 4.) I could
   not hear what Astley was saying. I opened the envelope and
   handed it to him. I could not hear what he said. I tried to stop
   the guns firing to hear it but that was hopeless. At last he handed
   me the envelope and pointed to it and I read what was on the
   outside of the envelope, and he said, after Mr Riel had closed the
   letter, he got it back and wrote on it with an indelible pencil, and
   he said you better read what that was.

Q. Then what took place? A. Astley said he had better go back with
   an answer, and I said no, there was no necessity. He said the
   prisoners might be massacred. I said there was no fear of that,
   that we would be there in half a minute. I went on and forced my
   way, brought the 90th, and dismounted the troops and gradually
   pushed on.

Q. And then the place was carried? A. Then the place was carried.
   By a series of rushes we forced our way on and the enemy dispersed altogether, but they still kept up a fire in the distance, but
   virtually all attempt at defence had ceased with the exception of
   a few stray shots now and then.

Q. Astley didn't return? A. No, he went down with us to the
   plateau.

Q. How many of your force was killed on that occasion? A. On that
   occasion there was six killed, I think, and twelve or thirteen
   wounded.

Q. That, practically, was the end of the campaign so far as your
   campaign was concerned? A. Practically, it was.

Q. How long after that was it before the prisoner was brought to
   you? A. That was the 12th. We halted the 13th and marched on
   the 14th, and I think it was on the 15th. I had heard he was on
   that side of the river and I marched as soon as I could, intending
   to go to Lepine's Crossing. On the way I heard of Riel and
   Dumont having been seen, and instead of going to Lepine's I
   turned and halted at Garriépy's crossing and sent out all the
   scouts I could spare with directions to search the woods as far as
   Batoche. On the 15th Riel was brought in by two scouts, Hourie
   and Armstrong, and brought to my tent, and when he entered the
   tent he produced a paper which I had sent to him, saying if he

surrendered I would protect him until his case was decided by the
Canadian Government.

Q. What was done with him when he was first brought in? A. He was
brought into my tent. Very few knew he was there. I kept him in
my tent all day. I had another tent pitched alongside and he was
put in that tent under charge of Captain Young with two sentries
with loaded arms and during that night Captain Young slept in
the tent.

Q. Had you conversation with the prisoner while he was there?
A. Yes, during the first day he was there I had conversation with
him.

Q. Did you invite any conversation from him? A. I daresay I asked
him one or two questions. He talked very freely to me.

Q. And did he make any representations as to his share in the
matter? A. No, I cannot hardly remember. I was writing at the
time and then I stopped writing and talked to Riel. The only one
thing I can remember particularly as to his share in the matter
was as I was leaving the tent. He said: 'General, I have been thinking whether, if the Lord had granted me as decided a victory as he
has you, whether I should have been able to have put it to a good
use.' That was the only thing he said as I left the tent. I had
talked a good deal with him on different matters.

Q. Then he was sent down with Captain Young? A. Yes. I telegraphed down to the Government to say Mr Riel was a prisoner
and to know what was to be done with him, and eventually I was
directed to send him to Regina which I did, under the charge of
Captain Young with twelve men and a sergeant.

Examined by MR GREENSHIELDS:

Q. You were in command of the forces in the North-West Territories? A. I was.

Q. In the course of that command did you issue any general instructions or proclamations to the inhabitants? A. Well, once while I
was at Fish Creek I sent a communication by an Indian to say
that the Government had no war against the half-breeds or
Indians, that those who had been forced against their will to
join Riel would be pardoned if they left and went to their
homes and reserves, but I said no pardon should be given to
Riel or his immediate aiders and abetters. It was something to
that effect.

Q. Was that proclamation issued over your name? A. Over my signature.

Q. About what time was that? A. That must have been between the 24th of April and the 5th of May, while we were lying at Fish Creek with the wounded.

Q. During the time Riel was in your tent did you have any conversation with him regarding his religious views? A. Well, yes, he talked a good deal about his religion.

Q. Did Astley make any remark to you at the time he brought these two messages that Riel wished as a condition of his surrender that he should be recognized as the head of the church he had formed at Batoche, or remarks to that effect? A. No, I don't think so. I remember Astley saying: 'Confound him, he is always bothering about his religion, he is anxious you should know about his religion,' or something like that.

Q. This was before you saw Riel? A. Yes.

Q. What did he say to you, that is Riel, when you had this conversation with him regarding religion? A. I could hardly tell you. It was a disconnected thing. He told me that Rome was all wrong and the priests were narrow-minded people. There was nothing particularly, except the ideas of an enthusiast on some religious point.

Q. Did he say to you he was a prophet? A. No.

Q. And endowed with the Spirit of God? A. No, nothing of that sort.

Q. Under what circumstances was the paper which you sent to Riel offering him protection sent? A. I don't exactly know what you mean. That, I think, was sent when Astley told me he was anxious to surrender.

Q. It was when Astley told you he thought he was anxious to surrender that you sent him that? A. I think I sent it out by a scout. I have got a copy of it in my book. I think I sent it by a scout.

Q. Was there not a man came on behalf of Riel, after the final charge and after Batoche had been carried, and stated to you Riel would be willing to give himself up under certain conditions? A. No; I have no recollection of that.

Q. Do you recollect having seen a man named Moïse Ouellette, who was one of the councillors of the government of the Saskatchewan? A. I don't remember him particularly.

Q. Do you remember he came to your camp and stated he knew where Riel was, and that he would surrender under certain conditions, and he didn't wish to be followed by anyone? A. Nothing of the sort. If any man had come and told me that, I would have seized him immediately.

Q. That is pretty good evidence he didn't come? A. Certainly.

Q. Your recollection is you gave that little piece of paper to a scout? A. Yes; with the hope it would reach Riel in some way or another.

Q. Do you recollect the date you gave him this paper? A. No; I cannot exactly say, but it must have been between the 12th and the 15th.

GEORGE HOLMES YOUNG sworn

Examined by MR BURBIDGE:

Q. You are an officer in the Winnipeg Field Battery? A. Yes.

Q. Were you with General Middleton's force before Batoche? A. Yes.

Q. In what position were you? A. I was Brigade Major of the Infantry Brigade.

Q. You were with the forces on arrival at Batoche? A. I was.

Q. Did you hear any firing about the time you arrived? A. As we supposed we were nearing Batoche we heard heavy firing from the steamer; that was early in the morning of the 9th of May. We heard the steamer firing and whistling for assistance.

Q. You were present during the fighting on the 9th, 10th, 11th, and 12th? A. Yes.

Q. Were you with the advance that went over the rifle pits in the last charge? A. I was.

Q. You were one of the first who went into a certain house I believe? A. Yes, sir.

Q. Can you describe that house? A. The house known as their council chamber.

Q. What did you find there? A. In the upstairs I found a large number of papers and books.

Q. Where did you find them? A. On the table where they had left them, fastened to the wall in paper clips and some in tin boxes and some in a small leather reticule; they were generally through the room in places of safety according to their importance.

Q. What did you do with them? A. I lashed the books and papers together with a rope and gave them to an artillery sergeant to take to Colonel Jarvis. Other papers were found besides those I found in the council chamber, and as they turned up I took possesion of them.

Q. Did you examine those papers? A. I did.

Q. Do you recognize that (5) as one of the papers? A. I do.

Q. Do you recognize that as one of the papers you found (6)? A. I do.

Q. Do you recognize that as one of the papers you found there (7)? A. I do.

Q. Do you recognize that as one of the papers (13)? A. I do.

Q. Do you recognize this as one of the papers you found there (16)? A. I do.

Q. Were you present when the prisoner was brought into camp? A. I was in the camp and saw him brought in.

Q. You were through the fight at Batoche? A. Yes.

Q. You saw the rebels fighting against the troops, against General Middleton? A. Yes.

Q. How were they armed? A. With rifles and shot guns.

Q. How many days after Batoche was Riel taken? A. The last day of Batoche was Tuesday the 12th, and the prisoner was brought into camp on the afternoon of Friday the 15th. He was brought by the scouts to the tent of the general and was held there for questioning.

Q. Was he afterwards put under your charge? A. I was sent for by the general, as I had known the prisoner in the rebellion of '69 and '70, to see if I would recognize him. I reported that there was no mistake as to his identity. About half-past nine word was sent that the general wanted me, and I went to the tent and the general told me that he wanted me to take charge of the prisoner and be answerable for his safe keeping. I had charge of him till I delivered him to Captain Dean on the 23rd of May.

Q. Had you frequent conversations with him during that time? A. Constantly.

Q. Did he speak freely and voluntarily with you? A. Yes, he talked all the time.

Q. You did not order him to make any statements to you? A. None at all.

Q. Did he speak at all in regard to the Indians he expected to act
with him. How many they were –

MR FITZPATRICK: I raise the formal objection to this part of the
evidence. This was a statement made by this man to this person who
was in charge of him.

HIS HONOR: What is your objection?

MR FITZPATRICK: A statement made by a prisoner when in custody to the person in charge of him is not admissible in evidence.

By MR BURBIDGE:

Q. Did you hold out any inducement to him to make a statement to
you? A. No.

Q. His statements were voluntary entirely? A. Yes.

Q. Did you offer any inducements or make any promises of any
kind? A. No.

MR FITZPATRICK: It is not admissible in evidence unless he made
it voluntarily.

By MR BURBIDGE:

Q. What did he say about the Indians? A. On Saturday the general
wished to know as to the movements of some bands who intended to join the rebel forces and the prisoner spoke about a
messenger, Chi-ci-cum, whom he had sent towards Prince Albert
and Battleford to bring men with him to Batoche. He gave this
information to the general as it might be possible to divert the
Indians from their intentions.

Q. Did he say anything about sending runners out to the bands?
A. Yes, in the North-West, and also towards Cypress Hills.

Q. Did he speak to you of any other aid he expected to receive?
A. I was instructed to speak about possible aid from Irish sym-
pathisers in the United States.

MR FITZPATRICK: Were you instructed to speak to him about
that? A. Yes.

MR FITZPATRICK: Then I object.

MR BURBIDGE: We will not say anything about that.

Q. Did he speak about the battles? A. About Duck Lake.

Q. What did he say about that? A. We had a conversation as to the
way it occurred. He insisted that Major Crozier fired first. After
the first fire he said that he had instructed his men to fire; he gave
theree commands to fire as he explained it. The first, as I remember, it was 'In the name of God who made us, reply to that.' They

fired and Crozier's men replied, and then he said 'In the name of God the Son who saves us, reply to that,' and the third was 'In the name of the Holy Ghost who sanctifies us, reply to that.' He spoke also on the circumstance that after Gabriel was wounded, a scalp wound, I think, he continued to load the guns of the men till stopped by the flow of blood and when he could not do that any longer he said 'My poor children what will you do, I can't help you any longer.' We spoke of Batoche after his capture, in reference to the death of an old man I saw lying dead on the face of the ravine, Donald Ross, I think was his name. He told me that as he was dying he called out for his relatives and children to come and see him before he died.

Q. Did he say anything about the disposal of his forces at the fight? A. We were conversing about his different lines of defences. He had three as I understood, a double line of rifle pits and a lower line again. He explained how the scouts were to fall back when pressed, that there were to be three in each pit. He said that he and Gabriel Dumont differed, that Gabriel's opinion was that the rebel right was the key of the position and should be defended. The prisoner's opinion was that the whole line should be especially defended. The matter was decided in council in favor of his view.

Q. Did he speak about the fighting qualities of the Indians? A. He said in the early part the movement was all carried on by the half-breeds, but when it came to fighting the Indians were the bravest of his soldiers. He was aware of the death of French, and of many other instances of the fight. I was positive from the instances he talked about he must have been opposite to me at different times.

Q. This conversation took place when he was under your charge? A. Yes.

By MR FITZPATRICK:

Q. The information given to you by the prisoner was intended to be given to the general, in reference to the Indians? A. Chi-ci-cum, yes.

Q. He gave the information for the purpose of enabling the general to take such measures as were necessary to prevent any difficulty with the Indians? A. He did.

Q. He gave that freely and voluntarily without pressure? A. Yes; entirely of his own accord.

Q. The fact that the prisoner gave himself up, necessarily tended to shorten the conflict, and avoid further spilling of blood? A. I thought he was captured by the scouts. I cannot express any opinion as to that. If he gave himself up it might have had that effect.
Q. You heard what the general said this morning? A. Yes.
Q. Your general impression was that Riel in every way desired to close hostilities? A. He gave us all the information that we pressed him for; sometimes he would branch out into other subjects to gain time to consider his answers.

MAJOR EDWARD W. JARVIS sworn
Examined by MR SCOTT:
Q. I understand you were in command of the Winnipeg Field Battery? A. Yes.
Q. On active service at the battle of Batoche? A. Yes.
Q. Were you there on the 12th of May? A. Yes.
Q. Through the whole four days? A. Yes.
Q. Were any papers handed to you during that time? A. Yes, towards the end of the engagement on the 12th, the last day of the engagement.
Q. By whom were they brought to you? A. By one of the staff-sergeants of the battery.
Q. Would you recognize the papers; did you examine them? A. I examined them, but not particularly. I examined them more particularly subsequently, about two days after, by order of the general.
Q. You would recognize them I suppose. Is that one of them (6)? A. Yes, that is one of them.
Q. Do you recognize that (5)? A. Yes, that is one of them.
Q. Do you recognize that (7)? A. Yes, that is one of them.
Q. Do you recognize that (13)? A. Yes, that is one too.
Q. Do you recognize this one (11)?
Q. Do you recognize this one (12)? A. That is also one of them.
Q. Do you recognize that one (16)? A. Yes, that is one of them.
Q. And this (15)? A. Yes, that was also among the papers.

MAJOR CROZIER sworn
Examined by MR OSLER:
Q. I believe you are an officer in the Mounted Police? A. Yes.

Q. At the time of this trouble commanding in the north district?
A. Yes.

Q. With headquarters at Battleford? A. Yes.

Q. Carlton was the principal outpost? A. Yes; the headquarters were at Battleford.

Q. Fort Carlton was the principal outpost? A. Yes.

Q. In command of? A. Superintendent Gagnon.

Q. I believe you arrived at Carlton on the 11th of March? A. Yes.

Q. You remained there till after the Duck Lake fight? A. Yes.

Q. What force had you immediately before the Duck Lake fight, at Carlton? A. We had fifty men on my arrival on the 11th, and I brought twenty-five men afterwards.

Q. And then? A. That was the full strength of the police.

Q. You were joined by some volunteers? A. By the Prince Albert volunteers about the 21st.

Q. I believe you heard there was trouble and you issued a proclamation? A. I did, sir.

Q. And then there was the engagement we had heard of? A. There was.

Q. Your terms, as given to your agents, were? A. Captain Moore and Thomas McKay, of Prince Albert, were the men that I sent out.

Q. With instructions? A. I told Captain Moore to tell the men whom he would meet from Riel that, as I believed many of the men had been led into this affair, I hoped they would disperse and go to their homes, and I believed that the Government would consider their case and would deal leniently with them, with the exception of the ringleaders, who would have to answer for their offence; that I would do all in my power to get an amnesty for the rank and file.

Q. Do you know how those terms were received of your own knowledge? A. I can tell what was told me.

Q. The result was that they still continued in arms? A. Yes.

Q. You organized an advance from Fort Carlton on the morning of the 26th? A. Yes; it was not an advance in the military sense of the word. I went out for the purpose of getting some provisions at a store at Duck Lake.

Q. Having sent out a smaller party in the morning who returned unsuccessful? A. Driven in.

Q. Then you were proceeding to get the provisions and you were met by a —? A. By a large party of rebels.

Q. Did you identify any of the party as leading? A. No.

Q. The result was a contest? A. Yes.

Q. Your force was fired upon? A. Yes.

Q. And several killed and wounded? A. Yes.

Q. Did you get the provisions? A. We did not.

Q. Why? A. We could not proceed; we were prevented by an armed force of rebels.

Q. Then did you receive a letter or communication after the fight on the 27th of March? A. I did.

Q. Who gave that communication (20) to you? A. Sanderson.

Q. Asking you to come for your dead. Had it this copy of the minute attached when you received it? A. Well I cannot swear to that. I don't recollect that minute, the other part I remember distinctly. I handed it to my commanding officer after receiving it.

Q. You do recollect getting this document purporting to be signed by the prisoner? A. Yes.

Q. That is in effect a letter asking you to send for your dead? A. Yes.

Q. Whom you had been compelled to leave upon the field? A. Yes.

Q. They were sent for? A. Not then; they were sent for afterwards.

Q. Who composed the forces that opposed you — were they all half-breeds? A. I don't think so; to the best of my knowledge they were not.

Q. Did you see any Indians? A. I saw men dressed as Indians and that looked like Indians.

By MR FITZPATRICK:

Q. When you reached the place where the fight took place you advanced yourself did you not? A. Yes, I did.

Q. A short distance in advance of your troops? A. Yes.

Q. You were met by one from the opposite side? A. Yes.

Q. Who was that? A. I do not know — he appeared to be an Indian.

Q. What became of that man? A. That man I heard was killed.

Q. Did you see him drop? A. I cannot say that I saw him drop.

Q. Was he the first man killed to your knowledge? A. I do not know.

Q. You did not see any of the men drop yourself? A. I cannot say that I did. My attention was engaged giving directions to my party.

Q. Your dead remained upon the field? A. Not the whole of them, some of the dead did.

Q. You knew that one of your men, Newett, remained wounded? A. Of course I knew it afterwards, but I did not know it at the time.

Q. To your knowledge that man was taken care of? A. Not to my
personal knowledge, though I believe he was from what I heard.
Q. Did you see the dead after the battle? A. No, I did not.
Q. Before they were interred? A. No.
Q. Did you see them on the field? A. I saw some, but the dead left
upon the field I did not see.

CHARLES NOLIN sworn
Examined by MR CASGRAIN:
(Mr Marceau was sworn as interpreter.)
Q. You live at St Laurent? A. At the present time, yes.
Q. You lived before in Manitoba? A. Yes.
Q. Do you know when the prisoner came into the country? A. Yes.
Q. About what time was it? A. I think about the beginning of July
1884.
Q. You met him several times between that time and the time of the
insurrection? A. Yes.
Q. Did the prisoner speak about his plans, and if so, what did he
say? A. About a month after he arrived he showed me a book
that he had written in the States. What he showed me in that
book was first to destroy England and Canada.
Q. And? A. And also to destroy Rome and the Pope.
Q. Anything else? A. He said that he had a mission to fulfil, a divine
mission, and as a proof that he had a mission he showed a letter
from the Bishop of Montreal, eleven years back.
Q. Did he say how he would carry out his plans? A. He did not say
how he would carry out his plans then.
Q. Did he tell you something after? A. He commenced to talk about
his plans about the 1st of December 1884.
Q. What did he tell you? A. In the beginning of December 1884, he
began to show a desire to have money, he spoke to me about it
first I think.
Q. How much did he say he wanted? A. The first time he spoke of
money I think he said he wanted $10,000 or $15,000.
Q. From whom would he get the money? A. The first time he spoke
about it he did not know any particular plan to get it, at the same
time he told me that he wanted to claim an indemnity from the
Canadian Government. He said that the Canadian Government
owed him about $100,000, and then the question arose who the

persons were whom he would have to talk to the Government
about the indemnity. Some time after that the prisoner told me
that he had an interview with Father André and that he had made
peace with the church, that since his arrival in the country he had
tried to separate the people from the clergy, that until that time
he was at open war almost with the clergy. He said that he went
to the church with Father André and in the presence of another
priest and the blessed sacrament he had made peace, and said that
he would never again do anything against the clergy. Father
André told him he would use his influence with the Government
to obtain for him $35,000. He said that he would be contented
with $35,000 then, and that he would settle with the Govern-
ment himself for the balance of the $100,000. That agreement
took place at Prince Albert. The agreement took place at St
Laurent and then Father André went back to his mission at
Prince Albert.

Q. Before December were there meetings at which Riel spoke and at
which you were present? A. Yes.

Q. How many? A. Till the 24th of February I assisted at seven meetings to the best of my knowledge.

Q. Did the prisoner tell you what he would do if the Government
paid him the indemnity in question? A. Yes.

Q. What did he tell you? A. He said if he got the money he wanted
from the Government he said he would go wherever the Government wished to send him. He had told that to Father André, if he
was an embarrassment to the Government by remaining in the
North-West he would even go to the Province of Quebec. He said
also, that if he got the money he would go to the United States
and start a paper and raise the other nationalities in the States. He
said before the grass is that high in this country you will see
foreign armies in this country. He said I will commence by destroying Manitoba, and then I will come and destroy the North-
West and take possession of the North-West.

Q. Did anyone make a demand in the name of the prisoner for the
indemnity? A. In the beginning of January the Government asked
for tenders to construct a telegraph line between Edmonton and
Duck Lake. I tendered for it.

Q. You withdrew your tender? A. Yes.

Q. Why? A. On the 29th of January the tenders were to be opened, on the 27th the prisoner came with Dumont and asked me to resign my contract in his favor, because the Government had not given him any answer to his claim for $35,000, so as to frighten the Government. The prisoner asked to have a private interview to speak of that privately with Dumont and Maxime Lepine. We went to Lepine's and it was then that Riel told me of his plans.

Q. What were his plans? A. The prisoner asked me to resign him my contract to show the Government that the half-breeds were not satisfied, because the Government had not given Riel what he asked for.

Q. Did he speak how he would realize his plans? A. Not there, I spoke to him.

Q. What did you say? A. I told him I would not sacrifice anything for him particularly, on account of his plan of going into the United States. I would not give him five cents, but that if he would make a bargain with me, with Lepine and Dumont as witnesses, I proposed to him certain conditions. I proposed that he would abandon his plan of going to the United States and raising the people, that he should abandon his idea of going to the States and raising an army to come into Canada. The second condition was, that he would renounce his title as an American citizen. The third condition was, that he would accept a seat in the House of Commons as soon as the North-West would be divide into counties.

Q. Were those conditions accepted by the prisoner? A. Yes; the next day I received a telegram; answer to a telegram from McDowall. The telegram said that the Government was going to grant the rights of the half-breeds, but there was nothing said about Riel's claim.

Q. Did you show the answer to Riel? A. I showed the reply I received next Sunday.

Q. That was in the month –? A. Of February.

Q. In the beginning of the month? A. Yes.

Q. What did the prisoner say? A. He answered, that it was 400 years that the English had been robbing, and that it was time to put a stop to it, that it had been going on long enough.

Q. Was there a meeting about that time, about the 8th or 24th of February? A. A meeting?

Q. At which the prisoner spoke? A. There was a meeting on the 24th of February, when the prisoner was present.

Q. What took place at that meeting, did the prisoner say anything about his departing for the United States? A. Yes.

Q. What did the prisoner tell you about that? A. He told me that it would be well to try and make it appear as if they wanted to stop him going into the States. Five or six persons were appointed to go among the people, and when Riel's going away was spoken about the people were to say 'no, no.' It was expected that Gagnon would be there, but he was not there. Riel never had any intention of leaving the country.

Q. Who instructed the people to do that? A. Riel suggested that himself.

Q. Was that put in practice? A. Yes.

Q. Did the prisoner tell you he was going to the United States? A. I was chairman of the meeting when the question of Riel's going away was brought up.

Q. In the beginning of March was there a meeting at the Halcro settlement? A. Yes.

Q. Were you present when that meeting was organized by him? A. The meeting was not exactly organized by the prisoner; it was organized by me; but the prisoner took advantage of the meeting to do what he did. The object of the meeting was to inform the people of the answer the Government had given to the petition they had sent in.

Q. Between the 1st of March and the meeting at Halcro was there an interview between the prisoner and Father André? A. Yes; on the 2nd of March.

Q. Those notes you have in your hand were made at the time? A. Yes, about the time. On the 2nd of March there was a meeting between Father André and the prisoner at the mission.

Q. At the interview between Father André and the prisoner, did the prisoner speak about the formation of a provisional government? A. About seven or eight half-breeds were there. The prisoner came about between 10 and 11 o'clock.

Q. What did he say to Father André? A. The prisoner was with Napoléon Nauld and Damase Carrière. The prisoner appeared to be very excited. He said to Father André: 'You must give me permission to proclaim a provisional government before twelve o'clock to-night.'

Q. What day was this? A. The 2nd of March.

Q. What then? A. The prisoner and Father André had a dispute, and Father André put the prisoner out of doors.

Q. What took place at the meeting at Halcro? What did you see? A. I saw about sixty men arrive there nearly all armed, with the prisoner.

Q. What day was that? A. 3rd of March.

Q. Were these men armed? A. Nearly all were armed.

Q. What did you do? A. That meeting was for the purpose of meeting the English half-breeds and the Canadians. When I saw the men coming with arms I asked them what they wanted and I said the best thing they could do was to put the arms in a waggon and cover them up so they would not be seen.

Q. The prisoner spoke at the meeting? A. Yes.

Q. What did he say? A. He said the police wanted to arrest him but he said these are the real police, pointing to the men that were with him.

Q. Did you speak at the meeting? A. Yes, I spoke at that meeting and as I could not speak in English I asked the prisoner to interpret for me. Before leaving in the morning the prisoner and I had a conversation. He had slept at my place that night. Before leaving I reproached him for what he had done the night before.

Q. On the 5th of March? A. The prisoner came with Gabriel Dumont to see me, he proposed a plan to me that he had written upon a piece of paper. He said that he had decided to take up arms and to induce the people to take up arms and the first thing was to fight for the glory of God, for the honor of religion, and for the salvation of our souls. The prisoner said that he had already nine names upon the paper and he asked me for my name. I told him that the plan was not perfect, but since he wanted to fight for the love of God I would propose a more perfect plan. My plan was to have public prayers in the Catholic chapel during nine days and to go to confession and communion and then do as our consciences told us.

Q. Did the prisoner adopt that plan? A. He said that nine days was too long. I told him that I did not care about the time and that I would not sign his paper. The prisoner asked me to come the next day to his house. I went, and there we discussed his plan. There were six or seven persons there.

Q. Did you propose your plan? A. He proposed his plan and then he proposed mine.

Q. Did you decide to have the nine days? A. We decided upon the nine days' prayers; that plan was adopted almost unanimously, no vote was taken upon it.

Q. Was the nine days' prayer commenced in the church? A. Yes, on the Sunday following.

Q. What day was that? A. The meeting at Riel's was on the 6th. I think it was on the 6th of March.

Q. When did the nine days' prayer commence? A. It was announced in the church to commence on the Tuesday following and to close on the 19th, St Joseph's day.

Q. Did the prisoner assist at the prayers? A. No, he prevented people going.

Q. When did you finally differ from the prisoner in opinion?
A. About twenty days before they took up arms. I broke with the prisoner and made open war upon him.

Q. What happened on the 19th? A. On the 19th of March I and the prisoner were to meet to explain the situation. I was taken prisoner by four armed men.

Q. Who were the armed men? A. Philip Garriépy, David Touron, Francis Vermette and Joseph Flemoine. I was taken to the church of St Antoine. I saw some Indians and half-breeds armed in the church.

Q. Did you have occasion to go to the council after that? A. During that night I was brought before the council.

Q. Was the prisoner there? A. Yes.

Q. What did he say? A. I was brought before the council about ten o'clock at night. The prisoner made the accusation against me.

Q. What did you do? A. I defended myself.

Q. What did you say in a few words? A. I proved to the council that the prisoner had made use of the movement to claim the indemnity for his own pocket.

Q. You were acquitted? A. Yes.

Q. You were in the church after that? A. The prisoner protested against the decision of the council.

Q. Why did you join the movement? A. To save my life.

Q. You were condemned to death? A. Yes.

Q. When were you condemned to death? A. When I was made prisoner I had been condemned to death, when I was brought to the church.·

Q. On the 21st of March were you charged with a commission? Do you recognize that (5)? A. Yes.

Q. Who gave you that? A. The prisoner himself.

Q. For what purpose? A. To go and meet the delegates of Major Crozier. I did not give them the document, because I thought it was better not.

Q. Do you remember the 26th of March, the day of the battle at Duck Lake? A. Yes.

Q. Was the prisoner there? A. Yes. After the news came that the police were coming, the prisoner started one of the first for Duck Lake on horseback.

Q. What did he carry? A. He had a cross.

Q. Some time after you left? A. Yes.

Q. You went to Prince Albert? A. Yes.

Q. In the beginning of December, 1884, the prisoner had begun speaking of his plans about taking up arms? A. Yes.

By MR LEMIEUX:

Q. You took a very active part in the political movements in this country since 1869? A. Yes. In 1869 I was in Manitoba. The prisoner is my cousin. In 1884 I knew that the prisoner was living in Montana. I understood that he was teaching school there. He had his wife and children there. I was aware there was a scheme to bring him into the country.

Q. You thought the presence of the prisoner would be good for the half-breeds, for the claims they were demanding from the Government? A. Yes.

Q. In that movement the Catholic clergy took part? A. The clergy did not take part in the political movements, but they assisted otherwise.

Q. The clergy of all denominations? A. Yes, all the religions in the North-West.

Q. You were not satisfied with the way things were going, and you thought it necessary to have Riel as a rallying point? A. Not directly, not quite.

Q. Who sent to bring him? A. A committee was nominated, and it was decided to send the resolution to Ottawa. We did not know whether the petition was right or whether we had the right to present it. We were sending to Ottawa, and they were to pass Riel's residence. When the time came we saw that we could not realize money enough to send them there, and the committee changed its decision. Delegates were sent to Mr Riel to speak about this petition, and they were to invite him into the country if they thought proper.

Q. Did the prisoner object to come? A. I don't know.

Q. Who were the delegates sent by the committee? A. Gabriel Dumont, Michel Dumas and James Isbester. The prisoner came with his wife and children and lived with me about four months.

Q. A constitutional movement took place in the Saskatchewan to redress the grievances? A. Yes.

Q. The half-breeds of all religions took part? A. Yes.

Q. The whites? A. Not directly, they sympathised very much with us. The whites did not take direct action in the movement, but sympathised greatly with the half-breeds.

The witness is asked during what length of time the political movement lasted and he says it commenced in March 1884, and continued until February or March 1885. He says that the prisoner, after having lived about three months at his place, went into his own house that he thinks was given to him by Mr Ouellette.

The witness is asked if in September the prisoner wanted to go, and the witness answers that he knows that the prisoner spoke of going, but he never believed that he wanted to go.

The witness is asked at what date about he ceased to have friendly relations with the prisoner, and he says about twenty days before the taking up of arms, which was about the 18th of March.

The witness is asked if in the month of February he thought yet Mr Riel could be useful to their cause, and he says that in that month he thought that if he acted constitutionally, he would be useful to their cause, but that as soon as he heard that the Government had refused the prisoner the indemnity that he claimed, that he said he had no more confidence in him as a leader in a constitutional way.

The witness is asked if after the Government had refused to pay him his indemnity that the prisoner pretended that he wanted to go, and he says yes.

The witness is asked how he can say, under his oath, that if he had no confidence in him, in the prisoner, why he acted with him to deceive the people, and the witness answers that he says what he saw and heard.

The witness is asked again to say how it is that having lost confidence in the prisoner he agreed with him to deceive the people and make them believe that he wanted to go when he knew he did not want to leave the country. He says that the prisoner came and asked him to do that because Captain Gagnon was there, and so as to impress the Government, and he says that he thought that at the time they expected that Mr Gagnon would be at the meeting and it would bring a satisfactory result for Mr Riel.

The witness is asked, in other words you wanted to put a false impression on Mr Gagnon so as to obtain a good result for Mr Riel, and the witness answers no, not at all.

The witness is asked if in 1869 he knew the prisoner well, and he says yes.

The witness is asked whether after that didn't they start a political movement with him in Manitoba. He says that in Manitoba in 1869 and 1870 he did not directly start any movement with the prisoner, and then he is asked if he did not act like he did in this case, if he did not start with them and abandon them, and he says yes. He says that he participated in that movement as long as he thought it was constitutional, but as soon as he saw it was not, he withdrew.

The witness is asked if subsequently to the rebellion and the abandonment that he made in 1870, if he was not appointed Minister of Agriculture, and he says in 1875 he was appointed Minister of Agriculture. He is asked if he was not looked upon as one of the leaders of the half-breeds of the Saskatchewan, and he says he was looked upon as one of the leaders.

The witness is asked if Father Fourmand did not want to stop Mr Riel from acting, and he says it may be so, but it is not to his knowledge. Witness says there was a meeting on the 24th February. He knows Father André spoke there, but he could not say if he asked the prisoner to remain. He says he may have said so.

The witness is asked if about that time in February there had not been a dinner at which the political situation of the Saskatchewan was discussed, and he says he knows of one on the 6th January. The witness says that at that time he spoke, but he did not speak much. He said something at that dinner, but he did not speak much.

The witness is asked if he can swear that at that dinner it was not spoken of, the grievances of the half-breeds, and the refusal of the Government to redress them, and the witness says that he was present at that dinner, and that to his knowledge he does not remember that there was any political speech at that.

The witness says that he had very frequent occasions to meet Riel conversing with him since March 1884, till the moment they disagreed.

Witness is asked if the prisoner ever told him that he considered himself a prophet, and he says yes.

The witness is asked if after the meal something strange did not happen, if there was not a question of the Spirit of God between the witness and the prisoner.

Witness says it was not after a dinner, but it was one evening, they were spending the night together at his house, and there was a noise in his bowels, and the prisoner asked him if he heard that, and the witness said yes, and then the prisoner told him that that was his liver, and that he had inspirations that worked through every part of his body.

The witness is asked if at that moment the prisoner did not write in a book that he was inspired of, and the witness answers that he did not write in a book, but on a sheet of paper; he said he was inspired.

The witness is asked whether he ever heard the prisoner speak of his internal policy in the division of the country, if he should succeed in his enterprise, and he says yes. He says that after his arrival the prisoner showed him a book written with buffalo blood, and the witness said that the prisoner in that plan said that after having taken England and Canada, he would divide Canada and give the Province of Quebec to the Prussians, Ontario to the Irish, and the North-West Territory he divided into different parts between the European nations. He says he does not remember them all, but the Jews were to have a part.

The witness says that he thinks he also spoke of the Hungarians and Bavarians. He says that he thought the whole world should have a piece of the cake, that Prussia was to have Quebec.

The witness says that since 1884 there was a committee which was called a council. Witness says he was one of the members of that committee or council. He was only an ordinary member – not president. Mr Andrew Spence was president. He was an English half-breed. He says that the council condemned him to death, and liberated him after and offered him a place in the council.

The witness is asked if he refused that position, and he says he did not refuse it, that he accepted it, but it was only to save his life, because he had been condemned to death.

The witness is asked if he was present at the meeting at Prince Albert, and he says he was not there, he was outside. He did not speak there.

The witness says that before the battle at Duck Lake he saw Riel going out with a crucifix about a foot and a half long, that the crucifix had been taken out of the next church near by.

The witness is asked if it is not true that when there was a question in the Saskatchewan of the police, the character of the prisoner changed completely, and that he became very excitable and even uncontrollable. And the witness says that whenever even the word police was pronounced, he got very excited.

The witness is asked if at the time it was said in the district that 500 police would be sent to answer the petition of the half-breeds, his character did not become very excitable, and he says that after that he did not see the prisoner, but that before that whenever the word police was pronounced, he got very excited. He says that what he said here was about the month of January or even February, and about that time Captain Gagnon passed in the country and stopped at the prisoner's house to enquire what was the road to St Laurent, and there was only the prisoner's wife and Mrs Dumont in the house, and when the prisoner came back and was informed that Mr Gagnon had been there, he got very much excited, and the women could not explain it what Gagnon had stopped there for, and he got very excited, and the population generally got excited too. He does not know whether the policemen had their uniforms on or not. He says he cannot say at what date that was that Gagnon passed there, but he says he heard of the 500 policemen coming to the country only after arms were taken up.

The witness says that one of his sons was arrested after the fight at Batoche, and that he was brought here to the barracks, and was released within the last few days.

The witness is asked if he had any influence, and he says he does not know what influence he could exercise. He says that at any rate he has been put at liberty since the witness came to Regina to give his evidence in this case.

PRISONER: Your Honor, would you permit me a little while —
MR JUSTICE RICHARDSON: In the proper time, I will tell you
when you may speak to me, and give you every opportunity — not
just now though.
PRISONER: If there was any way, by legal procedure, that I should
be allowed to say a word, I wish you would allow me before this
prisoner (witness) leaves the box.
MR JUSTICE RICHARDSON: I think you should suggest any question you have to your own counsel —
PRISONER: Do you allow me to say? I have some observation to
make before the court.
MR FITZPATRICK: I don't think this is the proper time, your
Honor, that the prisoner should be allowed to say anything in the
matter.
MR JUSTICE RICHARDSON: I should ask him at the close of the
case, before it goes to the jury.
MR FITZPATRICK: That is the time to do it.
MR JUSTICE RICHARDSON: I think you should mention it quietly
to your counsel, and if they think it proper for your defence, they
will put it.
MR FITZPATRICK: I think the time has now arrived when it is
necessary to state to the court that we require that the prisoner in
the box should thoroughly understand that anything that is done in
this case, must be done through us, and if he wishes anything to be
done, he must necessarily give us instructions. He should be given to
understand that he should give any instructions to us, and he must
not be allowed to interfere. He is now endeavoring to withhold
instructions.
MR JUSTICE RICHARDSON: Is there not this difficulty under the
statute, saying that he shall do so?
MR FITZPATRICK: I think the statute provides that he may make
statements to the jury.
MR JUSTICE RICHARDSON: The prisoner may defend himself
under the statute, personally or by counsel.
MR FITZPATRICK: Once he has counsel, he has no right to interfere.
MR ROBINSON: He has the right to address the jury. I am not
aware of any right till then.
PRISONER: If you will allow me, your Honor, this case comes to be
extraordinary, and while the Crown, with the great talents they have
at its service, are trying to show I am guilty — of course it is their

duty, my counsellors are trying – my good friends and lawyers, who have been sent here by friends whom I respect – are trying to show that I am insane –

MR JUSTICE RICHARDSON: Now you must stop.

PRISONER: I will stop and obey your court.

MR JUSTICE RICHARDSON: I will tell you once more, if you have any questions which you think ought to be put to this witness, and which your advisers have not put, just tell them quietly and they will put it, if they think it proper to do so.

MR FITZPATRICK: I don't think he ought to be allowed to say any more.

MR OSLER: The court understands that we are not objecting to the fullest kind of questions, we are only saying they should properly go through the counsel. We are not objecting, and I suppose we would be quite willing, if the prisoner's counsel are, that he should ask any particular question himself. We are perfectly willing. That is a matter between himself and his counsel.

MR FITZPATRICK: For the last two days we felt ourselves in this position, that this man is actually obstructing the proper management of this case, for the express purpose of having a chance to interfere in this case, and he must be given to understand immediately that he won't be allowed to interfere in it, or else it will be absolutely useless for us to endeavor to continue any further in it.

MR RICHARDSON: Is that a matter that I ought to interfere in? Isn't that a matter entirely between yourself and your client? Suppose you cannot go on and my ruling was called in question, and the question was raised, and the court allowed such and such a thing to be done?

MR FITZPATRICK: I don't pretend to argue with the court; it is not my practice, it is not my custom. I have stated to the court what I think of this case. I think the court here is bound by the ordinary rules of law, and so long as the prisoner is represented by counsel it is his duty to give such instructions to his counsel as to enable him to do duty to his case.

MR JUSTICE RICHARDSON: I admit he ought to do so, but suppose he does not, and suppose counsel think fit to throw up their brief.

MR FITZPATRICK: We are entirely free to do that, and that is matter for our consideration at the present moment if the prisoner is allowed to interfere. Of course, I have to take the ruling of the court.

MR JUSTICE RICHARDSON: I don't like to dictate to you, but it strikes me that now an opportunity should be taken of ascertaining whether there is really anything that has not been put to this witness that ought to have been put.

MR FITZPATRICK: We have very little desire to have questions put which we, in our discretion, do not desire to put. What has this court got to do with theories about inspiration and the division of lands, further than we have gone into it? However, I, of course, have to accept the ruling of the court as it is given, and then it will be for the counsel for the defence to consider the position.

MR ROBINSON: It must be quite understood that no rulings of the court are given with the desire or at the request or with the concurrence of the Crown. We have nothing to do in the shape of interference. We must not be drawn into the position that there is a ruling of the court on a question of that kind. I think it would probably be right for the court to ask the prisoner whether the case is or is not fully in the hands of the counsel. It is for the prisoner to say.

MR FITZPATRICK: We accept that suggestion.

MR JUSTICE RICHARDSON: Prisoner, are you defended by counsel? Are you defended by counsel? Are you defended by counsel? Answer my question, please, are you defended by counsel? Is your case in the hands of counsel?

PRISONER: Partly; my cause is partly into their hands.

MR JUSTICE RICHARDSON: Now, stop; are you defended by counsel or not? Have you advisers?

PRISONER: I don't wish to leave them aside. I want them, I want their services, but I want my cause to be, your Honor, to be defended to the best which circumstances allow.

MR JUSTICE RICHARDSON: Then you must leave it in their hands.

PRISONER: I will, if you please, say this reason: My counsel come from Quebec, from a far province. They have to put questions to men with whom they are not acquainted, on circumstances which they don't know, and although I am willing to give them all the information that I can, they cannot follow the thread of all the questions that could be put to the witnesses. They lose more than three-quarters of the good opportunities of making good answers, not because they are not able, not because they are not able; they are learned, they are talented, but the circumstances are such that they cannot put all the questions. If I would be allowed, as it was suggested, this case is extraordinary.

MR JUSTICE RICHARDSON: You have told me your case is in the hand of advisers.

PRISONER: Partly.

MR JUSTICE RICHARDSON: Now you must leave it there until you get through. I will give you an opportunity of speaking to the court at the proper time.

PRISONER: The witnesses are passing and the opportunities.

MR JUSTICE RICHARDSON: Tell your counsel.

PRISONER: I cannot all. I have too much to say. There is too much to say.

MR JUSTICE RICHARDSON: If there is any question not put to this witness which you think ought to be put, tell it to your counsel and they will say whether it should be put.

PRISONER: I have on cross-examination 200 questions.

MR ROBINSON: We had better understand this. Counsel for the Crown are taking no part. Our inclination is if counsel for the prisoner agree to it, to let the prisoner put any questions he pleases to the witness. We don't wish to interfere in any way between the prisoner and his counsel.

MR JUSTICE RICHARDSON: I can quite understand that, Mr Robinson, but if a man tells me he is defended by counsel, I think he ought to have a reasonable opportunity of stopping that defence when he pleases, and when he tells me he has stopped it then he takes the management into his own hands.

MR GREENSHIELDS: If he will just say that, that is all right.

MR JUSTICE RICHARDSON: At present I think I am right. I think both sides agree that my course is to say, either one or the other, counsel or prisoner, and while the counsel are there they have the conduct.

MR FITZPATRICK: Would your Honor allow us, say five minutes of a consultation?

MR JUSTICE RICHARDSON: I was just going to suggest that you should take a little time and that the prisoner should go with you.

(Adjournment takes place here in accordance with the suggestion.)

On the court re-assembling:

MR LEMIEUX: May it please your Honor, Mr Fitzpatrick, Mr Greenshields and myself are discharging as you understand very important duties before this court. The duties we are discharging

now may be public duties, because the prisoner having in our
province a number of friends, a number of people who knew him a
number of years ago, they thought that we should come here and
give him the benefit of our little experience and knowledge of the
law, that we may have from a number of years' practice at the bar.
Now since the beginning of the trial, we have done our very best to
help him. It appears that he is not well pleased, or it appears he
thinks we did not put all the questions to the witnesses that we
should have put. Well the law says that when a man appears by
counsel, that counsel must act for him during the whole trial. We
appeared for him, he acquiesced in our appearance –
MR JUSTICE RICHARDSON: Does it say that you must through
the whole trial?
MR LEMIEUX: Well as long as we are disavowed. We appeared for
the prisoner and he acquiesced in our appearance, our appearance is
on the record and if the prisoner insists upon putting to the witnesses questions, we object to it, and we moreover say that we will
not continue to act in the case as counsel. We think however it is too
late for him to now disavow or refuse.
MR ROBINSON: If the prisoner under the special circumstances of
this case deisres to join his counsel in conducting the examination or
cross-examination of witnesses, the Crown do not object to it.
MR JUSTICE RICHARDSON: My opinion of the course which the
court ought to follow has not changed in the interval. If this man
insists on putting a question, I don't think the court should refuse
him. It would be a matter between himself and his counsel. There
cannot be two.
MR FITZPATRICK: Does your Honor think that so long as there is
counsel on the record that a prisoner has got a right to put a question to a witness, otherwise than through the counsel?
MR JUSTICE RICHARDSON: He must take the consequences and
know what the consequences will be, and I think he does know for
I explained the consequences.
MR FITZPATRICK: Questions can only be put by a prisoner to a
witness in the presence of counsel after counsel have been
refused. If he wants to take that step, on him the responsibility
will lie.
MR JUSTICE RICHARDSON: Prisoner, do you understand the position these genetlemen tell you you are taking.

PRISONER: I do, my Honor, and I know from my good friends and my learned lawyers that it is a matter of dignity for their profession, and I consider if my intentions were not respectful for them and for the friends who sent them, I would commit a great fault against my friends and against myself; but in this case would ask your Honor if there is any possibility that I am allowed to put questions –

MR JUSTICE RICHARDSON: Listen to me for one moment. I say that I shall not stop you from putting a question. I could not stop you from putting a question, but if you do it, you do it with the knowledge that those gentlemen will abandon you at once. I think that is the position you gentlemen put it in, and you will have to take the responsibility of that.

These gentlemen who are opposing you do not, will not interfere.

PRISONER: I thank them for their liberality.

MR JUSTICE RICHARDSON: You must understand that, and I hope you do understand it. Now arrange with your counsel as to what course you will take.

PRISONER: I was going to ask if it is in any way possible that I should put questions to the witness, and my good lawyers being there to give me advice necessary to stop me when I go out of the procedure.

MR JUSTICE RICHARDSON: That is a matter between you and them. It is entirely a matter between you and them.

PRISONER: Your Honor, it is not because they don't put all the questions that they ought, but they don't know all the circumstances, and they cannot know them because they were far away.

MR JUSTICE RICHARDSON: Then if you think they are not properly instructed, I will give you an opportunity to instruct them, if they had not had an opportunity of getting proper information from you.

MR LEMIEUX: We don't want that. We have had full instructions. We cannot pretend to do anything of the kind. We have been here for two weeks in constant communication with him, and we can't learn anything more in a few hours.

PRISONER: The case concerns my good lawyers and my friends, but in the first place it concerns me, and as I think, conscientiously, that I ought to do this for me and for those who have been with me, I cannot abandon the wish that I expressed to the court, and I cannot abandon the wish that I expressed to retain my counsels, because they are good and learned.

MR JUSTICE RICHARDSON: Now, do you intend to retain your counsel?

PRISONER: Yes, and to help myself when they help me.

MR JUSTICE RICHARDSON: Do you wish to retain your counsel?

PRISONER: I wish to retain, first my chances of doing the best I can for myself, and then to take the help of those who are so kind to me.

MR JUSTICE RICHARDSON: But they say they won't help you unless you leave the whole case in their hands.

PRISONER: They ought to do it.

MR JUSTICE RICHARDSON: They cannot help you —

PRISONER: Yes, I know that. It is between them and me. I think I would throw away many good opportunities, your Honor. I hold this court thanks because you have retarded my trial for fifteen days, and after fifteen days, you have delayed eight other days, and even the court has been kind enough to furnish money to have witnesses, and it is because they show me impartiality. Since it is the first time that I speak before the court, it is my duty to acknowledge what I owe you in that way, because you could have refused it.

MR ROBINSON: Does the prisoner thoroughly understand that he will have an opportunity of addressing the jury?

MR JUSTICE RICHARDSON: It is in regard to putting questions to this witness.

MR OSLER: The simple way would be for him to suggest a question to the counsel.

MR FITZPATRICK: We have asked him half a dozen times to suggest, and he says he knows all about it himself.

MR JUSTICE RICHARDSON: Will you then suggest a question to your own lawyers? Don't read it out, but suggest to them. They will listen to you. One of the gentlemen will listen quietly to anything you wish to put.

PRISONER: All the witnesses for the Crown have nearly passed away from the box, and there is only a few. I have been insisting since yesterday on this, in the hope that they would make that concession to my own interest, and to the cause which they defend. I have been patiently waiting. As they have determined to go on, I will

assert that, while I wish to retain them, I cannot abandon my
dignity. Here I have to defend myself against the accusation of high
treason, or I have to consent to the animal life of an asylum. I don't
care much about animal life if I am not allowed to carry with it the
moral existence of an intellectual being.

MR JUSTICE RICHARDSON: Now, stop.

PRISONER: Yes, your Honor, I will.

MR JUSTICE RICHARDSON: If you have got any question which
has not been put to this witness, why can't you tell those gentlemen? (After a pause.) Very well, then, they don't think it proper to
put it. Now, I understand you to say that you wish to retain the
services of these lawyers throughout your defence – the rest of your
defence, don't I?

PRISONER: I want to ally the small ability I have to their great
ability.

MR OSLER: The statute 7 William IV says he shall make full defence by counsel.

MR JUSTICE RICHARDSON: That is the last Treason Act.

MR OSLER: Counsel is assigned by the court, and then he has also
the right to address the jury after the close of the case. It is a special
privilege in treason.

MR JUSTICE RICHARDSON: Well, the authority which has just
been put in my hands is this: Where after a witness has been fully
cross-examined by the defendant's lawyer, the court refused to let
the defendant examine, this was held not to violate the constitutional right of defence by himself. I think I shall have to tell you,
too, that you are in your counsel's hands, and if you and they cannot agree, then will come another question, whether the court will
not further interfere, and say counsel must go on.

PRISONER: By what has been said there, he shall make full
defence –

MR JUSTICE RICHARDSON: I will give you an opportunity of
addressing the court, not while the examination is going on, though,
of the witnesses.

PRISONER: After travelling 800 miles why shouldn't they travel the
other piece of allowing ten questions; it is the coronation of their
kindness.

MR JUSTICE RICHARDSON: Have you any questions to ask the
witness? (to counsel) Let the re-examination go on.

Examination of Mr Charles Nolin continued, through the interpreter.

The witness is asked if the council which he spoke of a while ago, and which was presided over by Mr Andrew Spence, was the same that condemned him to death, and he says no.

MR JUSTICE RICHARDSON: That is, the old council was not the council that condemned him to death?

Witness says that the council that condemned him to death was one that was called *'exovede.'*

Witness is asked if the prisoner had separated from the clergy, and he says completely. He says the half-breeds are people who need religion. Religion has a great influence on their mind.

The witness is asked if with religion the prisoner would have succeeded in bringing half-breeds with him, and the witness answers no, it would never have succeeded. If the prisoner had not made himself appear as a prophet, he would never have succeeded in bringing the half-breeds with him.

By MR LEMIEUX, re-cross-examination:

The witness is asked if the prisoner did not lose a great deal of his influence in that way, by the fact that he lost the influence of the clergy, and he says that at the time he gained influence by working against the clergy and by making himself out as a priest.

The witness is asked if he means that the people did not have confidence in their clergy, and he says no; but he says they were ignorant, and they were taking advantage of their ignorance and their simplicity.

PRISONER: I wish to put a question myself to the witness in the box, your Honor.

MR JUSTICE RICHARDSON: If your counsel see fit to put it, they will put it, and if not the witness is discharged.

MR LEMIEUX: I asked the prisoner if he had any questions to put to the witness through me, and he said he had none, that he would only put questions by himself.

PRISONER: I cannot abandon my wish, your Honor. I leave it to your consideration – my two wishes – of defending myself and of retaining them.

MR JUSTICE RICHARDSON: I have made this memorandum, that it may not be misunderstood: The prisoner asks to be allowed to put questions himself to the witness who has just been here, and his

214   The Queen *v* Louis Riel

counsel say that they manage his case, and object to the prisoner putting these questions as such. Mr Lemieux explains to the court that the witness has been specially asked to inform counsel or himself what he desires as to this witness, and I tell the prisoner that the court at this stage cannot allow both counsel and prisoner to manage the defence. While he has counsel, counsel must conduct, but at a proper stage, he has rights which the court will respect.

MR ROBINSON: I wish it to be understood in this way: I understand the prisoner to say that he declines to make his choice between allowing his counsel to examine witnesses and joining him in examination, that he wishes then to examine him, and that he wishes to ask himself directly such questions as he desires; and I understand counsel to say that they cannot accept the responsibility of conducting his case if he insists upon that.

Counsel for the defence say yes, that's it.

MR ROBINSON: We will assist the counsel for the prisoner in any way that is proper.

MR JUSTICE RICHARDSON: If it were an ordinary criminal case, I should not hesitate, but this is beyond the ordinary run of cases that I have had to do with in my whole career.

PRISONER: Have I to keep silent?

MR JUSTICE RICHARDSON: You can inform your counsel what you want. You have selected them and the court recognizes them.

PRISONER: Your Honor, I have another question to ask you. Can my counsel insist upon being my counsel if I thank them for their services?

MR JUSTICE RICHARDSON: They were the counsel who represented you at the start. They were recognized by you, and I don't think at this stage I should refuse to recognize them as having charge and the responsibility for the defence.

MR LEMIEUX: We accept the responsibility.

PRISONER: Your Honor, I have accepted them, but you all know why you accept defenders, it is to defend ourselves, and I think that since they have begun matters are taking a shape that would allow me to make the petition that I make presently to your honor and the court.

MR JUSTICE RICHARDSON: You might find yourself in this position: Suppose these gentlemen do not continue your defence, you might have counsel assigned by the court to defend you, and then you would be bound.

PRISONER: It is not against their dignity. I cannot see it in that light.

MR JUSTICE RICHARDSON: Proceed with another witness, please.

THOMAS SANDERSON sworn
Examined by MR ROBINSON:
There is a paper which has not been read yet, and which was proved by the witness Jackson. It is dated 1th May 1885. It is addressed to General Middleton.

Major General Fredrick Middleton
General — I have received only to-day yours of the 13th, but our counsel have dispersed. I wish you would let them quiet and free. I hear that presently you are absent. Would I go to Batoche, who is going to receive me? I will go to fulfil God's will.
LOUIS 'DAVID' RIEL, *Exovede*
15th May 1885

MR JUSTICE RICHARDSON: Was that document proved?
MR OSLER: It was proved by Jackson (19).
By MR ROBINSON:
Q. I believe you are a farmer living at Carrot River settlement?
A. Yes.
Q. Do you remember the 20th March last? Do you remember that day? A. I don't exactly remember the date.
Q. Well, do you remember Gordon coming to you? A. Yes.
Q. About when was that? A. I think it was about the 20th, I don't exactly recollect the date.
Q. Was it at your house? A. At my father's house.
Q. What did he desire you to do? A. To go with him — to conduct him to meet Colonel Irvine.
Q. He wished you to conduct him to meet Colonel Irvine? A. Yes.
Q. Where was Colonel Irvine represented to be coming from?
A. Coming from Qu'Appelle.
Q. And what were you to do; to show Mr Gordon the way? A. He did not know the way and requested me to take him through the woods to avoid the rebels.
Q. How far were you taken? A. To Hoodoo. Away as far as I possibly could to secure his safety and the safety of the despatches he carried.

Q. He was carrying despatches and he wished you to take him through the woods to avoid the rebels? A. Yes.

Q. How far did you go with him? A. To Hoodoo.

Q. How far is Hoodoo? A. About fifty miles. It is between Batoche and Humboldt.

Q. When did you get there? A. About noon of the following day.

Q. What did you find when you got there? A. I found Mr. Woodcock, who was then in charge of Hoodoo station, and another man whose name I don't know, who just came there with a load of oats.

Q. What do you mean by a station? Is it a mail station? A. A mail stopping place. There were also two other men with sleighs loaded with flour and goods for Carlton, I think, they told me.

Q. For whom? A. I think for the Hudson Bay Company, but I am not positive.

Q. Who were the men? A. Mr Isbister, and another I think who was called Campbell. I have seen the man often before, and I think that is his name.

Q. What happened while you were there? A. On towards evening, while I was out washing about the store I saw two half-breeds as I supposed coming along in jumpers, and I stepped inside and told Woodcock that the rebels were coming for us, and went out again and finished my washing, and then they drove up to the door, drove up along the road, got out of their jumpers and walked into the house, and I asked them what was going on at Batoche and they said nothing much, and I asked if Mr Riel was taking prisoners and they said they had got some, and I asked if they were getting a good deal of flour and he said they were getting a good deal, and I sat down to supper, and they went on conversing amongst themselves.

Q. Well, what else took place that you remember? A. At supper a few more came in. I said, getting pretty thick; I guess I will go outside and see if any more outside. I went outside and found about twenty or twenty-five armed men, and returned and finished my supper.

Q. What did you do next? A. There was one stepped up then and said he had a letter for Woodcock. I handed him the letter on a small slip of paper, and he read it. He handed it to me to read, and I think it stated that we have been told that you are going to furnish the police now coming up with hay and oats. If you do we will consider you a rebel – signed Garnot.

Q. Well, what else was said or done? A. I said that they hadn't ought to consider him a rebel at all, that he was simply performing his duty, and if Mr Irvine had orders to get hay and oats there, he would certainly have to get them given to him, and that I did not think they could consider him a rebel on such grounds or an enemy to them, with the idea probably of them getting them or leaving them there. They said anyway they had to take the prisoner and take him to Batoche, and I spoke up in his defence and they said they were going to take me also.

Q. Did they take you too? A. Yes.

Q. Now, was there a Mr Isbister there? A. Yes.

Q. And they took you both to Batoche? A. Yes.

Q. When did you get there? A. I should say about eleven or twelve o'clock. I am not positive.

Q. How many went with you? A. I think there was either seven or eight in my sleigh and about the same in Woodcock's.

Q. Armed? A. Yes.

Q. What did they do to Mr Isbister? A. I don't know. He was left there when I came away.

Q. You don't know whether they took his freight or not? A. I saw him next day in Batoche, and I think they did, but I am not positive.

Q. You got to Batoche about twelve I think? A. I did, about twelve.

Q. And what happened there? A. I was taken out of the sleigh and taken into the church.

Q. Whom did you see there? A. Well, I was not acquainted with any of them; I knew one was Gabriel Dumont; I had seen him before and knew him by sight.

Q. How many did you see? A. I should say about 300, around the church and in the church that night.

Q. That was the 21st? A. I think it was the 21st.

Q. Were they armed? A. Nearly all that I seen were armed.

Q. Were they all half-breeds or any Indians? A. Some Indians and some half-breeds; it was after night and I could not distinguish them.

Q. How long did they keep you? A. Dumont got up and made a speech of some length, I should say it took him about an hour, and afterwards an Indian got up and made a speech that lasted about half an hour, and then there was a good deal of talking and they took us away to the council house.

Q. Near the church? A. A little up the road from the church.

Q. What happened when you got there? A. There were several men around the lower storey, some eating, some talking and so on; and they kept me there till Mr Riel came.

Q. And what did he say or do? A. I was then conducted up stairs as I supposed into the council room. Mr Riel asked me what I –

Q. Were they sitting as a council around the table? A. I don't know, they were sitting around the table and around the house in all shapes possible.

Q. Was anybody acting as secretary? A. Yes, one whom I afterwards knew as Garnot was acting as secretary. Mr Riel asked me what I was about, and I told him I did not know what he meant; he says, what are you about, and I says I don't know, I don't know what you brought me here for; says he, where do you come from? I said, I come from Carrot River; he says, I consider you my enemy, and I says all right.

Q. Well, what more? A. He asked Mr Woodcock some questions. I am not positive to what the questions were, that is all that was said to him till morning.

Q. Well, what took place in the morning? A. In the morning I requested an interview with Mr Riel, and he gave me one; I asked him what I was brought there for, what he had against me, and he said he considered me an enemy, and I asked him why, and he said he considered all the people at Carrot River his enemies, and I told him I did not know any person there who was against him in the movement, before he took up arms, and when I left there they did not know he had taken up arms, and I said as far as I was concerned, I was not his enemy, although I would not take up arms to defend him, and I thought my best plan was to make some way to get out of there if I possibly could, for I was in a bad box. I was then taken to a house that I was told afterwards was Garnot's where I found other prisoners.

Q. And what took place then? A. I don't just recollect everything that took place, there was so much.

Q. Well, What conversation had you with the prisoner? A. With Riel?

Q. Yes? A. He came and asked me down that forenoon, I think it was in the forenoon and he wanted me to speak to him; he asked me if I knew there was any police coming, and I told him I thought there was but I did not know positively, and he said he had been told there were 500 coming, and he asked me if I thought it was true, and I told him I guessed it was, that I thought there was 500 coming; he asked me if I thought there was; I forget now how he mentioned it; anyway a deputation to settle his grievances was coming with them, and I told him I thought they were coming, something to that effect, that they were coming to try and settle this rebellion.

Q. A deputation was coming to try and settle the rebellion? A. Yes.

Q. You mean the 500 policemen were the deputation? A. No, I mean that there were other parties with the 500 policemen.

Q. Now, did he talk to you about his grievances, or what they were, or anything else? A. Not at that time.

Q. Well, when did he, if at any time? A. He did after the Duck Lake battle, and I think the day before. I had several conversations with Mr Riel. I could not just recollect what was said. He did talk to me about them after the Duck Lake battle, and I think the day before.

Q. Did he speak about his grievances, or what were the grievances? A. I couldn't state positively what he did claim as grievances. There were three grievances and other things. I don't exactly recollect what the conversation was.

Q. Were they general grievances or personal grievances? A. General grievances he spoke to me of.

Q. Well, what took place next; how long were you kept there? A. I think I was kept there till Wednesday in Batoche. I am not positive.

Q. And what happened there? A. Till the day before the Duck Lake fight, and I was then taken to Duck Lake.

Q. With an armed guard? A. With an armed guard.

Q. And where were you put there? A. In the up stairs of Mr Mitchell's house; at least I was informed it was Mitchell's.

Q. With other prisoners? A. Yes; Mr Peter Tompkins, Mr Lash, William Tompkins and Mr Woodcock.

Q. Did you see the people coming over — the body of the half-
breeds, and so on, coming to Duck Lake? A. I saw them leaving
Batoche and going to Duck Lake the night previous.

Q. About how many? A. I should say between 400 and 500.

Q. Was Riel with them? A. I did not see him.

Q. Did you see Riel at Duck Lake? A. Yes.

Q. When? A. Before going out to the battle, and coming back from
it.

Q. Did you see him actually go out to the battle? A. Yes; I saw him
going out of the yard towards where the police were coming.

Q. With others? A. With about between twenty and thirty men.

Q. And you saw him coming back from it? A. Yes.

Q. Well, when he came back did you hear him say anything? A. I
heard him speaking, but I could not understand him, for he spoke
in either French or Cree, I couldn't say which.

Q. Did he come up and speak to you at all? A. He did. After speaking to the men he came upstairs, and brought up Charles Newett,
the wounded man.

Q. What did he say about him? A. He told us he thought it was the
best thing he could do with a wounded man, that he thought we
would take better care of him than his own men would, and I
thanked him for bringing him up to us, and he then went
downstairs.

Q. Did he tell you anything about the battle? A. He did. After he
came back I asked him how many were killed, and he said nine
and he thought there were more, but nine were left on the field;
he thought a good many went away on the sleigh.

Q. Did he tell you anything else about the battle? A. I asked him
who fired first and he said the police, and he said he afterwards
then gave orders for his men to fire, three distinct orders.

Q. Did he say how he gave the orders? A. In the name of the Father
Almighty, I command you to fire, was the first time; at least I
think those are as near the words as I can repeat them. I think he
said the second time, in the name of Our Saviour who redeemed
us, I command you to fire; and the third time, in the name of the
Father, Son and Holy Ghost, I command you to fire.

Q. Then how long did you remain at Duck Lake? A. Till the
next day.

Q. And where were you taken then? A. I asked Mr Riel what he was
   going to do with the dead bodies the day of the battle, and he
   told me that he did not know, that they would consider. I said he
   ought to send some word to Major Crozier and let him know, and
   allow him to come and take away the bodies, and he said that he
   would consider the matter and see his council. Afterwards, he
   came back up there and I asked him what he was going to do, and
   he said they were afraid to send one of the men for fear Major
   Crozier would keep him prisoner. I told him if he would send me
   I would come back and give myself up again as a prisoner, and he
   would consider it, and he afterwards concluded to send one of
   the other men, and then finally he came himself and told me he
   would send me.

Q. Did he give you any letter to take? A. Yes.

Q. Is that the letter he gave you (showing witness a paper)? A. Well,
   I could not say, for I never saw the letter only while he was
   writing it, so that I could not actually give any evidence on the
   letter. I couldn't swear to it.

Q. You could not identify the letter or swear to the letter? A. No; I
   did not see it afterwards.

Q. Did you give the letter? A. I did.

Q. To whom? A. To Major Crozier.

Q. And what happened then? A. The next that happened I was detained by the police then and was not allowed to go back, as I
   had promised to do to Mr Riel.

Q. Did you assist in bringing the dead from the field? A. Yes.

Q. Well, did Riel ask you any questions after coming back from
   Duck Lake at all? A. Yes he asked me about the police. He had
   requested me while going with his message to tell the people (the
   volunteers) that he did not wish to fight them; that he wished
   them to remain neutral and afterwards help him to establish a
   government, and when I went back to Duck Lake I told him I had
   told the people this, which was a lie. I told him also that I was
   taken prisoner by Major Crozier and put into the cells, which was
   true, and that I was afterwards taken to Prince Albert by Major
   Crozier; that the volunteers there kicked because I was taken
   prisoner; that Major Crozier was afraid to stay and left Carlton
   and went to Prince Albert. That was lies also.

Q. That is the information you gave Mr Riel? A. That I gave Mr Riel.

Q. And then what happened to you? A. Well, before giving him this information he asked me about them and I told him that I refused to tell him anything about them without he told me whether I was to go back to the prisoners and whether I was to be allowed to go at large — go free — and he said I would be allowed to go free, so then I spun him a little yarn.

Q. Who wrote this letter that you took to Major Crozier? A. I could not say positively. Mr Riel was writing and so was Mr Garnot, and they had a great time getting up the letter, so I don't know which I should say.

Q. What do you mean by a great time? A. They wrote so many of them and destroyed them.

Q. They wrote more than one before they got one to suit them? A. Yes.

Q. And finally they finished one and gave it to you? A. Yes.

By MR GREENSHIELDS:

Q. At the time you were taken prisoner did Riel take any part in it? A. No, I did not see him.

Q. It was only after you had been taken prisoner that you saw him? A. Yes.

Q. At the time you spoke to him regarding the formation of a government did he give you any idea of what kind of a government he proposed forming? A. Yes; he said he was going to divide the country up into seven parts. One part was to be for the Canadian or white settlers, one-seventh, another seventh for the Indians, another seventh for the half-breeds, and he named over what he was going to do with the rest. I don't recollect the names of the people.

Q. Did he tell you he was going to give other sevenths to other nationalities, the Poles, Hungarians and Bavarians and Jews? A. No; he did not.

Q. Did you hear him say anything about giving a portion of it to the Germans? A. No; not to my knowledge, he named over, I think it was three-sevenths of it was to remain to support the Government.

Q. That was for himself, I suppose? A. Yes, I suppose so, for the government he was about to establish.

Q. Now, that was about the extent of the conversation with him regarding this government? A. Yes; that was about the extent of it.

Q. He did not say anything about expecting assistance from foreign powers in his undertaking? A. No; he did not.

Q. Did he talk to you anything about religion? A. Yes.

Q. What did he tell you about that? A. He told me he had cut himself loose from Rome altogether, and would have nothing more to do with the Pope, that they were not going to pay taxes to Rome. He said if they still kept on with Rome, they could not agree with the Canadians and white people who came there to live because their government would have to keep all Protestants out of the country, if they kept on with Rome.

Q. That is, if the Riel government kept on with Rome, they would have to keep all Protestants out of the country? A. Yes.

Q. And abandoning Rome, they would be able to allow Protestants to come into the country? A. Yes, that is what I understood from him.

Q. Well, did he mention anything to you about who was to succeed the Pope? A. He did not.

Q. Did he tell you he was going to play Pope for the North-West Territories? A. He did not.

Q. Well, did he explain to you any of his principles of the religion that he was founding? A. No; by the way he spoke to me, the religion was just the same, any more than he had cut himself from the Pope.

ROBERT JEFFERSON sworn
Examined by MR CASGRAIN:

Q. In the course of this last spring I believe you were in Poundmaker's reserve, were you not? A. I was.

Q. In his camp? A. In his camp.

Q. About what month? A. The end of March, and April and May. I don't believe it was the whole of May though.

Q. Last? A. Yes.

Q. Who is Poundmaker? A. He is one of the chiefs of the Cree tribe.

Q. Had he a band of Indians with him? A. He had a band of Indians.

Q. A large band? A. Yes, he had a large band.

Q. Do you recognise this letter (18) and if so, where did you see it? A. Well, I have seen it twice.

Q. Where did you see it the first time? A. I saw it the first time in the camp, and the second time was in the camp too.

Q. You saw it twice in the camp? A. Twice in the camp, yes — once after the capitulation and the other before.

Q. Whose hand was it in the first time you saw it? A. It was in the hands of Poundmaker.

Q. And the second time? A. The second time it was in the hands of Poundmaker.

Q. And the second time? A. The second time it was in the hands of Poundmaker's wife.

Q. How did it get there? Into the camp into Poundmaker's hands? A. It was brought in by Delorme and Chic-i-cum.

Q. What was his Christian name, do you remember? A. I could not say.

Q. He was a half-breed? A. He was a half-breed, yes.

Q. From where? A. From Duck Lake.

Q. Chic-i-cum is an Indian, isn't he? A. Yes.

Q. Do you remember the battle of Cut Knife? A. Yes.

Q. Was this before or after the battle of Cut Knife? A. It was before, considerably.

Q. Was it after the battle of Duck Lake? A. Yes, it was after the battle of Duck Lake.

Q. When was the battle of Cut Knife fought? A. I could not say the date.

Q. About what time? A. About the beginning of May.

Examined by MR GREENSHEILDS:

Q. Was Poundmaker reading this letter at the time that you saw it in his hands? A. No, he was not.

Q. Do you know whether he can read or not? A. I do.

Q. Does he read English? A. No.

Q. Does he read French? A. No, nor French, he does not read at all.

Q. What was he doing with the letter when you saw it in his hands? A. The letter was brought to him.

Q. Handed to him? A. Yes.

Q. In your presence? A. No.

Q. Did you see it brought to him? A. No, I could not say that I saw it brought to him.

Q. Well, how do you know the letter was brought to him? A. Well, everyone said it was brought to him.

Q. But you don't know anything about it yourself? A. I beg your pardon, I know it was brought to him. He said it was brought to him.

Q. Who said? A. Poundmaker.

Q. But you don't know of your personal knowledge it was brought to him? A. No, I did not see it brought to him.

Q. What was he doing with it when you saw it in his hands? Was he looking at it as a matter of curiosity or what? A. No, I believe he was going to put it away.

Q. Did he know what it was? A. O, yes, he knew what it was.

Q. He knew it was a letter, eh? A. He knew it was a letter.

Q. Did he ask you to read it for him? A. No, he did not.

Q. Do you know yourself now where he got that letter, or how he got it, of your own personal knowledge, not what he told you or anybody else told you, but of your own personal knowledge? A. No, I don't.

Q. You don't know anything about it, do you? A. No.

Q. You don't even know whether it was intended for Poundmaker or not, do you? A. Not of my own personal knowledge.

Re-examined by MR CASGRAIN:

Q. Was this letter read to Poundmaker? A. It was.

Q. By whom? A. By the man that brought it.

Q. Was it interpreted to him? A. It was interpreted to him.

By MR GREENSHIELDS:

Q. How do you know it was read to him? A. I heard them read it.

Q. Where were you when it was read? A. I was there when he read it.

Q. Do you understand French? A. I don't understand very much of it.

Q. Did you have the letter in your hand? A. I did, yes.

Q. Was it read in French to Poundmaker, or in English, or how, or German, or what? A. It was translated for him. I believe it was read in French to him first. I believe it was read in French first. I am not certain about it, though.

Q. How do you know it was translated to him? A. Well, I heard what was called a translation of it.

Q. What were you doing there about that time? A. I was listening.

Q. Now, how do you know it was translated, if you never read the letter? A. I never said I never read the letter.

Q. Well, did you ever read it? A. I did read it.

Q. Before or after it was translated? A. After this.

Q. After it was translated? A. After it was translated.

Q. Let us hear you read it now and tell us what is in it? A. But I have heard your translation here –

Q. You said you heard that translated, because you understood it.
Now, let us hear what that letter means, not what anybody told
you or what you heard, but we want to know what your knowledge of the contents of that letter is? A. (Reading the letter as
follows: — Since we wrote to you important events have occurred
to the half-breeds and savages and Indians of Fort Battleford and
vicinity. Since we wrote to you important events have occurred,
the police came to attack us, and we encountered them. God has
given us victory. Thirty half-breeds and five Crees have sustained
the battle against 120 men. After thirty-five or forty minutes of
fire, the enemy took flight. Bless God —)

Q. Now, did you read the letter before it was translated in language to
Poundmaker? A. No, I read it afterwards.

Q. And he read it over in French first of all to Poundmaker, and
then afterwards in English? A. Then afterwards in Cree. I think he
read it in French first, but I am not sure.

By MR JUSTICE RICHARDSON:

Q. Do you understand Cree? A. Yes.

MR ROBINSON: I think your Honor that that will be the last witness for the Crown. I am not quite sure till to-morrow, and of course
we will adjourn now, it being six o'clock.

Court here adjourned till ten o'clock, a.m., to-morrow.

Thursday, 30th July

Court opened at 10 A.M.

FATHER ALEXIS ANDRÉ sworn

Examined by MR LEMIEUX: (Mr F.R. Marceau being interpreter.)

Q. What is your name and religion? A. Alexis André, Oblat. I would
prefer to speak in French. I understand the English very well, but
speaking it is quite a different matter.

Q. You are the superior of the Oblats in the district of — ? A. Of
Carlton.

Q. For how long? A. Since seven years.

Q. Since how long have you been living in the country? A. I lived in
the country since 1865, in the Saskatchewan.

Q. Do you know the population and habits of the people? A. For
twenty-five years I have been continually with the half-breeds of

the Saskatchewan above and below. I was four years with the
same population in Dakota.

Q. You have been with the half-breeds, Catholic and Protestant?
A. They were mixed up in the colony, and I knew a great many
both of the Catholic and Protestant half-breeds, and had a great
many friends among the Protestants.

Q. Do you remember 1884 and 1885? Do you remember the events
of those years? A. Yes, very well.

Q. Do you remember the circumstances under which the prisoner
came into the Saskatchewan country in 1884? A. Yes, I remember very well.

Q. At that time there was an agitation in the Saskatchewan about
certain rights the half-breeds claimed they had against the Federal
Government? A. Yes, about three months before there was an
agitation amongst the English and French half-breeds.

Q. State what were the claims of the half-breeds towards the Federal
Government? A. At first I did not know what was the cause of
the agitation in the country.

Q. Afterwards? A. After, we knew from questioning the half-breeds
that they were going to see Riel.

Q. And finally Riel came into the country? A. Yes.

Q. In what month? A. About the 1st of July 1884.

Q. During the first months that he was in the country was there a
constitutional agitation going on? A. Yes, there were meetings
held amongst the French and English half-breeds, and at Prince
Albert there was a meeting at which I was present myself.

Q. Do you know that resolutions were passed and sent to the
Federal authorities? A. I did not know that resolutions were
passed at the meeting.

Q. Did you know of petitions and requisitions being sent to the
Federal Government? A. At that time I did not know of any,
only of the meetings and the speeches.

Q. At the assembly you were at did you take part? A. No. I was
there as a spectator and did not speak.

Q. You did not take any part? A. I was only there as a spectator.

Q. Did you yourself communicate with the Dominion Government?
A. At what time?

Q. I mean in regard to the rights and claims of the half-breeds.
A. Yes, I communicated.

Q. At what time? A. I am not sure at what time — in 1882 I did communicate.

Q. Since that have you communicated? A. Not directly.

Q. How did you communicate? A. I communicated directly in regard to Riel.

Q. Can you tell me in what manner you communicated? A. I communicated in December when Riel said he wanted to go out of the country because of the agitation that was existing in the country.

Q. Did you communicate after that? A. No. I communicated after the rebellion.

Q. With whom? A. The Minister of Public Works.

Q. The Hon. Mr Langevin? A. Yes, asking help for those who were in distress.

Q. What were the claims of the half-breeds? A. Since when; you must distinguish.

Q. From 1884 until the time of the rebellion? A. Since the arrival of the prisoner in the country?

Q. Yes? A. It would be difficult to tell that; they changed from time to time since the arrival of the prisoner.

Q. Before his arrival? A. They demanded patents for their land, demanded frontage on the river, and the abolition of the taxes on wood, and the rights for those who did not have scrip in Manitoba.

Q. In what way did the half-breeds put forth their rights before the arrival of the prisoner? A. By public meetings, at which I assisted several times myself.

Q. Did you take part yourself? A. Yes; at all those meetings.

Q. Were communications made with the Dominion Government, resolutions and petitions? A. I remember three or four times that there was.

Q. Did you get any answer to your communications? A. I think we received an answer once — perhaps we received an answer once.

Q. Was the answer favorable? A. No; it was an evasive answer, saying they would take the question into consideration.

Q. That was the only answer to a number of communications?
A. Yes. I know of another communication made by Monsignor Grandin to the same effect.

Q. Did he get a favorable response? A. No; I do not know of any.

Q. Do you know if there was an answer sent to Charles Nolin in regard to a petition sent to the Government? A. It was in regard to those meetings I was making reference. I only know as to one answer.

Q. Finally, after these petitions and resolutions had been adopted at the public meetings and sent to the Government, was there a change in the state of things that existed then? A. The silence of the Government produced great dissatisfaction in the minds of the people.

Q. To-day are the people in a better position than they were before in regard to the rights they claim? A. They have not yet received the patents for their land on the South Saskatchewan.

MR OSLER: I must object to this class of questions being introduced. My learned friends have opened a case of treason, justified only by the insanity of the prisoner; they are now seeking to justify armed rebellion for the redress of these grievances. These two defences are inconsistent. One is no justification at all. We are willing to allow all possible latitude, but they have gone as far as I feel they should go. We have allowed them to describe documents which they have not produced, and answers in writing, so that they might not be embarrassed, and that the outline of the position might be fairly given to the jury, but it is not evidence, and if my learned friend is going into it in detail, I think it is objectionable.

HIS HONOR: Supposing they are going to produce these writings?

MR OSLER: They could not be evidence. They would not be evidence in justification; that is admitted. It cannot be possible for my learned friends to open the case on one defence and go the jury indirectly upon another. Of course, it is not really any defence in law, and should not be gone into with any greater particularity. If this is given in evidence, we would have to answer it in many particulars, and then there would be the question of justifying the policy of the Government.

HIS HONOR: It would be trying the Government.

MR OSLER: It is as it were a counter-claim against the Government and that is not open to any person on trial for high treason. We have no desire to unduly limit my learned friend, but I cannot consent to trying such an issue as that here.

MR LEMIEUX: I do not want to justify the rebellion. I want to show the state of things in the country so as to show that the

prisoner was justified in coming into the country and to show the
circumstances under which he came.

HIS HONOR: Have you not done that already?

MR LEMIEUX: I have, perhaps, to the satisfaction of the court, but,
perhaps, others may not be so well satisfied.

MR OSLER: If you do not go any further we will withdraw our
objection.

MR LEMIEUX: I want to get further facts, not in justification of the
rebellion, but to explain the circumstances under which the accused
came into the country. I had a right to prove what I have already
proved a minute ago, I am entitled to prove other facts. If I was right
a moment ago, I should be allowed to put similar questions now.

HIS HONOR: The objection is not urged until you have gone as far
as the counsel for the Crown thought you ought to go.

MR LEMIEUX: It is rather late now to object.

MR OSLER: I warned my learned friends quietly before.

MR LEMIEUX: Well, I will put the question and it can be objected to.

Q. Will you say if the state of things in the country, the actual state
of things in the country in 1882, 1883 and 1884, and if to-day
the state of things is the same as in 1882, 1883 and 1884? If
justice has been done to the claims and just rights of the people?

MR OSLER: That question must be objected to, it could not have
had anything to do with bringing the prisoner here. I object first, as
a matter of opinion. Second, that it is a leading question. And third,
that it is irrelevant to the issue.

MR LEMIEUX: The most important objection is that it is leading.
As to the opinion of the witness, I should think his opinion is valu-
able, it is facts I want from the witness. I suppose he can give his
opinion based on the facts. If he says no, or yes, I will ask him why
and he will give me his reason why.

HIS HONOR: That will be a matter of opinion.

MR LEMIEUX: I will put the question and you can object to it.

Q. Do you know if at any time the Dominion Government agreed or
acceded to the demands made by the half-breeds and clergy
relative to the claims and rights that you have spoken of in the
preceding answer.

MR OSLER: I do not object to the question if confined to a date
prior to the 1st of July, 1884, the time he was asked to come into
the country, although the question is really irregular. I am not going

by strict lines, but I do object to his asking as regards the present
state of things. I do not object if he confines his questions to the
time prior to the prisoner coming to the country.

MR LEMIEUX: My question will show that the prisoner had reason
to come, if the people had confidence in him he had a right to come
and help them to try and persuade the Federal Government to grant
what had been refused them so far.

HIS HONOR: Your question is what, Mr Lemieux?

MR OSLER: I am willing that the question should be allowed if
limited to the time prior to July 1884.

HIS HONOR, to MR LEMIEUX: Is that the way you put it?

MR LEMIEUX: Yes.

MR OSLER: Then we withdraw the objection.

HIS HONOR: Then we will have his answer.

MR LEMIEUX: I want to put the question generally.

MR OSLER: It is so general and difficult to grasp in any way I won't
object.

MR LEMIEUX: Perhaps it is difficult to you but not to the witness.

Q. Will you state if since the arrival of the prisoner in the country up
to the time of the rebellion, the Government has made any
favorable answer to the demands and claims of the half-breeds?
A. Yes, I know that they have acceded to certain demands in
regard to those who did not have any scrip in Manitoba. A telegram was sent on the 4th of March last, granting the scrip.

Q. Before that time? A. Yes, regarding the alteration of the survey of
lots on the river, there was an answer from the Government
saying they would grant it, and that was an important question.

Q. What question then remained to be settled? A. The question of
patents, that has been settled also in a certain way, because Mr
Duck was sent and I went with him as interpreter.

Q. What other question remained? A. Only the question of wood,
timber.

Q. You know now that there is a commission sitting in regard to the
claims and petitions of half-breeds? A. Yes.

Q. Do you know how many claims and demands have been settled
by that commission since it has been in existence? A. In what
place? Is it in the north-West or in the district of Carlton?

Q. Generally? A. I do not know. I know for my own district.

Q. What do you know? A. I know that at Batoche they gave three scrips.

Q. Since the rebellion? A. About three weeks.

Q. At Duck Lake? A. Forty.

Q. Since the rebellion? A. Yes, about the same time.

Q. Do you know of any others? A. No, not in that district.

Q. You have had occasion to meet the prisoner between July 1884, and the time of the rebellion? A. Yes.

Q. What is the name of your parish? A. Prince Albert.

Q. You saw the prisoner there? A. Yes.

Q. Did you see him elsewhere? A. At St Laurent several times. I don't know how often, and I saw him at Batoche also.

Q. Have you had occasion to speak often to him on the political situation and on religion? A. Frequently, it was the matter of our conversation.

Q. Do you like to speak of religion and politics with him? A. No, I did not like to.

Q. Will you give me your reasons why you did not like to speak of politics and religion with him? A. Politics and religion was a subject he always spoke of in conversation, he loved those subjects.

Q. Did he speak in a sensible manner? A. I wish to say why I did not like to speak to him on those subjects. Upon all other matters, literature and science he was in his ordinary state of mind.

Q. Upon political subjects and religion? A. Upon politics and religion he was no longer the same man. It would seem as if there were two men in him, he lost all control of himself upon these questions.

Q. When he spoke of religion and politics? A. Yes, on those two matters he lost all control of himself.

Q. Did you consider after the conversations you have had with him that when he spoke on politics and religion he had his intelligence? A. Many times, at least twenty times, I told him I would not speak on those subjects because he was a fool. He did not have his intelligence of mind.

Q. Is that the practical result that you have found in your conversation with Riel on political and religious questions? A. It is my experience.

Q. You have had a good deal of experience with people, and you have known persons who were afflicted with mania? A. Before answering that, I want to state a fact to the court regarding the prisoner; you know the life of that man affected us during a certain time.

Q. In what way? A. He was a fervent Catholic, attending the church and attending to his religious duties frequently, and his state of mind was the cause of great anxiety. In conversation on politics and on the rebellion, and on religion, he stated things which frightened the priests. I am obliged to visit every month the fathers (priests) of the district. Once all of the priests met together, and they put the question: Is it possible to allow that man to continue in his religious duties? And they unanimously decided that on this question he was not responsible, that he was completely a fool on this question, that he could not suffer any contradiction. On the question of religion and politics we considered that he was completely a fool. In discussing these questions, it was like showing a red flag to a bull, to use a vulgar expression.

Cross-examined by MR CASGRAIN:

Q. I believe in the month of December 1884, you had an interview with Riel and Nolin with regard to a certain sum of money which the prisoner claimed from the Federal Government? A. Not with Nolin. Nolin was not present at the interview.

Q. The prisoner was there? A. Yes.

Q. Will you please state what the prisoner asked of the Federal Government? A. I had two interviews with the prisoner on that subject.

Q. The prisoner claimed a certain indemnity from the Federal Government, didn't he? A. When the prisoner made his claim I was there with another gentleman, and he asked from the Government $100,000. We thought that was exorbitant, and the prisoner said: Wait a little, I will take at once $35,000 cash.

Q. And on that condition the prisoner was to leave the country if the Government gave him the $35,000? A. Yes, that was the condition he put.

Q. When was this? A. That was on the 23rd December 1884.

Q. There was also another interview between you and the prisoner? A. There has been about twenty interviews between us.

Q. He was always after you to ask you to use your influence with the Federal Government to obtain this indemnity? A. The first

time he spoke of it was on the 12th December, he had never
spoken a word about it before, and on the 23rd December he
spoke about it again.

Q. He talked about it very frequently? A. On these two occasions
only.

Q. That was his great occupation? A. Yes, at those times.

Q. Is it not true that the prisoner told you he himself was the half-
breed question? A. He did not say so in express terms, but he
conveyed that idea. He said, if I am satisfied, the half-breeds will
be. I must explain this – this objection was made to him, that
even if the Government granted him $35,000, the half-breed
question would remain the same, and he said, in answer to that, if
I am satisfied the half-breeds will be.

Q. Is it not a fact he told you he would even accept a less sum than
the $35,000? A. Yes. He said, use all the influence you can, you
may not get all that, but get all you can, and if you get less we
will see.

Q. When he spoke of religion, the principal thing of which he spoke
was it not the supremacy of Pope Leo the XIII? A. Before the
rebellion, he never spoke directly on that question as to the
supremacy of the Pope.

Q. On that question he was perfectly reasonable? A. On religious
questions, before that time, he blamed everything. He wanted to
change mass and the liturgy, the ceremonies and the symbols.

Q. Do you pretend that every man who has strange ideas on religious
matters is a fool? A. No, I don't pretend that.

Q. A man may have particular views on religious matters and still
retain all his reason and intelligence? A. That depends on the way
in which he explains his ideas, and by his conduct in expressing
them.

Q. A man may be a great reformer of great religious questions without being a fool? A. I do not deny history, but the reformer must
have some principle which the prisoner never had.

Q. Is it not true that the prisoner had fixed principles in his new
religion? A. He had the principle that he was an autocrat in
religion and politics and he changed his opinions as he wished.

Q. Do you say he changed his religion as he wished? A. His ideas
changed. To-day he admitted this and to-morrow denied it. He
was his own judge in these matters. He believed himself infallible.

Q. Is it not a fact that the half-breeds are a people extremely religious? A. I admit the fact, very religious.

Q. Is it not true that religion has a great influence upon them? A. Yes.

Q. Is it not true that a man who tried to govern them by inducing them to completely change their religion or to do away with it would have no influence with them at all? A. Exactly, it was just because he was so religious and appeared so devout that he exercised such a great influence over them. I wish to explain this point, because it is a great point. With the half-breeds he never was contradicted, and consequently he was never excited with them and he appeared in his natural state with them. He did not admit his strange views at first. It was only after a time that he proclaimed them and especially after the provisional government had been proclaimed.

Re-examined by MR LEMIEUX:

Q. Is it not a fact that if any proposition was made to Riel, he became irascible and violent and almost uncontrollable? A. As far as personal experience goes he would not allow the least opposition at all. Immediately his physiognomy changed and he beame a different man.

Mr Casgrain objects to this evidence on the ground that it should have been given on the examination-in-chief.

PHILIP GARNOT sworn

Examined by MR FITZPATRICK:

Q. What is your name? A. Philip Garnot.

Q. Where do you live when you are at home? A. At Batoche.

Q. Where are you living at the present time? A. In Regina jail.

Q. Do you know Riel, the prisoner at the bar? A. I do.

Q. You have known him for how long? A. I saw him for the first time in Helena, Montana, about seven years ago.

Q. Did you see him at Batoche during the course of last summer or in the Saskatchewan district? A. I saw him last fall.

Q. What time last fall? A. In October.

Q. From that time up to the month of March last did you have occasion to see him frequently? A. No, I did not see much of him. I only saw him once or twice.

Q. During that time did you have any conversation with him? A. Not that I remember.

Q. No conversation whatever with him? A. I had some small conversation, but none that I can remember well.

Q. Do you remember during the course of last autumn and last
winter up to the month of March – do you remember having any
conversation with him on religious matters or on political
matters? A. No, I never had.

Q. No conversation whatever up to that time? A. I had some conversation, but not on religion or politics.

Q. Did you at any time talk to him on religion previous to his
arrest? A. I did. After the trouble, after the 18th March.

Q. Was he living at your house? A. No, but he came there occasionally and slept there sometimes.

Q. When he spoke to you of religion do you remember what he said
to you? A. I know he was talking to me about changing the Pope,
or something of that kind; wanting to name Bishop Bourget, of
Montreal, Pope of the new world, as he named it. He spoke to me
several things about religion that I cannot remember.

Q. Did he say anything to you about the Holy Ghost or the Spirit of
God? A. Yes, he said in my presence, not to me exactly, at a
meeting, that the spirit of Elias was with him.

Q. Did he say he had any of the divine attributes that are generally
attributed to Elias? A. That is what I think he meant by that.

Q. What did he say about it as far as you can recollect? A. He
wanted the people in the meeting to acknowledge him as a
prophet, and he gave them to understand he had the spirit of
Elias in him and that he was prophesying.

Q. Do you remember any of his numerous prophesies? A. I don't
remember them all.

Q. Do you remember any of them? A. I know every morning, almost
every morning, he would come in front of the people and say
such and such a thing would happen. I don't remember any of
them in particular.

Q. You said a moment ago he spent some nights at your house?
A. Yes, he slept once or twice at my house.

Q. During the nights he spent there did you notice anything remarkable about him? A. I know he was praying loud all night and kept
me awake sometimes.

Q. Everyone else was asleep in the house at the time? A. I was the
only other one in the house with him.

Q. Can you remember now the kind of prayers he delivered himself of? A. It was prayers he was making up himself. I never heard them before.

Q. You are a Roman Catholic? A. Yes.

Q. You are a French-Canadian? A. Yes.

Q. Had you ever heard any of these prayers before? A. I never heard them, except some of them. He would say the prayer 'Our Father,' but all the rest of the prayers I never heard before, except by him.

Q. During the time you saw him when he delivered himself of these prophesies you alluded to, what was his temper; how did he act when contradicted? A. He would not stand contradicition by anyone. He had to have his own way in everything.

Q. Was he very smooth tempered? A. No he was not smooth tempered.

Q. Irritable? A. Yes.

Q. Did he make any declarations to you as to what he thought him-self to be in the way of power or authority? A. No, he did not make any statement to me, but in my presence he made the declaration that he was representing St. Peter.

Q. Did he aspire to any particular gifts, or pretend he was endowed with the abilities of a poet, musician or orator? A. No.

Q. You did not hear him boast of his great intellectual qualities? A. No.

Q. Did he at any time communicate to you his views with reference to the way in which the country was to be divided in the event of his success? A. He did in my presence.

Q. Tell us what he said to you about that as far as you can remem-ber? A. He was talking about the country being divided into several provinces; one for the French, Germans, Irish, and I don't know what else. There was to be seven different nationalities.

Q. Do you remember anything else besides this you have men-tioned? What other foreigners? A. Italians.

Q. Hungarians? A. I can't remember particularly very well. I know it was seven different provinces and seven different nationalities.

Q. Did the plan he then stated appear to you a very feasible one? A. I did not believe he could succeed in that.

Q. Did he say he expected any assistance from these people? A. Yes, he espected assistance from them. He mentioned he expected the

assistance of an army of several nationalities, and I remember he
mentioned the Jews. He expected their assistance and money. He
was going to give them a province as a reward for their help. That
is what I understood him to say.

Q. Did he tell you how he had arranged that, or if he had made any
arrangement with the people? A. He might, but I don't
remember.

Q. In his conversation with you, or with others in your presence on
these subjects, did he at any time give you any intimation that he
had any doubt of his success or that any obstacle could prevent
him from succeeding? A. No, he always mentioned he was going
to succeed. That it was a divine mission he had, and that he was
only an instrument in the hand of God.

Q. When he talked of other matters than religion and the success of
his plans, how did he act and talk generally? A. I never noticed
any difference in his talk on other matters, because I never had
much intercourse with him only during the time of the trouble. I
met him once before that.

Q. Did he appear to be actuated by any friendship for other people,
or did he appear to be wrapped up in himself? Did he appear to
have any sympathy for anyone except himself, or did he appear
to think of anyone but himself, I mean during these times you
had conversations with him? A. I could not answer that question
because I don't understand rightly.

Q. When he spoke of religion and about the country in the different
interviews he had with you or others, did you understand that he
had any idea of thinking of the welfare of anyone at all except
himself; that he was the sole person to be considered? A. It
seemed as if he was working in the interest of the half-breed
population, and the settlers generally; he mentioned that.

Q. Did you communicate to anyone your impression of this man —
what you thought of him? A. I did.

Q. What did you think of him? A. I thought the man was crazy,
because he acted very foolish.

Cross-examied by MR ROBINSON:

Q. He had great influence over the half-breed population there,
hadn't he? A. Yes, he could do almost what he wanted with them.

Q. And you were one of those who followed him? A. No, I followed
him, but against my will.

Q. What do you mean? A. When a man has a stronger force than I
have, I have to follow him. He came to me with an armed force
and I had to go.

Q. Do you say you were forced to follow him by violence, is that
what you mean? A. I don't mean to say that I was forced exactly
by violence, he came and brought me from my house, he came
with armed men, and I saw there was no use resisting.

Q. Do you mean to say you followed him because of the armed men,
and that that was all that influenced you? A. Yes.

Q. He had great influence over all the French half-breed population? A. I always thought he had lots of influence amongst the
half-breeds.

Q. I believe they all looked to him as a leader and followed him?
A. Yes they did.

Q. They relied upon his judgment and advice? A. They did.

FATHER VITAL FOURMOND sworn (Arthur Lewis, sworn as
interpreter.)

Examined by MR LEMIEUX:

Q. Your profession? A. I am a priest at St Laurent, in the district of
Carlton, an Oblat father.

Q. For how long have you been a priest? A. Ten years. I arrived at
the place in the year 1875.

Q. Have you known the prisoner Riel since 1884? A. Yes; directly
since his arrival. I knew the prisoner by what I had heard, but I
never seen him till then.

Q. Since his arrival in the country have you had several conversations
with the prisoner up to the time of the rebellion? A. Very often.

Q. At St Laurent? A. At St Laurent, at Batoche, and during the war.

Q. Had you any conversation with the prisoner on religious and
political subjects? A. Very often.

Q. Were you present at the meeting which Father André spoke of in
which Riel's judgement and sanity was questioned? A. Yes; I was
present.

Q. Did you agree with the other fathers in the opinion as to the
sanity of the prisoner? A. It was me consulted the reverend fathers.

Q. Were you personally acquainted with the facts upon which you
based your opinion as to the insanity of Riel? A. I was personally
acquainted with the facts upon which they based their opinion.

Q. Will you please state upon what facts you based your opinion
   that the prisoner was not sane on religious or political matters?
   A. Permit me to divide the answer into two: the facts before the
   rebellion and the facts during the rebellion. Before the rebellion it
   appeared as if there were two men in the prisoner. In private conversation he was affable, polite, pleasant and a charitable man to
   me. I noticed that even when he was quietly talked to about the
   affairs of politics and government, and he was not contradicted
   he was quite rational; but as soon as he was contradicted on these
   subjects, then he became a different man and would be carried
   away with his feelings. He would go so far as to use violent expressions to those who were even his friends. As soon as the rebellion commenced, then he became excited and was carried away
   and he lost all control of himself and of his temper. He went so
   far that when a father contradicted him, he became quite excited
   and had no respect for him, and he often threatened to destroy
   all the churches. He says there is danger for you, but thanks for
   the friendship I have for you I will protect you from any harm.
   Once I went to St Antoine and there I met a number of priests,
   and Riel says, I have been appointed by the council to be your
   spiritual adviser. I said that our spiritual adviser was a bishop and
   that Mr Riel would not be him. There is only one way you can be
   our adviser, the only way you can become so is by shooting us,
   the only way you can direct us is by shooting us, and then you
   can direct our corpses in any way you like; that was my answer to
   him. (The interpreter states that he does not feel qualified to
   correctly interpret the evidence, and Mr Casgrain proposes that
   they translate the evidence given by the defence, and Mr Fitzpatrick that given by the Crown, which is agreed to.) Witness
   continues: He had extraordinary ideas on the subject of the
   Trinity. The only God was God the Father, and that God the Son
   was not God; the Holy Ghost was not God either; the second
   person of the Trinity was not God and as a consequence of this
   the Virgin Mary was not the mother of God but the mother of
   the Son of God. That is the reason why he changed the formula
   of the prayer which is commonly known as 'Hail Mary.' Instead
   of saying 'Hail Mary, mother of God,' he said 'Hail Mary, mother
   of the Son of God.' He did not admit the doctrines of the church,
   of the divine presence; according to his ideas it was not God who

was present in the host, but an ordinary man 6 feet high. As to his political ideas, he wanted first to go to Winnipeg and Lower Canada and the United States and even France. He said he will take your country even, and then he was to go to Italy and overthrow the Pope and then he would choose another Pope of his own making.

MR OSLER: Your Honor, we would prefer the interpretation should be done by a regular interpreter. I don't think it is within the ordinary rules of evidence that it should be done as it now is; it is a question whether, even if consented to as in this case, it would be binding in a criminal case.

Court here adjourns for lunch.
On court resuming, Louis Bourget was appointed interpreter.

Q. Before adjournment you said that Riel had said that he was going down to Winnipeg, then he was going to the Province of Quebec, then he was going to cross the ocean and go to Paris and Rome and have a new Pope elected; he would get one appointed or appoint himself as Pope? A. Yes, he said something to that effect.

Q. Have you made up your mind about the prisoner being insane as far as religious matters are concerned? A. We were much embarrassed at first, because sometimes he looked reasonable and sometimes he looked as a man who did not know what he was saying.

Q. Finally? A. We made up our minds there was no way to explain his conduct but that he was insane, otherwise he would have to be too big a criminal.

Q. As the agitation was progressing did you notice a change in his conduct, in his mind? A. A great change, he was a great deal more excitable.

Q. At the time of the rebellion you formed the opinion that he was insane? A. Yes, I can tell some facts to that effect.

Q. If it is not too long, will you tell us what it is? A. Once he was asked by the people to explain his views on religion or religious matters so that they could see through them. When he found out the clergy were against him, that he was contradicted, he turned against the clergy, particularly against me, and opposed the clergy, and kept following me into the tents wherever I would go. He compelled me to leave the place, go down to the river and cross to the other side. There were several women there who came to shake hands with me. The prisoner had a very extraordinary expression upon his face, he was excited by the opinion he gave upon religion. The prisoner spoke to the women and said: 'Woe unto you if you go to the priests, because you will be killed by the priests.' All of a sudden, when I came to the boat, which was not very easy to get into, the prisoner, with great politeness, came up and said: 'Look out, father, I will help you to get on the boat.'

Q. In an instant he passed from great rage to great politeness, in very few minutes? A. Yes, the first time I was at Batoche I was brought before the council by the prisoner.

Q. When you first came to Batoche were you friends with the prisoner? A. Yes, I was.

Q. You repeat what you have already said that in matters political and religious the prisoner was not in his mind? A. Yes.

Q. And could not be controlled? A. Yes.

Q. And was not sane? A. Yes.

Q. What happened at the council house when he brought you there? A. I was made to render an account of my conduct as a priest, and on several other matters against the provisional government. The prisoner got very much excited and called me a little tiger.

Q. Why did he call you a little tiger? A. I do not know, I suppose because I contradicted him. It was about ten o'clock when I asked to go, late at night, and then the prisoner became very polite and offered a carriage to convey me. The council was in the room above. There was a stairs I had to go down, and I had a parcel in my hands, under my arm. With extraordinary politeness the prisoner took the parcel and said 'Father, you may hurt yourself.'

Q. Did he ever show you a little book in which he had written those prophecies in the blood of the buffalo as to the future of this country? A. I heard of it but I never saw it. The prisoner never spoke to me about the book.

By MR CASGRAIN:

Q. It was when the prisoner was contradicted that he became uncontrollable? A. Yes, that is what I said.

Q. It was then the prisoner became uncontrollable? A. Yes, and at other times too.

Q. The half-breeds did not contradict him upon religious matters?
A. Some of the half-breeds did contradict him.

Q. A great number? Most of the half-breeds followed him in his religious views? A. I cannot say; most would be too many.

Q. A great number? A. Yes, and several did not dare to express their views.

Q. Before the rebellion began he was quiet and sane in mind? A. Yes, relatively, except sometimes when he was contradicted, as I said this morning.

Q. When do you fix the commencement of the rebellion? A. 18th of March. The prisoner came himself and proclaimed the rebellion.

Q. He made you take an oath of neutrality towards the provisional government during the rebellion? A. No, there was no oath, but there was a written promise concerning the exercise of the ministry.

Q. Was it in terms of neutrality towards the provisional government? A. Yes.

Q. You said there was no other way to explain his conduct than to say he was insane or a great criminal, and you would rather say he was insane — rather than say he was insane — rather than say he was a great criminal you would say he was insane? A. I did not say that, but in my mind it was the best way to explain it.

Q. You had naturally a great deal of friendship with the prisoner? A. I could not have had much friendship, because I did not know him at the beginning, and afterwards when I became acquainted with him, the friendship was broken off.

Q. Between the time when he came into the mission and the time you had a rupture with him, is it not true that you and he were friends — that you had a great deal of friendship for him? A. Yes, as I would have for you.

Q. Religion has a great influence on half-breeds? A. In what sense?

Q. In a general way; they are a religious people by instinct? A. Yes, religion has great influence with them.

FRANCOIS ROY sworn (Louis Bourget, interpreter)
Examined by MR FITZPATRICK:

Q. You are a doctor of medicine? A. Yes.

Q. In the city of Quebec? A. Yes, I belong to Quebec.

Q. What is your position in Quebec? A. For a great number of years
I have been medical superintendent and one of the proprietors of
the lunatic asylum at Beauport.

Q. How long have you been connected with the asylum as superintendent? A. More than fifteen or sixteen years.

Q. You are also a member of the society of America — of the
Society of the Superintendents of the Insane Asylums of
America? A. Yes.

Q. During these fifteen or sixteen years your duties caused you to
make a special study of diseases of the brain? Is it not true that it
has been necessary for you to make a special study of diseases of
the brain? A. Yes; it was my duty to go to the principal asylums
in the United States and see how the patients were treated there.

Q. Had you any connection with the asylum of Beauport in 1875
and 1876? A. Yes.

Q. You were at that time superintendent of the asylum? A. Yes.

Q. In those years, or about that time, did you have occasion to see
the prisoner? A. Certainly; many times.

Q. Where did you see him? A. In the asylum.

Q. Can you tell the date? A. Yes, the date was taken from the
register when I left Quebec.

Q. What date is that? A. I took the entry from the register in the
hospital in the beginning of this month.

Q. Was he admitted with all the formalities required by law? A. Yes.

Q. Will you tell me what time he left the asylum? A. He was discharged about the 21st of January, after a residence in the house
of about nineteen months.

Q. Had you occasion to study at that time the mental disease by
which the prisoner was affected at that time? A. Yes.

Q. Did you have relations with him during that time, and did you
watch him carefully during that time? A. Not every day, but very
often.

Q. Can you say now what mental disease the prisoner was then suffering from? A. He was suffering from what is known by authors
as megalomania.

Q. Will you give the symptoms of this disease? A. Many of the symptoms of that disease are found in the ordinary maniac. The particular characteristic of this malady is, that in all cases they show

great judgment in all cases not immediately connected with the
particular disease with which they suffer.

Q. Will you speak from memory or by referring to the authors, what
are the other symptoms of this disease? A. They sometimes give
you reasons which would be reasonable if they were not starting
from a false idea. They are very clever on those discussions, and
they have a tendency to irritability when you question or doubt
their mental condition, because they are under a strong impression that they are right and they consider it to be an insult when
you try to bring them to reason again. On ordinary questions
they may be reasonable and sometimes may be very clever, in fact
without careful watching they would lead one to think that they
were well.

Q. Was he there some weeks or months before you ascertained his
mental condition? A. Yes. I waited till then to classify him as to
his mental condition. We wait a few weeks before classifying the
patient.

Q. Does a feeling of pride occupy a prominent position in that
mental disease? A. Yes, in different forms, religion, and there are
a great many with pride; we have kings with us.

Q. Is the question of selfishness or egotism prominent in those
cases? A. Yes.

Q. Are they liable to change in their affections rapidly? A. Yes,
becuase they are susceptible to the least kind of attraction.

Q. In that particular malady are the patients generally inclined to be
sanguine as to the success of their projects? A. The difficulty is to
make them believe that they will not have success; you cannot
bring them to change that, it is a characteristic of the disease.

Q. Are people who suffer from this particular form of disease liable
to be permanently cured or are they liable to fall back into the
old malady? A. Generally remain in that condition; they may
have sensible moments and then intermission would interfere.

Q. In a case of this kind could a casual observer without any medical
experience form an estimate as to the state of the man's mind?
A. Not usually, unless he makes a special study of the case; there
is more or less difference in each case.

Q. What is the position of the mind of a man suffering from this
disease in reference to other subjects which do not come within

the radius of his mania? A. They will answer questions as any
other man with the sense of reason; it is only when they touch
the spot of their monomania that they become delirious.

Q. You stated that the prisoner left the asylum in 1878? A. In
January 1878.

Q. Have you ever seen him from that time till yesterday? A. No,
never.

Q. Do you recognize him perfectly as the same person who was in
your asylum in 1876 and 1878? A. Yes.

Q. Were you present at the examination of the witnesses that took
place to-day and yesterday? A. Partly.

Q. Did you hear the witnesses describing the actions of the prisoner
as to his peculiar views on religion in reference to his power, to
his hoping to succeed the Pope, and as to his prophecies, yesterday and to-day? A. Yes.

Q. From what you heard from these witnesses and from the symptoms they prove to have been exhibited by the prisoner, are you
now in a position to say whether or not at that time he was a man
of sound mind? A. I am perfectly certain that when the prisoner
was under our care he was not of sound mind, but he became
cured before he left, more or less. But from what I heard here
to-day I am ready to say that I believe on these occasions his
mind was unsound, and that he was laboring under the disease so
well described by Dagoust.

Q. Do you believe that under the state of mind as described by the
witnesses and to which you referred that he was capable or
incapable of knowing the nature of the acts which he did? A. No,
I do not believe that he was in a condition to be the master of his
acts, and I positively swear it and I have people of the same
character under my supervision.

Q. Will you swear from the knowledge you have heard? A. From the
witnesses.

Q. That the man did not know what he was doing or whether it was
contrary to law in reference to the particular delusion? A. No,
and for another reason the same character of the disease is shown
in the last period, the same as when he was with us, there is no
difference, if there was any difference in the symptoms I would
have doubts, but if it was of the same character so well described

by Dagoust, who is taken as an authority and has been adopted in France as well as in America and England.

Q. The opinion you have formed as to the soundness of his mind is based upon the fact that the symptoms disclosed by the witnesses here yesterday and to-day are to a large extent identical with the symptoms of his malady as disclosed while he was at your asylum? A. Yes.

By MR OSLER:

Q. You are one of the two proprietors of the asylum? A. Yes.

Q. It is a private asylum under Government supervision? A. It has the character of a private asylum as to the condition of the board of the patients, but it is a public institution in that sense of the word. We receive patients by order of the Government.

Q. But it is a private asylum as far as its financial basis is concerned? A. No, because it is ruled by the Government.

Q. Is it owned by the Government or by the proprietors? A. By the proprietors.

Q. It is only subject to inspection by the Government? A. To inspecting and visiting besides.

Q. Is the profit or loss of the establishment borne by the proprietors. A. Yes, by the proprietors.

Q. What is the extent of your accommodation? How many patients? A. I do not know whether you have a right to ask these questions.

Q. How many patients have you got? A. Sometimes the number increases and sometimes it diminishes according to the discharges. I think there would be an average of from 800 to 900.

Q. It is from the profit of keeping these patients that the proprietors make money? A. And to pay expenses and the interest upon a large capital put in.

Q. You are paid by the Government and paid by private patients? A. When we have them.

Q. And the proprietors manage it as a place to cure, and where they board these thousand people? A. We have a place to cure and take care of those poor people who cannot take care of themselves.

Q. Who manages the institution? A. There is a medical superintendent.

Q. Who manages the financial part of the institution and looks after the bread and the butter of the patients? A. We have a treasurer to look after that.

Q. You have a medical superintendent to look after the medical department? A. Yes, and we have the rules and regulations of the house.

Q. The proprietors only have a general supervision? A. More than that, I, myself, am a specialist.

Q. You are quite a specialist in keeping a boarding house? A. No.

Q. You have to look after that? A. No.

Q. Who looks after the financial part? A. My co-associates.

Q. You do not look after that? A. No.

Q. You look after the patients? A. Yes, I take a special interest in the insane and those who require treatment.

Q. Will you tell me whether you ever prescribed or looked personally after the prisoner? A. I did.

Q. Under what name was the prisoner in your asylum? A. Under the name of La Rochelle.

Q. Under what name does he appear in your books? A. That is it.

Q. Did you know his right name? A. No, I was not present when he entered the first day.

Q. Have you got the papers with you under which you held him? A. I have this memorandum book.

Q. I want to see the papers? A. No, I have not brought the books.

Q. Have you any papers showing what disease he had and under whose certificate he was confined? A. I cannot give you what I have not got.

Q. There are papers and certificates filed? A. Those papers are kept by the Provincial Secretary, and I would have had to get them from him.

Q. Where did you make that note from? A. From the register taking the exact date.

Q. Is it from that register only that you are able to speak of the case? A. No, it is only a help to my memory and so as to be exact as to dates.

Q. Among the thousand patients that were there at the time he was, you have a perfect recollection of his symptoms? A. Yes, because he was a special case and that gave me a good deal of care.

Q. Did you enquire into his former history? A. No, except as to the fact of his disease.

Q. You did not get the history of the patient? A. I asked some questions as to the condition of his character and his disease.

Q. You found out what his name was? A. He confessed to me who he was.

Q. That violence was after he was admitted into the asylum? A. Yes.

Q. All this treatment would appear in the books, there would be a history of the case? A. Not always, it depends, it is in a medical book.

Q. You have no book or copy of the book here? A. No.

Q. You have brought us nothing? A. Except what I am able to tell you from memory.

Q. You knew a long time before that you were going to be examined as a witness in this case, you had been talked to about it shortly after the capture of the prisoner? A. No, I was asked by telegraph.

Q. You were seen by the friends of the prisoner shortly after he was arrested? A. No.

Q. When were you spoken to about giving evidence at the trial? A. Some days before the trial came on.

Q. Did it strike you that it would be important to have a written history of the case, the cause of his commitment; did it not strike you that that would be a matter of importance in considering a case of this kind? A. No, I thought they would ask me my opinion of the case.

Q. That is what you thought would be satisfactory? A. I never thought of coming at all at first.

Q. At the time he was there, you attended how many cases personally in a year? A. I saw the most important cases, and took a great deal of interest in them on account of the responsibility of the treatment.

Q. And the others would carry out the treatment? A. They would consult me and I would consult them.

Q. How many superintendents have you got? A. None, co-associates.

Q. How many patients had you under your immediate treatment in the year 1877? A. I am not able to tell you.

Q. One hundred cases? A. No, we have not 100 cases of acute mania under our hands, fortunately.

Q. How many did you have under your personal treatment? A. The cases of which I made a special study are acute mania.

Q. How many of such cases would you have in a year? A. Not many, fortunately.

Q. How many in a year? A. Twenty-five or thirty would be about the average of acute cases.

Q. We will speak of 1877, can you give us the names of those men whom you treated in 1877? A. I will give you some of the names. I cannot tell you all. If you mentioned the names, I would know about them.

Q. The treatment of those persons is gone from your mind? A. More or less.

Q. You see the value of written testimony here? A. There are certain cases.

Q. You did not know that this man was Riel? A. I heard that he was, and he himself admitted to me that his name was Riel.

Q. Who put him in the asylum? A. The Government.

Q. On whose certificate? A. The Government.

Q. On what medical certificate was he put in? A. I do not know, it is the Department of the Provincial Secretary. We admit them as sent by the Government.

Q. You are paid by the Government? A. Yes.

Q. That is the Local Government of Quebec? A. Yes, they see that everything is correct; they have a special physician for that.

Q. You say the main feature of this disease is what? What is the leading feature of this disease do you say? Do you say that it is a fixed idea incapable of change? A. That is one thing I may say.

Q. Will you answer the question? Do you say that the leading feature of the disease is a fixed idea incapable of a change by reason? A. It did not succeed in changing.

Q. I ask you is that the leading feature of the disease? A. That is one of the features.

Q. Is it the leading feature? A. It is one of them – it is one of the characteristic features.

Q. A fixed idea with a special ambition, incapable of change by reasoning? A. Yes; we did not succeed in changing the idea of the patient.

Q. Well, that fixed idea is beyond his control? A. I would not be prepared to say entirely.

Q. If it is beyond his control, he is an insane man? A. Yes.

Q. Is not this fixed idea beyond his control? A. Yes.

Q. If within his control, it is an indication of sanity? A. That he was trying to get better, he may have had intermissions in which he understood his condition.

Q. If it is subject to control, it is not a fixed idea, that is what we have agreed upon as the leading characteristic, do you understand? A. I do not know what you are after.

Q. If this idea is subject to control, then this man is sane? A. There may be intermissions when he can control himself because then the insanity disappears.

Q. And then there is a lucid interval? A. Yes.

Q. During the period of the insanity the idea possesses the man and it is not controllable? A. No.

Q. Is that the leading feature of the disease? A. Partly.

Q. Do you know of any other? A. I am not an expert in insanity.

Q. Can you give me any other leading feature of the disease? A. I have no other feature to give.

Q. That is the only one you can describe? A. I gave you the features and characteristics of the disease well enough.

Q. I am going to keep you to that unless you want to enlarge upon it. I am going to build my theory upon that. You can enlarge it as much as you like now, but do not go back upon me afterwards. Is there any other leading feature of the disease? A. I have given you the principal characteristics of his disease.

Q. I want to get the peculiar characteristic of this form of mania. A. They have intermissions sometimes for months and sometimes for days. The least contradiction excites them.

Q. There is a class of healthy intermissions. Sometimes a man likes beer and sometimes whiskey. I want to get the characteristics that distinguish him from a healthy man, not those that we have in common with the insane. A. We always answer reasonably, but when a man comes and pretends to know everything and talks nonsense we expect that, to a certain extent, he has lost his reason.

Q. We want to get at the leading characteristic. You have given us one feature. Is there only the one feature. If there are any other features say so? A. I won't give you any.

Q. Will you stick to it? A. Yes.

Q. Then what leading idea not subject to change by reason is it that you have fixed upon the evidence yesterday and to-day bringing you to the conclusion that he is of unsound mind? A. It is because of some symptoms.

Q. Tell me the symptoms that brings you to the conclusion that this man is within the rule you have laid down. Tell me the facts that bring him within that rule? A. The facts are that he has always kept that characteristic.

Q. Answer that question? A. —

MR FITZPATRICK: This witness has been speaking in English for some time past. If the witness does not understand the questions properly he should answer the questions in French.

MR OSLER: If the man wants to hide himself under the French he can do so.

Q. You understand what I mean? A. Speak to me in French.

MR OSLER: It will be for the jury to say whether he is making the change at his own suggestion or at that of the counsel on the other side.

Q. Having given a rule to test this insanity, what fact is there disclosed in the evidence which leads you to say that the prisoner comes within the rule? A. That part of the evidence given by the clergy to-day shows in a positive manner that the prisoner has manifested symptoms that we meet with in megalomania.

Q. That is no answer to my question. I want the fact on which you bring the prisoner within the rule that you have laid down? A. I want to take the fact proved by the evidence.

Q. Tell me the fact upon which you rely? A. The prisoner gets his theory from the idea that he has a mission.

Q. Do you understand that to be the fixed idea not controllable by reason? A. I believe so because reason has never so far succeeded in changing that idea that he has.

Q. Is that the only reason you have for saying that the prisoner is insane? A. It is, and I believe it to be sufficient.

Q. Is it consistent laboring under an idea not controllable by reason would abandon that idea for $35,000.

MR FITZPATRICK: I object to that. That has not been proved.

HIS HONOR: What is the question?

MR OSLER: Is it consistent with a man, having an idea not controllable by reason, that he will abandon that idea for $35,000? Let that be a hypothetical question.

MR FITZPATRICK: I object to the question.

HIS HONOR: He can put hypothetical questions.

MR OSLER: My learned friend must know that the question is regular, and should not interfere at a critical part of the examination so as to give the witness a cue.

MR FITZPATRICK: I did not have any such intention. We have the right to object, and we intend to exercise that right.

MR OSLER: You should not exercise it in such a way as to give the witness a cue. That is the second cue that you have given the witness. You gave him a cue in regard to speaking in French.

Q. Will you answer the question: Is it consistent with the leading feature of this disease, an idea not controllable by reason, that he should abandon that idea for money? A. I think it is possible that the prisoner might want to obtain the money to obtain the object he has in view.

Q. It may be consistent if he wants the money for the object which he wishes to obtain? A. Yes.

Q. Do you say that the answer is consistent with the idea that he is not able to control his actions? A. Yes, it gives it more strength.

Q. Wherein does that differ from the idea of a sound mind? A. It is very important in this case particularly. The patient shows great ability in taking the necessary means to accomplish the particular mission that he believes has been given to him. He was reasoning from a false basis, and that is a characteristic of this disease.

Q. Do you agree with this proposition: 'An insane delusion is never the result of reasoning and reflection?' A. I don't understand what you want to get at.

Q. I want you to give an answer. Do you agree with that proposition, that 'An insane delusion is never the result of reasoning and reflection?' A. I believe that he makes false reasoning from a false principle.

Q. Is delusion produced by reasoning and deduction? A. It has been by hallucinations and –

Q. That is not an answer to my question. I want to know whether a delusion – an insane delusion – may be the result of reasoning

and deduction, or is it always the production of the disease?
A. Sometimes, not always. Sometimes by false inspiration.

Q. Sometimes by sane inspiration? A. Yes.

Q. You won't answer my question? A. I have done my best.

Q. Have you not the capacity to understand it? A. That may be your opinion.

Q. Take an insane delusion in a man's head, can it be brought by reasoning and deduction, or is it the outcome of the disease? A. It is the consequence of his disease.

Q. And, therefore, it has nothing to do with reason and deduction? A. I believe that when the patient is under the influence of hallucination he is quite beyond control.

Q. You say it is the first principle of irresponsibility whether it is the result of disease, or whether it is the result of reason (distorted reason if you will) it is only by disease that the insane delusion is produced? A. Yes, by the disturbance of the brain which there is in every case.

Q. And it is by reason of its being a product of the disease that it is not controllable? A. It is a consequence of it.

Q. Why do you say this prisoner during this time had no knowledge of right from wrong? A. I say that the prisoner was under the influence of his delusion that he had a special mission to fulfil.

Q. From what facts in evidence do you say that the prisoner could not distinguish between right and wrong? A. They never could prove to him that that mission never existed.

MR FITZPATRICK: It is impossible for us to accept such translation as is now being given of the evidence.

MR GREENSHIELDS: The last two questions have not been translated properly.

MR OSLER: We have done everything we could to procure a translator. We did not want one for our part of the evidence and it was for the defence to produce one in tendering a witness whose evidence had to be translated.

MR FITZPATRICK: I say it is entirely wrong, it should be taken down in French.

MR OSLER: It has been taken down in French as well as in English.

MR FITZPATRICK: It has gone to the jury in English.

MR OSLER: The witness can explain himself in English but was told not to do so, it is not my difficulty.

MR FITZPATRICK: I think the Act of 1880 provides for the use of both languages.

HIS HONOR: The court can take the best interpreter to be had.

MR FITZPATRICK: All right, if you say so.

MR ROBINSON: When they hear it improperly translated they should say so and it can be repeated.

WITNESS: It could not be proved to him that the mission did not exist.

HIS HONOR: Is that answer correct? A. Yes.

MR OSLER: Is that the only reason why you say the prisoner could not distinguish between right and wrong.

HIS HONOR: The reporter had better read the question to him and see whether it has been correctly translated.

Reporter, reading from the notes. 'From what facts in evidence do you say that the prisoner could not distinguish between right and wrong?' A. They never could prove to him that the mission never existed.

HIS HONOR: Is that the proper answer? A. Yes.

Q. Is that the only reason why you say the prisoner could not distinguish between right and wrong? A. I give that as one of the reasons.

Q. Give me any other reasons? A. The reasons given by the last witness.

Q. I want you to state the facts that the witnesses spoke of from which you came to your conclusion? A. The facts are that he believed he had a mission to fulfil in the North-West.

Q. What evidence have you that that was an insane delusion because he stated that he had a letter from the bishop containing such an allegation? A. I never heard that he was inspired by such a letter.

Q. Do you say that any man claiming to be inspired is insane so as not to distinguish between right and wrong? A. It is possible.

Q. Is it a true proposition scientifically? A. The proposition, as given by the patient, is not always reasonable.

Q. Might it not be evidence of fraud on the part of the man making it? A. But when the same idea has been sustained, at different times, without reason —

Q. When the idea is sustained from time to time, it is only sustained with insanity, is that the answer? A. Yes, particularly with that kind of delirium.

Q. Do you know the history of Joseph Smith, the Mormon, would you consider him insane? A. No, I do not know his history.

Q. Do you know anything of Brigham Young. would you call him insane? A. To my mind he was more or less insane.

Q. Would you call Brigham Young's idea of prophetic inspiration inconsistent with a knowledge of what was right and wrong? A. It would require an examination. If you send him to the asylum for a few months, I will make a study of the case.

Q. Does not the whole evidence sustain the theory that it was a skilful fraud? A. I don't think so. I saw the prisoner at my place. He always retained the impression that he had a mission when he could have none and he had nothing to gain by it.

Q. I am asking the general question whether the evidence, upon which you have formed your opinion, is not consistent with a skilful fraud? A. It might be possible there might be such an understanding, but it is not my opinion.

Q. It may be that it is consistent with skilful fraud? A. There is no evidence in this case that can prove that there was fraud.

Q. Do you say the evidence is inconsistent with a skilful fraud? A. When I had the prisoner under my care —

Q. I am asking about the facts in evidence upon which you formed your opinion? A. In the mental condition of the prisoner, I think he is not.

Q. That is not an answer at all. Can you give me any answer? A. Put another question or in another way.

Q. If you cannot answer it in English or French, I may as well let you go. You can go.

DR DANIEL CLARK sworn
Examined by MR FITZPATRICK:

Q. You belong to Toronto, do you not? A. I do

Q. What is your position there, doctor? A. Superintendent of the Toronto Lunatic Asylum.

Q. Have you had any experience in the treatment of the insane? A. A small experience.

Q. Limited to how many years, doctor? A. Between nine and ten years.

Q. Has it been your fate to attend occasionally as an expert in cases of lunacy? A. Yes, very often.

Q. Have you had any occasion to examine this prisoner here at the bar? A. I examined him three times, twice yesterday and once this morning.

Q. Did you attend at the examination of the other witnesses in this case yesterday and to-day? A. I did.

Q. From what you have heard from the witnesses here in court, and also from the examination which you have made of the accused, are you in a position to form any opinion as to the soundness or unsoundness of his mind? A. Well, assuming the fact that the witnesses told the truth, I have to assume that — assuming also that the prisoner at the bar was not a malingerer — that is English I believe — then of course there is no conclusion that any reasonable man could come to, from my standpoint of course, than that a man who held these views and did these things must certainly be of insane mind.

Q. Do you consider, doctor, that a person suffering from such unsoundness of mind as you say this man is suffering from, is incapable of taking the nature of the acts which they do? A. Why, the insane understand, many of them, the nature of the acts which they do, except in dementia cases and melancholia and cases of mania even; they often know what they do and can tell all about it afterwards; it is all nonsense to talk about a man not knowing what he is doing, simply because he is insane.

Q. Do you think that that man was, in the circumstances detailed by the different witnesses, in a position to be able to say or be able to judge of what he was doing as either wrong or contrary to law? A. Well, that is one of the legal metaphysical distinctions in regard to right and wrong, and it is a dangerous one, simply because it covers only partly the truth. I could convince any lawyers if they will come to Toronto Asylum, in half an hour, that dozens in that institution know right and wrong both in the abstract and in the concrete, and yet are undoubtedly insane; the distinction of right and wrong covers part of the truth; it covers the larger part of the truth, but the large minority of the insane do know right from wrong. It is one of those metaphysical subtilties that practical men in asylums know to be false.

Q. There are some lawyers who think it is false also? A.,Well, the lawyers find it in the books, and they take it for granted it must be correct.

Q. Do you consider from the knowledge which you now have of this individual that at the time the events detailed by the witnesses here took place, that is to say, in March, April and May last, that he was laboring under such a defect of reason from disease of the mind, that he did not know that what he was doing was wrong? A. I think he did know; I think he was quite capable of distinguishing right from wrong.

Q. Quote the particular acts, doctor. A. Well, quote the particular acts; I presume 'if you were to ask him to define what is right and what is wrong, he could possibly give you a very good definition, as far as I could judge from my examination of him.

Q. Was he in a position to be able to say at that time, and to act that time as an ordinary sane man would have done? A. Assuming the evidence given by the witnesses, he did not act as a sane man would have done, for this reason that no sane man would have imagined that he could come into the Saskatchewan, and that he could gather around him such a force as would enable him to become monarch of this country, that it could be divided up into seven divisions, giving it to different nationalities. He was not an ignorant man. He was not like an Indian who never read the newspapers and knew nothing about the country around him. He had travelled, he had been in Ottawa, he had been in the United States, and he knew all about the power of Britain and the Dominion, and for him to imagine that he could come here and raise a few half-breeds in the Saskatchewan and keep up a successful warfare, and divide the country in seven divisions, with different nationalities, was certainly not a thing that a man with an ordinary understanding would ever think he could succeed in.

Q. So that you think at that time the man was certainly insane, and of unsound mind? A. Assuming the statements made, I think so.

Q. To be true? A. Yes.

Q. You take into consideration, of course, in this opinion, all the evidence given as well by the doctor as by the other witnesses? A. Yes; and I assume, of course, as I said before, that not only the evidence given is correct, but that he was not a deceiver. I might say, if the court will allow me, that when I come to cases of this kind, I am not subpoenaed for one side more than another. I am here only subpoenaed to give a sort of medical judicial opinion, and, therefore, I stand in that capacity.

MR JUSTICE RICHARDSON: That is well understood, Dr Clark.

Cross-examined by MR OSLER:

Q. Then, doctor, he would know the nature and quality of the act that he was committing? A. He would know the nature and the quality of the act that he was committing, subject to his delusions assuming them to be such.

Q. He would know the nature and quality of the act that he was committing, and he would know if it was wrong? A. If it was wrong, based upon his delusion; yes.

Q. And all the facts are quite compatible with a skilful shamming by malingering? A. Yes I think so. I think that no one – at least I say for myself, of course – that in a cursory examination of a man of this kind who has a good deal of cunning, who is educated, that it is impossible for any man to state from three examinations whether he is a deceiver or not. I require to have that man under my supervision for months, to watch him day by day, before I could say whether he is a sham or not.

Q. Months under your supervision to say whether he is a sham or not? A. Yes.

Q. And really the only ground upon which you would form an opinion as to his insanity is the commission of the crime? A. No, not the commission of the crime. I form an opinion of his insanity from the statements made by the witnesses both anterior to the crime and since that time.

Q. But you told the court and jury just now that what struck you was the insane idea of seeking to take possession of the country and divide it into provinces? A. Yes, that is one idea.

Q. That gave you the greatest idea of his insanity? A. One, and then another one was he was a Roman Catholic, and among Roman Catholic people, among people attached to their priests, and he went among that people endeavoring to conciliate them, as he supposed, in order to get them educated up in any schemes he had in view, and yet he goes to work and he says at once, I want to depose the Pope.

Q. But did you notice also this, that he gets people to follow him? A. Some of them do.

Q. Yes, but he got people to follow him with their guns? A. They followed him, on another basis.

Q. They elected him prophet? A. Yes, and he told me this morning
   he was a prophet, and he knew the jury would acquit him,
   because he knew what was coming beforehand.

Q. Then don't you think that that is perfectly consistent with such
   leading spirits as Joseph Smith and Brigham Young? A. No, it is not.

Q. Not consistent? A. No; and I will tell you the reason why.

Q. Well I don't want the reason, beyond your opinion? A. Well, it is
   not consistent.

Q. It is consistent, however, with fraud? A. Consistent with fraud.
   Yes, anything is consistent with fraud that is not discovered.

Q. You cannot say that it is not fraud? A. I cannot.

Q. And there is nothing here to show you, in the state of his intellect, that he was not able to distinguish between right and wrong,
   and know the quality of the act which he was committing?
   A. No, I say that I think that he knows what right is from wrong,
   subject to his delusions; but, mind you, I want to add to that,
   that many of the insane know right from wrong.

Q. And you know, doctor, very well, that there is a class of insanity
   that is held responsible to the law? A. You know I am not
   allowed to say anything about the responsibility legally —

Q. You know that there is a conflict between the courts and the
   doctors? A. I know there is.

Q. And you know that the doctors have an idea that all mental
   disease should be acquitted of crime? A. No, they don't all. For
   instance, Maudsley has written a small book on the responsibi-
   lities of the insane. He is a most prominent man in England.

Q. He brings in, and the doctors have a tendency, have they not, to
   bring in as irresponsible a very much larger class than the courts
   and lawyers? A. I think not. I think, of late years, that such men
   as Maudsley, Buchnell and Schuch, &c., and some of these recent
   investigators, lean to the idea that insanity *per se* does not absolve
   from responsibility. You have got to take each case on its own
   merits.

Q. There is a large class of insane people or cranks? A. Well. No, you
   cannot say, or cranks, because a crank is a different man altogether. A crank is a man who is normally a peculiar man from
   his birth upwards. An insane man is a man who has become so,
   out of unusual conduct from disease.

Q. I did not bracket them together, I put them in the alternative?
A. You said 'or' crank. I thought you meant lunatic-crank.

Q. I put them as coming up to each other's border line? A. I see.
I thought you had an equation.

Q. It is so that a large number then, I should say of insane
persons, ought to be responsible to the law? A. There are some
that are.

Q. For they know right from wrong, and know the nature and
quality of the act they perform? A. When I speak about responsibility, it is said that the court should decide —

Q. That is when you are examined in chief, but on cross-examination
we have a little more liberty? A. I see.

Q. You have been an expert witness in criminal cases? A. Yes.

Q. How frequently? A. Well, I don't know, perhaps nine or ten
times, perhaps more. I don't remember exactly the number.

Re-examined by MR FITZPATRICK:

Q. You said a moment ago that the conduct of this man might be
consistent with the conduct for instance of such a man as Smith
or Young, and you were about to make a distinction between the
two, and you were stopped? A. Oh! Smith and Young were
religious enthusiasts. They carried out consistently their system.
If you read Brigham Young's Bible, or if you read Mahomet's
Koran if you like, or if you read any of those books issued by
those men, who are religious enthusiasts, you will find that consistently with common sense, they have tact and discretion to
carry on successfully till the end of their lives without intermission, a successful crusade of this kind, and their books contain
sufficient consistency throughout to show you that these men
were sound in mind as much as nature provided them with a
sound mind, that is the different.

Q. Do you find anything of that kind in the present case? A. Oh, no,
I don't think he would make a very good Brigham Young, or El
Mahdi.

Q. You say that he is quite capable of distinguishing right from
wrong, subject to his delusions? Subject to his particular
delusions? A. Yes.

MR LEMIEUX: This closes our defence, your Honor.

MR ROBINSON: We have some witnesses in rebuttal.

DR JAMES M. WALLACE sworn

Examined by MR OSLER:

Q. Doctor, what is your position? A. I am medical superintendent of the Asylum for the Insane at Hamilton, Ontario.

Q. An institution having about how many patients, on the average? A. Somewhere over 600.

Q. How long have you been making a branch a specialty of the study of the insane? A. I have been in charge of that asylum nearly nine years, but I have been studying insanity for a few years more than that.

Q. For more than nine years? A. Yes.

Q. And you see every variety of it I suppose? A. All shades and variety.

Q. Now, do you devote yourself to the medical branch of it? A. Entirely.

Q. You have nothing to do with keeping the hotel or boarding house? A. Well, I have the general superintendence of the house; but I devote nearly all my time to the medical department of the asylum.

Q. Have you been listening to the evidence in this case? A. Yes.

Q. Have you examined or had an opportunity of seeing the prisoner? A. I saw him for about half an hour, that is, alone, not in court.

Q. And you have been here during the —? A. During the sitting of the court.

Q. Have you formed an opinion of his mental responsibility, of his sanity or insanity? A. I have so far as my time and opportunities enabled me to do so.

Q. What is that opinion? A. I have not discovered any insanity about him, no indication of insanity.

Q. What would you say then in view of the evidence and your examination? Is he of sound mind or is he not? A. I think he is of sound mind.

Q. And capable of distinguishing right from wrong? A. I think so.

Q. And know the nature and quality of any act which he would commit? A. Very acutely.

Cross-examined by MR FITZPATRICK:

Q. You have no doubt whatever in your mind from the examination you have made of this man during half an hour, and from the evidence which you heard here, that he is of perfectly sound mind? A. Well, I should qualify, I should qualify my answer to that question. I have only had a limited examination of him, and in any case of obscure mental disease, it sometimes takes a very long time before one can make up their mind; but from what I have seen of him, I say that I have discovered no symptoms of insanity.

Q. So what you say now, doctor, is purely and simply this, not that he is not insane, but that you have not been able to discover any symptoms of insanity? A. That is what I say, I say I have not discovered it. It would be presumption for me to say he is not insane, from the opportunities that I have had; but at the same time my opinion is pretty fairly fixed in my mind that he is not insane.

Q. You are aware that a great many cases exist in which men are found to be perfectly insane without its being possible to discover any trace of insanity, are you not? A. O, sir, I have had patients in my asylum for weeks sometimes before I found any symptoms of insanity.

Q. You are aware also, are you not, that there have been cases in England in which men were examined for a whole day, and cross-examined by such men as Erskine for instance, perfectly insane, and during the whole day it was impossible for Erskine to discover that the man was insane? A. Yes, I daresay such cases may exist. I am quite certain such cases have existed.

Q. You are quite certain such cases are in existence? A. Yes.

Q. Therefore you are obliged to say that all that you have discovered in this case, or all that you are in a position to say is that you have not discovered any traces of insanity? A. That is all that my conscience will allow me to say.

Q. You have heard of that particular form of mental disease known as megalomania probably? A. Yes.

Q. Would you tell us what are the symptoms which are the characteristics of this disease? A. That is a simple complication. That is a term which is scarcely ever used, and I think it is only used by one writer. I don't remember any other who uses it in the English language, and he simply introduces it and says —

Q. But one writer uses that name? A. Only one that I can think of at the present time in the English language, and he says that it is a condition in which the patient has delusions, grandiose delusions, delusions of greatness, and most commonly complicated with that form of insanity called paralytic insanity or gentle paralysis.

Q. You are aware that this particular form of insanity is characterized, among other things, by extreme irritability on the part of the patient? A. Not megalomania. Megalomania simply applies to grandiose ideas. It can have no other definition than that. And these definitions allow me to explain are delusions; they are delusions such as a person holding or believing himself to be a king or possessed of immense wealth, and that the world is at his feet. These are the kind of delusions that are meant by megalomania, as I understand them, and it has not any other meaning that I know of.

Q. The delusions are that he is rich? A. Yes.

Q. And powerful? A. Yes.

Q. A great general? A. Yes.

Q. A great minister? A. He may be a great anything and everything.

Q. A great prophet? A. Yes.

Q. Or divinely inspired, or that he is a poet or a musician, in fact that he is an egotist, and a selfish man? A. Yes.

Q. But you are quite sure that the character of irritability is not one of the characters of this malady? A. It is not a malady, it is merely a symptom.

Q. That is a form of mental disease? A. It is not a mental disease, it is only a symptom of mental disease.

Q. You have heard of a book written and published by Dagoust, a French writer? A. I have heard of it, but I have never read it.

Q. He is an author of repute, is he not? A. I think so, but I don't read much French.

Q. Would you allow me to read to you what this author says. Talking of megalomania, he says: 'What characterizes this particular form of mental alienation is exaggeration of the sentiment of personality. Expanse of passions,' he says 'is one of the consequences of it.' He says: 'Megalomaniacs are happy, satisfied with themselves, and speak without limit of their own personality (now here is the part I speak to you about), the individual is susceptible, irritable, he is seized with sudden fury when he is at any time opposed in his ideas? 'A. Well, isn't that speaking of gentle paralysis – the insanity of gentle paralysis?

Q. It is under the heading 'megalomania,' with the plate showing the different characters? A. I understand that, but there are a vastly large number of manias, puerpuomania and all that sort of thing.

Q. Would you keep to megalomania, that is what we now refer to, that is what the book refers to, and that is what I refer to? A. I stated that megalomania was one of the complications or symptoms of paralytic insanity, and that that you read, of course, is one of the accompaniments of paralytic insanity too, irritability and all that that you stated. They are always found in connection with each other.

Q. And you now say that irritability is one of the characteristics of megalomania? A. No, I don't. Megalomania, as far as I understand it, is one of the complications of paralytic insanity, and this irritability is also another symptom of paralytic insanity.

Q. We will just narrow the facts down to exactly what we have in evidence, that the extreme irritability was one of the characteristics of this megalomania? A. Simply.

Q. And the book shows, that I now hold in my hand, it is one of the characteristics? A. I think we do not understand each other yet.

Q. I am waiting for light? A. I have stated that megalomania is a symptom commonly found in paralytic insanity; irritability and all those other symptoms are also symptoms found in the same disease.

Q. So that now, irritability being one of the characteristics of paralytic insanity, and megalomania being one of the branches of paralytic insanity, you now say irritability is one of the characteristics of megalomania? A. Oh, but we find megalomania in other diseases, and we find megalomania is simply mania.

Q. But in megalomania irritability is laid down by the book as one of the characteristics, at all events? A. Yes.

Q. So that now, doctor, you are of the opinion that the idea of grandeur and of power is not to be found anywhere except in cases of parlytic insanity? A. Oh, yes; we find it in simple mania. We find it in simple mania, but these are fixed delusions; these are fixed delusions, and persons who hold them say they are, believe themselves to be kings and queens or great leaders or wealthy people. They may be great in anything and great in everything, and they actually believe this and act upon their belief, constantly act upon their belief.

Q. Did I understand you to say, doctor, that the idea of grandeur is
exclusively a symptom of paralytic insanity, that that is not to be
met in other cases? A. No; I have just stated now that you will
find delusions of grandeur in other forms of insanity.

Q. Now is it not a fact that in cases of megalomania one of the
characteristics, one of the very essential characteristics, is that the
individual who suffers from that particular form of mental disease
is able in a very large measure to hide the disease from any person
who endeavors to find it out? A. Well, insane persons are able, as
I said before, to conceal their delusions sometimes for a length of
time, but a person suffering from megalomania does not attempt
to do it; he is too proud to expose his delusion.

Q. So that one of the characteristics of it is pride? A. Yes.

Q. Is there a case in which a man, for instance, would be under the
insane delusion that he was destined to fill a great mission, that
he was in a position to take possession of a country such as this
one is – would not that man be in a position to take such means
as would be necessary to arrive at his ends, and to take those
means with a great amount of shrewdness and precaution?
A. That is quite inconsistent with my idea of megalomania. As I
said before, my idea of megalomania is, as defined by Clouston,
for instance, that man is already in possession of all these things,
and he does not want any more.

Q. So that your idea is, doctor, that a man who is suffering from this
particular disease is not in a position, and it is utterly impossible
for him to take any steps to arrive at the conclusion which he
pretends he ought to arrive at? A. Oh, he does not require any
plans at all; everything flows into him; he is the greatest man in
the world, and everything is subservient to him; wealth comes
into him; he does not want, and he can command everybody and
they will obey him.

Q. So that he does not make any calculations at all, and does not
adopt any means at all to arrive at his end? A. Not at all.

Q. It is one of the characteristics of the malady that he is unable to
do that? A. Not unable; because he does not ask to do it; he is so
self-possessed and so self-contented.

Q. Now, doctor, we will just read this little book again on that
subject: 'it is so much the more dangerous that he still retains
the necessary faculty to be able to make calculations which are

necessary to arrive at his ends'? A. But is that speaking of megalomania?

Q. Under the chapter entitled 'Megalomania? 'A. Well, would you allow me to quote from Clouston? He is speaking of mental depression, and he says, there are a few cases of depressed feeling with exalted intellectual condition. Many persons exaggerate their former notions of wealth and position by way of contrast with their present misery. I had a woman, in excited melancholia, groaning all the time, and then considered herself a queen; and another a king, and of immense wealth. Some cases are of the nature of what the French call megalomania, that is, expansive grandiose, exalted state of the mind, which, as a mental symptom, is best seen in gentle paralysis, coupled with ideas of persecution, and with depressed feeling, especially at times.

Q. Do you think there is anything in what you have read there that is inconsistent with what I have read to you, that contradicts that? A. Well, there is nothing contradicts it; but I say that megalomania is —

Q. That is simply an interpretation of what this book has said here? A. Well, we are not very far apart; we are only apart this far, that you wish to contend for megalomania as a disease, while I contend that it is only a symptom.

Q. We are not talking about symptoms of diseases at all, I ask you was that one of the symptoms of megalomania and you said that it did not exist in a case, and the book says that it does? A. You are not giving me justice.

Q. I don't mean to do you an injustice. I don't mean to adopt any bullying process, it is not my habit and I don't do it, I don't pretend to set my knowledge against yours in a matter of this kind, you are free to explain it. This megalomania was called formerly intellectual monomania, was it not? A. Yes, it is a monomania.

Q. It came under that general class of cases formerly? A. Yes.

Q. Now, one of the symptoms of that malady — you have heard of a book written by Ducelle? A. No, I never heard of that.

Q. You don't know Legrand Ducelle, a French author? A. No, I never heard of that.

Q. You don't know Legrand Ducelle, a French author? A. No, I don't know the book.

Q. You never heard of a book of that kind, at all events I cannot put the authority in evidence as you say you don't know it, but I might ask you, for instance, whether or not that particular form of disease which I have spoken to you about, that is intellectual monomania, that insane persons believe they are in constant intercourse with God, and they believe themselves to be inspired, and believe themselves to be prophets, and their hallucinations are such that they suppose they are in constant intercourse with the Supreme Being? A. Yes, I have known patients of that kind.

Q. Have you ever heard of — (giving the name of another French author)? A. I don't want to hear of any French authors. I never read them.

Q. You never get that far? A. No.

Q. Persons suffering from delusions of grandeur are perfectly harmless as a rule are they not? A. No; as a rule they are not. Not always. They sometimes are and sometimes they are not.

Q. In cases in which they would be harmless, would you put two of these persons together in the same ward? A. I never put two together anywhere. I never put two lunatics together anywhere. They are always kept, either one, or more than two.

Q. Would you put more than two together? A. Yes.

Q. Without any impropriety whatever? A. Yes. Our buildings are put up with a view to that.

Q. I don't know if you understand my question — I suppose several persons suffering from the same, two kings and a queen or two queens, you would put all those persons together in the same ward? A. They might be or they might not.

Q. You would not see any objection in that? A. There would be no impropriety in putting them together, I think not.

By MR OSLER:

Q. Where the disease exists, is the idea, the result of disease, fixed and constant? A. It is the result of the disease.

Q. But is it fixed or intermittent? A. In those cases they are fixed.

Q. So that when a person has taken herself a queen, she remains a queen? A. She usually dies a queen.

Q. In her own idea? A. Yes.

Q. And she is a queen to everybody to whom she talks? A. Yes.

Q. Not sometimes a queen and sometimes otherwise? A. No.

DR JUKES sworn
Examined by MR ROBINSON:

Q. You are at present the medical officer attached to the Mounted
Police force? A. I am the senior surgeon of the Mounted Police.

Q. And how long have you been in medical practice? A. Thirty-five
years.

Q. Have you devoted your attention to insanity at all specially or
not? A. Never specially. There are cases, of course, occasionally
will come under the notice of every general practitioner, but as a
special study I have never done so.

Q. Every medical practitioner, I suppose, has his attention more or
less directed to it? A. Occasionally I have been called upon to
certify in cases of insanity.

Q. You are also surgeon to the gaol here I am told? A. At present
until a gaol has been erected in the North-West Territories, the
guard room at Regina constitutes the gaol, the guard room headquarters constitutes the gaol.

Q. In that capacity insane persons would pass under your hands –
any person supposed to be insane? A. Yes. I remember during the
last three years a number of persons of unsound mind have been
sent there as a place of confinement.

Q. And in that way they have come under your observation?
A. They have come under my observation for the time.

Q. Now, you know the prisoner I believe? A. Yes.

Q. How long have you known him? A. I don't remember the exact
day that he was brought to Regina, but I think it must have been
between the 20th and 24th May.

Q. But whatever it was – between the 20th and 24th? A. About that
time I am not sure.

Q. Since that time how often have you seen him? A. I have seen him
almost every day. There have been one or two or perhaps three
days that I have missed seeing him, owing to pressure of other
business, other work at that time, but I have seen him uniformly
every day.

Q. As a rule you have seen him every day, although you have missed
two or three or four days during that time? A. Yes.

Q. Then you have had an opportunity I suppose of observing his
mental condition? A. I would speak to him on every occasion in

passing him, and he has generally acquainted me with what he conceived to be his wants and his necessities, and I would examine into the condition of his physical — the general health and ascertain how his diet was agreeing with him, and things of that kind, such as came under my special duty, and occasionally he would speak to me on other matters, occasionally he would delay me and speak to me on other subjects.

Q. Then have you formed an opinion as to his mental state? I am speaking now of his insanity — sanity or insanity? A. I have never seen anything during my intercourse with Mr Riel to leave any impression upon my mind that he was insane.

Q. Then as I understand you believe him to be sane? A. I believe him to be sane so far as my knowledge of such matters goes. I have seen nothing to induce me to believe otherwise.

Q. I suppose you have had your attention directed to that part of his character more or less, I mean to his mental condition more or less? A. No, I have never seen anything to make me question his mental condition, and therefore have never led the conversation under any circumstances to draw out any possible insane notion. I have never made any effort to do so, because my duty was otherwise.

Q. What I mean is, doctor, you have heard, I suppose, from time to time, rumors that there was an assertion of the unsoundness of his mind? A. I have heard it rumored that he had been formerly insane and that he had been confined, I think, in the Beauport Asylum, and I have heard it also rumored that it was the intention to bring forward a plea of insanity in his defence on the present occasion, that is a general rumor.

Q. Therefore, I suppose you have had this thing in your mind, that is all, that part of his condition in your own mind in speaking to him? That is all that I mean? A. Yes; Oh, I have always watched him very carefully so as to notice if possible any appearance of unsoundness of mind, and if I had noticed it, I would have placed him under special treatment as far as my knowledge enabled me to do, or have advised further treatment for him as I have done in other cases.

Cross-examined by MR FITZPATRICK:

Q. You said, doctor, that you had not made any endeavor to ascertain during the intercourse which you had with Mr Riel, whether or not he suffered from any particular mental disease, did you? or any form of insanity or any mental disease, unsoundness of mind? A. I never specially examined him as a lunatic. I never made a special examination of him as a lunatic.

Q. You never made any special endeavor to discover whether or not he was suffering from any particular form of mental disease? A. Never any special endeavor, anything beyond ordinary conversation of the day.

Q. Is it not a fact that there are, doctor, forms of insanity which are not discoverable except after considerable endeavors have been made to discover them? A. Yes; it is so, unquestionably, that you may converse with a man continually and not be aware of his insanity until you touch accidentally, or some other person touches accidentally upon that point upon which he is insane.

Q. Had you been informed at any time of the particular mental disease from which Mr. Riel was supposed to have been suffering? A. I don't think I ever knew as much of it as I have learned here.

Q. So that you never made any endeavor to? A. I never did, that is, I never spoke to him specially with regard to what he believes to be his mission, knowing that many very sane men might be so, and yet the man might be perfectly sane.

Q. So that you have no doubt at all, doctor, from the evidence that you have heard here given by the different witnesses who were examined, the conduct of Mr Riel is perfectly compatible with a perfectly sound mind? A. Well, I regret to say that my hearing is rather imperfect in the court room, and that I have not been able to hear so well as I could wish the translations that were made to the examinations in French, but so far as my understanding has gone of the evidence which has been given, I have heard nothing which would satisfy me that he was of unsound mind. I have heard nothing which might not be accounted for by other causes, that for instance, of fraud or deception. A man might really believe that he had a mission, as many great men have believed, or he might only pretend for a purpose that he had that belief.

Q. A man might also labor under the insane delusion that he had a mission? A. He might also labor under the insane delusion, but the fact of his laboring under that insane delusion would not necessarily imply that he was otherwise insane or incompetent either to perform business in a successful manner or to be responsible for his actions. That would be my own judgment.

Q. But *quoad* the particular delusion, in so far as the particular delusion under which he is suffering is concerned, he would be still responsible in your opinion, doctor. Supposing for instance that a man labored under the delusion that his neighbor was a savage dog and was endeavoring to destroy him and bite him, and that he killed his neighbor, he might be perfectly sane in other respects? A. You misunderstand me if you think I entertain that opinion.

Q. That is not the opinion you entertain? A. Certainly not.

Q. So that if a man is laboring under an insane delusion the acts which he does while he is under that insane delusion *quoad* the particular delusion he is not responsible for? A. If a man is clearly – if it can be proved that a man is acting – if it is proved that the man is acting under an insane delusion, then any act I should consider which he performed under that delusion, any act having special relation to his delusion I should consider that he was not personally responsible for, if it could be shown clearly that that delusion was an insane one, and that it was not rather a feigned one for a purpose.

Q. So that if it can be proved that a man is laboring under an insane delusion that he was in direct communication with the Holy Ghost and was acting under the direct inspiration of God and he was bound to do a certain act, and he did it, would he be responsible for that act? A. Views on subjects of that kind are so different even among those who are confessedly sane, that it is hardly one on which I could base an opinion. There are men who have held very remarkable views with respect to religion and who have been always declared to be insane until they gathered together great numbers of followers and became leaders of a new sect, then they became great prophets and great men. It is extremely difficult to tell how far a delusion of that kind may begin as a direct attempt at fraud and may at last so take possession of a man's mind that he may believe himself divinely inspired. I think that cases of that kind could be produced – and it would depend very much upon the mental condition of a man whether he were responsible. If it could be shown that he was clearly insane, he is clearly irresponsible on that point. That would be my own view.

Q. So that if it can be clearly shown that he was laboring under a delusion that he was divinely inspired from God, you think he would not be responsible for his action? A. Responsible for what?

Q. Responsible for his actions in connection with delusion of course? A. What actions would they be, such actions as what?

Q. Such actions as he might do for the purpose of carrying out his insane delusion? A. Well, take Mahomet for instance, that was exactly Mahomet's belief. He believed and few believed with him, even of his own people, that he was divinely inspired, but he acted upon his belief and he carried his whole belief with him. He believed it and he carried it out at the point of the sword and with the whole world, and he convinced the people of what, if he had failed, would have been simply regarded as a delusion of his own mind.

Q. So that you think the conduct of Mr Riel perfectly compatible with the conduct for instance of a man like Mahomet or a man like Smith or a man like Young? A. No, I don't regard him so far as I understand them – Mr Riel's views in that light. My opinion is rather, in regard to Mr Riel, if you will allow me to say it, as far as I have been able to judge from my own personal knowledge, that he is a man of great shrewdness and very great depth, and that he might choose, knowing the great influence which he exercised over these people who had a much inferior education to his own, that they regarded him in the light almost of a Saviour, I have thought that he might have assumed for the purpose of maintaining his influence with them, more than he really believed.

Q. That is your impression, doctor? A. I have thought that it might be so. I don't think it is, for I have never heard him on the subject. I have never heard him speak on that subject, and I gather that knowledge only from a general knowledge of what has taken place and from personal knowledge which I acquired in speaking with Mr Riel, but never on that subject.

Q. And of course that knowledge is also based upon a very imperfect hearing of the evidence? A. Of this evidence to-day – on this evidence to-day it is not based. I had a very imperfect hearing of the evidence of to-day. I am speaking only of the general judgment I formed in my own mind entirely apart from the evidence as given in this room. That is what I speak of.

Q. That is entirely outside of what you have heard here? A. Yes, not — let me observe — contrary to what I have heard, though it may be contrary to what I have not heard.

Q. So that now, doctor, you are perfectly aware, are you not, that insane men have exhibited very great shrewdness in some respects? A. Yes.

Q. Now, are you in a position to say, doctor, on your oath, that this man here is not insane? A. I am in a position to say that after a very considerable amount of conversation with him and daily communication with him, I have never spoken to him on a single subject on which he has spoken irrationally.

Q. And you have never spoken to him on the particular subjects with reference to which he is supposed to have his delusions? A. Name the subject?

Q. On religion, and on his mission with reference to the North-West Territories? A. I have never spoken to him on either.

MR OSLER: We may, your Honor, be able to shorten our evidence in reply, if it would be convenient to adjourn now (5 P.M.). It is impossible to close the case to-night, and it would be a matter of convenience if your Honors would adjourn now.

MR LEMIEUX: We agree if your Honors consent to it. We don't want to be responsible.

Court here adjourned till 10 A.M.

Friday and Saturday, 31st July and 1st August 1885

CAPTAIN HOLMES YOUNG recalled
Examined by MR ROBINSON:

Q. We have heard from you as to the part you took in this rebellion and I need not go over that again. The prisoner was in your charge for a certain time? A. Yes.

Q. When was he given in your charge? A. On the evening of the 15th May.

Q. By whom? A. By Major General Middleton commanding the forces.

Q. What were your instructions, what were you to do with him? A. I was responsible for the prisoner to hold him. On Sunday after-noon I received instructions to leave with him for Regina.

Q. Was it on Sunday afternoon that he was given into your charge?
A. He was given into my charge on Friday and remained in my charge till Sunday, when I received the order I have mentioned. We left on Monday at 11:30.

Q. When did you deliver him out of your charge? A. I delivered him here on the 23rd of May.

Q. From the time he first came under your charge till the 23rd of May he was constantly in your charge? A. Yes.

Q. Day and night? A. Yes.

Q. Had you much conversation with him about himself and his conduct and the part he took in the rebellion? A. We conversed almost constantly and very freely.

Q. Upon what subject? A. He conversed on almost every subject connected with the rebellion.

Q. Well then, will you tell us what you think material and of importance in his conversation regarding the rebellion and his own conduct and the part he took in it? A. During the term of eight or nine days that I was living with him entirely, there was an immense amount of conversation. I have no notes to help me in speaking and my remarks may be a good deal rambling.

Q. Well, tell us? A. He did not speak in reference to Fish Creek, he spoke in reference to Duck Lake, as I said the other day.

Q. Did he speak in reference to his general view and the conduct of the campaign? A. In reference to his general view as to the conduct of the campaign he expressed himself in this way, that he was not so foolish as to imagine that he could wage war against Canada and Britain, but he hoped by the first success to compel the Canadian Government to consider the situation or accede to his demands. He placed it in this way: He hoped to surround and capture Major Crozier's force and with them as hostages to compel the Canadian Government to consider the situation, but they failed in that.

Q. Did he say how he failed to capture Crozier? A. A battle occurred and the police retired. He was attempting, as I said, to surround the police force, but the fight commenced and the police retired. He spoke in reference to attacking the column advancing from Qu'Appelle to the front. He said he did not imagine he could fight the army in the field and the reason he did not adopt guerilla warfare was that he hoped by remaining quiet to induce the general to send a small force or to come ahead with a small force himself, and he hoped to capture that small force, and with them as hostages to compel the Canadian Government to consider the situation. They failed in that, and then he made the attempt to capture the steamer *Northcote*, his intention being when he had captured those on board, also as hostages, to compel the Canadian Government to consider the situation. He said he did not sever communication with the east by telegraph, because he hoped to use the telegraph when he captured the hostages.

Q. Those were the general views he expressed as to the situation and the system on which he intended to carry on the campaign and hoped for success. Did he talk about religious matters? A. I noticed that when the conversation was reaching a point that might be of great importance and if he wished for time to answer or to evade the point, the conversation immediately returned on religious matters.

Q. He seemed to use his views on religious matters in that way? A. I so regarded it.

Q. Did he express any special views about religion when he did turn the conversation? A. We had a conversation on the subject of the days of the week, and on the subject of the reformed church.

Q. Tell us any views he expressed on those subjects? A. His view as to hell was, that God's mercy was too great to be sinned away by any person during the short time he had to live. He said there was a period of punishment, and after that, the person would be forgiven. In reference to the reformed church and the days of the week, he said, that when the Christian church emerged from Paganism, it brought some of the remains of Paganism with it, and he instanced the days of the week. He wished to purify religion in Canada, and particularly in the North-West of those parts.

Q. Any other matter? A. He especially mentioned about the infallibility of the Pope. I do not think he referred to any other dogma of the church except that. He desired that the government of the church might be local in Canada. Once or twice the conversation went back to the days of 1869 and 1870, and he spoke in reference to Archbishop Taché as a friend who had been very good to him, and he did not wish me to understand him as saying anything against Archbishop Taché or Bishop Bourget, of Montreal, because he felt that they were personal friends; but he felt that he was right, and even personal friendship would have to give way.

Q. Are there any other general topics on which you conferred with him, and on which he gave you any information? A. He talked about the Indians in different parts of the country, about the Irish aid from the United States, about the battle of Batoche and several incidents that occurred there. He spoke about the rebellion of 1869-70. During the trip in waggons from Saskatoon to Moose Jaw he talked on almost every circumstance and subject. One day when we camped at noon, in moving around the campground to place sentries, I saw some Indian signs, which I destroyed. I called his attention to them, and he said it was possible they might have been left there by a lodge of Indians going from the Cypress Hills to help him at Batoche.

Q. Is there anything else that occurs to you? Of course you cannot relate all the conversation. Was there any other subject upon which you had conversation that you recollect? A. When we found the books and papers in the council room, we found the word *'exovede.'* This bothered us a great deal. I could not translate it at all, and one of the first things I asked the prisoner was, what the meaning of that was. He wrote the meaning of the word in my notebook. He wrote also the meaning of his mission in the notebook.

Q. Do you remember what it was? A. He said that everyone had a mission, and that his mission was to accomplish practical results. The meaning of the word *'exovede'* was, he said, from two Latin words, *ex* from, *ovede* the flock – that the councillors were members of the flock. He himself professed not to be from *exovede*; that there was an *exovede* outside of him with a president.

Q. Does anything else occur to you? I don't wish you to give all the conversations. If you tell us what is important and material, that will be satisfactory to me? A. That is all I can think that will have any bearing on the case. There was a great deal of conversation.

Q. From first to last of these conversations with you, did you observe anything to arouse a suspicion or indicate that he was of unsound mind? A. None at all, certainly not. I found that I had a mind against my own, and fully equal to it; better educated and much more clever than I was myself. He would stop and evade answering questions with the best possible advantage.

Q. The idea of mental aberration, unsoundness of mind, never occurred to you? A. I believe it was for a purpose what has been given as a reason for insanity.

Q. Did he profess to you to have the Spirit of God or the power of prophesy? A. No, never to me.

By MR GREENSHIELDS:

Q. What experience have you had in dealing with people of unsound mind? A. None at all.

Q. You are only speaking now from the conversations you had with the prisoner? A. Merely from the nine days I lived with him.

Q. You never had a medical education in that respect? A. No.

Q. You do not consider yourself in a position to give an opinion as to the sanity? A. I could not give a medical opinion, but I consider that during the nine days I was living with him I would know if I was living with a lunatic.

Q. Did you hear Dr Clarke state that it would take three or four months to find out whether a person was insane in many cases? A. I did.

Q. Do you think you are as clever as these doctors who have stated that? A. I think, living with them as I did, it would be different.

Q. Did you hear the doctor say it would require constant conversation with the person to discover? A. Not constant; such intercourse as the superintendent of an asylum would have.

Q. Have you got that little book he wrote in? A. The counsel for the Crown have it.

Q. You stated that he told you his mission was to produce practical results? A. Yes, the exact words are in the little notebook.

Q. You gave him the book and asked him to write in it? A. He asked for my book to write in, so that it would be correct, and that there would be no misunderstanding about it after.

Q. Did he tell you what the practical result of his mission was to be? A. He spoke frequently of the annihilation of the Métis by the Hudson Bay Company and the Mounted Police. I wanted to get at the meaning of the annihilation, but I could not succeed; he evaded me.

Q. The practical results did he explain to you? A. His explanation was that he wanted to save the people of the North-West from annihilation.

Q. That was the practical result of his mission, as you gathered in conversation with him? A. He evaded me, he could not come down to particulars.

Q. Did he tell you anything as to dividing the territories among different nationalities? A. No, the first I heard of that was in the court room.

Q. You stated that he said he was not foolish enough to imagine that he could wage war against England and Canada? A. I asked him how he expected, with 700 or 800 men, to wage war against three millions of people.

Q. You included England? A. Yes, as being the governing country. (Notebook handed to witness, who reads.) 'I have a mission, so has everybody for me. I understand my mission in this way, to bring about practical results.'

Q. I understand there is something in your book in reference to the word 'exovede'? A. It is lengthy.

Q. No matter, let us have it? A. It is as follows: *Exovede* from, Latin word *exovede*, flock; from two latin words, *ex*, which means from, and *ovede*, flock. That word I made use of to convey that I was assuming no authority at all. And the advisers of the movement took also that title, instead of councillors or representatives; and their purpose for doing so was exactly the same as mine, no assumption of authority. We considered ourselves a part of society and near us, another part of the same society attempted to rule over us improperly, and, by false representations and through bad mismanagement of public affairs, were injuring us greatly, at the same time they were obtaining the ear of the Government. They were turning all the press against us. The situation was leading us simply to annihilation. Without assuming any authority than that which exists by itself in the condition of our nature we recurred to the right of self-preservation and those who agreed to act together in the protection of their existence, threatened in so many different ways, took the names of *exovedes.* So that having their distinctive title for the time being and to be known as the men of the movement, when the crisis would be over, the reaction would be as slight as possible; for the reason that what would have been undertaken and accomplished under the sound authority of good sense could have no other result than good ones, and consequently the movement prove to be less a disturbance than a remedy to some things which were previously

going too far in the wrong. Several times it is true, we made use
of the words, 'representative members of the council,' but we had
to do it, until the word *exovede* was understood and until it would
begin to become usual amongst even the men of the movement.
So the council itself is not a council, and being composed of
exovedes we have called it the *exovedate.*

GENERAL MIDDLETON recalled
Examined by MR ROBINSON:
Q. General Middleton, you have been examined already in this
case — on what date did you say Riel came into your custody?
A. On the 15th of May, I think.
Q. And how long was it before he left your camp? A. On the
morning of the 19th.
Q. So he was with you almost four days? A. Yes, three or four days.
Q. And during that time had you much conversation with him?
A. No, not much. I had more conversation with him the first day
than any other for I had him for the first part of the day, in fact
nearly the whole day, in my tent, until I prepared another place
for him, so that I really talked more with him on that day than
any other.
Q. That was immediately after his capture? A. Yes.
Q. Can you give us any general idea what your subjects of conversation with him were and what he said about himself, his party and
his plans? A. Well, I didn't ask him much about them. I remember
asking him some questions similar to what Captain Young has
told you. I remember asking him why he confined himself to
cutting the telegraph wire only between Frog Lake or between
that station and Prince Albert, why he confined himself to only
removing that and not removing the other wire all around me,
and, as near as I can remember, his answer was that he only
wanted to cut off the police from Prince Albert, and that he
thought he might deprive them of being able to communicate
with the rest of Canada and that he probably would want to use
it himself. And then I asked him how he came to think he would
be able to wage war against Canada with England at its back
because I said England would of course have come to the front
had Canada been beaten, that it would have been impossible for
him to hope to succeed against Canada, and he gave me very

much a similar answer, that he didn't expect to be able to beat
them, but he thought that by dint of showing a good bold front
that he would probably get better terms from the Government,
and he seemed to have an indefinite idea, a sort of idea of taking
everybody prisoner he could lay hold of, that he thought he
could take Major Crozier, and he said he hoped to take me prisoner, and that he then would have got better terms.

Q. Taking hostages in point of fact? A. Yes, hostages. That was the
general view, I think, by means of which he would obtain better
terms.

Q. Is there anything else he said to you on this subject that you
remember? A. No, I cannot really remember anything more.

Q. Did he speak to you on religious subjects? A. Yes.

Q. What were his views? A. He very often turned the conversation to
religious subjects. He told me some of his views. Some of them I
had nothing to say against. I used to listen to what he had to say.
He told me Rome was all wrong and corrupt, and that the priests
were narrow-minded and had interfered too much with the
people, and other of his ideas were excessively good. He told me
he thought religion should be based on morality and humanity
and charity. He talked in that sense and style.

Q. You cannot remember anything else just now that he said to
you? A. No.

Q. During all your intercourse with him did you see anything whatever to indicate any suspicion of unsoundness of mind in him?
A. No, I cannot say I did – on the contrary.

Q. Did it occur to you there was any reason to imagine the man was
not perfectly sound in mind? A. No, I should say on the contrary
he was a man of rather acute intellect. He seemed quite able to
hold his own upon any argument or topic we happened to touch
upon.

Q. That idea never occurred to you? A. Of course I had heard constantly before about reports of his insanity. I heard for instance
one or two of the people that escaped from him, scouts, half-
breeds, one man I remember told me 'Oh, Riel is mad, he is a
fool, he told me what he was doing at Batoche.' So that I really
had heard it, but I came to the conclusion he was very far from
being made or a fool.

Q. That was your conclusion? A. Yes, that was my conclusion.

Examined by MR GREENSHIELDS:

Q. Did that man say what Riel was doing at Batoche? A. Nothing. He simply said Riel was a fool and shrugged his shoulder.

Q. The letters addressed to you by Riel were signed by him *Exovede*? A. I believe they were – no, I don't think they were; you have them there.

Q. Of course you never had seen Riel previous to his surrender on the 15th? A. Never.

REV CHARLES BRUCE PITBLADO sworn
Examined by MR OSLER:

Q. You live in Winnipeg and are a clergyman? A. Yes.

Q. Were you on the boat when the prisoner was brought down the Saskatchewan? A. I was on the *Northcote* with Riel.

Q. From what date and for how long? A. We were on the boat Monday, Tuesday and part of Wednesday.

Q. Were you in his company otherwise? A. I accompanied him to Regina.

Q. How many days were you on the way altogether? A. Five days. We came here on Saturday and had left on Monday.

Q. Had you any conversation with him? A. Several conversations with him.

Q. On what subjects? A. Well, on various subjects, on the rebellion, as I call it, also on his religious views, and we spoke of various other subjects.

Q. Did he give you his plans, his schemes, what he hoped to get by the rebellion? A. Yes, his general scheme was this: He hoped to induce the Government to make a treaty with him or with the half-breeds of the North-West similar to the treaty they had made with the half-breeds of Manitoba. That was what he stated to be his chief object.

Q. How did he hope to accomplish that with his force? A. He told me first of having sent his bill of rights or representation of his grievances to the Government.

Q. How did he hope, with his organization to get what he wanted? A. It would be necessary for me to tell just how the matter progressed.

Q. No, we only want what is material? A. Well, he hoped to get the police in his power, so that whilst they were held, I suppose as

hostages, he said simply while he held them, that he might negotiate with the Government while they were in his power.

Q. Then did he say how that failed? A. He explained how that failed
at Duck Lake.

Q. Did he tell you what his object was at Duck Lake? A. His object
was to get hold of the police so that whilst they were in his power
he might negotiate with the Government.

Q. Then failing that what was his next plan? A. To meet General
Middleton's forces at Fish Creek and if they suffered reverses, of
which he was pretty confident they would, that he would then
send word to the Indians and whilst the troops in the country
were busy with the Indians, who he felt confident would rise,
that then he would be able to negotiate with the Government.
That is substantially the plan as it impressed itself on my mind.

Q. The second plan was to meet him at Fish Creek and then raise the
Indians and whilst the country was engaged with the Indians to
carry on negotiations with the Government? A. That is substantially what I understood it to be.

Q. Failing that, what did he expect to do? A. Well, if that failed, and
of course it did fail, he still hoped to meet General Middleton at
Batoche, and he would be able to hold him at bay long enough to
negotiate with the Government.

Q. These were his three different steps? A. His three different steps.

Q. All ending with the one object? A. Yes, to get a treaty with the
Government.

Q. Now you had a conversation with him how frequently? A. I had
them off and on during the whole of that time. I could not tell
the number. We often spoke together.

Examined by MR GREENSHIELDS:

Q. How long did you say you had been with him altogether?
A. From Monday to Saturday; from the time they started from
Garriépy's Crossing till we came to Regina.

Q. You never had seen or met Mr Riel before that time? A. Never.

CAPT RICHARD DEANE sworn

Examined by MR BURBIDGE:

Q. You belong to the North-West Mounted Police? A. Yes.

Q. Has the prisoner been in your charge? A. Yes, since the 23rd of
May last.

Q. Have you had occasion to visit him fequently? A. Yes, I have seen
   a good deal of him from first to last.

Q. Since that time up to the present? A. Yes.

Q. You have conversed with him? A. Yes.

Q. Principally on what subjects? A. Chiefly subjects affecting prison
   discipline and as to his diet and concessions as to liberty. All
   requisitions must be made to me.

Q. Have you been always able to grant them to him? A. Well, not
   always.

Q. When refused did he show any excitemeñt or irritability? A. No;
   his manner was most polite and suave and he never altered his
   manner in the least.

Q. From the observation you had of him have you seen anything to
   indicate he is not of a sound mind? A. Nothing whatever.

Q. Anything to indicate the contrary? A. Yes, I think so; he always
   gave me the impression of being very shrewd.

JOSEPH PIGGOTT sworn

Examined by MR OSLER:

Q. You are a member of the North-West Mounted Police? A. Yes.

Q. What is your position? A. Corporal.

Q. You have had charge of the prisoner? A. Yes.

Q. Since when? A. Twenty-second May.

Q. Have you been his keeper? A. I have.

Q. Did you see him daily? A. Many times a day.

Q. Have you conversed with him? A. I didn't converse with him.

Q. You have had frequent opportunity of observing him? A. Yes.

Q. Have you seen anything in his conduct to show he is not of sound
   mind? A. No, sir, I always considered him of sound mind.

Q. You have heard him speak? A. Often sir.

Q. And he speaks with good reason? A. With reason and politeness.

MR OSLER: That is the close of the evidence in reply.

ADDRESS TO THE JURY BY THE DEFENCE

MR FITZPATRICK: May it please your Honors, gentlemen of the jury:
In the month of March last, towards the end of that month, a cry of
alarm spread throughout the country, which was flashed with the
rapidity of lightning all throughout the Dominion of Canada. A

rebellion was supposed to exist in this section of the Dominion. It
was said that the country was placed in peril. Men from the north
and from the south, and from the east and from the west, men rose
and rallied around the flag of their country ready to do or die.
Clerks left the stools of their countinghouses, mechanics left their
shops, and all stood ready to do or die in defence of their country.
In this peaceable, law-abiding country the hum of industry to a
certain extent ceased and it was superseded by the tread of armed
men, and the sounds and strains of martial music. Men came, as I
said, from all parts of the Dominion to this section of the country.
War, to a certain extent, prevailed for a short time. Cut-Knife Hill,
Fish Creek, Batoche – all those battles were fought – and as a result
we find to-day the prisoner at the bar now stands indicted for high
treason. We find him now indicted for treason, for an offence, not
one of those ordinary criminal offences for which men are generally
arraigned before the tribunals of their country, but we find him
arraigned for an offence which is peculiarly an offence against the
Government. As during the so-called rebellion all the forces of the
State were put in motion to suppress it, so to-day all the machinery
of the law is put in motion for the purpose of reaching this man, the
prisoner at the bar. We have, as in case of the so-called rebellion,
forces taken by the Government from all sections of the country. We
find them appealing to all those learned and eminent in our profession. We find men brought here from the east and from the west,
from the north and from the south, for the purpose of vindicating
the cause of the Goverment. Gentlemen, allow me to say it, even in
their presence the Government has exercised a wise discretion in
their choice. On the other hand, the flint-locks of the rebels at
Batoche, these weak arms that they then had are presented to you
to-day by the flint-lock counsel who are now acting for the prisoner.
You now see, gentlemen, arrayed on one side all the forces of the
Government, and on the other side all the weakness of the rebels at
Batoche. You now see the storm raging furiously around this man's
head. You now see the waves rising ready to engulf him, but, gentlemen, if we have but the flint-locks of Batoche in our hands, if we
have nothing else at our disposal but our weak talents, when I look
around me I see a silver lining to the cloud, and the storm which is
rising so furiously around this man, and that silver lining I see there
before me in you, good men and true. I say, gentlemen, that,

notwithstanding this man may be weak, and notwithstanding that the Government has arrayed all its talents against him, I see in that the semblance of an English jury, this one grand right that you shall say to the Government, thus far shalt thou go and no further; thou shalt not touch one single hair of this man's head except in justice and in fair play, and not one single hair of his head shall you allow to be touched unless it is in accordance with the well understood principles of law and of justice, and of equity, and especially of fair play. Gentlemen, as I said when I opened this case, what I now have before me is but a shred of that proud institution known as a British jury. What I now see before me is but a shred of it, but even a shred of that jury is sufficient to save a man, when that shred is woven by such material as that that I now see before me. You have but the shred of a jury, but it is sufficient, I trust, in this case, to see that justice is done.

In this case you have heard a very brilliant statement made of a case for the prosecution. You have seen, gentlemen of the jury, the learned counsel who opened the case for the Crown state to you all the events which he intended to prove. You have seen in his hands – and he is truly master of the art – you have seen how in his hands the wounds of our citizen soldiers who died at Duck Lake and at Fish Creek – how they were made to do the duty for the Crown. You have seen how their bloody corpses were made to do duty for the Crown. You have seen how their bloody corpses were appealed to, how the blood-stained snow was brought to your presence – all that has been done.

First, gentlemen, we must limit ourselves to a plain statement of the facts and ask you to bear in mind but two things. In the first place, to what extent, and how was this rebellion carried on as it has been described here? What proof has been given before you by the Crown of the overt acts of treason laid at the door of this man. And secondly, to what extent is he responsible for those acts?

I know, gentlemen, that it would be extremely right for me now here to say a word of praise for those citizen soldiers who at the call of duty left their homes and firesides and came here to fight a battle for what they thought was right – I know, gentlemen, that it would be right for me to say a word about them, but I know, gentlemen, that all I can say can never be equal to the task which I see imposed upon myself, for I know that the names of Fish Creek and of

Batoche and of Cut Knife Hill shall be inscribed in letters of gold on
the annals of the history of our country. I know that the names of
those men who died in those battles shall be written on something
more durable than marble or stone, that they shall be engraved on
the hearts of their grateful countrymen; but, gentlemen, in the face
of all this, is it possible that no voice shall be heard, no voice shall be
heard to say a word in favor of the vanquished? Is it possible that in
a country like this, that all men shall cringe to power, that all men
shall be on the side of victory, and that no voice shall be heard to
plead the cause of the vanquished? Shall we resemble the Romans of
old after the fight of the gladiators and say, victory to the victors,
life to the victors and death to the vanquished? No, gentlemen, I
know that such shall not be the case here, and I know that when I
plead for those unfortunate men, for those men who died on the
side of the rebels at Duck Lake, Fish Creek and Batoche — I know
that I plead for good men and brave, men who died fighting for what
they thought was right; men who died for what they thought was
fair and just, and if they were misguided, they were none the less
brave men and men looked upon as our fellow citizens and to have
done honor to our common country.

Now, gentlemen, it is probably right for me to say here that no
one of any nationality, of any creed, whatever may be the source
whence he derives the blood in his veins, can justify the rebellion,
but it may, at the same time, be proper for me to say, to draw your
attention to the fact that criminal folly and neglect would have gone
unpunished had there been no resistance. It is right for me to say,
gentlemen, that the Government of Canada had wholly failed in its
duty towards these North-West Territories — and here I may as well
remark that, while I speak of the Government, I speak not with the
eye of a politician; when I speak of the Government, all parties are
identical and the same in my eyes — I say that the Government of
Canada wholly failed in its duty towards these North-West Territories, and I say, gentlemen, that it is a maxim of political economy
that the faults of those whom we have placed in authority necessarily injuriously affect ourselves, and it is thus that we are made the
guardians of each other's rights. The fact that the Government and
the people placed in authority have committed faults towards the
North-West to a large extent do not justify the rebellion; but, gentlemen, if there had been no rebellion, if there had been no resistance,

is there any one of you that can say to-day, is there any one of you
that can place his hand on his conscience and honestly say that the
evils under which this country has complained would have been
remedied? I know, gentlemen, that it is not right to preach treason,
and it is no part of my duty to do it. I know that it is probable some
of the doctrines may be looked upon as socialistic, but I say that the
plant of liberty requires the nourishment of blood occasionally. I
say, gentlemen, look at the pages of history of our country, look at
the pages of the history of England, and tell me if there are in all
those bright annals any that shine brighter than those that were
written by Cromwell at the time of the revolution? Tell me, gentlemen, if the liberties which Britons enjoy to-day were bought too
dearly, even with the life blood of a king? I say that they were not.
Let us now look at the position of this country. We find that this
country originally was the exclusive property of the Indians. We find
that this country, in the wise decree of Providence, had been originally left to them. Then we find, gentlemen, that this country,
being entirely in their possession, the Provinces of Canada now were
settled by people from the other side. We find these people animated
with that desire which necessarily actuates all these descendants of
Englishmen and Frenchmen that desire to go and conquer and see
worlds unknown, that those people spread out over those fertile
regions and came in contact with the Indians and formed alliances
with them, and became part and parcel of themselves – an act of
union between the English and French settlers in Canada and the
Indian aborigines of this part of the country; and we have that race
now known as the Métis. We have the Indians in possession, and then
we find the Government of Canada and England coming here, and
how do they treat the Indians? Do we find the Government treating
them with buckshot and with cannon ball? No. Guided by that
humane policy that has always been an essential attribute of England, we find treaties being made with the Indians. We find their
rights acknowledged, and we find arrangements being made with
them whereby certain rights are secured to them, and in return they
give up portions of the country to the English. Then we find the
Indians travelling towards the land of the setting sun. We find the
Indian leaving the land that has been formerly his, and hunting
ground, and receding in the face of the onward march of civilization.
We find the Indian, as he says himself, leaving his happy hunting
grounds, and, as a poet has already said, saying to the bones of his

forefathers as they lie beneath the sod, rise up, march on with us toward the land of the setting sun, where we also shall set at some day not now far distant.

Then, gentlemen, as I tell you, we have the half-breeds. We have the half-breeds who by their blood represent and form the distinctive characteristic of union between the Indian and the white man. We have the half-breed, the result of the union between the Indian, the representative of savagery, and the white man, the representative of civilization. We have therefore, gentlemen, this bond of union between civilization and the Indian, and I say gentlemen, that that bond of union represented by the Métis has been one of the greatest factors in the civilization of the Indian. I say that this bond of union which is represented by the Métis has done more for the North-West country than anything that has ever been done for it heretofore.

Why is it that this country has not been the scene of so many Indian wars as we have seen ravaging the United States? Why is it that this country here as to its Indian policy, has been such a great success? Why is it that the Indian policy of our Government has been so successful? It is purely and simply because of the fact that the half-breed always stood between the Indian and his fellow white man. The half-breed was the distinctive characteristic intermediary between the two. And gentlemen, it is impossible for us to find any better illustration of that principle than has been afforded us by this last unfortunate war. In the whole of this war, what do we find? When we find the savage instincts of the Indians roused, when we find them roused up ready to do and commit acts of the utmost brutality, what do we find standing between him and his fell designs? Where do we find the man that is brave enough and plucky enough to say thus far shalt thou go and no farther? You have found it in the case of the half-breeds. You have found the half-breed always standing between the Indians and the white men. You have found the half-breed standing between the Indian and the white man. You have found the half-breed standing between the Indians and Mrs Delaney and Mrs Gowanlock. You have found the half-breed standing between the Indians and the priests. You have found the half-breed − in the case of those very prisoners brought here − you have always found the half-breed standing between the white man and the Indians, and always on the side of civilization and the side of mercy, and always on the side of humanity.

Now, gentlemen, what rights those men have had by virtue of
their Indian origin, what rights those men have acquired by virtue of
the services which they rendered to the Government, how were
those rights respected?

It is not necessary for me to go any further than simply to put
the question: And what was the condition of affairs in this country
at the time, at the beginning of this constitutional agitation? We
find, gentlemen, that those men after being deprived of their means
of subsistence by reason of the fact that the chase would no longer
furnish them support, the support they had previously obtained
from it — we find those men, gentlemen, turning their attention to
pastoral pursuits and giving their attention to agriculture. We find
those men entering into possession of those small portions of land, a
very small portion of God's inheritance, of that inheritance which
had been given to their Indian ancestors. We find them entering into
possession of those lands, and imbued with the ideas which their
forefathers had given to them, they settle on those lands, they
endeavor to cultivate them, they endeavor to make a home for themselves. After they had been in possession of those lands, we find
certain grievances crop up, certain difficulties arise between the
Government and themselves, and then what next? Then they begin to
think if they can find in the annals of history any people who have
ever occupied the same position as themselves. They begin with the
limited knowledge which they have, to ask themselves whether or
not they can find a comparison, they can find a people situated as
they were, so as to see how those people acted, and how they obtained a redress of their rights. Their sphere is limited, those ignorant
half-breeds of the Saskatchewan had not, as you and probably a
great many others here have, travelled through Europe, across the
waters and gone into the United States, and gone around the world,
with enlarged ideas — the sphere of their knowledge was limited, but
they looked around themselves, and the first thing they saw was
Manitoba. The first thing they saw was Manitoba, and they said to
themselves, why, here in Manitoba, the people were situated as we
are, they had about the same rights, the same privileges as we had
before Canada came into their country, and they said to themselves,
why, with those rights, what resulted? What position are they in to-
day? What is the difference between their position and ours? They
said their position is entirely different from ours, as entirely

different as day is from night, they are in the full enjoyment of all
the privileges of the British constitution. They are in full enjoyment
and peaceable possession of their lands. They have been conceded
titles. Titles have been conceded by the Government to them, by
which they have the muniments of title to the little patch of land
they have tilled. How did they come by all this? How did they
acquire it? Then some of the old men in this district begin to think
so far back as 1870, when a difficulty arose there between the
Government and the people – a difficulty arose in which there was
one man who guided the movement, from which movement a successful issue was obtained, and they said, the man that did so much
for the half-breeds there, the man that obtained for them their rights
surely will consent to do as much for us, the man who acted in Manitoba and gained for the Manitobans, for our brothers of that district,
their rights and their privileges, will surely do as much for us as he
did for them. Then the word goes around and the name of Louis
Riel suggests itself to every person, and they begin to find out where
this man is. They say to themselves, a man who played such an
important part at that time as he did, that man surely will help us.
But perhaps he may now be placed in a situation where he is above
and beyond want. He may now be placed in a position where he must
necessarily have benefited very largely by what he did in Manitoba,
and they say, they may possibly have said to themselves, well, perhaps, we cannot get him, but we will try at all events. They had to
choose a deputation, and they sent that forth They find out where
Riel is, and they send a deputation to ask him to come up and help
them in their agitation, and where do they find Louis Riel? Is he a
gentleman living in the lap of luxury? Is this the man who will be
represented to you and who has been represented to you as a selfish,
ambitious man, with no desire in the world but for selfishness and
for egotism – this man who has been represented to you as the man
who endeavors to seek himself first and everyone else after? Where
do they find this man? Not, as I said, rolling in the lap of luxury.
No, gentlemen of the jury, he occupied the humble position of a village schoolmaster; he was there with his wife, an humble Cree
woman, with his little children there in Montana, endeavoring to
earn for them their daily bread by the sweat of his brow as a schoolmaster; he was there acting as a schoolmaster among those people
and endeavoring to earn his modest pittance, and, gentlemen, he is

asked, and from there he comes up to join this movement – he does
not hesitate. He does not, before he leaves there, stipulate that he
shall be paid for his services. He does not tell those men: You want
me to leave my country; you want me to leave this home that I have
made for myself and you want to bring me back there in the hands
of enemies, to a certain extent. He does not stipulate for a payment.
He says: No, you are my brethren; the same blood that runs through
my veins runs through yours, and any services that I may be able to
give you are free to command, and he went with them. Then he
comes into the country, and when he is there how does he act? He
takes part in this movement; he assists his fellow men in their agitation; he attends at all the meetings; he gives his views on the political
situation, and then, gentlemen, we are told at a sudden moment a
break takes place. Then, you will be told by the Crown, there is the
transition from constitutional agitation to open armed rebellion, and
I have no doubt that some beautiful theories will be expounded to
you on the art of constitutional agitations. You will be told probably, in very eloquent terms, that the British constitution is elastic
enough to enable men to obtain the redress of all their rights, to
obtain the redress of all their rights by means of constitutional
political agitation. I say, gentlemen, all that is very true, and all that
may appear to you as very forcible argument; but there is one thing
you must remember when it is said to you – there is one thing I beg
of you to remember when my voice shall have ceased to be heard by
you, and that is that when they talk of constitutional agitation in
England, when they talk of the representative institutions of England, when they tell you what might be done in England and in
Canada, you must remember that the North-West Territories cannot
come in under that rule; you must remember that constitutional
agitation, as understood by those books as represented to you by the
officers of the Crown, is perfect when the people are makers of their
laws; when the people elect their representatives and send them to
Parliament and have a voice in the affairs of the administration of
the body politic – if you were represented in Parliament, if you had
rights, if you had grievances, and you had people to represent you in
Parliament, what would you have to do? You would agitate, you
would constitutionally agitate. You would politically agitate. You
would have your representative in the House of Parliament come
among you, and you would say, we have those grievances, we insist

on those grievances being redressed, and you are there at Ottawa in the Federal Parliament for the purpose of having those grievances redressed, you are there for the purpose of expressing to those people who are down in Ottawa, what our views are and how we want the law administered, in so far as we are concerned. That would be constitutional agitation. That would be perfect agitation. That would be a perfect answer to any argument that I might have advanced on constitutional agitation; but when you are in the North-West Territories very nearly 2,000 miles away from those who make the laws under which you are governed — very nearly 2,000 miles away from the people who make the laws for you, and in the making of which laws you have no voice, over which you have no control, in which representative institutions you have no one to represent you — here you have those Métis, gentlemen of the jury, you have those unfortunate Métis of the Saskatchewan 2,000 miles away from Ottawa, 2,000 miles away from this representative House of Parliament and without one single representative either constitutional or otherwise to represent them, without one single voice to be raised in their favor. You have the fact that those men have been in this territory, and that this country has been in the hands of the Dominion of Canada for the last fourteen or fifteen years, you have that fact and you have the fact that during all that time those men have not been able to get one single representative, not been able to take any part direct or indirect in the management of their affairs, of their own affairs or the affairs of their country. Now, where is the constitutional agitation? How can you be told on those facts that those men could constitutionally act? Could you be told that on those facts they could have endeavored to obtain a redress of their wrongs by this constitutional agitation? I say, gentlemen of the jury, the situations are entirely different, that which was constitutional agitation in England cannot be considered as constitutional agitation here and what is considered constitutional agitation in Canada, in any other part of the Dominion of Canada, cannot be considered as applying to the North-West Territories, for the situations are entirely different.

You have seen, gentlemen, from the evidence adduced before you, how Mr Riel acted throughout the whole of this movement. You have seen he took part in the different political meetings that were held, and what his conduct was during that time. You have

been told of this meeting at Nolin's — you have been told of this
meeting at Prince Albert — you have been told how at the meeting at
Nolin's this man in the month of January last stood up, and in
terms, the very essence of loyalty, proposed the health of Her
Majesty the Queen. You have been told how at Prince Albert, at a
meeting held there, this man said, let us agitate, let us agitate by constitutional means. We must obtain the redress of our wrongs during
five years, but if we do not obtain it at the end of five years, we will
agitate for five years more, and probably at the end of ten our voices
shall have been able to pierce from the Saskatchewan Valley down
to the House at Ottawa; but, gentlemen, at a given moment, in the
beginning of March, as I said when I opened, an appeal to arms took
place, and here I confess I tread on dangerous ground. Either this
man is the lunatic that we his counsel have tried to make him, or he
is an entirely sane man in the full possession of all his mental facul-
ties, and was responsible in the eyes of God and man for everything
that he has done. If he is a lunatic, we, in the exercise of a sound
discretion, have done right to endeavor to prove it. If he is a sane
man, what humiliation have we passed upon that man, we his
counsel endeavoring, despite his orders, despite his desire, despite his
instructions, to make him out a fool. If he is a sane man, gentlemen
of the jury, if he is the sane man that the Crown will endeavor to
represent him, are there any redeeming features in his character and
in his conduct of this rebellion? Are there any redeeming features in
what he has done in connection with it which necessarily appeal to
the sympathies and to the judgment? Here we find this man taking
part in this, acting in concert with a naturally excitable population,
acting with them in entire sympathy with the movement which
began long before he came into the country or had anything to do
with it. At a given moment — if he is a sane man — that movement,
like all other popular movements, got ahead of him, got beyond his
control. Then, gentlemen, did he after fanning the flame, did he
after fomenting the trouble, like some others, turn his back on the
men whom he had put into the trouble and into the difficulty? Did
he like some of the men who stood in that box — did he after
fomenting the discord, after inciting those unfortunate men to rebellion, after placing their necks in the halter — did he stand back or
stand from under and endeavor to save himself? Did he play the part
of the coward or the traitor? Did he play the part of the sycophant

who comes and kneels at the feet of the Government, endeavoring to
seek a victim amongst his friends and relations? Did he, gentlemen of
the jury, with all this magnanimity which has been represented to
stand on other heads, with all this glory, has been endeavored to be
put on the heads of other people? Did he fly and leave women and
children to be massacred? and did he fly from the hands of justice,
or did he stand his ground like a man, and did he come before the
representatives of Her Majesty and say, if any is to suffer, let me
suffer; if anyone is to be punished, let me be punished; if any victim
is to be found, I am the victim that is to go upon the scaffold; and I
fought for liberty, and if liberty is not worth fighting for, it is not
worth having?

Gentlemen, you will be told men have been brought into that box
and endeavors have been made to excite the public mind with enthusiasm about certain soldiers who acted throughout this rebellion; a
man has been brought into that box to come here and tell you how
he took part in that agitation, to tell you how he fanned the flame as
I said and how afterwards, sycophantic like, he bent his knees and
adored the rising sun. You have been told throughout this country
that this person and that person who took part in the rebellion was a
hero, that they were all heroes but this unfortunate man; but when
the time comes to show the true spirit of the hero, did this man run
away? Did this man endeavor to seek safety in flight or did he come,
as General Middleton said himself, in the box, and deliver himself up
freely and voluntarily ready to bear the consequences of his acts?
But, gentlemen, I have stated those facts to you simply to show you
that no matter how you look at the character of Louis Riel, there
are to be found in it redeeming features; but, gentlemen, I still maintain that it was a wise movement on our part, that we were justified
by the facts, that our views have been borne out by the evidence,
and that we were bound in our instructions as representing this man
to say that he is entirely insane and irresponsible for his acts, and
will now proceed to examine that branch of the case. Here it may be
well for me to remind you somewhat of the history of this man's
life. You know, gentlemen, that he is himself a half-breed. You
know that he is himself a descendant of those Indians of whom the
poet has said that their untutored minds see God in the clouds and
hear His voice in the winds. You know, gentlemen, that a descendant
of those Indians is endowed with that mysticism which forms an

essential element of their religious character. He has descended from
the Indians and one of those Métis of whom I spoke to you a moment ago. He lived in this country for a considerable period of time
and took part — as matter of history, I might state this to you — in
the Manitoba movement in 1870. As a result of that movement the
unfortunate man was afflicted with a disease of the mind and so far
did it go that it became necessary to keep him in a lunatic asylum.
You know that we find here proved that he was in a lunatic asylum
from the year 1876 to 1878. That is a fact about which there can be
no dispute. It now becomes necessary for us to see whether or not
this man is suffering from any form of mental disease which is
known to the books and known to authors who have treated on this
subject. We have stated that this man was suffering from that form
of disease known as megalomania. It is not necessary for me to tell
you more than that the characteristic symptom of this disease is an
insane, an extraordinary love of power and extraordinary develop-
ment of ambition, a man that is acting under the insane delusion
that he is either a great poet or a god or a king or that he is in direct
communication with the Holy Ghost; and it may be well for me here
to remind you that I do not speak here of my own authority. I tell
you here that from books, the most reputed authorities on this
subject, one of the distinguishing characteristics of this disease is
that the man might reason perfectly and give perfect reasons for all
that he does and justify it in every respect, subject always to the
insane delusion. They are naturally irritable, excitable, and will not
suffer that they can be contradicted in any respect. Let us now see,
gentlemen, whether, under the evidence that has been brought here
before you, we find proof of the existence of those symptoms which
are described as characteristic of the malady which we contend this
man is suffering from; and, in the first place, it may be well, perhaps,
before I enter upon that branch of the case in detail, to remind you
that in all cases of crime, it is essential, I might almost say, for the
jury to enable them to arrive at a proper conclusion, to examine into
the motive, the determining motive which can have brought a man
to commit a crime. You take a case of murder, you always see in a
case of murder, if you find a man accused of murder, you naturally
ask yourself well what can have been the determining cause, the
motive which can have guided that man in the commission of the
crime? Was it jealousy, was it desire of gain, was it hatred, was it

passion? There is some motive, there is some moving, guiding motive
which must necessarily be account for.

Now, gentlemen, bearing that fact in mind, you know that human
depravity has not gone so far that a man will commit a crime of
mere wantonness, without any motive, without any object whatever
in view? Now here, what object could Louis Riel have in this rebellion? What motive could he have in view. If you are told that this
was a vain, ambitious man, and the object this man had in view when
he did all those things was his desire for gain, his desire for power,
and you say the man was sane, that the man was perfectly sane; let
us examine together how it is possible to consistently say that this
man, if he was sane, could have ever thought to obtain the object of
his ambition, the wealth which he is supposed to have desired, by
adopting the means which they pretend he did adopt. Here is a man
in the valley of the Saskatchewan in the midst of a tribe of men, in
the midst of a people who were devoutedly attached to their church,
a people who were not armed, who did not have any power to obtain any of the essential attributes, any of the things requisite to
enable them to levy war. You have this man who is represented to
you by the witnesses who come into the box and who expect you to
believe them; this deep, designing, cunning man; you have this man
who is gifted with extraordinary powers that one of the witnesses,
who is an extremely intelligent man, said, that he was afraid to risk
himself against him; you have this man who is represented to you as
a villain of the first water, a deep, designing rascal, with intelligence
of the very highest calibre; you have this man represented to you as
going coolly to work for the purpose of obtaining his ambition by
enrolling four or five hundred poor unfortunate Métis, with flint-
locks, with guns, with limited ammunition, and, as General Middleton said, attacking the whole power of the Dominion of Canada,
with a power of Britain behind her back. Now you have this deep,
designing man – remember you have this man here with wonderful
intellect, this man here with a wonderful judgment, actually undertaking to effect the purpose of obliging Canada to grant him his
requests. You have this man here, this deep, designing, cunning man,
this man with wonderful intellect, expecting to succeed in forcing
the Dominion of Canada, backed by England, to accede to his
demand with four or five hundred Métis at his back. You have in
addition to that this cunning man, this man with full knowledge of

the character of his fellow-men, of the Métis; this man with full
knowledge of the fact that those men were devout, most devout;
that they were men attached to their religion; you have this man
told that he endeavored to succeed in his purposes and to effect his
object by directly assailing those beliefs, that creed which those men
had been taught as they were children, which those men loved,
which those men adored, which those men had been taught as they
were children and which had grown up and formed an essential part
of their natures; you are told, gentlemen, that this man, this deep,
designing, cunning man, would have adopted that method to achieve
his object. Oh, gentlemen, I think I could show you how a deep,
designing man would have achieved his object better than this under
those circumstances; I think I can show you how much more easy, if
Riel is the man he is represented to be by the Crown, how he could
have achieved his object in a different method from this.

Here is this man brought into the country, this man who had
succeeded in Manitoba who had the whole force of the Métis st his
back, who had behind him not only the French half-breeds, but also
the English half-brreds, you see this man coming into the country,
who is the embodiment in person of those deprived of their rights
and their privileges, and you see this man doing what? What did he
do? What did the ordinary common dictates of reason tell him to
do? What did ordinary common sense tell him to do? Why did he
not do as he said he wanted to do at Prince Albert, lie low and continue on fomenting this movement, and continue on guiding this
movement, and is it possible to expect that in the course of time the
North-West is not going to have its rights? Is it possible to tell me
that the North-West Territories shall not form essentially and really a
part of the Dominion of Canada as it now forms part of it nomi-
nally? Is it possible that there is no future for the North-West Territories? Is it possible that some day the North-West Territories shall
not play a part in this Dominion? If ever a day arrives, and I think
every man of you in the box hopes it will arrive very soon, if ever
that day arrives where would Louis Riel be, what would have become of him? Would there have been any position in this country to
which this man might not have aspired? Would there have been any
position in this country which that man might not legitimately hope
to obtain? Had he simply exercised the ordinary dictates of prudence and caution and common sense, all he had to do was to stay

with the Métis and remain in possession of their confidence and then necessarily, of absolute necessity, would he some day have acquired, have arrived at the highest pinnacle of his ambition, whatever it might have been. And, gentlemen, is that not much more reasonable, would that not be the way a reasonable man would have acted? Would that not be the way a reasonable man should have acted? Would that not be the way that you or I or any other man of common sense would have acted? Now, gentlemen, so far as religion is concerned, you were told this man took advantage of the religious nature of the half-breeds. He understood thoroughly their nature, he understood thoroughly their character, and he knew full well that by playing upon their religious notions that by playing upon their religion, he would necessarily achieve his purpose. If he understood so well their religious character, if he knew what their religious character was why did he not side with the priests? Why did he not ascertain what their desire was? If to help him. He knew the priests wanted to help him. He knew, gentlemen, that the priests could not be an obstacle in his way. The priests could not have any ambition outside of ministering to the wants of their parishioners. The priests could not have any ambition to represent this country in any political position. The priests could not otherwise than be mere stepping stones for him to rise into power. If he understood the character of his fellowmen as a deep, designing, cunning man would have understood them, had he understood the character of the Métis as to their devoted religious character as that man of superior intellect, as he is represented to be, would have understood them, would he have taken such steps as are proved here to have alienated from him the sympathies of the half-breeds? And there is the point given in evidence, about which there can be no dispute, a matter of fact about which there can be no dispute, which it is impossible to controvert; and I may as well tell you here that I should have begun probably by that, that in all that I say I speak under the direction of the court. I speak under the direction of the distinguished magistrate who presides over this trial, and if any statements of fact are made by me which are not entirely correct, I beg of him, as a duty towards you and towards myself, to correct me.

After having said so much, I now proceed to tell you that if this man was the deep, designing, cunning rascal that he is represented to be, this man of superior intellect, he would have understood the

Métis character better than he did. He would have known their religion was so deeply rooted in them, that it was impossible for a crazy lunatic to eradicate it. He would have known, gentlemen, that those men could not have been imposed upon, and, as a matter of fact, he did not impose upon them. You saw the witness in the box, you saw that venerable clergyman, gentlemen, who came into the box, and who stated to you and to all of us, that the half-breeds followed Riel in very limited numbers. He says that there was not half of them followed Riel in his religious movement. Now, gentlemen, you have two facts which I say are inconsistent with the theory that this man can be the deep, designing rascal that he is represented to be, that this man can be of such superior intellect as to almost impose upon the general commanding the forces, and the subordinate, Captain Young. I say, gentlemen, it is impossible, because if he was, in the first place he would not have gone astray in the means he would have used to achieve his purpose. He would not have attempted, with a handful of half-breeds — three hundred or four hundred is the greatest number we have heard — many of them unarmed except with a few flint locks, he would not have endeavored, with those men, to force Canada to grant him his rights. He would not have endeavored, with those men, to force the power of Britain to come down before him and to seek terms from him. No such thing could have been achieved, and he would not have either endeavored to take the half-breeds from their alliance, or from their allegiance to their religion, by adopting such means as he eventually alienated their entire sympathy from him.

But, gentlemen, if his conduct is entirely inconsistent with the possession of a sound mind, is it not consistent with the possession of an unsound mind? And here I may as well tell you that you are entire masters of the fact in this case, that all the evidence given here is given for the purpose of enabling you to arrive at a conclusion, that you are not to take your verdict from me, from the Crown nor from the court; that the oath which you have taken, as you understand thoroughly, obliged you, when you came into the box, to stand indifferent as you stood unsworn, and the true deliverance made between our Sovereign Lady the Queen and the prisoner at the bar, according to your conscience and to your judgment.

Therefore, gentlemen, you have these facts in evidence, that this man, laboring under the insane delusion that he at some future

day would have the whole of the North-West Territories under his
control, and being thoroughly convinced that he was called and
vested by God, for the purpose of chastising Canada and of creating
a new country and a new kingdom here, acting under that insane
delusion, what do we find him doing? We find him then taking such
steps as would enable him to carry out the object which he then had
in view. We find this man believing himself to be inspired by God
and believing himself to be in direct communication with the Holy
Ghost, believing himself to be an instrument in the hands of the
Lord of Hosts. We find him with forty or fifty men going out to do
battle with against the forces of Canada. If the man was sane, how is
it possible for you to justify such conduct as that? If the man was
insane you know it is one of the distinguishing characteristics of his
insanity that he could see no opposition of his objects, that he believed himself to be under the guidance of the Lord of Hosts, and
natural reason, he could reason naturally, subject to his insane delusion, he reasoned naturally that the All Powerful will necessarily give
him the victory no matter what may be the material that may be
placed in his hands, no matter how inadequate that material may
appear to a sane man, I, knowing that I am inspired by the Almighty, knowing that I am the instrument in the hands of God, I
know that I will necessarily gain the victory; and he goes forth and
gives battle with these men. Therefore, gentlemen of the jury, you
have one illustration of the insanity, of the unsoundness of this
man's mind in those very facts. Then I know what you will be told
in answer to that immediately, 'Oh, but here is this $35,000 that he
was ready to take, and this money he was willing to receive from the
Government, and the case of the Métis, the case of the half-breeds
was nothing in his eye, provided the person, Louis Riel, was safe.'
Well, gentlemen, may I remind you of the evidence which was given
on that point by us. Need I remind you of the evidence which was
given on that point by two men, the only two men who spoke to it,
and that is Charles Nolin and Father André, the priest. You will find,
gentlemen, that both of those men said that he wanted $35,000. Was
it for the purpose of putting it into his pocket? Was it for the purpose of leaving Canada and going away and living in the United
States in ease and luxury with this money? Was it for the personal
gratification and the personal advantages of Louis Riel that he
wanted this money? You remember the evidence, and I need not

remind you of it. You remember that he said he wanted that money for the purpose of enabling him to carry out his mission, and he wanted to go to the United States to found a newspaper, as he said, and with that newspaper to rouse up the foreign nations to enable him to come in here and take possession of the country. Now, in that fact alone is evidence of his insane delusions, there is evidence that there is the manner which is characteristic of this delusion, of this malady, and which enables men to reason properly and to achieve the object which they have in view, always subject to their insane delusions.

I told you yesterday, I had occasion to put it before to you, that those men subject to this malady can reason perfectly, and as Dr Clarke said, subject always to their delusions. He reasoned perfectly. He says: 'I want to get this money, I want it to help me in my object and I want to attain that object and I know that I can attain it, and I necessarily will attain it.' That is the only interpretation which can be put on it, and that is the only interpretation which can reasonably be put on that demand of $35,000. Then, gentlemen, you have the evidence of the insanity given to you by Dr Clarke, and by the clergyman and several of the Crown witnesses, whose names I do not want to repeat, and I do not want to detain you any unnecessary length of time; but, gentlemen, I do not think it necessary for me to extend, to go in at any length into this evidence further than to say Dr Roy proved this man was in his asylum in the year 1878; and here I may as well draw your attention to the fact that this witness is a man who has been for some fifteen years in constant study of mental diseases. I may as well draw your attention to the fact that this man came 2,000 miles here at the request of the Crown as well as of the defence for the purpose of giving evidence in this case.

I may as well draw your attention to the fact that this man is a foreigner and an alien at least in language to us. He is a man, gentlemen, who possesses the characteristic politeness of his race, a man who is possessed of the characteristic politeness of the French race, and who comes here into the box prepared to make himself agreeable to all, and being so, as you saw yesterday, he endeavored, being at a difficulty, to give his evidence in such a manner as it could be thoroughly understood by you. I do not want to refer any more to his evidence.

You now have Dr Clarke, who was examined afterwards. He gave you his experience. He has told you what he knows about asylums. He was examined in his own language, and he had that advantage over Dr Roy. You heard his evidence as he gave it. You heard that he was not very closely cross-examined. I noticed that he was not very closely cross-examined, and he gave his evidence and told you what he thought about this man's mind. Now, what interest had Dr Roy and Dr Clarke in coming here for the purpose of deceiving you, gentlemen? What interest have either of those men got in coming here 2,000 miles to step in that box in this great public case when they know that every word they say will be spread broadcast through Canada and the United States? What interest have those men got in coming here and perjuring themselves? What interest have those men got in coming here and saying anything that is not true? You have heard the evidence given by these men. You have seen them. You are sufficient judges of human nature to be able to say whether or not those men are telling the truth. In addition, gentlemen, you have heard the remark made by Dr Clarke that struck me as being peculiarly applicable to this case. You have heard the remark which was made by him, when he said that this man, if this man was sane, he took very insane methods to arrive at his objects, when he began by making the remark of the very purpose which he had in view, by means of which he showed if he was perfectly sane. For instance, he gave to you the illustration, he illustrated his remarks by referring to his religion, and he said that necessarily if he was sane his religious duties would tend to alienate the sympathies of the half-breeds.

Now, gentlemen, on the other hand, you have the evidence of those priests, you have the evidence of the Crown witnesses. Of course, it is not for me to say anything about the witnesses that were brought here before you. You have seen them. It is for you to judge of their characters. It does not properly behoove me, a man occupying my position, to praise any person. All that I can say is, so far as I have been able to judge, all the witnesses that were examined here in the examination-in-chief acted like men who appeared to me brought here on behalf of the Crown who wanted to tell the truth, men who really astonished me. I was really astonished when I heard about the perils which some of those men had met, I was really filled with admiration for their bravery and their courage, and I know, gentlemen, that no number of men, no men who have confronted difficulties that those men have confronted, no men who have gone through perils and the risk those men have gone through is a liar or a coward. Therefore, gentlemen, I know that those gentlemen who were examined for the Crown tell the truth. I know that, as far as they could, they gave their evidence to the best of their ability, and, gentlemen, I know also that those men, with the exception of one, who has branded himself for all time, were foreigners and strangers to this man, but, with true instincts of British justice, they did what they could do to get fair play, and they gave him no thrust in the back. I cannot say anything for the other one.

So far as our witnesses are concerned, gentlemen, so far as our witnesses are concerned, I think I can say as much for them. I think our witnesses told honestly all they could to tell the truth. Then you have those two priests brought into the box, who tell you their impressions, who tell you that, in so far as their knowledge of this man went, they could not call him anything else than a fool; that as far as they could go, as far as their knowledge went — and they were a little guarded in their statement — they said they could not think of him otherwise than as a fool, and they have been in positions to judge of him. They had daily intercourse with him from the month of July last up to month of March; they had been able to follow him day by day, step by step, to follow him in his movements, to see how easy the movement increased, when the agitation continued, and when he was carried away by the violence of his passions — when, from one day to another, how quickly, swiftly the agitation stepped into armed rebellion, because you will remember there was no transition.

Now, gentlemen, in the face of this, you have the evidence of the Crown and that evidence is given to you by men, who to the best of their skill and ability come here and tell you what they know — and no one can be expected to tell you anything that he does not know. For instance, if a man has not read French books, he cannot tell you what is in them; but gentlemen, you must remember this fact, that those men come here and tell you they have a very limited knowledge of this man, that their intercourse with him has been extremely limited, and they will tell you, what? Not that he is sound, they will not on their oath undertake to swear positively this man is not of

unsound mind, but they will tell you, gentlemen, that all they can
tell you is that they have not been able to discover any symptoms of
insanity. You all know, gentlemen, the story of my countryman who
was being tried for murder, an Irishman, like myself, being tried for
murder, and two witnesses pretended to swear positively that they
had seen him do the deed, that they saw him commit the murder:
Well, my countryman turns round and says, is that all the evidence
you have got? The Crown says yes. Well, he says I can get eighty
men who will swear that they did not see me do it. That is about the
way it is in this case. We have men who swear positively to the unsoundness of this man's mind, and we have a great many more who
say they did not see any traces of insanity, they can find no traces of
insanity. Now, gentlemen, with all due deference and respect for the
great skill and ability of the Crown witnesses, which skill and ability
I do not intend to contest, I mean to say that they are men of extraordinary pretensions, and that their pretensions are quite equal to
their extraordinary abilities; but, gentlemen, with all due deference
and respect, I have heard also other men, very eminent men, equally
eminent with the Crown witnesses, I have heard of a man called
Erskine who is well known as the greatest lawyer the bar of England
has ever produced, who was Lord Chancellor of England, and I can
tell you, gentlemen, that there was a case came up in England, a case
of James Hadfield, of whom you have probably heard, indicted for
treason, for having shot one of the Georges, in the Hay Market
Theatre. The case was identical with the present one, and in that
case the plea of his insanity was set up. Erskine, in that case states
his experience in another case in which a man had been confined in
the Hawkestone Asylum in England and had been discharged as
cured. After his discharge he took an action of damages against the
authorities in the asylum who had kept him there, saying that he had
been confined as a lunatic when he was of perfectly sound mind. At
the trial, Erskine, who appeared for the authorities of the asylum,
had the man in the box and cross-examined in every possible way
and manner so as to endeavor to show that the authorities were perfectly justified in what they had done and that the man was a lunatic. He kept him there for twenty-four hours and examined him
persistently during twenty-four hours, and during the whole of that
time he could not discover that he was insane, and the only way
they got on to it, was that this man was in his belief Jesus Christ,

and acted under that insane delusion. He was perfectly rational, perfectly reasonable on all other subjects, but the very moment they touched that subject that he was Jesus Christ, of course the man was off his feet and there was an end to it, and at the end of the day after Mr Erskine had given the man up the doctor came and said that that was his belief, and when they got him on to that the case was at an end.

Then I know, gentlemen, another case which is also told about another man who believed that he corresponded with a princess in cherry juice, that he had been confined in a tower and the princess used to sail along a river which ran at the foot of the tower, and when she would pass he used to throw down letters to her, and she would receive them, and he labored under that insane delusion that he was in love with the princess, and he was confined in an asylum. In this case it was Lord Chief Justice Mansfield about whom you have heard, who acted. They examined the man a whole day and never could discover his insanity until by fortuitous events he brought out that this was his particular malady, and when they discovered that there was an end to it.

Now I know what the Crown will tell you. They will say yes, but there was one vulnerable point in those men, and when that vulnerable point was touched, then of course the whole game was up and the insanity became apparent, and that no such thing as that has been made to appear in this case; but in that last case I spoke to you about, after the case was dismissed, after it had been made apparent that the man was insane, of course the action was dismissed, and then as he had gone through two different obstructions on his way to the asylum, he took a new case out and had the authorities of the asylum tried the second time for the offence that he pretended that they had committed towards him, and of course, then you see the difficulty that cropped up. In the first place of course it was known, and they endeavored to cross-examine this man and endeavored by every means in their power to get him into some craze that he had exhibited in the first case in order to show his insanity.

Well, gentlemen, it is narrated in the books and laid down here, that they examined that man for days and days and never could get him to talk about his insanity, never could discover any traces of insanity, notwithstanding they knew the particular delusion existing – the particular delusion under which he labored, and it became so apparent, he went so far that it was utterly impossible for them to arrive at it, and they had to take the depositions given in the previous case. Been found in the council chamber. What proof have we got here now that these documents were ever used for any purpose whatsoever, or for the purposes which have been ascribed to this man? What proof have we got that those documents were issued, and that an appeal was made to those savage hordes to rise in their fury for the purpose of exterminating the whites? What proof have you got before you that any such things was done? What proof have you got before you to justify such an appeal as was made to you? You have got but one single act, you have got the proof of a letter which was sent to Poundmaker, you have got a proof that a letter was found in Poundmaker's camp, and what proof have you got of that? Do you not think that it is rather a strange proceeding that this letter should have been found in Poundmaker's camp, that this letter should have been found in the possession of Poundmaker who is now, gentlemen of the jury, as is well known, a prisoner in the hands of the Crown, that this letter should have been sent to him for the purpose of inciting the devilish passions as an Indian, and to say that no proof has been brought before you that that letter was read to Poundmaker, excepting a bystander who says that he heard something or other of the kind being said to him. The man who read the letter to him is not produced; and why is Poundmaker not here and put into that box and examined as a witness? Why was Poundmaker not produced here by the Crown and examined as a witness to prove that he got this letter, that he read it and that he understood it, understood the purport of it? Why were Big Bear and the other Indians to whom this man is supposed to have written not brought here? They are within a stone's throw of this very building, they are here under the control of the Crown, and if this man is guilty of the savagery of which he is accused, if this man is the contemptible bad rascal that he is represented to you to be by the Crown, why is it not proved? Why is it not proved so that we may all understand the position that we occupy so that we may all know the true inwardness and character of this man? Why make the statements and not prove them? Why are those Indians not produced? You know, gentlemen, that special provision exists for the examination of men like that? Special provisions exists for their swearing, and special provisions exist in the laws of this country providing that even if a man does

not believe in God, if he is an infidel and does not believe in God, he
may still be examined as a witness. Now, gentlemen, why are those
men not examined? Why was the best proof of that criminal act not
adduced? Why were those Indians not brought before you here and
examined? Why were those that were within a stone's throw of this
building not brought here, and men brought from Poundmaker's
reserve to prove that fact? What is the reason of that, can you find
any justification for it? Can you find any excuse for it? I say you
cannot, gentlemen, and I say we have the right to exact that when
such a terrible accusation as that is made against a man, the very best
possible evidence should be given so that there can be no doubt
about it, I say that such a statement as that is of the character to
alienate the sympathy of every right-minded man, if he is sane; I say
that such a statement as that is of a character to go very far towards
putting the rope around this man's neck and putting him to the gallows, and it is of such a nature as to alienate the sympathy of every
right-thinking man in the community.

I say this statement when made must be proved and proved
beyond controversy proved beyond doubt, and bring it into this
case and prove it, in the second case. Now, gentlemen, those are
historical facts. Those are facts that are to be found in all the books
which treat on medical insanity and those are facts which show to
what extent cunning is an essential ingredient of insanity, to what
low cunning those people can resort; and you will find other cases of
that kind in all the books which treat on those subjects. Now, in
view of those facts, will it be considered acting in a very improper
manner towards the doctors for the Crown if I say it is possible that
they made a mistake? It is quite possible that they have made a mistake, and Dr Wallace has told you himself that he has had many in
his asylum for months at a time before he could discover any symptoms of insanity. Now, if he has been in that position, gentlemen of
the jury, if he has been in that position himself with others, and in
this case he has had one-half hour interview with this man, saw him
for just half an hour and then saw him in court here, and he has
heard the evidence, and he is not able to say that he is insane, is that
very conclusive, gentlemen of the jury, is that very conclusive evidence? Is that evidence that would justify you in saying that this
man is of unsound mind? You have heard Mr Young and General
Middleton — I do not wish unnecessarily to refer to them. They have

said what they thought was true. They gave you their opinions. I
leave you to appreciate the value of those opinions in view of the
facts that I have stated to you.

Now, gentlemen, I say that the conduct of Louis Riel throughout
the whole if this affair is entirely inconsistent with any idea of
sanity, but is entirely consistent with his insanity. As I said to you a
moment ago in speaking at the opening of this case, the fact of his
delivering himself up is one of the characteristics of a man suffering
from the insanity from which he is suffering, because he cannot
appreciate the danger in which he is placed. It is impossible for him
to appreciate the danger in which he places himself, and he never
sees that there is any possibility that any harm can happen to him. If
that man was perfectly sane, gentlemen, if that man was perfectly
sane in doing as he did do, then you have to say whether or not, as I
said before, there are not some redeeming features about this man's
character, in the heroic act which he did in delivering himself up to
Middleton. On the other hand if he is insane, as I contend he is, you
see then the proof, for any man of ordinary prudence knows that
this man could have escaped and could have evaded the officers of
the law and the soldiers. Notwithstanding all that, he comes and
gives himself over to General Middleton and is prepared to take the
consequences, no matter what they are. I say that that is one of the
characteristics of his malady, that that is one of the proofs of his
insanity and that is one of the characteristics which are laid down in
all the books, as being characteristic of the disease of those men who
believe themselves to be in constant intercourse with God, because
they think God is always around them, that He is constantly taking
care of them and that no harm of any kind can befall them. Now,
gentlemen, in the opening of this case, a great deal was said to you
about letters which were written to the Indians, a great deal has been
said to you about the attempt made by this man to raise up savage
warfare in this country, and to deluge the whole country with blood,
letting forth the savage hosts upon your wives and children and upon
all the inhabitants of this country. Now, gentlemen, after having said
that, will you tell me what proof you have had of it. After having
produced before you documents enumerable, as having, and I say
the proof has not been brought here, that the best proof of that
would have been either from the man who brought this letter to
Poundmaker – and his abscence has not been accounted for – or

Poundmaker himself, to show that he got such a letter. He could
identify the appearance of the letter at all events, and no such proof
as that has been given. I say, gentlemen of the jury, if that proof
could have been given, it would have been given, because you know
and I know, that no more eminent men in their profession could be
found throughout Canada than the men who act for the Crown in
this case – no more eminent right-minded or fairer men in Canada
could be found than they are, and I know if they could have made
that proof they would have made it, and I know it is because they
could not make it that they did not do it, for you have seen that no
stone has been left unturned by them in this case. I do not say that
they have exceeded their duty, but I know, gentlemen, they have
neglected nothing, and if they have neglected that, they had a reason
for it – it was because they could not do it. You see, gentlemen, this
letter is brought to you, this savage appeal that is made to these men
to spread themselves all over the country, and spill the blood of
those innocent people, this appeal is made to those men: all you do,
do it for the love of God under the protection of Jesus Christ, and
the Virgin, St Joseph and St Jean Baptiste. Be assured faith works
miracles. That is the letter which contains this appeal that has been
made so much of and by which the public mind of this country has
been so terribly excited against this man. Now, gentlemen, my task
is at an end. I know I leave this case safely in your hands. This man,
gentlemen, the prisoner at the bar, is an alien in race and an alien in
religion, so far as you and I are concerned. This man, gentleman, so
far as you are concerned entirely in both, and so far as I am concerned in one; this man, gentleman, as I have stated to you is in your
hands, without the provisions of an ordinary trial by jury as understood elsewhere. This man is in your hands without the provisions
which the humane laws of England have made for people like him in
Manitoba, and in the Province of Quebec, where he would have the
right to have one-half people of his own nationality. But, gentlemen,
I do not complain of that. I do not complain. I tell this man with
confidence that justice will be done him, and I know that when I go
home to my country, and when I am asked as to what has taken
place here, when I am asked about this country, I will safely be able
to say that this is the land, gentlemen, that free men till, that sober
suited freedom choose, this is the land that where first with friends
or foes a man speak the thing he will, I will tell them that I have

come here a stranger myself in a strange place; I will tell them that I
have come here to plead the cause of an alien in race and an alien in
religion; I will tell them that I spoke to British subjects, that I appealed to British jurors, and that I knew full well that the principles
of English liberty have always found a safe resting place in the hearts
of English jurors. I know, gentlemen, that right will be done. I know
you will do him justice, and that this man shall not be sent to the
gallows by you, and that you shall not weave the cord that shall
hang and hang him high in the face of all the world, a poor confirmed lunatic; a victim, gentlemen, of oppression or the victim of
fanaticism.

HIS HONOR: Prisoner, have you any remarks to make to the jury, if
so, now is your time to speak?

MR LEMIEUX: May it please your Honors. At a former stage of the
trial you will remember that the prisoner wished to cross-examine
the witnesses, we objected at the time, thinking that it was better for
the interest of the prisoner that we should do so. The prisoner at this
stage is entitled to make any statement he likes to the jury and he
has been so warned by your Honor, but I must declare before the
court that we must not be considered responsible for any declaration
he may make.

HIS HONOR: Certainly, but he is entitled, and I am bound to tell
him so.

PRISONER: Your Honors, gentlemen of the jury: It would be easy
for me to-day to play insanity, because the circumstances are such as
to excite any man, and under the natural excitement of what is
taking place to-day (I cannot speak English very well, but am trying
to do so, because most of those here speak English), under the excitement which my trial causes me would justify me not to appear as
usual, but with my mind out of its ordinary condition. I hope with
the help of God I will maintain calmness and decorum as suits this
honorable court, this honorable jury.

You have seen by the papers in the hands of the Crown that I am
naturally inclined to think of God at the beginning of my actions. I
wish if you — I do it you won't take it as a mark of insanity, that
you won't take it as part of a play of insanity. Oh, my God, help me
through Thy grace and the divine influence of Jesus Christ. Oh, my
God, bless me, bless this honorable court, bless this honorable jury,
bless my good lawyers who have come 700 leagues to try to save my

life, bless also the lawyers for the Crown, because they have done, I am sure, what they thought their duty. They have shown me fairness which at first I did not expect from them. Oh, my God, bless all those who are around me through the grace and influence of Jesus Christ our Saviour, change the curiosity of those who are paying attention to me, change that curiosity into sympathy with me. The day of my birth I was helpless and my mother took care of me although she was not able to do it alone, there was some one to help her to take care of me and I lived. To-day, although a man I am as helpless before this court, in the Dominion of Canada and in this world, as I was helpless on the knees of my mother the day of my birth.

The North-West is also my mother, it is my mother country and although my mother country is sick and confined in a certain way, there are some from Lower Canada who came to help her to take care of me during her sickness and I am sure that my mother country will not kill me more than my mother did forty years ago when I came into the world, because a mother is always a mother, and even if I have my faults if she can see I am true she will be full of love for me.

When I came into the North-West in July, the first of July 1884, I found the Indians suffering. I found the half-breeds eating the rotten pork of the Hudson Bay Company and getting sick and weak every day. Although a half-breed, and having no pretension to help the whites, I also paid attention to them. I saw they were deprived of responsible government, I saw that they were deprived of their public liberties. I remembered that half-breed meant white and Indian, and while I paid attention to the suffering Indians and the half-breeds I remembered that the greatest part of my heart and blood was white and I have directed my attention to help the Indians, to help the half-breeds and to help the whites to the best of my ability. We have made petitions, I have made petitions with others to the Canadian Government asking to relieve the condition of this country. We have taken time; we have tried to unite all classes, even if I may speak, all parties. Those who have been in close communication with me know I have suffered, that I have waited for months to bring some of the people of the Saskatchewan to an understanding of certain important points in our petition to the Canadian Government and I have done my duty. I believe I have done my duty. It has

been said in this box that I have been egotistic. Perhaps I am egotistic. A man cannot be individuality without paying attention to himself. He cannot generalize himself, though he may be general. I have
done all I could to make good petitions with others, and we have
sent them to the Canadian Government, and when the Canadian
Government did answer, through the Under Secretary of State, to
the secretary of the joint committee of the Saskatchewan, then I
began to speak of myself, not before; so my particular interests
passed after the public interests. A good deal has been said about the
settlement and division of lands a good deal has been said about
that. I do not think my dignity to-day here would allow me to mention the foreign policy, but if I was to explain to you or if I had
been allowed to make the questions to witnesses, those questions
would have appeared in an altogether different light before the court
and jury. I do not say that my lawyers did not put the right questions. The observations I had the honor to make to the court the day
before yesterday were good, they were absent of the situation, they
did not know all the small circumstances as I did. I could mention a
point, but that point was leading to so many that I could not have
been all the time suggesting. By it I don't wish it understood that I
do not appreciate the good works of my lawyers, but if I were to go
into all the details of what has taken place, I think I could safely
show you that what Captain Young said that I am aiming all the
time at practical results was true, and I could have proved it. During
my life I have aimed at practical results. I have writings, and after
my death I hope that my spirit will bring practical results.

   The learned lawyers for the Crown have produced all the papers
and scribbling that was under their hands. I thank them for not having brought out those papers which are so particular to myself,
though as soon as they saw what they were they should not have
looked at them. I have written not books but many things. All my
papers were taken. I destined the papers to be published, if they
were worth publishing, after my death. I told Parenteau, one of the
prisoners, to put all my books under ground. He did not do it. At
that time they acknowledged my orders, that is why I say so. He did
not put my books away in time and I am not sorry. I say I thank the
learned lawyers for the Crown for having reserved so many things;
and if, by the almighty power of God, I go free from this trial, I have
such confidence in British fairness that all my papers will be

returned me, at least the originals, and if copies are wanted I will be willing to give them.

No one can say that the North-West was not suffering last year, particularly the Saskatchewan, for the other parts of the North-West I cannot say so much; but what I have done, and risked, and to which I have exposed myself, rested certainly on the conviction, I had to do, was called upon to do something for my country.

It is true, gentlemen, I believed for years I had a mission, and when I speak of a mission you will understand me not as trying to play the roll of insane before the grand jury so as to have a verdict of acquittal upon that ground. I believe that I have a mission, I believe I had a mission at this very time. What encourages me to speak to you with more confidence in all the imperfections of my English way of speaking, it is that I have yet and still that mission, and with the help of God, who is in this box with me, and He is on the side of my lawyers, even with the honorable court, the Crown and the jury, to help me, and to prove by the extraordinary help that there is a Providence to-day in my trial, as there was a Providence in the battles of the Saskatchewan.

I have not assumed to myself that I had a mission. I was working in Manitoba first, and I did all I could to get free institutions for Manitoba; they have those institutions to-day in Manitoba, and they try to improve them, while myself, who obtained them, I am forgotten as if I was dead. But after I had obtained, with the help of others, a constitution for Manitoba, when the Government at Ottawa was not willing to inaugurate it at the proper time, I have worked till the inauguration should take place, and that is why I have been banished for five years. I had to rest five years, I was willing to do it. I protested, I said: 'Oh, my God, I offer You all my existence for that cause, and please to make of my weakness an instrument to help men in my country.' And seeing my intentions, the late Archibishop Bourget said: 'Riel has no narrow views, he is a man to accomplish great things,' and he wrote that letter of which I hope that the Crown has at least a copy. And in another letter, when I became what doctors believed to be insane, Bishop Bourget wrote again and said: 'Be ye blessed by God and man and take patience in your evils.' Am I not taking patience? Will I be blessed by man as I have been by God?

I say that I have been blessed by God, and I hope that you will
not take that as a presumptuous assertion. It has been a great success
for me to come through all the dangers I have in that fifteen years. If
I have not succeeded in wearing a fine coat myself I have at the same
time the great consolation of seeing that God has maintained my
view; that He has maintained my health sufficiently to go through
the world, and that he has kept me from bullets, when bullets
marked my hat. I am blessed by God. It is this trial that is going to
show that I am going to be blessed by man during my existence, the
benedictions are a guarantee that I was not wrong when by circumstances I was taken away from adopted land to my native land.
When I see British people sitting in the court to try me, remembering
that the English people are proud of that word 'fair-play,' I am confident that I will be blesssed by God and by man also.

Not only Bishop Bourget spoke to me in that way, but Father
Jean Baptiste Bruno, the priest of Worcester, who was my director
of conscience, said to me: 'Riel, God has put an object into your
hands, the cause of the triumph of religion in the world, take care,
you will succeed when most believe you have lost.' I have got those
words in my heart, those words of J.B. Bruno and the late Archbishop Bourget. But last year, while I was yet in Montana, and while
I was passing before the Catholic church, the priest, the Reverend
Father Frederick Ebeville, curate of the church of the Immaculate
Conception, at Benton, said to me: 'I am glad to see you; is your
family here?' I said: 'Yes.' He said: 'Go and bring them to the altar, I
want to bless you before you go away.' And with Gabriel Dumont
and my family we all went on our knees at the altar, the priest put
on his surplice and he took holy water and was going to bless us, I
said: 'Will you allow me to pronounce a prayer while you bless me?'
He said: 'Yes, I want to know what it is.' I told him the prayer. It is
speaking to God: 'My Father, bless me according to the views of Thy
Providence which are bountiful and without measure.' He said to
me: 'You can say that prayer while I bless you.' Well, he blessed me
and I pronounced that prayer for myself, for my wife, for my children, and for Gabriel Dumont.

When the glorious General Middleton fired on us during three
days, and on our families, and when shells went and bullets went as
thick as mosquitoes in the hot days of summer, when I saw my

children, my wife, myself and Gabriel Dumont were escaping, I said that nothing but the blessing without measure of Father Frederick Ebeville could save me, and that can save me to-day from these charges. The benediction promised to me surrounded me all the time in the Saskatchewan, and since it seems to me that I have seen it. Captain Deane, Corporal Prickert, and the corporal of the guard who have been appointed over me have been so gentle while the papers were raging against me shows that nothing but the benediction of God could give me the favor I have had in remaining so respected among these men. To-day when I saw the glorious General Middleton bearing testimony that he thought I was not insane, and when Captain Young proved that I am not insane, I felt that God was blessing me, and blotting away from my name the blot resting upon my reputation on account of having been in the lunatic asylum of my good friend Dr Roy. I have been in an asylum, but I thank the lawyers for the Crown who destroyed the testimony of my good friend Dr Roy, because I have always believed that I was put in the asylum without reason. To-day my pretension is guaranteed, and that is a blessing too in that way. I have also been in the lunatic asylum at Longue Pointe, and I wonder that my friend Dr Lachapelle, who took care of me charitably, and Dr Howard are not here. I was there perhaps under my own name.

Even if I was going to be sentenced by you, gentlemen of the jury, I have this satisfaction if I die – that if I die I will not be reputed by all men as insane, as a lunatic. A good deal has been said by the two reverend fathers, André and Fourmand. I cannot call them my friends, but they made no false testimony. I know that a long time ago they believed me more or less insane. Father Fourmand said that I would pass from great passion to great calmness. That shows great control under contradiction, and according to my opinion and with the help of God I have that control. Mr Charles Nolin, when he went into the box, did not say that he was sworn with me in all the affairs that I did. Far from taking them as insane affairs, he was in them under the cover of an oath with four of us. He did not say that in the box. My word is perhaps not testimony, but if he was asked in the box to say if there was an oath taken he could not deny it, and he would have to name the four men, and he would have to name himself. When he speaks of resigning a contract in my favor, I did not ask it, the Government would not give it to me; besides, he was engaged in a movement against the Government, and to take a contract from the Government was certainly a weakness upon his part, and I told him not to compromise his cause, and I told him to withdraw instead of going ahead till we saw if we were going to be listened to at all. He wanted me to make a bargain and renounce my American citizenship. I told him that it was a matter of more strength that I should be an American citizen, not that I want to make any ground of it, but as it took place naturally and as the fact existed I wanted to take advantage of it as such. I told him: 'It is of advantage for you that you should have me an American citizen. I have no bargain to make with you about my American papers, no bargain on such a matter as that.' Mr Charles Nolin speaks of my ambition, and other witnesses also. There are men among the prisoners who know that last year Mr Renez and Mr Joseph Fourget came to the Saskatchewan and said that I could have a place in the council if I wanted it, and that it was a good chance for the half-breeds of the Saskatchewan. If I had been so anxious for position I would have grasped at this place, but I did not, and Mr Nolin has some knowledge of that. I speak of those things to defend my character, as it has been said that I am egotistical.

The agitation in the North-West Territories would have been constitutional, and would certainly be constitutional to-day if, in my opinion, we had not been attacked. Perhaps the Crown has not been able to find out the particulars, that we were attacked, but as we were on the scene it was easy to understand. When we sent petitions to the Government, they used to answer us by sending police, and when the rumors were increasing every day that Riel had been shot here or there, or that Riel was going to be shot by such and such a man, the police would not pay any attention to it. I am glad that I have mentioned the police, because of the testimony that has been given in the box during the examination of many of the witnesses. If I had been allowed to put questions to the witnesses, I would have asked them when it was I said a single word against a single policeman or a single officer. I have respected the policemen, and I do to-day, and I have respected the officers of the police; the paper that I sent to Major Crozier is a proof it: 'We respect you, Major.' There are papers which the Crown has in its hands, and which show that demoralization exists among the police, if you will allow me to say it in the court, as I have said it in writing.

Your Honors, gentlemen of the jury: If I was a man of to-day perhaps it would be presumptuous to speak in that way, but the truth is good to say, and it is said in a proper manner, and it is without any presumption, it is not because I have been libelled for fifteen years that I do not believe myself something. I know that through the grace of God I am the founder of Manitoba. I know that though I have no open road for my influence, I have big influence, concentrated as a big amount of vapour in an engine. I believe by what I suffered for fifteen years, by what I have done for Manitoba and the people of the North-West, that my words are worth something. If I give offence, I do not speak to insult. Yes, you are the pioneers of civilization, the whites are the pioneers of civilization, but they bring among the Indians demoralization. Do not be offended, ladies, do not be offended, here are the men who can cure that evil; and if at times I have been strong against my true friends and fathers, the reverend priests of the Saskatchewan, it is because my convictions are strong. There have been witnesses to show that immediately after great passion I could come back to the great respect I have for them.

One of the witnesses here, George Ness, I think, said that I spoke of Archbishop Taché, and told him that he was a thief. If I had had the opportunity I proposed I would have questioned him as to what I said, so that you would understand me. I have known Archbishop Taché as a great benefactor, I have seen him surrounded by his great property, the property of a widow, whose road was passing near. He bought the land around, and took that way to try and get her property at a cheap price. I read in the Gospel: 'Ye Pharisees with your long prayers devour the widows.' And as Archbishop Taché is my great benefactor, as he is my father, I would say because he has done me an immense deal of good, and because there was no one who had the courage to tell him, I did, because I love him, because I acknowledge all he has done for me; as to Bishop Grandin, it was on the same grounds. I have other instances of Bishop Taché, and the witness could have said that the Reverend Father Moulin: 'When you speak of such persons as Archbishop Taché, you ought to say that he made a mistake, not that he committed robbery.' I say that we have been patient a long time, and when we see that mild words only serve as covers for great ones to do wrong, it is time when we are justified in saying that robbery is robbery everywhere, and the guilty ones are bound by the force of public opinion to take notice of it. The one who has the courage to speak out in that way, instead of being an outrageous man, becomes in fact a benefactor to those men themselves, and to society.

When we got to the church of St Anthony on the 18th, there was a witness who said, I think George Ness, that I said to Father Moulin, 'You are a Protestant.' According to my theory I was not going to speak in that way, but I said that we were protesting against the Canadian Government, and that he was protesting against us, and that we were two protestants in our different ways.

As to religion, what is my belief? What is my insanity about that? My insanity, your Honors, gentlemen of the jury, is that I wish to leave Rome aside, inasmuch as it is the cause of division between Catholics and Protestants. I did not wish to force my views, because in Batoche to the half-breeds that followed me I used the word, *carte blanche.* If I have any influence in the new world it is to help in that way and even if it takes 200 years to become practical, then after my death that will bring out practical results, and then my children's children will shake hands with the Protestants of the new world in a friendly manner. I do not wish these evils which exist in Europe to be continued, as much as I can influence it, among the half-breeds. I do not wish that to be repeated in America. That work is not the work of some days or some years, it is the work of hundreds of years.

My condition is helpless, so helpless that my good lawyers, and they have done it by conviction (Mr Fitzpatrick in his beautiful speech has proved he believed I was insane) my condition seems to be so helpless that they have recourse to try and prove insanity to try and save me in that way. If I am insane, of course I don't know it, it is a property of insanity to be unable to know it. But what is the kind of mission that I have? Practical results. It is said that I had myself acknowledged as a prophet by the half-breeds. The half-breeds have some intelligence. Captain Young who has been so polite and gentle during the time I was under his care, said that what was done at Batoche, from a military point of view was nice, that the line of defence was nice, that showed some intelligence.

It is not to be supposed that the half-breeds acknowledged me as a prophet if they had not seen that I could see something into the future. If I am blessed without measure I can see something into the

future, we all see into the future more or less. As what kind of a
prophet would I come, would it be a prophet who would all the time
have a stick in his hand, and threatening, a prophet of evil? If the
half-breeds had acknowledged me as a prophet, if on the other side
priests come and say that I am polite, if there are general officers,
good men, come into this box and prove that I am polite, prove that
I am decent in my manner, in combining all together you have a
decent prophet. An insane man cannot withhold his insanity, if I am
insane my heart will tell what is in me.

Last night while I was taking exercise the spirit who guides and
assists me and consoles me, told me that to-morrow somebody will
come *t'aider*, five English and one French word *t'aider*, that is to
help you. I am consoled by that. While I was recurring to my God,
to our God, I said, but woe to me if you do not help me, and these
words came to me in the morning, in the morning someone will
come *t'aider*, that is to-day. I said that to my two guards and you
can go for the two guards. I told them that if the spirit that directs
me is the spirit of truth it is to-day that I expect help. This morning
the good doctor who has care of me came to me and said you will
speak to-day before the court. I thought I would not be allowed to
speak; those words were given to me to tell me that I would have
liberty to speak. There was one French word in it, it meant I believe
that there was to be some French influence in it, but the most part
English. It is true that my good lawyers from the Province of Quebec
have given me good advice.

Mr Nolin came into the box and said that Mr Riel said that he had
a noise in his bowels and that I told him that it meant something. I
wish that he had said what I said, what I wrote on the paper of
which he speaks, perhaps he can yet be put in the box. I said to
Nolin, 'Do you hear?' Yes, I said there will be trouble in the North-
West, and was it so or not? Has there been no trouble in the North-
West? Besides Nolin knows that among his nationality, which is
mine, he knows that the half-breeds as hunters can fortell many
things, perhaps some of you have a special knowledge of it. I have
seen half-breeds who say, my hand is shaking, this part of my hand is
shaking you will see such a thing to-day, and it happens. Others will
say I feel the flesh on my leg move in such a way, it is a sign of such
a thing, and it happens. There are men who know that I speak right.
If the witness spoke of that fact which he mentioned, to show that I

was insane he did not remember that perhaps on that point he is insane himself, because the half-breed by the movement of the hand, sometimes of his shoulders, sometimes his legs, can have certain knowledge of what will happen. To bring Sir John to my feet, if it was well reported it would appear far more reasonable than it has been made to appear; Mr Blake the leader of the Opposition is trying to bring Sir John to his feet in one way. He never had as much at stake as I had, although the Province of Ontario is great it is not as great as the North-West.

I am glad that the Crown have proved that I am the leader of the half-breeds in the North-West. I will perhaps be one day acknowledged as more than a leader of the half-breeds, and if I am I will have an opportunity of being acknowledged as a leader of good in this great country.

One of the witnesses said that I intended to give Upper Canada to the Irish, if he had no mystery he would have seen that Upper Canada could not be given to the Irish without being given to England; he rested only upon his imagination.

There is another thing about the partition of lands into sevenths. I do not know if I am prepared to speak of it here because it would become public information, there is so much at stake that if I explained that theory Canada would not very long remain in quiet.

Captain Deane has seen my papers, I have sent them somewhere but he has seen them, and after seeing them he came there and said that I was an intelligent man, and pretty shrewd. I have written these documents and they are in the hands of those whom I trust. I do not want to make them public during my trial; what I have made public during the sixty days we were in arms at Batoche. There have been three different times when the council decided to send men to the States to notify the nationalities to come to our assistance, but these three delegations waited for my orders and have not started; why? Because I had an object.

The half-breeds also knew that I told them that they would be punished, that I did not say it of my own responsibility, but that I said it in the same way as I have told them other things. It was said to me that the nation would be punished. Why? Because she had consented to leave Rome too quick. What was the meaning of that? There was a discussion about too quick; they said that they should do it at once. Too quick does not mean too soon, if we say yes, it

shows no consideration to the man. If God wants something, and if
we say yes, that is not the way to answer him. He wants the conscience to say: yes, oh my God, I do Thy will; and because the half-
breeds quickly separated from Rome, in such a quick manner, it was
disagreeable to God and they were punished, and I told them it
would happen; fifty of those who are there can prove it. But,you
will say, you did not put yourself as a prophet? The 19th century is
to be treated in certain ways, and it is probably for that reason I
have found the word '*exovede*,' I prefer to be called one of the
flock; I am no more than you are, I am simply one of the flock,
equal to the rest. If it is any satisfaction to the doctors to know
what kind of insanity I have, if they are going to call my pretensions
insanity, I say humbly, through the grace of God, I believe I am the
prophet of the new world.

I wish you to believe that I am not trying to play insanity, there
is in the manner, in the standing of a man, the proof that he is sincere, not playing. You will say, what have you got to say? I have to
attend to practical results. Is it practical that you be acknowledged
as a prophet? It is practical to say it. I think that if the half-breeds
have acknowledged me, as a community, to be a prophet, I have
reason to believe that it is beginning to become practical. I do not
wish, for my satisfaction, the name of prophet, generally that title is
accompanied with such a burden, that if there is satisfaction for
your vanity, there is a check to it.

To set myself up as Pope, no, no. I said I believed that Bishop
Bourget had succeeded in spirit and in truth. Why? Because while
Rome did not pay attention to us, he, as a bishop, paid attention to
us.

You have given me your attention, your Honors; you have given
me your attention, gentlemen of the jury, and this great audience, I
see that if I go any further on that point I will lose the favor you
have granted me up to this time, and as I am aiming all the time at
practical results, I will stop here, master of myself, through the help
of God. I have only a few more words to say, your Honors. Gentlemen of the jury, my reputation, my liberty, my life, are at your discretion. So confident am I, that I have not the slightest anxiety, not
even the slightest doubt, as to your verdict. The calmness of my
mind concerning the favorable decision which I expect, does not
come from any unjustifiable presumption upon my part. I simply

trust, that through God's help, you will balance everything in a conscientious manner, and that, having heard what I had to say, that you will acquit me. I do respect you, although you are only half a jury, but your number of six does not prevent you from being just and conscientious; your number of six does not prevent me giving you my confidence, which I would grant to another six men. Your Honor, because you appointed these men, do not believe that I disrespect you. It is not by your own choice, you were authorised by those above you, by the authorities in the North-West; you have acted according to your duty, and while it is, in our view, against the guarantees of liberty, I trust the Providence of God will bring out good of what you have done conscientiously.

Although this court has been in existence for the last fifteen years, I thought I had a right to be tried in another court. I do not disrespect this court. I do respect it, and what is called by my learned and good lawyers, the incompetency of the court must not be called in disrespect, because I have all respect.

The only things I would like to call your attention to before you retire to deliberate are: 1st That the House of Commons, Senate and Ministers of the Dominion, and who make laws for this land and govern it, are no representation whatever of the people of the North-West.

2nd That the North-West Council generated by the Federal Government has the great defect of its parent.

3rd The number of members elected for the Council by the people make it only a sham representative legislature and no representative government at all.

British civilization which rules to-day the world, and the British constitution has defined such government as this is which rules the North-West Territories as irresponsible government, which plainly means that there is no responsibility, and by all the science which has been shown here yesterday you are compelled to admit if there is no responsibility, it is insane.

Good sense combined with scientific theories lead to the same conclusion. By the testimony laid before you during my trial witnesses on both sides made it certain that petition after petition had been sent to the Federal Government, and so irresponsible is that Government to the North-West that in the course of several years besides doing nothing to satisfy the people of this great land, it has

even hardly been able to answer once or to give a single response.
That fact would indicate an absolute lack of responsibility, and
therefore insanity complicated with paralysis.

The Ministers of an insane and irresponsible Government and its
little one — the North-West Council — made up their minds to
answer my petitions by surrounding me slyly and by attempting to
jump upon me suddenly and upon my people in the Saskatchewan.
Happily when they appeared and showed their teeth to devour, I was
ready: that is what is called my crime of high treason, and to which
they hold me to-day. Oh, my good jurors, in the name of Jesus
Christ, the only one who can save and help me, they have tried to
tear me to pieces.

If you take the plea of the defence that I am not responsible for
my acts, acquit me completely since I have been quarrelling with an
insane and irresponsible Government. If you pronounce in favor of
the Crown, which contends that I am responsible, acquit me all the
same. You are perfectly justified in declaring that having my reason
and sound mind, I have acted reasonably and in self-defence, while
the Government, my accuser, being irresponsible, and consequently
insane, cannot but have acted wrong, and if high treason there is it
must be on its side and not on my part.

HIS HONOR: Are you done?

PRISONER: Not yet, if you have the kindness to permit me your
attention for a while.

HIS HONOR: Well, proceed.

PRISONER: For fifteen years I have been neglecting myself. Even
one of the most hard witnesses on me said that with all my vanity, I
never was particular to my clothing; yes, because I never had much
to buy any clothing. The Rev. Father André has often had the kindness to feed my family with a sack of flour, and Father Fourmand.
My wife and children are without means, while I am working more
than any representative in the North-West. Although I am simply a
guest of this country — a guest of the half-breeds of the Saskatchewan — although as a simple guest, I worked to better the condition of the people of the Saskatchewan at the risk of my life, to
better the condition of the people of the Saskatchewan at the risk of
my life, to better the condition of the people of the North-West, I
have never had any pay. It has always been my hope to have a fair
living one day. It will be for you to pronounce — if you say I was

right, you can conscientiously acquit me, as I hope through the help
of God you will. You will console those who have been fifteen years
around me only partaking in my sufferings. What you will do in
justice to me, in justice to my family, in justice to my friends, in
justice to the North-West, will be rendered a hundred times to you in
this world, and to use a sacred expression, life everlasting in the
other.

I thank your Honor for the favor you have granted me in speaking; I thank you for the attention you have given me, gentlemen of
the jury, and I thank those who have had the kindness to encourage
my imperfect way of speaking the English language by your good
attention. I put my speech under the protection of my God, my
Saviour, He is the only one who can make it effective. It is possible
it should become effective, as it is proposed to good men, to good
people, and to good ladies also.

ADDRESS OF THE CROWN COUNSEL

MR ROBINSON: There are two or three reasons peculiar to this case
why I shall find it unnecessary to occupy your time at such length as
is usual in trials of this description; it will not be necessary to go
over the evidence in detail for a reason we seldom find in cases of
this kind. As a general rule it is necessary for the representative of
the Crown at the conclusion of the case to go over the evidence in
detail and compare the different statements which are frequently
contradictory. But in this case, gentlemen, there is no contradiction,
there is no dispute, there is not a single witness whose word has been
doubted, there is not a single fact proved on the part of the Crown
which anybody has been called to contradict, and it stands therefore
as an admission, and an admission made by counsel for the defence
that the case as presented has been made out beyond all question —
there can be no doubt about that either on the documentary evidence or the evidence of the witnesses. What I have to do, therefore,
in the first place, is to address myself to the only defence which has
in reality been set up here, and I have next to show you, because I
think it right to show you, that every single allegation of my learned
friend's statement made to you in the opening of the case has been
proved to the very letter.

I must say before I proceed farther that I felt it hardly consistent with our position as counsel for the Crown to listen to a portion of the address of my learned friend Mr Greenshields and to a portion of the address of my learned friend Mr Fitzpatrick without a protest, but I listened in silence for two reasons: In the first place we have been anxious throughout this case to give to them every possible latitude, every possible privilege, every possible opportunity of placing their case fully and fairly, not only as we thought that the law might authorize them to do, but as they in their judgment might desire to do before you who are to judge of it; and in the next place when I reflected for a moment of the utter inconsistency of the defence which was set up, I thought I might listen to it in silence without neglecting any part of my duty. What my learned friend's address amounted to was practically this: They told you in fact that this rebellion was justifiable. My learned friend, Mr Greenshields, told you that the men responsible for the blood that was shed were the people who had refused the petitions of the half-breeds made under the direction and guidance of the prisoner at the bar.

In the next breath he told you that this rebellion was directed and carried on by an irresponsible lunatic.

If the only thing, gentlemen, that can be charged against the persons at the head of affairs, is that they hesitated to accede to the request presented to them through the hands and by the direction of a person whom my learned friends tell you is insane, surely they may be excused for their hesitation.

When my learned friend, Mr Greenshields, told you that the name of this prisoner would go down to posterity as that of a man who was justified in the action he has taken, he had to tell you in the next breath that he honored and praised the men who risked their lives to put down the rebellion. Gentlemen, is not that the very height of inconsistency? Are you to be told as sensible men that all credit and respect is due to those brave and loyal men who shed their blood and lost their lives to put down this rebellion, and at the same time that that man who organized this rebellion and who is responsible for it is to go down to posterity with an honored name, and as a victim of the wrongs of his country?

My learned friends must make their choice between their defences. They cannot claim for their client what is called a niche in the temple of fame and at the same time assert that he is entitled to

a place in a lunatic asylum. I understand perfectly well the defence
of insanity; I understand perfectly the defence of patriotism, but I
am utterly unable to understand how you can be told in one breath
a man is a noble patriot and to be told in the next breath that every
guiding motive of his actions, every controlling influence which he is
bound by his very nature to give heed to, is that of overweening
vanity, a selfish sense of his own importance and an utter disregard
to everything but his own insane power. There must be either one
defence or the other in this case.

Unfortunately it becomes my duty to show to you, that the case
which the Crown believes it has made out is, that this prisoner at the
bar is neither a patriot nor a lunatic.

But before I proceed further as to that, I would ask you in all
seriousness, as sensible men: do you believe that a defence of insanity could have any conceivable or possible applicability to a case
of this description?

I have here a book which is supposed to contain a record of every
case, at least of every reported case, in which the defence of insanity
has been set up, and I see my learned friends have the same book
before them too. And one thing is certain, that among those cases
there never has been a case in the least like this.

Now, gentlemen, just remember what you are told and what
you are asked to believe: The half-breeds of this district number, I
understand, some 600 or 700. I am speaking entirely of the French
half-breeds. I believe the English half-breeds are more numerous than
that.

In July 1884, the French half-breeds, believing that the prisoner
at the bar was a person in whose judgment, whose advice, whose
discretion they could trust and rely upon, sought him out in the
place where he was then living with a view of getting him to manage
for them their affairs, and to represent their grievances, and to endeavor to obtain for them those rights and that justice which they
believed to be theirs.

They sent men, I suppose, in whom they had confidence to ask
the prisoner to come for that purpose. They, in their intercourse
with him, discovered nothing wrong in his mind, no unsoundness in
his reason. The prisoner came here. He remained here from July
1884, till March 1885, and during all that time he was before the
public; he addressed, I think we have been told, seven meetings, and

there were, I suppose, many more in which he also participated. There was in the district a population of at least 2,000 altogether, for there were six or seven hundred French half-breeds and the English half-breeds outnumbered them. There can be no question, I say, that the prisoner at the bar addressed on public affairs at least two thousand people.

During that time was there ever a whisper of his insanity heard? Have you had one single soul who heard him during that time, one single person of the community among which he lived, and which believed in him; have you heard, I say, one single suspicion from any of them that the prisoner was insane?

The next thing we find in regard to these men is that under the guidance of the prisoner they embark in an enterprise full of danger and gravity. They place their lives and property under his control and direction, and trusting in his judgment they risk both in obedience to his advice, and we have not heard from any one of them that during all that time there was the smallest suspicion he was affected with any unsoundness of mind whatever.

Now, gentlemen, am I speaking reason or am I not speaking reason? Unless all reason and common sense has been banished from the land is it possible that a defence of insanity can be set up in the case of a person of that description? If so, I should like to know what protection there is for society, I should like to know how crimes are to be put down. I should like to know more; I should like to know if the prisoner at the bar is not in law to be held responsible for this crime, who is responsible? He was followed by some six or seven hundred misled and misguided men. Are we to be told that the prisoner at the bar was insane but that his followers were sane? Is there any escape from the one inevitable conclusion either that the prisoner at the bar was perfectly sane and sound in mind or that all the half-breed population of the Saskatchewan were insane. You must have it either one way or the other.

What in reality is the defence set up here; what in reality is the defence which you, as sensible men, are asked to find by your verdict? You are asked to find that six or seven hundred men may get up an armed rebellion with its consequent loss of life, its loss of property, that murder and arson and pillage may be commited by that band of armed men, and we are to be told they are all irresponsible lunatics.

It is my duty to put these facts to you plainly and strongly, because it is our duty to protect society, and all that I can say is that if
such a folly as finding this man insane is possible in this country,
you say in effect to men who desire to come here to live, that there
is no sufficient protection by law for either life or property or
liberty.

Are you prepared to say that? Because that is the single issue
placed before you by the counsel for the Crown; disguise it as you
like; speak of it as you like, that is the simple result and the plain
consequence.

Can you say with any reason that a man who has lived among his
fellow-men for eighteen months, probably the most prominent man
in the district, that he can live for that length of time without his
unsoundness of mind being found out, if his mind is unsound? Can
you say that this prisoner can, by any application of law, administered by reasonable men, be held to be irresponsible for his actions?
And if he is irresponsible are you to say, or are you not to say to all
the men who followed him in his crime 'it was your duty, it was
your business, living as you did so long with the prisoner, to know
more about this man's unsoundness of mind,' and his insanity; it was
your duty to know more about him than such witnesses as Capt.
Young and General Middleton, who have seen him just lately, who
can discover nothing unsound about him. Are you to tell these men
it was their duty to discover his unsoundness of mind and not to
follow him because he was a lunatic? If not then no one is responsible for this rebellion.

Now, with regard to the evidence which it is necessary for me to
refer to in this defence. I will first speak for a moment of the scientific evidence.

Medical men have it as their duty to investigate and discover
every kind and every degree of unsoundness of mind; that is a duty
which they take upon themselves, that is a duty which, I believe,
they are pursuing with increasing devotion and success as years go
on, but what medical men occasionally call unsoundness of mind
and what may be insanity in law are two different things entirely; it
is for the law to say what degree of unsoundness of mind will enable
a man to escape punishment for his acts; it is for medical men to
describe the different degrees of unsoundness of mind which may be
made to yield to medical treatment.

Now, in this case there is one absolutely conclusive fact proved, about which there can be no dispute, which is a complete answer to the defence of insanity. There is no question and no dispute of one thing, that the very essence of an insane impulse is that it is impervious to reason. The impulse of the insane man is such that you do not reason him into it and therefore you cannot reason him out of it. The moment you find the impulse which possesses a man yielding to reason, force or any motive, that moment that ceases to be an insane delusion. We hear of poor creatures in asylums who suppose themselves to be possessed of all the wealth of the world. Do you suppose if you went to one of them and offered him $100 in exchange for all the wealth he imagined himself possessed of, and if he accepted that, that you would have a lunatic before you? You might have an imposter, but the lunacy is at an end. Or if you go to the poor creature who thinks herself to be a queen and offer her $100 to give up her throne, and you find her willing to do so, you will no more discover a lunatic here than in the case I have just referred to. The most well known form of mania is what is called homicidal mania. That is a mania of which there are always instances in our asylums. The one idea, the one feeling and thought that possesses the man, is a desire to take human life, and that has more than once been set up as a defence to murder. Do you suppose if you find a man who had been paid $1,000 to commit a murder, or who says he would not commit a murder unless he got $1,000, and who then sets up as a defence this homicidal mania, do you think any jury would listen to him for a moment?

Now, what are the facts here? We are told that this man's controlling mania was a sense of his own importance and power; that he was so possessed with over-weening vanity and insane ambition that the one thing which he was unable to resist, which in his own mind justified all crimes, and was an atonement for all guilt, was his own sense of greatness and position and his own power. Well, gentlemen, is it not a fact that he expressly said that if he could get a certain sum of money he would give up this power and this ambition and go away. Now, my learned friend, Mr Fitzpatrick, has said to you all that can be said upon that head. He says he made that offer through Nolin, that what he desired to do with the money was to go to a foreign country and work out some schemes of conquest there. Gentlemen, did he say that to Father André, or to Mr Jackson? Am I right or am I wrong in suggesting to you that the prisoner at the bar was capable of adopting his arguments, his convictions to the men with whom he had to reason? He tells Nolin that he wished the money to go to a foreign country and work out his schemes, and why? Because he was one of his own people, one whom he believed to be in sympathy with his own schemes. Did he tell Father André anything of the kind? When he wanted Father André to get this money for him what was it he said to him? He said, if I get the $35,000 I will go, I will leave the country. Did he tell Father André he was going on any absurd schemes of conquest, that he was going to return with his army and devastate Manitoba? No, gentlemen, that was not said, and the reason why it was not said was because he knew it would ruin all his chances with Father André.

And in the same way he reasoned with Mr Jackson. Jackson is an Englishman, and the prisoner knew if he had told Jackson any of these absurd ideas it would have had no influence whatever with him. Well, gentlemen, we do not find that he did communicate those ideas to him. Now, then, what does this evidence show you so far as that is concerned? Does it show to you he was a man who controlled his mania and used it for his own purpose? If so, there is no mania about it; and if in any way that impulse was under his control then that very moment it ceased to be insanity. Now, gentlemen, is there any doubt in the facts of this case, that what I have told you is the truth, you have to judge for yourself; I am expressing no opinion. I am simply placing before you these simple facts. I am pointing out to you in the first place this so-called insanity had no such control on him that he was not perfectly willing to drop his insane theories for a sum of money, and secondly, when he desired to get that money the arguments which he used were adapted to the character and position of the person whom he wished to influence by them. There are other features in his character and conduct, but you must remember all I am here to discuss is what was his conduct and what was his character, what were his actions and what were his motives during this rebellion. There are, I say, other features connected with the prisoner's conduct which I think ought to be submitted to you to show that his mind was strong and clear, that he was not merely a man of strong mind but unusually long-headed, that he was a man who calculated his schemes and drew his plans with shrewdness, and was controlled by no insane impulse.

In the first place do you think his treatment with regard to the rising of the Indians is a piece of insanity? Do you think that the manner in which he addressed them to rise? Do you think the communications which he sent them were suited to their purpose, were adapted to answer the object he had in view? Or do you think you can discover in any one of these communications the insane ravings of an unsound mind? I shall come to this on another branch of the case in a few minutes.

Do you think when he told Mr Lash what he intended to do with him, that he might release the other prisoners, but he would not release him because he was a Government official, do you think that was a piece of insanity?

Do you think the manner in which he conceived this campaign, do you think the mode in which he was to carry it out, do you think these were proofs of any insanity? I would ask you, gentlemen, if he is to be declared insane in the conduct of this whole undertaking, who is to escape the charge of insanity and who is to be punished when a plea of insanity is set up?

The only peculiarity in this case is that some eight or nine years ago the prisoner was in a lunatic asylum, and I cannot help saying that the evidence we have had here on that subject was to my mind unsatisfactory. I should like to have known how, and under what circumstances, the prisoner was placed in that asylum, under an assumed name. I should like to know who were responsible for his being placed there. I should like to have seen the register and records which are kept in every asylum from week to week, and I should like to have seen not only why he was received into that asylum, but how he came to be discharged. All these things they have not thought it necessary to bring before you. I have in one respect to correct my learned friend, Mr Fitzpatrick, who stated that Dr Roy was brought here on the part of the Crown. He was not brought here on the part of the Crown. You have heard how Dr Roy came to be brought here. My learned friend stated at the opening of this case that they had not their evidence, that they desired to obtain certain witnesses, and the Crown said, if you desire to obtain witnesses we will use our own influence in procuring them, that is to say we will join you in telegrams to any witnesses whom you want to come here and we will pay their expenses, but Dr Roy was not in any sense called as a witness for the Crown. The crown concurred with my learned friends in calling him here because they believed it subservient to the cause of justice to do all in their power to give my learned friends every right assistance in getting the evidence which they believed to be necessary for their case.

I have nothing more to say in that respect except this: It has been said by learned judges over and over again that insanity is not a question which is only decided by experts. Any man of intelligence and sense, and ordinary capacity is said to be a perfectly good witness, and in many respects as capable to decide on cases of insanity as medical experts can be. A man like Captain Young, who was asked what experience he had with regard to insanity, and who answered, 'I think I should know if I had been living eight days with a lunatic' – the evidence of that man is just as good and strong in law, and to many minds would be considered stronger than the evidence of medical experts, because as a rule they have better opportunities of observation. The medical experts have none of them had any opportunity of observing the prisoner at the bar and his state of mind at the only time when his state of mind is in question, at the time when his crimes were planned and carried out. Our witnesses are men who saw him at that very time and who observed his demeanor, who had much better opportunities of observing him.

Now, gentlemen, if a man's mind is weak, if a man's mind is likely to give way, I ask you when is it more likely to give way? (If the one thing that possessed this man's mind was his ambition and vanity, and a sense of his own power and importance.) I should like to know, I say, when his mind was more likely to give way than when all his schemes collapsed, all his ambition was frustrated and he found himself helpless in the hands of his opponents? And that was the time we had the opportunity of observing his demeanor. Did he then show any signs of unsoundness of mind? Can you fancy any stronger test of a man's unsoundness of mind, anything more likely to cause an inherent weakness to become apparent? Every scheme in life which he may be supposed to have formed, every hope he had cherished, every desire he had wished to see gratified, all these were dashed to the ground, and do we see he then showed any signs of insanity, or any evidence of that excitement under which he is supposed to be laboring? Or do we, from the beginning to the end, until this whole thing had failed, and until his guilt or innocence became the question, do we ever find the defence of insanity hinted at or suspected by any human being who came in contact with him?

Gentlemen, as to latent insanity, all I can say is this: There are cases of latent insanity; human nature is always fallible, but if it be possible in any civilized community for a man to go through the career which the prisoner at the bar has had, for a man to exercise all that influence over his fellow-creatures which he has exercised, and if sensible men are then to be told that during that time he was practically irresponsible, then all I can say is that there is no safety for society — can be no safety for society at all. If we are to be told that these six or seven hundred men who entrusted themselves to his guidance were all a band of lunatics, following a lunatic leader, and that they are not responsible for murder, pillage, arson, spread throughout this country, then all we can say is that it is not a country for human beings to live in.

You may give every consideration you desire to the arguments of my learned friend, give them the fullest consideration, give them every consideration which by any possibility you in the exercise of your reason can think them entitled to, but, gentlemen, it is my duty to ask you not to forget the other aspect of the case, not with any degree of feeling or emphasis, but to place it before you as a fact you must consider upon the evidence.

I have little more to say upon the question of insanity, except so far as it is connected with the other branches of the case. My learned friend, Mr Fitzpatrick, closing with an eloquent description of a free land, with which many of us are familiar with, uses these words: That it is a land where a man may speak the thing he will, what seems to him right. Gentlemen, I wish the prisoner at the bar had confined himself to speaking what he thought to be right. It is not for what he spoke that he is in this situation; it is entirely for the acts he did, and the crimes he committed that throws upon us the painful duty of trying him here. If he had only considered this was a free land and a land where free speech will always get a man his rights, there would have been no difficulty or trouble in the matter. It was just because he was not contented with constitutional agitation, just because he desired to carry on armed rebellion, to have his own way, just because he was not contented with that constitutional agitation which others are satisfied to follow; it was for this reason that he occupies the unhappy position in which he finds himself to-day.

Gentlemen, my learned friend in opening this case to you, opened it as I thought, strongly, clearly and emphatically, but if there is one

duty more incumbent on the counsel for the Crown than another it
is to say nothing to a jury which they are not prepared to support in
evidence, it is to make no statement which may possibly influence
their mind, which the evidence will not carry out.

Now, gentlemen, let us see whether those few important and
material features in this case to which my learned friend called your
attention have or have not been proved beyond all doubt or
suspicion.

In the first place my learned friend, Mr Fitzpatrick, has represented to you; I cannot say he has represented it, but he has argued
to you, that this is a case in which the prisoner started with no intention, with no expectation or desire for anything beyond constitutional agitation, that he was, as it were, overtaken by the situation,
that the situation got beyond him. Gentlemen, does the evidence
afford even the shadow of a foundation for such a statement. You
will remember it was on the 26th of March before hostilities of any
kind broke out. Now, what does the evidence show in that respect?
You will remember in the first place, according to the evidence of
Nolin, he spoke of taking up arms as long ago as December. Very
severe attacks have been made upon the character and evidence of
Nolin. I will only say this, that in so far as Mr Nolin's evidence is
concerned, in one of the most important features it was corroborated to the letter by Father André. And I will say this further for
him, that as far as the constitutional agitation was concerned, he
sympathized with it and went along with it until unconstitutional
means were employed, when he declined to go any further with the
prisoner in his criminal course, in consequence of which he was tried
for his life but escaped. Is Nolin to be censured for that course he
took? He was wrong, I believe, to accept the leadership of the prisoner at the bar under any circumstances, but he was perfectly right
and he did the duty of a loyal citizen in seceding altogether when
unconstitutional means were employed, and he further did the duty
of a loyal citizen when he placed in the hands of the Crown such
information as he could afford.

On the 3rd of March the prisoner at the bar is accompanied by
sixty armed half-breeds to the Halcro settlement, and there he
made use of the expression, 'They talk to us about the police, but
here are our police,' pointing to the armed men. The next thing we
find is that on the 5th of March and on the 6th, he told Nolin that

he had decided to take up arms, that that was his view of the proper course. We hear Nolin dissented from that, and we hear that they disagreed. (And you must remember that they are isolated people and their ways are not in some respects our ways.) They agreed I say that it was better to have a novena or nine days' prayer in order to avert the trouble and agitation which was in the settlement. Riel, the prisoner, seems to have said it was too long a time, but the novena was carried against him.

Gentlemen, if in all he had done he was sincere and truthful, would not the prisoner at the bar heartily have joined in that prayer? What would his conduct have been? Would he not have attended this nine days' prayer and earnestly addressed his thoughts to avert from this country the bloodshed which he foresaw was coming upon it? What did he do? That novena was appointed at his suggestion to begin on the 9th of March and end on the 19th, and what was his course in the meantime? If Nolin's evidence is to be believed the prisoner did what he could to prevent the people from going to the church where these prayers were being said; and we find that before the 19th of March came under his direction and guidance armed rebellion had broken out, and Nolin was taken prisoner and in custody in his hands.

Well, gentlemen, it may be painful but we must test religion by its fruits, and I must ask you what is your opinion on that question, which has been proved beyond all doubt, whether these ways were our ways or the ways of others. I ask you if the prisoner had been sincere would he not have joined heartily in that attempt to avert the disaster which was coming upon the country in the same manner as all his fellow men desired and hoped to avert it, and would he have precipitated the disturbance as he did before these days of prayer were over? Now these are the facts; it is for you to draw your conclusion as to what is a fair inference from them.

But however you may view that, the next thing we find is that on the 18th and 19th, a week before hostilities broke out, and on the 18th more especially, speaking to Dr Willoughby, he told him that in one week from that day the police would be wiped out of existence. He told Dr Willoughby he would let him know who would do the killing in this country. He said: 'You know Louis Riel's history.' Well, gentlemen, I am content to drop the history of Louis Riel. I am content it should be buried in oblivion, and I shall say nothing

more to you about that. He told him the last rebellion would be
nothing to this one. He said the time had now come when he was to
rule this country or perish in the attempt. Well, gentlemen, is that
the talk of a man whom the situation has overwhelmed, or the talk
of a man who was the creature of circumstances?

The next thing we find is that on the 18th pillage and robbery is
committed on inoffensive citizens. We find two stores are robbed,
Walters' & Baker's and another, Kerr's. We find both these stores
looted and pillaged. We find the prisoner coming to the nearest of
these stores and demanding arms and ammunition. Can we fancy
anything more premeditated and designed? We find the preparations
made for war just as patiently and quietly as they are in the case of
two nations who have declared war against each other. On the 18th
he told Mr Lash that the rebellion had commenced and that they
intended to fight until the whole Saskatchewan valley was in their
hands. He told him on the 26th he had sent an armed body to capture the Lieutenant Governor, that he had waited fifteen years and
at last his opportunity had arrived.

The witness Tompkins tells you that, being arrested on the 19th
of April, he heard the prisoner at the bar address his followers in
these words: 'What is Carlton; what is Prince Albert? March on my
brave army!'

We find on the 21st he took the most deliberate step which could
be taken, not in words but in writing. This which I have in my hand
is a document in the prisoner's own handwriting. On the 21st he
addresses Major Crozier, then commandant of the Mounted Police at
Carlton, this summons: 'The councillors of the provisional government of the Saskatchewan have the honor to communicate to you
the following conditions of surrender: You will be required to give
up completely the situation which the Canadian Government have
placed you in at Carlton and Battleford, together with all Government properties. In case of non-acceptance we intend to attack you
when to-morrow, the Lord's Day, is over, and to commence without
delay a war of extermination upon all those who have shown themselves hostile to our rights.'

Can you fancy anything more deliberate, or more prepared, anything carried out with more plain intention and preparation? You
will remember, gentlemen, that that was five days even then before
open hostilities had broken out. It was not, therefore, one day or

one week; it was not one week or two weeks, but it was at least a period of three weeks, during which armed rebellion was in the contemplation and intention of this prisoner. We do not see men armed without an object; we don't hear incendiary speeches addressed to armed men without a purpose, and we certainly don't find summonses to surrender to those who are appointed to guard the public peace, and threaten them with a war of extermination, unless those who address those summonses are fully prepared to go into the rebellion which they contemplate. Well, then gentlemen, on the 21st that letter was addressed to Major Crozier. There was no want of fair warning, and everything was done on the part of the authorities to try if it might not be possible to arrest this prisoner and his misguided followers in their criminal course.

Major Crozier took what was probably the most judicious course, in spreading far and wide proclamations that if those who had begun this movement would only go peaceably back to their homes they should be let off, and their leaders only be required to answer for it. The prisoner and his followers must have been aware of that, and they had that opportunity of withdrawing from the course upon which they had entered.

The next thing we find is that open hostilities break out and blood is shed. Now, gentlemen, how did that come to happen? What were these men doing, the police and volunteers of Prince Albert — what were they doing, when they were attacked by an armed band and many of them slain? They were simply discharging the duty of true and loyal citizens, in endeavoring to protect property and to keep the peace. I ask you what crimes these unfortunate men had committed whose bodies were left on the battlefield that day: just the crime of being loyal and brave subjects.

Gentlemen, if we are to speak of religion, I must confess I never heard religion so used as we have heard it to-day. It was said by two or three, I forget how many witnesses, that the prisoner declared to them, that he said to his followers: In the name of God the Father, fire, and three men are laid out, it may be dead; in the name of God the Son, fire; in the name of the Holy Ghost, fire, and nine bodies are left on the field, and the prisoner returns to do what? To lament the loss of life? No, gentlemen, to rouse the cheers of his soldiers and thank God for his victory, and praise them for their shooting. Now, when we talk of humanity we must look to facts. We have no

right to shirk duties that are incumbent upon us, and it is our duty
to bring before you plainly all those facts, which are undeniable, and
to ask you to draw from them what you consider to be the fair and
proper inference. We have heard of humanity, and credit has been
claimed for humanity. You remember what the prisoner said to two
witnesses after Fish Creek, where more blood was shed – that being
then urged to make peace, he said: 'No, we must yet have another
fight, and then our terms will be better.' Well, gentlemen, human life
is sacred, and the position of the prisoner is a terrible one, but when
we are asked for sympathy for a person in his position, those only
can ask us to respect the sacredness of human life who respect it
themselves. Has there been any respect for human life in this rebellion, or any humanity shown? Has there been any reason or justification for the criminal acts which have been committed? These are
questions which each one of you must ask himself, and which you
must decide according to the evidence laid before you?

Well, gentlemen, we have the evidence to show that this rebellion
was designed contrived, premeditated and prepared, that it was
carried out with deliberation and intention, that it was the result of
no sudden impulse, that it was no outburst of passion, but it was
clearly, calmly, and deliberately opened and carried out.

Then the next thing we find, or the next feature which I must call
your attention to, is that which my learned friend has argued. We
say this was not a rebellion got up and carried out from mistaken
motives of patriotism, but that the leader was actuated by selfish
motives. You have heard the evidence of Astley, who tells you that
at the battle of Batoche the prisoner wanted him to go and see the
general and contrive some means by which he could be introduced
to him, that he might then explain to him that he was the founder of
this new religion, and that the councillors were responsible for the
war, and he said to Astley, 'you know I have never borne arms.'
Astley points to the contrary, that he had borne arms. Now, if he
did say that, was that the act of an honest man, a brave man, or a
true man? Was it right in him as an honest and a brave man to get it
represented not that he but his followers were responsible for the
rebellion, and that his share in the business was religious only?
You have further the evidence of Astley, who tells you that in his
conversation with the prisoner at Batoche the principal thing
in the prisoner's mind seemed to be his own grievances. Jackson

tells you the same story, and Nolin confirms it and so does Father
André.

My learned friend also stated to you that wherever we find there
was a question of leniency and extreme measures the prisoner's voice
was always for the latter. His treatment of McKay, does that bear
out this assertion or not? McKay went with great self risk, and in-
curred great danger, to the enemy's camp, among a band of armed
men, saying that he did not come as a spy, but as one of Her
Majesty's soldiers, and he came to warn them against their criminal
measures. I cannot forbear in passing here to mention that it is well
for this country that we had among us men like Mr McKay and one
or two others. If it hadn't been for the praiseworthy conduct of Mr
McKay before the rebels many others would have flocked to the
rebellion, and which then would have had greater chances of success.
You remember the charge made against Mr McKay, and you remember the manner in which it was met, and you remember the expressions with which it was accompanied. It is well, I say, we had in the
country men like McKay, men who deserve so well of their country.

It is well, too, we have had in this country a man whose conduct,
I think, entitles him to all credit. I refer to Mr Astley; for it is to my
mind by no means clear that the gallantry of the troops would have
rescued the prisoners at Batoche if it had not been for his conduct
there. Gentlemen, when he got to the camp of General Middleton his
own life was safe, and it was the act of a brave man that Astley, after
he had saved himself, did not hesitate again to risk his own life in his
praiseworthy desire to serve the cause of humanity.

Gentlemen, what do we find with regard to the treatment of Mr
McKay? He was tried for his life because he had attempted to teach
reason and sense to his fellow half-breeds. We find the prisoner at
the bar brought the charge against him, and said it was his blood
they wanted, and McKay having spoken for himself that Champagne
got up and said: 'We want no blood here; we want only our rights,'
and the prisoner then left the room and went away.

Are you satisfied if it hadn't been for Champagne McKay would
be where he is to-day? Are you satisfied that the evidence bears out
fully that feature of the case to which my learned friend called your
attention?

Well, gentlemen, there is but one more feature to which I must
call your attention. My learned friend, Mr Fitzpatrick, has said that

the prisoner and those who were responsible for the rebellion, cannot be fairly accused of any attempt to incite the Indians, of any attempt to induce them to take up arms. Gentlemen, is there any foundation for that statement of my learned friend that there is no proof that the documents we find in his handwriting were ever made use of?

Do you think, gentlemen, that men at a time of that sort would write out statements which they do not entertain? Do you think they put in writing and sign with their own names plans which they don't intend to carry out, or do you think that these words which I find in that document, No. 112, in the handwriting of the prisoner, signed by himself, and in which I find these expressions, are without intent:

'Take all the ammunition you can in whatever store they may be; murmur, growl and threaten; raise up the Indians; do all you can to put the police in an impossible position.'

Do you think the letters to Poundmaker, found in his camp, which it is shown was sent to him by a half-breed, in Riel's own handwriting, telling him of the victory over the police at Duck Lake, and thanking God for their success: 'If it is possible, and you have not yet taken Battleford, destroy it; take all the provisions and come to us; your number is such that you can send us a detachment of forty or fifty men.' Do you think that that, sent as it was to an Indian chief, was not intended to raise him to take up arms and go on the warpath and assist in this rebellion?

My learned friend, Mr Fitzpatrick, must have forgotten what is due to a prisoner when he charged those who were acting for the Crown with some warmth for not having called Poundmaker to prove the receipt of that document. He was good enough at the same time to say that those who were conducting the case for the Crown were persons who understood fair play. It was because we did understand fair play, because it would have been improper to have called Poundmaker to swear to that, that we did not call him. If we had attempted to put Poundmaker in the box to prove the receipt of this document we should have been asking Poundmaker to declare on his oath his own complicity in this rebellion and Poundmaker would have to say to us 'I decline to answer your questions,' and any judge would have said to those who acted for the Crown, 'gentlemen, you had no business to put a man in that position.' Now that is our answer on the part of the Crown to the charge that we didn't call the prisoners to prove their own guilt out of their own mouth. It was because we respect the law, because we wanted fair play that we didn't attempt to call anyone here except the one person who is free from any charge of complicity in this rebellion, and who was bound to prove the taking of that letter to Poundmaker.

Well, gentlemen, I think I have almost done; but it is right to say to you these few words: When we hear rebellion as we do hear it, sometimes lightly spoken of, when we read rebellion sometimes lightly written about, do these people, gentlemen, who speak of armed rebellion as a thing to be spoken of in that way, do they think what it means? Not what it may mean, but what it must mean; not what it may mean in theory but what we know it by sad experience it is in fact.

Armed rebellion means the sacrifice of innocent lives, it means the loss of fathers, brothers, sisters, parents, the destruction of many homes, and still more the lifelong bitter desolation of many human hearts, and gentlemen, we must not allow ourselves for one moment to speak lightly of anything which necessarily involves these terrible consequences.

If this scheme had succeeded, gentlemen, if these Indians had been roused, can any man with a human heart contemplate without a shudder the atrocities, the cruelties which would have overspread this land.

Those who are guilty of this rebellion and those who have not a proper excuse, have taken the step upon their own heads, and they must suffer the punishment which the law from all time, and which the law for the last five centuries has declared to be the punishment of the crime of treason.

Now, gentlemen, the Crown in this case has a double duty to perform. In the first place, to see that the prisoner has had every impartiality and fair play and every consideration which it was in their power to give him, and which the law afforded him. Let there be no mistake about that. If this fair play has not been granted, if this trial has not been impartial, if we have omitted any part of our duty, all I can say is that the prisoner's life has been in our hands quite as much as in the hands of the learned gentlemen for the defence.

But, gentlemen, we have another duty to perform; we have the cause of public justice entrusted to our hands; we have the duty of

seeing that the cause of public justice is properly served, that
justice is done.

I will leave this case with confidence in your hands.

The Crown asks only what is just, and the Crown believes justice
will be done. That is all the public and all the community have ever
asked, and to that the public and the community are fully entitled
and that they believe they will receive.

THE JUDGE'S CHARGE

MR JUSTICE RICHARDSON: Gentlemen of the jury, that this is an
important case and will require your very serious consideration, there
can be no shadow of doubt. The duties which devolved upon those gentlemen who had the prosecution in hand, are ended. They have called
their witnesses, and you have heard what they have had to say; in addition to that – and this is the only case in which it is permitted – you
have heard from the mouth of the accused what he has to say.

The remainder of the case rests with yourself and me. My duty is
to show you, to place before you as well as I can, what the law is, to
refresh your memory as to the evidence which has been given *pro*
and *con*, and then leave the determination upon that evidence to
yourselves.

Now, the charge against the prisoner is, as I told you, a very serious one. It is the most serious one in the whole criminal category.
It is the charge of high treason. In order that I may not be mistaken,
that I may not misplace any words, it will be right for me to read to
you what high treason is. The charge of high treason, which is laid
against the prisoner, is that of levying war against Her Majesty in her
realms in these territories. It is founded upon a very old English
statute, one on which is based the whole law of treason, and which
was passed in the reign of Edward III: 'When a man do levy war
against our Lord the King in his realm, or be adherent to the King's
enemies in his realm, giving to them aid and comfort in the realm or
elsewhere and thereof he proveably attainted of open deed by the
people of their condition, that this shall be one ground upon which
the party accused of the offence and legally proved to have committed the offence, shall be held to be guilty of the crime of high
treason.'

Now, in order to constitute the crime of high treason by levying war, a standard authority lays down this: 'To constitute high treason by levying war, there must be insurrection, there must be force accompanying that insurrection, and it must be for the accomplishment of an object of a general nature. And if all these circumstances are found to concur in any individual case that is brought under investigation, that is quite sufficient to constitute a levying of war.' The charge upon which the prisoner is upon his trial is under that statute, that clause of the statute, and it charges him with levying war upon Her Majesty at the locality of Duck Lake, North-West Territories, also at Fish Creek, and also at Batoche. Having refreshed your memory as to the evidence which was supplied on the part of the Crown, and which you have heard on the part of the defence, it will be your duty to say whether that has been proved or not. If it has not been proved, if the evidence has not brought it home conclusively to this man, he should be acquitted. If it has been brought home to the prisoner, then another question turns up which you will have most seriously to consider, is he answerable?

My intention now is to read the evidence which has been taken. I feel it my duty to do so, from the way it has been given, and after I have read it, to draw your attention to it and to make a few observations that occur to me, which may be useful to yourselves in arriving at a conclusion. Before I read the evidence, I may remark that before the prisoner can be convicted you must be satisfied that he was implicated in the acts charged against him. It must be brought home to him, otherwise he is entitled to be acquitted. If you are satisfied that he was implicated in the acts in which he is said to have been implicated, he must as completely satisfy you that he is not answerable by reason of unsoundness of mind.

You will recollect that there are two points which you must consider; first, was this man implicated, supposing him to be sane, in the acts charged against him? It is for the Crown to satisfy you upon that. If he was so implicated, are you satisfied, from what has been shown, that he is not answerable?

(Portions of the evidence read by his Honor, and the Court adjourned at six o'clock.)

Saturday, 1st August 1885

Court opened at 10 A.M.
His Honor continues to read portions of the evidence to the jury,
after which he says:
Gentlemen of the Jury:In opening my remarks to you yesterday
afternoon, I explained to you that an important duty devolved upon
us, one share of it upon myself and the other upon yourselves. My
part of that duty being to see that you recollect the evidence placed
before you, and that any salient points that struck me as important,
and that might assist you in your deliberation, are brought to your
notice, and also that the law as it relates to this case is laid fairly
before you, and then I will leave it to you to determine upon the
evidence as to the guilt or innocence of the prisoner. I explained to
you that the features of this case differ from ordinary cases, in that
it presents for your consideration, first, the question whether or not
(what is in legal phraseology) the 'overt acts' charged have been committed, and whether the prisoner was a participant in those acts. If
that has not been brought home to the prisoner, if the Crown has
not satisfied you conclusively upon that point, the prisoner should
be acquitted out and out. If, on the other hand, you feel that he was
so implicated, you have to determine the further question, whether
it has been shown with equal conclusiveness that this man was not
answerable for the commission of the acts charged against him.

Before proceeding with my remarks, I think I ought to digress for
a few moments. Reference has been made to the question of jurisdiction. With that we have really nothing to do, we have simply to
perform the duties imposed upon us by law. Still it may not be out
of place to tell you how that duty comes to be imposed on us.

In the first place, Great Britain owning these territories transferred the administration of peace, order and the good government
of them to the Dominion Parliament. That was in 1871. The Parliament of Canada accepted this charge, and in 1875 passed their first
law, by which the prisoner would have been tried in the territories
by the chief justice, or one of the judges of the Queen's Bench of
Manitoba, with a stipendiary magistrate beside him and a jury of
eight. This was brought into force in 1876, but for some reason,
possibly owing to difficulties in its working, was altered in 1877. It
was altered by providing that instead of a judge from Manitoba being

sent here, the court should be held in the territories, and presided
over by a stipendiary magistrate and two justices of the peace, with
the intervention of a jury of six, that is in cases of capital offences.
It having been found inconvenient, and probably, in some cases,
impossible to get the number of magistrates required in all places,
the statute of 1880 was passed, reducing the number of magistrates
sitting with the stipendiary magistrates to one, and there the law
stands. The council for the defence, in the exercise of their duty,
and I think in a proper manner, and at a proper time, objected to the
jurisdiction of this court. They deemed it right to say that the law is
not such a law as the Parliament of Canada can pass, and that therefore this court has not jurisdiction to try this case. It may perhaps
strike you as strange, but at the same time all the counsel knew it as
lawyers that while it was a proper time for them to make that objection, I sitting here could not say whether they were right or wrong in
their opinions, and why? I will tell you, because in the Act of 1877,
when Parliament altered the law relieving the provincial judges from
coming into the territories to hold such courts, a provision was made
which does not exist in any of the Provinces, that if the accused felt
aggrieved on his trial, there should be an appeal to the Court of
Queen's Bench in Manitoba. They did not allow this right of appeal
to the Crown, it is a special privilege given to those accused of capital offences. Having accepted a commission under the law, it would
strike one as strange that I should take it upon myself without anything further to say that the Parliament of Canada had exceeded
their power and should not have passed that Act. I was not called
upon to do that. That question had been disposed of within a few
days before this objection was raised. In deciding that the Court of
Queen's Bench held that the Act of Parliament of Canada passed in
1880, was not *ultra vires* that is that the Parliament of Canada did
not exceed their powers in passing it, and therefore it would have
been a piece of utter impertinence on my part to question their
decision. At the same time the exception was very properly put on
the record and at the proper time.

   You have heard, and are masters of the evidence, and therefore I
will be very brief in making what remarks I have to make to you.
The questions really for you to determine are, first, are you satisfied
that there was a rebellion? If you are satisfied that there was a rebellion, as I think you must be, the first question I will ask then is it

brought home conclusively to you that the prisoner at the bar was implicated? In charges of this sort there are no classes, no accessories, all are principals. If you are conclusively convinced that the prisoner was implicated, then has anything been shown here to relieve him from responsibility? His counsel urged that at the time he committed the acts charged he was of unsound mind, that he did not know what he was doing, and for that reason he should be acquitted. This question of unsoundness of mind has given rise in former years to a very great deal of consideration. I heard a case referred to yesterday which resulted in a great scandal in Great Britain. That was not the only case, it was followed some years afterwards by a case involving still greater scandal. The law has been put in such a shape now that when the question was set up, judges may be able to tell the jury fixedly in words what their duties are in regard to responsibility for crime when insanity is set up as a defence. As to insanity, as you saw yesterday, doctors differ as do lawyers. Month by month I may say, week by week, additions are made to classes of mania, new terms are used, branches which were under the simple category of mania come out with new names. I heard a name given in evidence yesterday that I never heard before, megalomania, but it seems to be accepted as a symptom or as a fixed branch of insanity, but it is not every man who is pronounced insane by the doctors and who from charity or kindness should be placed under restraint and be put in one of the asylums; it is not I say, every one of them that is to be held free from being called upon to answer for offences he may commit against the criminal law.

The line is drawn very distinctly, and where the line is drawn I will tell you shortly. Before doing so, and to assist you in your deliberations, let me draw your attention to some points suggested to my mind by the evidence. You recollect the statements as to the prisoner's appropriating property, and making prisoners of others simply because they, to his idea, opposed him in his movements. It has been suggested by the Crown, in reference to the $35,000, that it tends to show that this was all a scheme of the prisoner's to put money in his own pocket. Be that as it may, one of the witnesses, Nolin, speaks distinctly as to the $35,000, and on that branch of his evidence we have his corroborated by the priest Father André, and further by Jackson. Then you have heard the evidence given by Captain Young as to the conversations he had with the prisoner.

Witness after witness gave evidence as to what occurred in March,
at the time of the commencement of this rebellion. Some of
them speak of the prisoner being very irritable when the subject
of religion was brought up. It appears, however, that his irritability
had passed away when he was coming down with Captain Young,
as we do not hear anything of it then. Does this show reasoning
power?

Then at what date can you fix this insanity as having commenced? The theory of the defence fixes the insanity as having
commenced only in March, but threats of what he intended to do
began in December. Admitting that the insanity only commenced
about the time of the breaking out of the rebellion, what does seem
strange to me is that these people who were about him, if they had
an insane man in their midst, that some of them had not the charity
to go before a magistrate and lay an information setting forth that
there was an insane man amongst them, and that a breach of the
peace was liable to occur at any moment, and that he should be
taken care of. I only suggest that to you, not that you are to take it
as law, I merely suggest it to you as turning upon the evidence.
Having made the remarks I have, I am simply called upon to tell you
what is legal insanity, insanity in the eye of the law, so far as crime is
concerned. The Crown must in all cases, particularly such as this,
bring home conclusively the crime charged to the prisoner. If the
Crown has done that, on the prisoner rests the responsibility of relieving himself from the consequences of his acts. The law directs me
to tell you that every man is presumable to be sane and to possess a
sufficient degree of reason to be responsible for his crimes until the
contrary be proved to your satisfaction. And that to establish a defence on the ground of insanity, it must be clearly proved that at the
time he committed the act, the party accused was laboring under
such defective reasoning from a diseased mind as not to know the
nature and quality of the act he was committing, or that if he did
know it, that he did not know that he was doing wrong. That I pro-
pound to you as the law.

If the evidence conclusively satisfies you that the prisoner was
implicated in these acts or in any of them I may say, has it been
clearly proved to you that at the time he committed those acts he
was laboring under such defective reasoning caused by disease of
the mind as not to know the nature and quality of the act he was

committing, or if he did know it, that he did not know that he was
doing wrong? If the evidences convinces you and convinces you conclusively that such was the case, then your duty is to acquit the prisoner on that ground, and you are required to declare that he is
acquitted by you on account of such insanity.

I think I have reduced my remarks within the smallest possible
compass. You have been kept close at this case since Tuesday morning, and I cannot conceive that any further remarks would be of any
assistance to you. On you rests the responsibility of pronouncing
upon the guilt or innocence of the prisoner at the bar. Not only
must you think of the man in the dock, but you must think of
society at large, you are not called upon to think of the Government
at Ottawa simply as a Government, you have to think of the homes
and of the people who live in this country, you have to ask yourselves, can such things be permitted? There was one point I intended
to have mentioned but which has escaped me. You will bear in mind
that the law of the land under which this trial is held was objected to
on behalf of the prisoner, and he has a perfect right to object to it,
but the law of the land was in existence years before he came into
this country three years ago, that Act came into force in 1875, and
the law which he is said to have broken has been in existence for
centuries, and I think I may fairly say to you that if a man chooses
to come into the country, he shall not say, I will do as I like and no
laws can touch me. A person coming into the country is supposed to
know the law, it is his duty. We have the law given to us and we are
called upon to administer it. I, under the oath that I have taken, and
you, under the oath administered to you on Tuesday morning, are to
pass between this man and the Crown. If therefore the Crown has
not conclusively brought guilt home to the prisoner, say so, say that
you acquit him simply by reason of that.

On the jury returning, after having retired to consider their verdict,
the clerk of the court says, gentlemen are you agreed upon your
verdict? How say you, is the prisoner guilty or not guilty?

The jury find the prisoner guilty.

CLERK: Gentlemen of the jury, hearken to your verdict as the court
records it, 'You find the prisoner, Louis Riel, guilty, so say you all.'
The jury answer 'guilty.'

A JUROR: Your Honors, I have been asked by my brother jurors to recommend the prisoner to the mercy of the Crown.

MR JUSTICE RICHARDSON: I may say in answer to you that the recommendation which you have given will be forwarded in proper manner to the proper authorities.

MR ROBINSON: Do your Honors propose to pass sentence now? I believe the proper course is to ask the sentence of the court upon the prisoner.

MR JUSTICE RICHARDSON: Louis Riel, have you anything to say why the sentence of the court should not be pronounced upon you, for the offence of which you have been found guilty?

PRISONER: Yes, your Honor —

MR FITZPATRICK: Before the accused answers or makes any remarks, as suggested by your Honors, I would beg leave to ask your Honors to kindly note the objections which I have already taken to the jurisdiction of the court.

MR JUSTICE RICHARDSON: It is noted, Mr Fitzpatrick. You understand of course why I cannot rule upon it.

MR FITZPATRICK: It is simply so as to reserve any recourse the law may allow us hereafter.

PRISONER: Can I speak now?

MR JUSTICE RICHARDSON: Oh, yes.

PRISONER: Your Honors, gentlemen of the jury —

MR JUSTICE RICHARDSON: There is no jury now, they are discharged.

PRISONER: Well, they have passed away before me.

MR JUSTICE RICHARDSON: Yes, they have passed away.

PRISONER: But at the same time I consider them yet still there, still in their seat. The court has done the work for me, and although at first appearance it seems to be against me, I am so confident in the ideas which I have had the honor to express yesterday, that I think it is for good, and not for my loss. Up to this moment I have been considered by a certain party as insane, by another party as a criminal, by another party as a man with whom it was doubtful whether to have any intercourse. So there was hostility, and there was contempt, and there was avoidance. To-day, by the verdict of the court, one of those three situations has disappeared.

I suppose that after having been condemned, I will cease to be called a fool, and for me, it is a great advantage. I consider it as a

great advantage. If I have a mission – I say 'if,' for the sake of those
who doubt, but for my part it means 'since,' since I have a mission, I
cannot fulfil my mission as long as I am looked upon as an insane
being – human being, as the moment I begin to ascent that scale I
begin to succeed.

You have asked me, your Honors, if I have anything to say why
my sentence should not be passed. Yes, it is on that point particularly my attention is directed.

Before saying anything about it, I wish to take notice that if there
has ever been any contradiction in my life, it is at this moment, and
do I appear excited? Am I very irritable? Can I control myself? And
it is just on religion and on politics, and I am contradicted at this
moment on politics, and the smile that comes to my face is not an
act of my will so much as it comes naturally from the satisfaction
that I proved that I experienced seeing one of my difficulties dis-
appearing. Should I be executed – at least if I were going to be
executed – I would not be executed as an insane man. It would be a
great consolation for my mother, for my wife, for my children, for
my brothers, for my relatives, even for my protectors, for my countrymen. I thank the gentlemen who were composing the jury for
having recommended me to the clemency of the court. When I expressed the great hopes that I have just expressed to you, I don't
express it without grounds. My hopes are reasonable, and since they
are recommended, since the recommendation of the jury to the
Crown is for clemency, it would be easy for me, your Honor, to
make an incendiary protest and take the three reasons which have
been reasonably put forward by my good lawyers and learned
lawyers about the jury, about their selection, about the one who
selected them, and about the competency of the court; but why
should I do it since the court has undertaken to prove that I am a
reasonable man? Must not I take advantage of the situation to show
that they are right, and that I am reasonable? And yesterday, when I
said, by repeating the evidence which had been given against me,
when I said in conclusion that you had a decent prophet, I have just
to-day the great opportunity of proving it is so. Besides clearing me
of the stain of insanity, clearing my career of the stain of insanity, I
think the verdict that has been given against me is a proof that I am
more than ordinary myself, but that the circumstances and the help
which is given to me is more than ordinary, are more than ordinary,

and although I consider myself only as others, yet by the will of
God, by His Providence, by the circumstances which have surrounded me for fifteen years, I think that I have been called on to
do something which, at least in the North-West, nobody has done
yet. And in some way I think, that, to a certain number of people,
the verdict against me to-day is a proof that maybe I am a prophet,
maybe Riel is a prophet, he suffered enough for it. Now, I have been
hunted as an elk for fifteen years. David has been seventeen, I think
I will have to be about two years still. If the misfortunes that I have
had to go through were to be as long as those of old David, I would
have two years still, but I hope it will come sooner. I have two
reasons why I would ask that sentence should not be passed upon
me, against me. You will excuse me, you know my difficulty in
speaking English, and have had no time to prepare, your Honor, and
even had I prepared anything, it would have been imperfect enough,
and I have not prepared, and I wish you would excuse what I have to
say, the way which I will be able to perhaps express it.

The troubles of the Saskatchewan are not to be taken as an isolated fact. They are the result of fifteen years' war. The head of that
difficulty lies in the difficulty of Red River. The troubles of Red
River were called the troubles of the North-West, and I would like to
know if the troubles of the Saskatchewan have not the name of
being the troubles of the North-West. So the troubles of 1869 being
the troubles of the North-West, and the troubles of 1885 being still
the troubles of the North-West, the suggestion comes naturally to
the mind of the observer if it is a continuation. The troubles of the
North-West in 1885 are the continuation of the troubles in 1869, or
if they are two troubles entirely different — I say they are not.
Canada — no, I ought not to say Canada, because it was a certain
number of individuals, perhaps 700 or 800, that can have passed for
Canada, but they came to the Red River, and they wanted to take
possession of the country without consulting the people. True, it
was the half-breed people. There were a certain number of white
pioneers among the population, but the great majority were half-
breeds. We took up arms against the invaders of the east without
knowing them. They were so far apart of us, on the other side of the
lakes, that it cannot be said that we had any hatred against them. We
did not know them. They came without notification, they came
boldly. We said, who are they, they said, we are the possessors of the

country. Well, knowing that it was not true, we done against those
parties coming from the east, what we used to do against the Indians
from the south and the west, when they would invade us. Public
opinion in the States helped us a great deal. I don't mean to say that
it is need to obtain justice on this side of the line that the States
should interfere, but, at that time, as there was no telegraph communication between the eastern Provinces and the North-West, no
railroad, and as the natural way of going to Canada was through the
United States, naturally all the rumors, all the news, had to pass by
the States, and on their passage they had to meet the remarks and
observations of the American people. The American people were
favorable to us. Besides, the opposition in Canada done the same
thing, and said to the Government: Well, why did you go into the
North-West without consulting the people? We took up arms, as I
stated, and we made hundreds of prisoners, and we negotiated. A
treaty was made. That treaty was made by a delegation of both
parties. Whether you consider that organization of the Red River
people at that time a provisional government, or not, the fact is that
they were recognized as a body tribal, if you like to call it, as a social
body with whom the Canadian Government treated. Did they treat
with them as they treated with Indians? It will be for them to say,
but they didn't. Since Sir John A. Macdonald and the late Sir George
Cartier were delegated by the Dominion Government to meet our
delegates, delegates who had been appointed by me, the president –
that is the name that was given to me by the council, the president
of that council – that our delegates had been invited three times,
first by Donald A. Smith, a member of the Privy Council at that
time, second by the Rev. Mr Thibault (the late Rev. Mr Thibault),
third by Archbishop Taché, who had been called from Rome for the
purpose of pacifying the North-West, when those three delegates had
invited us to send delegates, we thought that it was safe to send delegates, and I appointed the Rev. Father Richot, now curate of St
Norbert, in Manitoba, I appointed the late Judge Black, who died in
Scotland, I appointed Alfred H. Scott, he is dead also, and those
three delegates started, with our bill of rights of twenty conditions,
to go and put it before the Canadian Government, and when our
delegates came to Ottawa, the Government wanted to treat them as
Indians I suppose. Father Richot said: If you don't give me, in
writing, my acknowledgment as a delegate, I will go back, and you

will go with your bayonets to the North-West, acknowledged my
status, I am invited, and I come. And what was the answer? Our
delegates had been invited three times, how were they received in
Canada? They were arrested – to show exactly what is the right of
nations. They were arrested, they had a formal trial, but the fact
remains that they were arrested, and the protest of the Rev. Father
Richot is still in the document. However, there was a treaty. Sir
John A. Macdonald was delegated, the late Sir George Cartier was
delegated to treat with the people, Sir John A. Macdonald was delegated. The late Sir George Cartier was delegated to treat with the
people, with those three delegates. Now, how were they acknowledged? Were they acknowledged as the delegates of Riel? Oh, no,
they were acknowledged as the delegates of the North-West. The late
Mr Howe, in his acknowledgment of the delegates, and in notifying
them who had been delegated by the Canadian Government to treat
with them, told them that they were acknowledged as the delegates
of the North-West. Then it was the cause of the North-West that
they represented. It is acknowledged by the Canadian Government
by that very same fact that fifteen years ago the treaty of which I
am speaking was a treaty of the North-West, of the delegates of the
North-West, and if, by trying to say that it was the delegates of the
North-West, they wanted to avoid the fact that I was no being at all,
the whole world knows that it is not so; they cannot avoid me. And
Sir John A. Macdonald himself, in the report of the committee of
enquiry about those very same troubles – the committee sat in
1874 – Sir John A. Macdonald said, I think we acknowledge Riel in
his status of a governor. What was the treaty? Was it an Indian
affair? If it had been an Indian affair Manitoba would not have been
as it is, would not be as it is. We have the Manitoba Act. There was
an agreement between the two delegates how the whole North-West
interest would be considered and how the Canadian Government
would treat with the North-West. And then, having settled on the
matters of principle, those very principles, the agreement was made
that those very principles would be inaugurated in Manitoba first.
There was a province erected with responsible government; the
lands, they were kept by the Dominion. As the half-breed people
were the majority of Manitoba, as at their stage of civilization they
were not supposed to be able to administer their lands, we thought
that at that time it was a reasonable concession to let them go, not

because we were willing to let them go, but because it seemed im-
practicable to have the administration of the lands. Still, one of the
conditions was that the lands were that the people of the North-West
wanted the administration of their lands. The half-breeds had a
million, and the land grant of 1,400,000 acres owned about
9,500,000, if I mistake not, which is about one-seventh of the lands
of Manitoba. You will see the origin of my insanity and of my
foreign policy. One-seventh of the land was granted to the people, to
the half-breeds of Manitoba — English and French, Protestant and
Catholic; there was no distinction whatever. But in the sub-division,
in the allotment of those lands between the half-breeds of Manitoba,
it came that they had 240 acres of land. Now, the Canadian Government say that we will give to the half-breeds of the North-West 240
acres. If I was insane I would say yes, but as I have had, thank God,
all the time the consciousness that I had a certain degree of reason, I
have made up my mind to make use of it, and to say that one-
seventh of the lands in Manitoba, as to the inauguration of a principle in the North-West, had to bring to the half-breeds of the
North-West at least as soon as possible the guarantee for the future
that a seventh of the lands will also be given to them; and seeing and
yourself understanding how it is difficult for a small population, as
the half-breed population, to have their voices heard, I said what
belongs to us ought to be ours. Our right to the North-West is
acknowledged, our co-proprietorship with the Indians is acknowledged, since one-seventh of the land is given us, but we have not the
means to be heard. What will we do? I said to some of my friends if
there is no other way we will make the people who have no country
understand that we have a country here which we have ceded on
condition. We want a seventh of the lands, and if the bargain is not
kept, it is null and void, and we have no right to retreat again. And if
we cannot have our seventh of the lands from Canada, we will ask
the people of the States, the Italians, to come and help us as emi-
grants. The Irish, I will count them. Now, it is my turn; I thank you.
I count them, and I will show you if I made an insane enumeration
of the parties. I said we will invite the Italians of the States, the Irish
of the States, the Bavarians of the States, the Poles of the States, the
Belgians of the States, and if they come and help us here to have the
seventh, we will give them each a seventh; and to show that we are
not fanatics, that we are not partizans, that we do not wish only for

the Catholic, but that we have a consideration for those who are not
Catholics. I said we will invite the Danes, we will invite the Swedes
who are numerous in the States, and the Norwegians, to come
around, and as there are Indians and half-breeds in British Columbia,
and as British Columbia is a part of the immense North-West, we said
not only for ourselves, but speaking of our children, we will make
the proposition, that if they help us to have our seventh on the two
sides of the Rocky Mountains, they will each have a seventh, and if
the Jews will help us, on condition that they acknowledge Jesus
Christ as the son of God and the only Saviour of human kind, and if
they will help us with their money, we will give them a seventh; and
I said also, if the principle of giving a seventh of the lands in the
North-West — if the principle of giving a seventh of the lands in the
North-West to the half-breeds is good, it ought to be good in the east
also, and I said if it is not possible that our views should be heard,
we will meet as American citizens. I will invite the Germans of the
States, and I will say if you ever have an opportunity of crossing the
line in the east, do it, and help the Indians and the half-breeds of the
east to have a revenue equivalent to about one-seventh. And what
would be the reward of the Germans? The reward of the Germans
would be, if they were successful, to take a part of the country and
make a new German-Indian world somewhere in British North
America; but that is the last resort, and if I had not had a verdict of
guilty against me, I would have never said it. Yesterday it is just
those things that I have just avoided to say; when I said I have a
reason to not mention them, and when I said, as one of the witnesses
said, that my proclamation was in Pembina, I think I am right,
because of this trial you see that my pretension is, that I can speak a
little of the future events. My trial has brought out the question of
the seventh, and although no one has explained the things as I do
now, still there is enough said about the seventh of the land and that
the division of the lands into seven, seven nationalities, while it
ought to have been said between ten nationalities, that by telegraph
to-day my proclamation is in Pembina, truly, and the States have my
idea; they have my idea. The Fenian element, without any tangible
object, have crossed the lines several times for the only sake of what
they called revenge, but now that Riel, whose name is somewhat
prominent for fifteen years, is known to be in his trouble for life and
death, for himself and his nationality, now that my trial gives me a

certain increase of the celebrity, now that those questions are appearing now before the public, that there is a land league in the
States, that that very same element which possesses Fenianism is still
there, and quiet, because they have no plan, because they have no
idea around which gather their numbers, and when they catch at it
do they think that they will smile? And Gabriel Dumont on the
other side of the line, is that Gabriel Dumont inactive? I believe not.
He is trying to save me from this box. This is no threat. I have
written it. I have written a document of that kind and put it in the
hands of Captain Deane three weeks ago. This is not an inspiration
of the moment. I have the right to thank God for the provision of
what happens to-day, but there is another means. I don't wish that
means, these means. I don't wish them to call the people from the
States on this side of the line. No, I wish it only if there is no other
possibility, if there is no other resort, of course that is my wish. The
last remedy, although it may be extreme, is always a remedy, and it
is worth something to try it. But if there is justice, as I still hope, oh,
dear, it seems to me I have become insane to hope still. I have seen
so many men in my position and where are they? But Lepine has
had his scaffold also in Manitoba, and he was not executed. Why?
Because he was recommended to the clemency of the court. The
idea of the seventh, I have two hands, and I have two sides to my
head, and I have two countries. I am an American citizen and I have
two countries, and I am taken here as a British subject. I don't abandon my idea of the seventh. I say because the other is an extreme
and extremity, I don't wish for it until extremities have come, and I
have, coming to extremities just now, but there are some hopes yet
for me, my heart is full of hope; but my friends, I suppose that
many of them think that I am gone. If Canada is just with me, if
Canada respects my life, my life, my liberty and my reputation, they
will give me all that they have taken from me, and as I said yesterday, that immense influence which my acts are gathering for the last
fifteen years, and which, as the power of steam contained in an
engine will have its sway, then what will it do? It will do that Riel
will go perhaps to the Dominion ministry, and there instead of
calling the parties in the States, he will by means, constitutional
means of the country, invite the same parties from Europe as emigration, but let it be well understood that as my right has been
acknowledged as a co-proprietor of the soil with the Indians, I want

to assert that right. It is constitutionally acknowledged in the
Manitoba Act by the 31st clause of that Act, and it does not say to
extinguish the Indian title. It says two words, extinguishing, and
1,400,000 acres of land, two words and as each child of the half-
breeds got one-seventh, naturally I am at least entitled to the same.
It is why I spoke of the seventh for the Indians, not of the lands but
of the revenue as it increases. But somebody will say, on what
grounds do you ask one-seventh of the lands? Do you own the
lands? In England, in France, the French and the English have lands,
the first was in England, they were the owners of the soil and they
transmitted to generations. Now, by the soil they have had their
start as a nation. Who starts the nations? The very one who creates
them, God. God is the master of the universe, our planet is his land,
and the nation and the tribes are members of His family, and as a
good father, he gives a portion of his lands to that nation, to that
tribe, to everyone, that is his heritage, that is his share of the inheritance, of the people, or nation or tribe. Now, here is a nation strong
as it may be, it has its inheritance from God. When they have
crowded their country because they had no room to stay any more
at home, it does not give them the right to come and take the share
of all tribes besides them. When they come they ought to say, well,
my little sister, the Cree tribe, you have a great territory, but that
territory has been given to you as our own land, it has been given to
our fathers in England or in France and of course you cannot exist
without having that spot of land. This is the principle God cannot
create a tribe without locating it. We are not birds. We have to walk
on the ground, and that ground is encircled of many things, which
besides its own value, increases its value in another manner, and
when we cultivate it we still increase that value. Well, on what principle can it be that the Canadian Government have given one-seventh
to the half-breeds of Manitoba? I say it must be on this ground, civilization has the means of improving life that Indians or half-breeds
have not. So when they come in our savage country, in our unculti-
vated land, they come and help us with their civilization, but we
helped them with our lands, so the question comes: Your land, you
Cree or you half-breed, your land is worth to-day one-seventh of
what it will be when civilization will have opened it? Your country
unopened is worth to you only one-seventh of what it will be when
opened. I think it is a fair share to acknowledge the genius of

civilization to such an extent as to give, when I have seven pair of socks, six, to keep one. They made the treaty with us. As they made the treaty, I say they have to observe it, and did they observe the treaty? No. There was a question of amnesty then, and when the treaty was made one of the questions was that before the Canadian Government would send a governor into Manitoba an Imperial amnesty should be proclaimed so as to blot out all the difficulties of the past. Instead of proclaiming a general amnesty before the arrival of the governor which took place on the 2nd of September 1870, the amnesty was proclaimed the 25th April 1875, so I suffered for five years unprotected, besides I was expelled from the House twice. I was they say outlawed, but, as I was busy as a member of the east, and had a trial in the west, I could not be in two places, and they say that I was outlawed, but no notification was sent to my house of any proceedings of the court. They say that I was outlawed and when the amnesty came five years after the time that it should have come, I was banished for five years and Lepine deprived of his political rights forever. Why? Because he had given political rights to Manitoba? Is that all? No. Did the amnesty come from the Imperial Government? Not at all. It came from our sister colony in the east, and mind you, to make a miracle of it I said the one being great, and Riel being small, I will go on the other side and I am banished. It is a wonder I did not take and go to Mexico. Naturally I went to the States, amnesty was given by the Secretary of State at Ottawa, the party who treated with us. That is no amnesty. It is an insult to me. It has always been an insult to me. I said in Manitoba two years ago that it was an insult and I considered it as such, but are there proofs that amnesty has been promised? Yes, many. Archbishop Taché the delegate who has been called, the prelate who has been called from Rome to come and pacify the North-West received a commission to make, to accomplish that pacification, and in general terms was written his commission, and when he came into the North-West before I sent delegates, he said I will give you my word of honor as a delegate, that there will be an Imperial amnesty, not because I can promise it on my own responsibility, but because it has been guaranteed to me by the representative of the Crown and the Ministers themselves, the Minister of the Crown, and instead of the Imperial amnesty came the amnesty of which I spoke and besides, an amnesty came five years too late, and which took the trouble of banishing me five years more.

MR JUSTICE RICHARDSON: Is that all?

PRISONER: No, excuse me, I feel weak and if I stop at times, I wish you would be kind enough to —

But the last clause of the Manitoba Act speaks also a little of the North-West, speaks that a temporary government will be put into the North-West until a certain time, not more than five years, and, gentlemen, the temporary government, how long has it lasted now? How long has it existed now? For fifteen years, and it will be temporary yet. It is against the Manitoba, it is against the treaty of the North-West that this North-West Council should continue to be in existence, and against the spirit of the understanding. Have I anything to say against the gentlemen who compose the North-West Council? Not at all, not more than I had yesterday to say against the jury and to say against the officials of this court, whom I respect all, but I speak of the institutions. No; I speak of the institutions in the North-West. The Manitoba treaty has not been fulfilled, neither in regard to me, neither in regard to Lepine. Besides the population of the half-breeds who have found in the troubles of the North-West in Manitoba in 1870, and who have been found in the troubles of the North-West, what right have they to be there? Have they not received their 240 acres? I suppose that the half-breeds in Manitoba in 1870 did not fight for 240 acres of land, but it is to be understood that there were two societies who treated together; one was small, but in its smallness it had its rights. The other was great, but by its greatness it had no greater rights than the rights of the small, because the rights is the same for every one, and when they began by treating the leaders of the small community as bandits, as outlaws, leaving them without protection, they disorganized that community. The right of nations wanted that the treaty of Manitoba should be fulfilled towards the little community of Red River in the same condition that they were when they treated. That is the right of nations, and when the treaty would have been fulfilled towards that small community in the same state as when it was when she treated, then the obligations would have been fulfilled and the half-breeds might have gone to the North-West, the Saskatchewan, and have no right to call for any other things for themselves, although they had a right to help their neighbors if they thought that they were in a bad fix, because charity is always charity. Now I say that the people of Manitoba have not been satisfied, nor the leaders nor the people, because during those five years, which elapsed between 1870 and 1875, there were laws made and those laws they embraced the people, the half-breed people, and because they hadn't their rights, because the leaders were always threatened in their existence, the people themselves did not feel any security and they sold their lands, because they thought they would never get first that seventh of the lands. They sold their lands because they saw they had no protection and they went east. What have they received in receiving the 240 acres? They have received 240 acres of land, and as a matter of fact I can prove that by circumstances many – one-half of them – sold for half of the price, $50 or $40, $60 or $25, and to show the state in which they had been kept those who came from the Red River and the half-breeds of Red River who were in the Red River trouble of 1870, appeared to be a wonder of egotism and of unreasonableness because they appeared to be in the troubles of 1885, which are the continuation of the troubles of the Red River. The amnesty has not been given by the right parties. Amnesty has not been given to Lepine, one of the leaders, who was then, as Dumont is to-day and myself. I was allowed to come back into the country after ten years; after I would be completely deprived of the chances which I had in 1870 to do something for my people and myself and for emigration, so as to cut down my influence forever. It is why I did not come at that time, and thought I would never come to the country. Did I take my American paper, put my papers of American naturalization during my five years' banishment? No, I did not want to give to the States a citizen of banishment, but when my banishment had ex-pired, when an officer at Battleford – somewhere on this side of the line, in Benton – invited me to come to the North-West I said: No, I will go to an American court, I will declare my intention, now that I am free to go back, and choose another land. It sored my heart. It sored my heart to say that kind of adieu to my mother, to my brothers, to my sisters, to my friends, to my countrymen, my native land, but I felt that in coming back to this country I could not re-enter it without protesting against all the injustice which I had been suffering, and in doing it I was renewing a struggle which I had not been able to continue as a sound man, as I thought I was, I thought it better to begin a career on the other side of the line. In Manitoba is that all about the amnesty? No, my share of the 1,400,000 acres of land, have I received it? No, I have not received it. My friends, my mother have applied to have it. No, I could not. Everyone else could apply for theirs. Father, mother, would apply for their sons and that was all right, but for my honor, to apply for me it was not, I did not get it. Last year there was a proof. Here, in the box, not long ago when I asked an indemnity, I was refused. Was that indemnity based on a fancy? I wanted my lands in Manitoba to be paid. Besides, when they treatied, the treaty was completed on the 31st May 1870, it was agreed to the 24th June, and Sir Geo. Cartier had said, let Riel govern the country until the troops get there, and from the 24th June till the 23rd August I governed the country in fact, and what was the reward for it? When the glorious General Wolseley came he rewarded me in saying Riel's banditti has taken flight, and he wanted to come during the night, at midnight, so as to have a chance to raise a row in Fort Garry and to have a glory to call for in the morning, but heaven was against him then. It rained so much that he could not get there during the night, and he had to come at ten o'clock next morning. He entered one door of Fort Garry while I left the other. I kept in sight of him. I was small. I did not want to be in his road. But, as I knew he had good eyes I say I will keep at a distance, where I can be seen, and if he wants to have me, he will come. A general knows where his enemy is, ought to know, and I kept about 300 yards ahead of him. While he was saying that Riel's banditti had taken flight, Riel was very near. That has been my reward. When I speak of an indemnity of $35,000, to call for something to complete the $100,000, I don't believe that I am exaggerating, your Honor. In 1871 the Fenians came in Pembina. Major Irvine, one of the witnesses, I was introduced to him, and when I brought to the governor 250 men, Governor Archibald was then anxious to have my help because he knew that we were the door of Manitoba, and he said as the question of amnesty came he said if Riel comes forward we will protect him. 'Pour la circonstance actuelle,' we will protect him. As long as we need him, we will protect him, but as soon as we don't want him, as soon as we don't need him, we want him to fall back in the same position he is to-day, and that answer had been brought because it had been represented that while I would be helping the Government the parties would be trying to shoot me in the back. 'Pour la circonstance actuelle,' they said, I will protect him. What reward have I had by that? The first reward that I had was that that took place in the first days of October 1871, before the year was ended.

Of course they gave the chance to Riel to come out. A rebel had a
chance to be loyal then. My friends, my glorious friend in Upper
Canada, now the leader of the opposition, Mr Blake, said, we must
prevent Mr Riel from arriving. When he was Minister in Upper
Canada he issued a proclamation of $5,000 for those who would
arrest Riel. That was my reward, my dowry, but the Canadian
Government, what reward would they give me? In the next year
there was going to be an election – 1872. If Riel remains in the
country for the elections, it will be trouble, and he has a right to
speak. We have made a treaty with him, we do not fulfil it; we
promise him amnesty; he is outlawed; we take his country and he
has no room even to sleep. He comes to our help. He governs the
country during two months and the reward is that he is a bandit. He
comes to the help of the Government with 250 men and the reward
is $5,000 for his head. It was at that time that I took the name of
David and didn't I take it myself? The hon. judge of the court at
Manitoba, Mr Dubuc, to-day is the one who gave me the name of
David. When I had to hide myself in the woods and when he wanted
to write me that he should write me under the name which would
not be known, so that my letter could come to me, and I may say
that in that way it is a legal name. From that point of view even, and
I put in a parenthesis, why I have a right, I think as a souvenir of my
friend in Upper Canada who caused the circumstances, who brought
me that name, to make nothing special about it, and besides, when
the King of Judea was speaking of the public services of David didn't
he refer us to refer to him in that way? Yes, he did, and as something similar I thought it was only proper that I should take the
name of David, but it was suggested to me in a mighty manner, and I
could not avoid it. The Canadian Government said, well, Riel will be
in the elections here, and he will have the right with all those grievances to speak, and he will embarrass the Government, so they called
on my great protector, Archbishop Taché, I don't know what; but in
the month of February 1872, Archbishop Taché came to me and
said the authorities in Lower Canada want you to go on the other
side of the line until the crisis is passed. Well, I said, if the crisis is
concerning me only, it would be my interest to go there, but I am in
a crisis which is the crisis of the people of the country, and as it concerns the public besides me I will speak to the public as the public
are speaking to me, but the Archbishop gave me so good reason that
although I could not yield to those reasons, I came to a conclusion

with him, and I said, my Lord, you have titles to my acknowledgment which shall never be blotted out of my heart, and although my
judgment in this matter altogether differs from yours, I don't consider my judgment above yours and what seems to me reasonable
might be more reasonable, although I think my course of action
reasonable, perhaps yours is more reasonable. I said if you command
me, as my Archbishop, to go, and take on your shoulders the responsibility of leaving my people in the crisis I will go, but let it be
known that it is not my word, that I do it to please you, and yet
after you command me to do it — to show that in politics when I am
contradicted I can give way, and they offered me £10 a month to
stay on the other side of the line. I said to be in gaol I have a chance
here in Manitoba, and I want something. They asked me how much I
wanted, and I said how long do you want me to stay away? Well, he
said, perhaps a year, I tell you beforehand that I want to be here
during the elections; that is what I asserted. I want to be here during
the elections and it was agreed that they would give £800; £400 to
Lepine, £400 to me, £300 to me personally, £300 for Lepine, £100
for my family, £100 for Lepine's family. That makes £800. How was
it agreed that I should receive that money? I said to his lordship that
the Canadian Government owe me money, they libel me, and even
on the question of libel, they do it so clearly that it does not need
any trial to come to judgment. They have a judgment and will they
make use of it? They owe me something for my reputation that they
abuse every day. Besides I have done work and they never paid me
for it. I will take that money as an account of what they will have to
pay me one day. It was agreed in that manner and the money was
given me in the chapel of St Vital in the presence of Mr Dubuc,
judge now, and when I did not know at that time where the money
came, surely came from, and when the little sack of £300 of gold
was handed me there on the table, I said to his lordship, my Lord, if
the one who wants me to go away was here, and if I had to treat him
as he is trying to treat me, this little sack of gold ought to go
through his head. That was my last protest. At that time, but before
the election, public opinion was so excited against the one who had
taken the responsibility of advising my leaving, that he called me
back, and during the elections I was present, it was three years to-
day. I am rewarded for what I have done through those three years.
Sir George Cartier in 1872, just in that summer was beaten in

Montreal. I speak of him not as a man of party, I speak of him as a
Canadian, as public man. He was beaten by Mr Jetté, of Montreal, by
1,200 majority, and they came to me. My election was sure in
Provencher. I had fifteen or twenty men against me, and they came
to me. Riel, do you want to resign your seat? I have not it yet. Oh,
well you are to get it. Allow George Cartier to be elected here, and I
said yes, to show that if I had at the time any inclination to become
insane when I was contradicted in politics. But Lower Canada has
more than paid me for the little consideration, great as my consideration, but that little mark I considered it a little mark of consideration, a little mark of a great consideration for them. The
people of Manitoba hadn't their government inaugurated at that
time, they had a sham government. It was to be erected. It was to be
inaugurated after 1871. After the 1st January 1871, but we went on
in 1874 and it was not inaugurated. As long as Riel was there, with
his popularity, if the proper institutions had been inaugurated, Riel
would have come in the House, the Provincial House, and of course
it was considered to be a damage so as to keep me back. They did
not give the people their rights, when it was constitutionally agreed
they should have done. I struggled not only for myself but I struggled for the rights, for the inauguration of the principles of responsible and constitutional government in Manitoba. That was conceded
about the time I was banished. While I was in the States was I
happy? Yes, I was very happy to find a refuge, but I have met men
who have come to me several times and say, here, look out, here is a
man on the other side of the line, and he is trying to take a revenge
at you, when you water your horses, because they have left stains as
much as possible on my name. I could not even water my horses on
the Missouri without being guarded against those who wanted my
life. And it is an irony for me that I should be called David.

Last year when I was invited, instead of coming to this country, I
could with the plan that has appeared to me, I could have communicated with the Fenian organizations, I could have sent my books; I
did not do it; and as a proof of it, while I had no means at all to
communicate with my brother, you will see in Manitoba, letters to
my brother Joseph where I speak of my books, that I could get any
amount of money for that book if I wished it to be published, but
that I thought that there was a better chance on this side of the line.
And what chance is it? What I said, constitutionally speaking, if Riel

succeeded that he should one day, as a public man, invite emigration
from the different parts of the different countries of the world, and
because this North-West is acknowledged to be partly his own, as a
half-breed of this population, to make bargains for this North-West
here with the Canadian Government, in such a way so that when the
English population has had a full and resasonable share of this land,
other nationalities, with whom we are in sympathy, should have also
their share of it. When we gave the lands in Manitoba for one-
seventh, we did not explain, we gave it to the Canadian Government,
but in giving it to the Canadian Government it does not mean that
we gave it with all the respect that I have for the English population,
the Anglo-Saxon race, we did not give it only for the Anglo-Saxon
race. There is the Irish in the east and the French in the west, and
their proportion in the Canadian Government ought to receive a
reasonable proportion of this land which is bought here; and it is
hardly the same to give to some French-Canadians in the North-West
and none at all to the Irish. I don't speak here to call the sympathies,
because I am sentenced; I speak sound sense. I follow the line of
natural and reasonable sympathies, but behind my thought, perhaps,
you would be inclined to believe that it is a way formed to try to
work against the English – no, I don't. I believe that the English
constitution is an institution which has been perfected for the
nations of the world, and while I speak of having in future, if not
durig my lifetime after it, of having different nationalities in the
North-West here, my hope that they will succeed is, that they will
have it amongst them, the great Anglo-Saxon race. As among the
nations of Europe 2,000 years ago, the Roman people were the leading race, and were teaching the other nations good government; that
is my opinion of the Anglo-Saxon race. I am not insane enough to
regard the great glory of the Anglo-Saxon race God has given to that
race, and when God gives something to somebody it is for a good
purpose, and because God gave glory to England, it is because He
wanted the Anglo-Saxon race to work for His own glory, and I
suppose it is not finished yet; they will continue – the Roman
empire at the time of the decade existed 400 years – still the king.
The Anglo-Saxon, the British empire, if it has come to its highest
point of glory, it may be called the king; but it is so great that it will
take many hundred years, and fully as many as 400 years to loose its
prestige, and during that time I hope that this great North-West, with

British influence will, by the emigration of which I speak, good
government. But will I show insanity in hoping that that plan will be
fulfilled? I will speak of the wish of my heart, I have been in what is
called, asserted to be wrong to-day; I have been proved to be the
leader. I hope that before long that very same thing which is said
wrong will be known as good, and then I will remain the leader of it;
and as the leader of what I am doing. I say my heart will never abandon the idea of having a new Ireland in the North-West by constitutional means, inviting the Irish of the other side of the sea to come
and have a share here; a new Poland in the North-West by the same
way, a new Bavaria in the same way, a new Italy in the same way,
and on the other side in Manitoba, and since Manitoba has been
erected it has been increased since 1870 at least by 9,500,000 acres
of land; now it is 96,000,000, say there is 86,000,000 millions
about, acres of land to which the half-breeds' title has not been ex-
tinguished, a seventh gives 12,000,000 of those lands and I want the
French-Canadians to come and help us there to-day, to-morrow – I
don't know when. I am called here to answer for my life, to have
time that I should make my testimony, and on the other side of the
mountains, there are Indians and as I have said half-breeds, and there
there is a beautiful island, Vancouver, and I think the Belgians will
be happy there, and the Jews who are looking for a country for
1,800 years, the knowledge of which the nations have not been able
to attain yet. While they are rich and the lords of finance, perhaps,
will they hear my voice one day, and on the other side of the mountains, while the waves of the Pacific will chant sweet music for them
to console their hearts for the mourning of 1,800 years; perhaps will
they say is the one thought of us in the whole Cree world, and if
they help us there on the other side between the great Pacific and
the great Rockies to have a share? The Jews from the States? No;
what I wish is the natural course of emigation, that is what I want;
my thoughts are for peace. During the sixty days that I have been in
Batoche, I told you yesterday that there were three delegations
appointed by the *exovede* to send on the other side for help, but
there I did not see the safety that I was looking for, not that I dis-
trust my countrymen, but such a great revolution will bring immense
disasters, and I don't want during my life to bring disasters except
those which I am bound to bring to defend my own life, and to
avoid to take away from my country, disasters which threaten me

and my friends and those who have confidence in me, and I don't
abandon my ancestors, either the acknowledgment that I have from
my ancestors. My ancestors were amongst those that came from
Scandinavia and the British Isles, 1,000 years ago. Some of them
went to Limerick and were called Reilson, and then they crossed
into Canada and they were called Riel; so in me there is Scandina-
vian, and well rooted; there is the Irish, and there is the French, and
there is some Indian blood. The Scandinavians, if possible, they will
have a share, it is my plan, it is one of the illusions of my insanity, if
I am insane, that they should have on the other side of these mountains, a new Norway, a new Denmark, and a new Sweden, so that
those who spoke of the lands of the great North-West to be divided
into seven, forgot that it was in ten. The French in Manitoba, the
Bavarians, the Italians and the Polands — the Poles and the Irish in
the North-West, and then five on the other side too. I have written
those things since I am in gaol, those things have passed through the
hands of Capt. Deane, they are in the hands of the Lieutenant
Governor, and something of it has reached Sir John, I think, I don't
know. I did not hide my thoughts, I went through the channel of
natural emigration, of peaceful emigration, through the channel of
constitutional means, to start the idea, and if possible to inaugurate
it, but if I can't do it during my life I leave the ideas to be fulfilled in
the future, and if it is not possible, you are reasonable men and you
know that the interests that I propose are of an immense interest,
and if it is not, if the peaceful channel of emigration is not open to
those races into the North-West, they are in such numbers in the
States that when you expect it least, they will perhaps try to come
on your borders and to look at the land, whether it is worth paying
it a visit or not. That is the seventh of the lands, that is about the
seventh of the lands. So you see that by the very nature of the evidence that has been given here when the witnesses speak of a seventh
of the land, that very same question originates from 1870, from the
troubles of Red River which brought a treaty where the seventh of
the lands took its existence, and I say if this court tries me for what
has taken place in the North-West they are trying me for something
which was in existence before then. This court was not in existence
when the difficulties of which we speak now in the Saskatchewan,
began; it is the difficulties of 1869, and what I say is, I wish that I
have a trial. My wish is this, your Honor, that a commission be

appointed by the proper authorities, but amongst the proper
authorities of course I count on English authorities, that is the first
proper authorities; that a commission be appointed; that that commission examines into this question, or if they are appointed to
try me, if a special tribunal is appointed to try me, that I am tried
first on this question: Has Riel rebelled in 1869? Second question.
Was Riel a murderer of Thomas Scott, when Thomas Scott was
executed? Third question. When Riel received the money from
Archibshop Taché, reported to be the money of Sir John, was it cor-
ruption money? Fourth. When Riel seized, with the council of Red
River, on the property of the Hudson Bay Company, did he commit
pillage? Fifth. When Riel was expelled from the House as a fugitive
of justice in 1874, was he a fugitive of justice? As at that time I had
through the member for Hochelaga, now in Canada, and through Dr
Fiset, had communications with the Government, but another time,
through the member for Hochelaga, Mr Alphonse Desjardins, I had
asked from the Minister of Justice an interview on the 4th of March,
and that interview was refused me. In the month of April I was expelled from the House. Lepine was arrested in 1873, and I was not;
not because they did not want to take me. And while I was in the
woods waiting for my election Sir John sent parties to me offering
$35,000 if I would leave the country for three years, and if that was
not enough to say what I wanted, and that I might take a trip over
the water, besides over the world. At the time I refused it. This is
not the first time that the $35,000 comes up, and if at that time I
refused it was it not reasonable for me that I should think it a sound
souvenir to Sir John? Am I insulting? No, I do not insult. You don't
mean to insult me when you declare me guilty; you act according to
your convictions, I do also according to mine. I speak true. I say
they should try me on this question, whether I rebelled on the Saskatchewan in 1885. There is another question. I want to have one
trial; I wish to have a trial that will cover the space of fifteen years,
on which public opinion is not satisfied. I have, without meaning
any offence, I have heard, without meaning any offence, when I
spoke of one of the articles I mentioned, some gentlemen behind me
saying, 'yes, he was a murderer.' You see what remarks. It shows
there is something not told. If told by law it would not be said. I
wish to have my trial, as I am tried for nothing; and as I am tried for
my career, I wish my career should be tried; not the last part of it.

On the other side I am declared to be guilty of high treason, and I give myself as a prophet of the new world. I wish that while a commission sits on one side a commission of doctors should also sit and examine fully whether I am sane, whether I am a prophet or not; not insanity, because it is disposed of, but whether I am a deceiver and impostor. I have said to my good lawyers, I have written things which were said to me last night and which have taken place to-day; I said that before the court opened. Last night the spirit that guides and assists me told me the court will make an effort — your Honor, allow me to speak of your charge, which appeared to me to go on one side — the court made an effort, and I think that word is justified. At the same time there was another thing said to me; a commission will sit; there will be a commission. I did not hear yet that a commission is to take place. I ask for it. You will see if I am an impostor thereby. The doctors will say when I speak of these things whether I am deceiving. If they say I am deceiving, I am not an impostor by will. I may be declared insane because I seek an idea which drives me to something right. I tell you in all what I say in most things I do, I do according to what is told to me. In Batoche any things which I said have already happened. It was said to me not far from here and that is why I never wanted to send the half-breeds far, I wanted to keep them, and it was said to me I will not begin to work before 12 o'clock, and when the first battle opened I was taking my dinner at Duck Lake. When the battle began it was a little after 12 o'clock. I will not begin to work before 12 o'clock, and what has happened? And it was said to me if you do not meet the troops on such a road, you will have to meet them at the foot of a hill, and the half-breeds facing it. It is said my papers have been published. If they have been published, examine what took place, and you will see we had to meet General Middleton at the foot of the hill. It was also told me that men would stay in the 'belle prairie,' and the spirit spoke of those who would remain on the 'belle prairie,' and there were men who remained on the 'belle prairie.' And he admits it was looked upon as something very correct in the line of military art, it was not come from me or Dumont, it was the spirit that guides me.

I have two reasons why I wish the sentence of the court should not be passed upon me. The first, I wish my trial should take place as I said, whether that wish is practical or not, I bow respectfully to

the court. I ask that a commission of doctors examine me. As I am
declared guilty I would like to leave my name, as far as conscience is
concerned, all right. If a commission of doctors sits and if they
examine me, they can see if I was sincere or not. I will give them the
whole history, and I think while I am declared guilty of high treason
it is only right I should be granted the advantages of giving my
proofs whether I am sincere, that I am sincere. Now, I am judged a
sane man, the cause of my guilt is that I am an impostor, that would
be the consequence. I wish a commission to sit and examine me.
There have been witnesses around me for ten years, about the time
they have declared me insane, and they will show if there is in me
the character of an impostor. If they declare me insane, if I have
been astray, I have been astray not as an impostor, but according to
my conscience. Your Honor that is all what I have to say.

SENTENCE

MR JUSTICE RICHARDSON: Louis Riel, after a long consideration
of your case, in which you have been defended with as great ability
as I think counsel could have defended you with, you have been
found by a jury who have shown, I might almost say, unexampled
patience, guilty of a crime the most pernicious and greatest that man
can commit. You have been found guilty of high treason. You have
been proved to have let loose the flood-gates of rapine and bloodshed, you have, with such assistance as you had in the Saskatchewan
country, managed to arouse the Indians and have brought ruin and
misery to many families whom if you had simply left alone were in
comfort, and many of them were on the road to affluence.

For what you did, the remarks you have made form no excuse
whatever. For what you have done the law requires you to answer.
It is true that the jury in merciful consideration have asked Her
Majesty to give your case such merciful consideration as she can
bestow upon it. I had almost forgotten that those who are defending
you have placed in my hands a notice that the objection which they
raised at the opening of the court must not be forgotten from the
record, in order that if they see fit they may raise the question in the
proper place. That has been done. But in spite of that, I cannot hold
out any hope to you that you will succeed in getting entirely free, or

that Her Majesty will, after what you have been the cause of doing, open her hand of clemency to you.

For me, I have only one more duty to perform, that is, to tell you what the sentence of the law is upon you. I have, as I must, given time to enable your case to be heard. All I can suggest or advise you is to prepare to meet your end, that is all the advice or suggestion I can offer. It is now my painful duty to pass the sentence of the court upon you, and that is, that you be taken now from here to the police guard-room at Regina, which is the gaol and the place from whence you came, and that you be kept there till the 18th of September next, that on the 18th of September next you be taken to the place appointed for your execution, and there be hanged by the neck till you are dead, and may God have mercy on your soul.

The court rose.

EXHIBITS

EXHIBIT NO. 1
Batoche, 12th May 1885
If you massacre our familes we are going to massacre the Indian agent and others, prisoners.
LOUIS 'DAVID' RIEL, *Exovede*
Per J.W. Astley, *bearer*

ENDORSEMENT ON EXHIBIT NO. 1
12th May 1885
Mr. Riel: I am anxious to avoid killing women and children, and have done my best to avoid doing so. Put your women and children in one place, and let us know where it is and no shot shall be fired on them. I trust to your honor not to put men with them.
FRED MIDDLETON, Comdg. N.W. Field Forces

EXHIBIT NO. 2
Batoche, 12th May 1885
Sir: If you massacre our families we will begin by Indian Lash and other prisoners.
LOUIS 'DAVID' RIEL, *Exovede*
Per F.E. Jackson, bearer

EXHIBIT NO. 3

Batoche, 12th May 1885

Major General Middleton: General, your prompt answer to my note shows that I was right in mentioning to you the cause of humanity. We will gather our families in one place, and as soon as it is done we will let you know.

I have the honor to be, General, your humble servant,

LOUIS 'DAVID' RIEL

EXHIBIT NO. 4

I do not like war, and if you do not retreat and refuse an interview, the question remaining the same the prisoners.

EXHIBIT NO. 5

St Anthony, 21st March 1885

To Major Crozier, Commandant of the Police Force at Carlton and Battleford

Major: The councillors of the provisional government of the Saskatchewan have the honor to communicate to you the following conditions of surrender: You will be required to give up completely the situation which the Canadian Government have placed you in, at Carlton and Battleford, together with all government properties.

In case of acceptance, you and your men will be set free, on your parole of honor to keep the peace. And those who will choose to leave the country will be furnished with teams and provisions to reach Qu'Appelle.

In case of non-acceptance, we intend to attack you, when tomorrow, the Lord's Day, is over; and to commence without delay a war of extermination upon all those who have shown themselves hostile to our rights.

Messrs. Charles and Maxime Lepine are the gentlemen with whom you will have to treat.

Major, we respect you. Let the cause of humanity be a consolation to you for the reverses which the governmental misconduct has brought upon you.

LOUIS 'DAVID' RIEL, *Exovede*

Réné Parenteau, chairman	Jean-Baptiste Parenteau
Chas. Nolin	Pierre Henry
Gab. Dumont	Albert Delorme
Moïse Ouellette	Dum. Carriere

Albert Monkman	Maxime Lepine
Bte. Boyer	Bte. Boucher
Donald Ross	David Tourond
Amb. Jobin	Ph. Garnot, secretary

St Anthony, 21st March 1885

To Messrs. Charles Nolin and Maxime Lepine

Gentlemen: If Major Crozier accedes to the conditions of surrender, let him use the following formula, and no other: 'Because I love my neighbor as myself, for the sake of God, and to prevent bloodshed, and principally the war of extermination which threatens the country, I agree to the above conditions of surrender.'

If the Major uses this formula and signs it, inform him that we will receive him and his men, Monday.

Yours,

LOUIS 'DAVID' RIEL, *Exovede*

EXHIBIT NO. 6

A calamity has fallen upon the country yesterday. You are responsible for it before God and man.

Your men cannot claim that their intentions were peaceable since they were bringing along cannons. And they fired many shots first.

God has pleased to grant us the victory, and as our movement is to say our rights our victory is good; and we offer it to the Almighty.

Major, we are Christians in war as in peace. We write you in the name of God and of humanity to come and take away your dead, whom we respect. Come and take them to-morrow before noon.

We enclose herein copy of a resolution adopted to-day by the representatives of the French half-breeds.

True copy, Ph. G.

EXHIBIT NO. 7

Aux Métis du Lac Qu'Appelle

Dear Relatives: We have the pleasure to let you know that on the 26th of last month, God has given us a victory over the mounted police. Thirty half-breeds and five Cree Indians have met 130 policemen and volunteers. Thanks to God, we have defeated them. Yourselves, dear relatives, be courageous; do what you can. If it is

not done yet, take the stores, the provisions, the ammunitions.
(Then follow two or three lines not intelligible.)

EXHIBIT NO. 8 (translation)
God has always taken care of the half-breeds. He fed them for many
days in the desert. Providence enriched our prairie with the buffalo.
The plenty in which our fathers lived was as wonderful as the
heavenly manna. But we were not sufficiently grateful to God, our
good Father, hence it is that we have allowed ourselves to fall into
the hands of a Government which only thinks of us to pillage us.
Had he only understood what God did for us before Confederation,
we should have been sorry to see it coming. And the half-breeds of
the North-West would have made conditions of a nature to preserve
for our children that liberty, that possession of the soil, without
which there is no happiness for anyone; but fifteen years of suffering, impoverishment and underhand, malignant persecution have
opened our eyes; and the sight of the abyss of demoralization into
which the Dominion is daily plunging us deeper and deeper every
day, has suddenly, by God's mercy as it were, stricken us with
horror. And the half-breed people are more afraid of the hell into
which the Mounted Police and their Government are openly seeking
to drive us, than of their firearms, which, after all, can only kill our
bodies. Our alarmed conscience have shouted out to us: Justice commands us take up arms. Dear relatives and friends, we advise you to
pay attention. Be ready for everything. Take the Indians with you.
Gather them from every side. Take all the ammunition you can,
whatsoever storehouses it may be in. Murmur, growl, and threaten.
Stir up the Indians. Render the police of Fort Pitt and Battleford
powerless. We pray God to open to us a way to go up. And when we
get there, as we hope, we shall help you to take Battleford and Fort
Pitt. Have confidence in Jesus Christ. Place yourselves under the protection of the Blessed Virgin. Implore St. Joseph, for he is powerful
with God. Commend yourselves to the powerful intercession of St.
John the Baptist, the glorious patron of the Canadians and half-
breeds. Be at peace with God. Keep His commandments. We pray
Him to be with you all and to make you succeed.

Try and give to the half-breeds and Indians of Fort Pitt, as
quickly as possible, the news we send you.

EXHIBIT NO. 9 (translation)
To the Indians; to the half-breeds
The half-breeds and Indians of Battleford, and environs
Dear Brothers and Relatives: Since we wrote to you, important
events have taken place. The police have attacked us; we met them
and God gave us the victory; 30 half-breeds and 5 Indians fought
against 120 men, and after 35 or 40 minutes, they took to flight.
Bless God with us for the success he has kindly granted us. Rise; face
the enemy, and if you can do so, take Battleford – destroy it – save
all the goods and provisions, and come to us. With your numbers,
you can perhaps send us a detachment of 40 or 50 men. All you do,
do it for the love of God, and in the protection of Jesus Christ, the
Blessed Virgin, St Joseph and St John the Baptist, and be certain
that faith does wonders.
LOUIS 'DAVID' RIEL, *Exovede*
(in pencil) signed by the members of council

EXHIBIT NO. 10 (translation)
To our brothers, the English and French half-breeds of Lake
Qu'Appelle and environs
Dear Relatives and Friends: If you do not know it already, we shall
tell you the reasons that induced us to take up arms. You know that
time out of mind our fathers have defended, at peril of their lives,
this land which was theirs and is ours. The Ottawa Government took
possession of our country. For 15 years they have made sport of our
rights, and offended God by overwhelming us with acts of injustice
of every kind. The officials commit every species of crime. The men
of the Mounted Police are the scandal of the whole country, by their
bad language and their bad actions. They are so corrupt that our
wives and daughters are no longer safe in their neighborhood. The
laws of decency are to them a subject for pleasantry. Oh, my
brothers and friends, we should at all times have confidence in God;
but now that evil is at its height, we specially require to commend
ourselves to our Lord. Perhaps you will see things as we see them.
They steal our country from us, and then they govern it so badly,
that if we let things go on it would soon be impossible for us to be
saved. The English half-breeds of the Saskatchewan are with us heart
and soul. The Indians are coming in and joining us from all sides.
Buy all the ammunition you can; go and get it, if necessary, on the

other side of the line. Be ready. Do not listen to the offers the Ottawa Government make you. Those offers are robbers' offers. Sign no papers or petitions. Let your trust be in God.

(translation) St Anthony, 25th March 1885
To Our Relatives: Thanks for the good news you have taken the trouble to send us. Since you are willing to help us, may God bless you.

Justice commands us to take up arms. And if you see the police passing, attack them, destroy them (and written across the first part of this letter, in English, afterwards:) 'Notify the Wood Indians not to be taken.'

EXHIBIT NO. 11 (translation)
I will not begin to work before twelve hours.
Our Relatives: Thanks for the good news you have taken the trouble to send us. Since you are willing to help, God bless you. And if you see the police passing, stop them, disarm them. Justice commands us to take up arms. Then warn the Wood Indians not to let themselves be surprised, but rather to be on their guard; to take ammunition from all the posts of the company, at Lac des Noisettes and Fish Lake.

Mr F. X., Batoche
The French half-breeds have taken up arms to a man. Not one of our people is against us. Tell our relatives, the Indians, to be ready to come and help us, if needed. Take all the ammunition of the company.

EXHIBIT NO. 12 (translation)
Trust in God and the circumstances which Providence is now producing in the Saskatchewan. We shall not forget you. If promises are made to you, you will say that the time for promises is past.

A time has come when we must have proof for everything. Pray. Be good, keep the commandments of God and you shall want for nothing.

EXHIBIT NO. 13
Dear Relative: We thank you for the good news that you took the trouble to send us. Since you are willing to help us, may God bless you in all what is to be done for our common salvation.

Justice commands to take up arms. And if you see the police passing by, stop it and take away their arms.

Afterwards notify the Wood Indians that they might be surprised; let them be ready to all events, in being calm and courageous, to take all the powder, the shot, the lead, the posts and the cartridges from the Hudson's Bay store, at Nut Lake and Fishing Lake. Do not kill anybody. No, not molest nor ill-treat anybody. Fear not, but take away the arms.

LOUIS 'DAVID' RIEL

EXHIBIT NO. 14

Gentlemen: The councillors of the half-breeds now under arms at St Anthony have received your message of the 22nd of March 1885.

They thank you for the sympathy with which you honor them even in this crisis, and of which you have given ample proof before.

Situated as you are it is difficult for you to approve (immediately) of our bold but just uprising, and you have been wise in your course.

Canada (Ottawa) has followed with us neither the principles of right nor constitutional methods of government. They have been arbitrary in their doings. They have usurped the title of the aboriginal half-breeds to the soil. And they dispose of it at condition opposed to honesty. Their administration of our lands, is which are already weighing altogether false – and which are already weighing very hard on all classes of the North-West people. They deprive their own immigrants of their franchises, of their liberties, not only political but even civil, and as they respect no right, we are justified before God and man to arm ourselves to try and defend our existence, rather than to see it crushed.

As to the Indians, you know, gentlemen, that the half-breeds have great influence over them. If the bad management of Indian affairs by the Canadian Government has been fifteen years without resulting in an outbreak, it is due only to the half-breeds who have up to this time persuaded to keep quiet. But now that the Indians, now that we ourselves are compelled to resort to arms, how can we tell them to keep quiet? We are sure that if the English and French half-breeds unite well in this time of crisis, not only can we control the Indians, but we will also have their weight on our side in the balance.

Gentlemen, please do not remain neutral. For the love of God help us to save the Saskatchewan. We sent to-day a number of men with Mr Monkman to help and support (under as it is just) the cause of the aboriginal half-breeds. Public necessity means no offence. Let us join willingly. The aboriginal half-breeds will understand that if we do we do so much for their interests we are entitled to their most hearty response.

You have acted admirably in sending copy of your resolutions to Carlton as well as to St Anthony. We consider that we have only two enemies in

The French half-breeds believe that they are only two enemies. Coshen and Carlton. Dear brethren in Jesus Christ, let us avoid the mistakes of the past.

We consider it an admirable act of it has been an admirable act of prudence that you should have sent copies of your resolutions to the police in Carlton and to the men of St Anthony.

We dear brothers in Jesus Christ, let us avoid the mistakes of the past, let us work for us and our children, as true Christians.
LOUIS 'DAVID' RIEL, *Exovede*

If we are well united the police will surrender and come out of Carlton as the hen's heat causes the chicken to come out of the shell. A strong union between the French and English half-breeds is the only guarantee that there will be no bloodshed.

EXHIBIT NO. 15
Resolved first that, when England gave that country to the Hudson Bay Company two hundred years ago, the North-West belonged to France as history shows it.

And when the Treaty of Paris ceded Canada to England no mention of any kind was made of the North-West.

As the American English colonies helped England to conquer Canada they ought to have a share of conquest, and that share ought to be the North-West, since commercially and politically the United States Government have done more for the North-West than ever England did, we ought to have.

Resolved, first, that our union is, and always will be most respectuous towards the American Government, their policy, their interest and towards the territorial Government of Montana as well.

2nd That our union will carefully avoid causing any difficulty whatever to the United States and will not conflict in any way with the constitution and laws of the Government. It is doubtful whether England really owns the North-West, because the first act of government that England ever accomplished over that North-West was to give it as a prey to the sordid monopoly of the Hudson Bay Company, two hundred years ago.

Her second act of government of any importance over that country was to give it in 1870 as a prey to the Canadians.

Our union is, and always will be most respectful towards the American annexation, against England and Rome, Manitoba French-Canadians.

EXHIBIT NO. 16
The French half-breed, members of the provisional government of the Saskatchewan, have separated from Rome and the great mass of the people have done the same.

If our priests were willing to help us, and up to this time our priests have shown themselves unwilling to leave Rome. They wish to govern us in a manner opposed to our interest and they wish to continue and govern us according to the dictates of Leo XIII.

Dear brothers in Jesus Christ, for the sake of God come and help us so that the enterprise against Rome may be a success and in return we will do all in our power to secure our political rights.

EXHIBIT NO. 17
Dear Relatives: We have the pleasure to let you know that on the 26th of last month God has given us a victory over the Mounted Police.

Thirty-five half-breeds and some five and six Cree Indians have met hundred and twenty policemen and volunteers.

Thank God, we have defeated them. Yourselves, dear relatives, be courageous. Do what you can. If it is not done, take the stores, the provisions and the munitions. And without delay come this way, as many as it is possible. Send us news.

LOUIS 'DAVID' RIEL, *Exovede*

Moïse Ouellette   Damas Carrière
J. Baptiste Boucher   Emmanuel Champagne

Donald Ross	Pierre Henry
Baptiste Parenteau	Pierre Garriépy
Maxime Lepine	Albert Monkman
Charles Trottier	Ambrose Jobin

The Mounted Police are making preparations for an attack; they are gathering themselves in one force, and no delay should exercise; come and reinforce us.

EXHIBIT NO. 18 (translation)
To the Half-breeds and Indians of Battleford and environs
Since we wrote you, important matters have occurred. The police came and attacked us. We met them. God gave us the victory. Thirty half-breeds and five Crees fought against one hundred and twenty men. After a fight of thirty-five or forty minutes, the enemy took to flight.

Bless God with us for the success He has kindly granted us. Rise. Face the police. If you possibly can, if the thing is not already done, take Fort Battleford. Destroy it. Save all the goods and provisions and come to us. With your numbers you can send us a detachment of forty to fifty men.

All that you do, do it for the love of God under the protection of Jesus Christ, of the Blessed Virgin of St Joseph, and of St John the Baptist.

Be certain that faith works wonders.
LOUIS 'DAVID' RIEL, *Exovede*

Pierre Parenteau	Donald Ross
Charles Trottier	Pierre Garriépy
Bte. Boucher	Damas Carrière
Pierre Henry	Antoine Jobin

EXHIBIT NO. 19
15th May 1885
Major General Fred. Middleton
General: I have received only to-day yours of the 13th instant. My council are dispersed. I wish you would let them go quiet and free. I hear that presently you are absent. Would I go to Batoche, who is going to receive me? I will go to fulfil God's will.
LOUIS 'DAVID' RIEL, *Exovede*

EXHIBIT NO. 20

Duck Lake, 27th March 1885

To Major Crozier, Commanding Officer, Fort Carleton

Sir: A calamity has fallen upon the country yesterday, you are responsible for it before God and man.

Your men cannot claim that their intentions were peaceable, since they were bringing along cannons. And they fired many shots first.

God has been pleased to grant us the victory, and as our movement is to save our lives, our victory is good, and we offer it to the Almighty.

Major, we are Christians in war as in peace. We write in the name of God and of humanity to come and take away your dead, whom we respect. Come and take them to-morrow before noon.

We enclose herein a copy of a resolution adopted to-day by the representatives of the French half-breeds.

LOUIS 'DAVID' RIEL, *Exovede*

Albert Monkman	J. Bte. Boucher
Gabriel Dumont	Damos Carrière
Norbert Delorme	Bte. Parenteau
Pierre Garriépy	Pierre Parenteau
Donald Ross	Amt. Jobin
Moïse Ouellete	David Tourond
Maxime Lepine	P. Garnot, secretary

(copy of minute)

That a prisoner be liberated and given a letter to the commanding officer at Carlton, inviting him in the name of God and of humanity to come and take away the bodies of the unfortunate who fell yesterday on his side in the combat; that far from being molested he will be accompanied by our condolences in the fulfilment of that sorrowful duty, that we will wait till to-morrow noon. Moved by Mr Monkman, seconded by Mr Jean Baptiste Boucher, and unanimously carried.

Dated 27th March 1885

Ottawa, 15th March 1886

Upon the reference of an Address of the Honorable the House of Commons, dated the 3rd March, instant, for copies of all documents forming the record in the case of Her Majesty against Louis Riel, tried at Regina, including the jury list, the names of the jurors challenged, and by whom they were challenged, the list of the jurors empanelled, the motions and affidavits filed, the evidence, the incidents of the trial, the addresses of counsel, and of the prisoner, the charge of the judge, the names of the judges or assistant judges who tried the case, the names of the counsel for the prosecution and for the defence, and, in short, of every document whatsoever relating to the trial, and also of the verdict, and of the recommendation to mercy of the court. The undersigned has the honor to transmit herewith a complete transcript of the record and proceedings in the case.

A. POWER, for D.M.J.